# PRAIRIE RISING

## Indigenous Youth, Decolonization, and the Politics of Intervention

In 2016, Canada's newly elected federal government publicly committed to addressing the longstanding abuse and social and material deprivation suffered by Indigenous communities across the country. Does this outward shift in the Canadian state's approach to the injustices facing Indigenous peoples reflect a "transformation with teeth," or is it merely a reconstructed attempt at colonial Indigenous-settler relations?

*Prairie Rising* provides a series of critical reflections on the changing face of settler colonialism in Canada through an ethnographic investigation of Indigenous-state relations in the city of Saskatoon. Jaskiran Dhillon uncovers how various groups, including state agents, youth workers, and community organizations, utilize participatory politics in order to intervene in the lives of Indigenous youth living under conditions of colonial occupation and marginality. In doing so, she sheds light on the changing forms of settler governance and the interlocking systems of education, child welfare, and criminal justice that sustain it. Dhillon's nuanced and fine-grained analysis exposes how the push for inclusionary governance ultimately reinstates colonial settler authority and raises troubling questions about the federal government's commitment to justice and political empowerment for Indigenous Nations, particularly within the context of the everyday realities facing Indigenous youth.

JASKIRAN DHILLON is an assistant professor of global studies and anthropology at The New School in New York City.

JASKIRAN DHILLON

# PRAIRIE RISING

## Indigenous Youth, Decolonization, and the Politics of Intervention

UNIVERSITY OF TORONTO PRESS
Toronto Buffalo London

ISBN 978-1-4426-4692-6 (cloth)
ISBN 978-1-4426-1471-0 (paper)

♾ Printed on acid-free, 100% post-consumer recycled paper.

---

**Library and Archives Canada Cataloguing in Publication**

Dhillon, Jaskiran K., 1974–, author
Prairie rising : indigenous youth, decolonization, and the politics
of intervention / Jaskiran K. Dhillon.

Includes bibliographical references and index.
ISBN 978-1-4426-4692-6 (cloth)    ISBN 978-1-4426-1471-0 (paper)

1. Indian youth–Government policy–Saskatchewan–Saskatoon.
2. Indian youth–Government policy–Canada.    3. Indian youth–
Saskatchewan–Saskatoon–Social conditions.    4. Saskatoon (Sask.)–
Ethnic relations.    I. Title.

E98.Y68D55 2017    305.235089'97071    C2016-908096-X

---

This book has been published with the help of a grant from the Federation
for the Humanities and Social Sciences, through the Awards to Scholarly
Publications Program, using funds provided by the Social Sciences and
Humanities Research Council of Canada.

University of Toronto Press acknowledges the financial assistance to its
publishing program of the Canada Council for the Arts and the Ontario Arts
Council, an agency of the Government of Ontario.

**Canada Council   Conseil des Arts
for the Arts   du Canada**

ONTARIO ARTS COUNCIL
CONSEIL DES ARTS DE L'ONTARIO
an Ontario government agency
un organisme du gouvernement de l'Ontario

Funded by the   Financé par le
Government   gouvernement
of Canada   du Canada

*In memory of my extraordinary parents,*
*Surjit Kaur Dhillon and Sukhdev Singh Dhillon.*
*And for Rekha and Larkin,*
*who carry us forward, into the future.*

**ris·ing** adj. 1. Ascending, sloping upward, or advancing: a rising tide. 2. Coming to maturity; emerging: the rising generation.

*The Free Dictionary*


One enters a room and history follows; one enters a room and history precedes.

– Dionne Brand, "Opening the Door:
An Interview with Dionne Brand"


Maybe it went on a few generations like this. Just holding on.
Waiting for something better.
Just breathing.

– Leanne Simpson, "For Asinykwe"


Writings of light assault the darkness, more prodigious than meteors.
– Jorge Luis Borges, "Boast of Quietness"

# Contents

# Figures

# Preface and Acknowledgments

The year 2015 marked the election of Canada's twenty-third prime minister: Justin Trudeau. Notably, Trudeau's entry into federal politics came armed with a rainbow-coloured cabinet and bold promises of a "renewed" relationship between Indigenous peoples and the settler state of Canada. Trudeau's gesturing towards the recalibration of settler governance, however, is not unique. This claim has been voiced before. Indeed, the Canadian state's current preoccupation with Indigenous peoples – who they are and how to "address" their political demands, the threats they pose to a white settler order – can be traced back to the making of Canada as a settler state, to the struggles that mark the conquest, seizure, and occupation of Indigenous land. It is part of a long line of settler state ideologies and schemes to manage the intractable "Indigenous problem" that so powerfully confronts the hubristic portrayal of Canada as a humanitarian nation cleansed of colonial rule, both at home and abroad, and profoundly challenges settler sovereignty as a fait accompli.

The most recent extension of liberal tactics to recalibrate Indigenous–settler state relations takes shape through the burgeoning of reconciliation and recognition politics that attempt to right the wrongs of the past by inviting Indigenous peoples to participate at greater and greater levels in dominant state institutions – a move the state positions as tangible evidence of Indigenous people's political power to govern their own lives. Why then, we might ask, are Indigenous peoples across Turtle Island, still in 2017, *continuing to fight* for the return of their stolen lands (many of which are caught up in state-sanctioned extractive projects threatening the existence of life), the reigniting of nation-to-nation relationships, the end of state violence against Indigenous women and girls, and for self-governance situated in and through Indigenous ways of knowing, governance systems, and social histories? It is because the Canadian state's assertions about crafting a new relationship with Indigenous peoples doesn't speak to the vision of decolonization and freedom articulated and practised by Indigenous political actors and communities on the ground. This is a different story than the one Canadian political agents – across a broad spectrum – tell themselves and the public about what needs to be done to alter the power dynamics of this relationship.

It is against this backdrop that *Prairie Rising* enters. This book, at its core, aims to (re)direct our gaze back to the settler colonial project itself and to push us to be attentive, first and foremost, to the lives of Indigenous youth that are caught up in the reinvention of settler governance and subsequent reinscription of colonial power through the discourse and practice of participation. The questions I ask in this book include the following: What does "participation" mean to Indigenous people who have very limited choices but are being told that they should, or that they do? How is the notion of "choice" mobilized for those who are defined by a particular stage of life, those who are young? What are the ways that the lives of Indigenous young people continue to be shaped by the settler colonial practices of the state, even in the wake of these new governing logics?

*Prairie Rising* takes up an ethnographic dissection of the ruse of "participation" and "choice" operating within a white settler society to showcase how these governing logics are not, in fact, predicated on "inclusion" but rather find their footing in present-day incarnations of "elimination." Indigenous youths' lives are situated on the frontiers of contemporary settler colonial institutions, discourses, and policies. State-sanctioned social programming for them, albeit through an invitation extended to Indigenous peoples to take part in the creation of these modes of intervention, continues to cause material harm, forecloses possibilities for Indigenous self-determined futures, and redirects our attention away from colonial racism in the here and now. This, I argue, is ultimately not a project of "making good citizens" – of addressing the now well-documented and publicized "crisis" facing Indigenous youth in Canada – but rather reconstructed colonial statecraft that seeks to target Indigenous youth for the end goal of reproducing and maintaining the settler colonial state project and the multitude of social and political practices that weave it together.

\* \* \*

In some regards, my journey to this book began without my knowing. It is unquestionably anchored in my experience of growing up in rural Saskatchewan where the first inklings of my political sensibility began to take shape. Over the nearly two decades that followed my departure from this small town, I continued deepening my learning through direct work with youth and by engaging in critical thinking about (in) justice, colonialism, marginalization, violence, rights, and decolonization, through ongoing conversations with numerous (and wise) advocates, scholars, friends, and family members. Eventually, I found my way to the ethnographic encounters that form the core of what you are about to read.

Although it is my name alone that graces the cover of this book, the binding together of these pages was only made possible through the efforts and thoughtfulness of many. I extend my heartfelt thanks and profound gratitude to the Indigenous youth whose lives sit at the centre of this account, and who have taught me such difficult and important lessons about intention, politics, power, freedom, and change by sharing the realities of their day-to-day lives with me. I am humbled by their courage, heartened by their strength, and inspired by their ability to keep fighting.

I would also like to express sincere thanks to all of the people in Saskatchewan (youth workers, organizers, artists, government employees, academics, educators, film-makers, and city officials) who opened their doors to me and provided me with the opportunity to learn from them. I hope the story that unfolds in the following pages reflects some of the hard work and commitment to the lives of Indigenous youth that exists out there, while also making clear the long, winding, and complicated journey of seeking justice many of us find ourselves on, often without any assurance of what lies ahead. The work of justice and decolonization requires that we always be reflective about the implications (deliberate and unintended) of our ideas and strategies for social transformation.

The conceptual orientation of this project has benefited from intense dialogue and debate with many of my mentors, colleagues, and friends. From my early days as an undergraduate student at the University of Saskatchewan where I first began to map colonialism in Canada, partly due to a class on Aboriginal Justice I took with the late Patricia Monture-Angus in one of my first semesters, to present-day discussions of the critical politics raised by this book, I am greatly indebted to many individuals for their time, energy, and understanding. Ritty

· Lukose at New York University, Kathleen D. Hall at the University of Pennsylvania, and Michael Marker at the University of British Columbia were particularly instrumental in bringing this project to fruition and have been tireless supporters and readers of my work. Their commentary, feedback, and mentorship greatly enhanced the integrity of this book in myriad ways.

I have also learned, in extraordinary measure, from a host of brilliant writers and thinkers whose perspectives and ideas are integrated throughout this book (there are simply too many to list here). Their intellectual guidance and theoretical critiques were essential in helping me to develop the arguments that you will find throughout *Prairie Rising*. I was grateful to be able to draw upon their work and learn from their vast expertise. In this sense, this book stands as a contribution to a growing body of scholarly work, with thematic interests in Indigenous life, politics, and the problematics of settler colonialism, that is expanding the scope of critical, anti-colonial inquiry across various literatures and disciplinary formations (youth studies, Indigenous studies, political anthropology, settler colonial studies, women and gender studies, and political theory). These are thinkers and advocates pushing the scope and boundaries of traditional academic disciplines and perhaps more importantly, doing the hard and essential work of decolonizing the academy. And to my anonymous reviewers, a huge thanks and deep appreciation for sharing your incredible insight, vast knowledge, and intellectual prowess – all of which enabled me to make this book even stronger.

At my home institution in New York City, The New School, I would like to thank wonderful colleagues who have helped to guide and encourage me through the final stages of writing this book – Siddhartha Deb, Jonathan Bach, Miriam Ticktin, Gustav Peebles, Radhika Subramanium, Laura Liu, and Joseph Heathcott have all offered support in different ways. My students at The New School have also assisted in expanding my thinking about the questions I raise throughout this account, and have encouraged me to consider and consider again, the implications of this work. They never stop asking difficult questions and demanding complicated answers. Special recognition to the students of Lang in Cambodia 2012 – Ashley Vidal, Noah Strouse, Shelley Green, Christina Hiras, Jordan Lapolla, Fiona Mahurin, and Kristen Turner – your consistent and collective good wishes did more than you realize. And a big thank you to all of my students in Global Studies and the Graduate Program in International Affairs who have helped me refine my anti-colonial curriculum, been willing to take risks, and who have been generous with their peers and me as we walk through learning together. Brenna Smith, Veija Kusama-Morri, and Jamey Jesperson – you are students turned comrades and friends. I thank you for that.

My former research assistant, colleague, and friend Mila Shopova deserves an immense thank you for her meticulous work in preparing the manuscript. Her careful and close readings enabled me to see things that I otherwise would have never seen. And her brilliance, encouragement, and friendship during the final stages of writing were a big part of how this book came into being. Thank you Mila, for everything.

Less easy to pin down in a long list of "thank yous" are all of my friends across multiple continents. As anyone who has produced something of this magnitude is aware, friends are essential to sustaining the passion and dedication required to reach the finish line. Anu Belgaumkar, Torsten Tabel, Angela Failler, Roger Bristol, John Makinson, Lori Carlson, Ponheary Ly, Todd Wolfson, Panos Grames, Peter Bloom, Veronica Eisner, Pratistha Pandya, Adam Bonilla, Shenid Bhayroo, and Amy Bach – thank you. Annabel Webb, Asia Czapska, Sue Delanoy, Marc Longjohn, John Noon, and Lori Waselchuk have spent endless hours listening to me talk about many of the troubling questions and tensions that frame this book. They have been tremendously generous and patient with their feedback and support. Andrea Summers has been an unwavering champion of this book and my work more generally, for which I am so grateful. A special shout out to Marcel Petit for sharing his spectacular photographs of the prairies with me and for making me laugh on my grey days. And to Jarrett Martineau for the constant stream of remote signals and music that helped keep me grounded and my eyes on the horizon. Big props to Katerina Zacharia for keeping me close to the story I wanted to tell and to Annabel (again!), for always reminding me that I had what it takes to push this book through the goal post and for offering insight and reassuring words every time I asked. Shout outs to my friends would be incomplete without my expressing the immense satisfaction and joy I have found writing and thinking with Siku Allooloo – your bravery, tenacity, and strength have been an inspiration to me and I look forward to continuing to build with you. And to Francois Paulette: thank you for sharing your wisdom and experience, for opening up your home and treating me like family, and for teaching me how to be a better person.

And lastly, I would like to express my deep and overwhelming gratitude to my family for their love and for always being there whenever

I needed them. I lost both of my parents during the completion of this manuscript – a reality that produces an unmooring of a whole new order and for which one can never prepare. Sukhdev Singh Dhillon and Surjit Kaur Dhillon were the parents that patiently waited for my ambitions to become a reality. They were the ones who always reminded me that in life there are no short cuts when the stakes are high. It was, and still is, an important lesson, Mom and Dad. I dedicate this work to you.

To my sisters Raman Dhillon and Simrata Dhillon, all of my nephews (Keiran, Kahlil, Ishaan, and Ashwin), and the Bakos crew, including Tarsch, Amber, and Shara – I couldn't have done this without you. Thank you for providing much needed spaces of respite, allowing me to bring my laptop and suitcase of books on every family trip for the last eight years, and for reminding me that what I do matters. My deep gratitude to Gordon Richardson who took such wonderful care of our two daughters, as only he can, while I was away doing the research for this book and for continuing to support my research, teaching, and advocacy. And a special thank you to Noreen Richardson, grandmother extraordinaire, for never failing to assist whenever I needed a hand.

But perhaps my biggest accolades are reserved for my daughters, Rekha and Larkin Dhillon-Richardson, who have lived through the experience of this project alongside me in the most intimate ways. With all of their beauty and precociousness, Rekha and Larkin put up with my absences while I was away doing research and were unfailingly patient with me while I finished the final stages of writing, often providing comic relief and always acting as my champions. They have grown up with a mom constantly on the move, always pushing them to ask hard questions, but loving them fiercely every step of the way. "Mom, any idea when the book will be done?" – a phrase heard all too often throughout our household.

Rekha and Larkin also helped me find words when I thought there were none to be found and willingly offered their youthful insight about these very complicated issues whenever I arrived at an impasse that seemed insurmountable. Not surprisingly, their ideas often contained more wisdom and clarity than one would imagine – in them lies the possibility for a different, better world. As they grow older, I hope they will come to understand that this work was also for them.

Philadelphia, 2016

# PRAIRIE RISING

Indigenous Youth, Decolonization, and the
Politics of Intervention

# Introduction: Urban Indigenous Youth and Participatory Politics in the Paris of the Prairies

My cell phone rings as I meander along the path. It is Nitânis. "Where are you?" she asks, her voice hurried and louder than normal. "Closer than you think," I respond, laughing.

Collapsed into a government file, Nitânis's labyrinthine existence would look something like this: Family breakdown. Child welfare apprehension. Attempted suicide. Sibling death. Addiction. Rape. Gang involvement. Teen pregnancy. Criminality. Street life. Fetal alcohol spectrum disorder. Homelessness. Service resistance (revolving door syndrome). Post-traumatic stress disorder. Drop out. Prison. Welfare. Mental illness. Runaway. Probation. Truancy. The institutions of the state that acted on her were manifold; the intrusions spanned close to twenty-five years. Formal government intervention began from the time Nitânis was two years old and was apprehended when her biological parents "disappeared."[1] Shortly thereafter, she was placed in an adoptive home, with white parents, and lived there with one of her siblings, separated from her other brothers and sisters. A few years later, Nitânis entered the complicated terrain of foster care after she discovered the body of her sibling, who had committed suicide. Her adoptive parents determined they could not adequately support her bouts of "acting out," which commenced following this traumatic loss, and she began bouncing among family foster placements, group homes, and life on the street. As a ward of the state, social workers played a primary role in determining Nitânis's fate from this point forward.

In one setting, foster parents forced Nitânis to live in the basement, quarantined from the "real" children and entertained by an old black and white television set. For nutrition, she received a bologna sandwich in a paper bag that was dropped on the first step of the staircase leading down to the basement. "Garbage food," she called it. In another home, located in a rural community, her foster dad sexually assaulted her and was never charged. She ran away. All of her foster care placements were with white families.

Nitânis was exploited by men who commodified her body and threatened to break her spirit through repeated acts of sexual violation and emotional harm. This violence started when she was 11, building on many prior experiences of sexual assault. In order to secure her most basic needs, Nitânis, along with other girls, was forced to "turn tricks" in a place named "Bubble Gum Avenue." For a short while, she lived with a group of friends in a single hotel room on the Westside of Saskatoon, in a neighbourhood where no one asked questions if you could pay with cash. They divided up expenses for room, board, and drugs. Each girl was responsible for generating her share of the required costs – it was how they survived. Today, most of these girls are dead.

At 15, Nitânis ended up in prison, and her record of criminal charges began to metastasize. She served three consecutive years in youth detention for one of the charges. Daily school attendance had long since been interrupted, and she never returned to formal education after the age of 12.

* * *

I have no prior knowledge of this place. Near the edge of a small city, my car crosses the boundary between asphalt and gravel approximately two hours after I start driving. I enter the sprawling institutional grounds through a leaf-canopied narrow road that dead-ends into the South Saskatchewan River before curving left. A vast expanse of buildings, each announcing its purpose with typical government signage, demarcates the territory of the Prairie North Regional Health Authority. Surrounding the buildings are grassy fields covering about as much space as a medium- to large-sized city park. The fields contain a modest golf course, and several flower gardens with benches for patients to sit. Apart from a solitary older man wandering around and collecting stray golf balls in a brown canvas bag, the grounds are absent human activity.

When I reach the parking lot, I see Nitânis standing in front of the main psychiatric hospital. It is a majestic looking brick structure, erected in the first decade of the 1900s. Light refracts off evenly spaced rectangular windows as I acquaint myself with the unfamiliar surroundings. Standing several stories high, the hospital receives patients and guests alike through a grand, arched entrance way, consisting of heavy wooden doors atop a wide cement staircase. A large white sign saying "visiting hours" is clearly visible to outsiders as they approach – a reminder that some of us are free to leave and others stay behind. I park my car in one of the many vacant stalls (does anyone ever come to visit?), take a few deep breaths, and slowly open the door. I turn around and wave to Nitânis, who walks over to me in her crispy white pants and salmon pink sweatshirt (with matching flip-flops), her eyes clear and a big smile on her face. She is average height, with hair the colour of chestnuts and skin a wheatish brown with a tinge of gold. We hug for a few moments in the windy, fresh air of the central plains, pausing under the promise of an endless summer sky. I am happy to see her.

My connection to Nitânis began almost a decade ago while I was carrying out a national research/advocacy project in Canada examining how young women and girls who live in poverty experience education. Nitânis was in her late teens, a young Indigenous woman among countless young Indigenous women, who was attempting to transcend the structural violence enveloping her existence since early childhood.[2] At the time of our first meeting, she was part of a social program for youth who are deemed victims of sexual exploitation.[3] The program was based on the premise that by drawing on the experiential knowledge of youth, a more effective public awareness campaign could be developed to address this issue. As a participant, Nitânis routinely gave presentations based on her lived experience with sexual violence and spoke about her life in local community organizations and schools. The program also included a series of activities – talking circles and outings, among others – that were meant to offer counsel and guidance as these youth attempted to transition to a better life. Frequently, the program hosted cooking nights, where participants prepared meals and ate together. The program supervisor told me this was an attempt to create a sense of togetherness and offer them an opportunity to develop life skills that were not purely about survival (budgeting, nutritional awareness, hygiene, etc.). Nitânis was eager to speak to me about her experiences with schooling. She helped me understand all of the reasons why she did not receive her high school diploma. I listened. We kept in touch, and I made a point of seeing her whenever I returned to Saskatchewan. Over time, I learned the events, big and small, that cumulatively comprised her life story.

I learned how Nitânis's body, mind, and spirit[4] were entangled with the bureaucratic realities and often competing agendas of the criminal justice, child welfare, and education systems. I learned how she bounced like a ping-pong ball from service provider to service provider to service provider. Somewhere along the way, we decided to count and arrived at an approximate tally of forty-seven government representatives who had participated in decisions about her future. In the eyes of the state, Nitânis is (simultaneously) a youth offender to be punished for the societal wrongs she has committed; a child in search of guardianship; a kid who needs a place to live; a teenager who needs food to eat; a student mandated to receive formal education; an addict requiring rehabilitation; a young woman demanding a medical doctor; a mother seeking parental support and custody of her children; a young adult suffering from mental illness; a victim of sexual abuse and exploitation; and a worker requiring a job that will eventually support her day to day life.

Nitânis, however, is also an *Indigenous* youth – a status to be understood within the broader structure of domination-framing Indigenous–state relations in Canada. A government committee, dedicated to the creation of a national strategy that aims (ostensibly) to redress the injustices of Indigenous lives, recognizes the existence of her endemic marginalization while distancing itself from the roots of this deprivation. Hers is an ecological kind of suffering that appears to have no clear beginning, no tangible end, and no readily diagnosable cause. A final report by the Canadian Parliament, *Urban Aboriginal Youth – An Action Plan for Change*, boldly asserts,

> The Committee believes that a genuine window of opportunity exists to implement the kind of positive change needed to ensure another generation of Aboriginal youth is not sacrificed on the altar of narrow policy thinking. The Committee has worked out a realistic plan of action, and detailed concrete steps, which, if implemented in a serious and dedicated fashion by the federal government, can lead to meaningful reform and long lasting solutions. In addition, due to the jurisdictional issues relating to Aboriginal people who reside off reserve and in urban areas, the Committee recognizes that several of the measures outlined will require close collaboration among various levels of government and *must include the substantive participation* of Aboriginal groups to be successful. In that spirit of cooperation, the Committee anticipates the thoughtful response of those who wish to continue working to achieve the aspirations of urban Aboriginal youth. (Canada, Standing Senate Committee on Aboriginal Peoples 2003, v; emphasis added)

Perhaps participation is the answer to rectifying the "narrow policy thinking" Nitânis has experienced in her many encounters with the state.

And now, on this summer day, Nitânis and I walk side by side on the grounds of the psychiatric facility, the latest government institution in which she has become enmeshed. "Do you want me to give you a tour? I can introduce you to some of my friends and show you what I have been doing." I tell her I would love a tour of the place where she is conducting the daily business of her life. I know she is looking hopefully towards the future ("Maybe I will actually get to realize some of my dreams," she tells me over lunch). We ascend the staircase and push our way through the heavy double doors, stepping into the foyer of a spacious entrance where a middle-aged woman with light-coloured hair and a pale complexion sits stationed behind a desk. "This is Jas," she says to the front desk receptionist. "I want to show her around." I sign in, a process which includes providing details of the date and time of my arrival and expected departure and presenting my government issued identification for inspection. A few moments later, the receptionist gives us clearance and reminds Nitânis that we are not allowed to enter any of the patients' private rooms.

Nitânis and I begin our journey through the wide, maze-like hallways that stretch on and on, tall ceilings set alight by industrial-style fluorescent bulbs. A cornucopia of posters is pasted unevenly across the walls, illustrating the range of activities open to patients. At one of the busier intersections sits a chalkboard providing information about the patients' dinner menu for the week. In rainbow letters, it informs us that mashed potatoes, beef, green beans and corn, and chocolate cake are on the list tonight. Nitânis and I move up and down the layers of the building, each floor reflecting a different part of the routine she is adopting – exercise facilities on some; recreation, art spaces, and counselling rooms on others.

Throughout our walk, Nitânis stops to introduce me to people with whom she has developed deep relationships. "This is my good friend Sara," she explains when acquainting me with a young, red haired woman. Sara is standing behind an orange counter that separates a closet like canteen from the recreational space that makes up the remainder of a large room. I extend my arm to shake Sara's petite hand. "I am happy to meet you Sara, Nitânis has told me about you." Sara's lips curve into a nascent grin and her eyes shift to the ground. She coils her fingers together, her long hair now partially shielding her face. I look over at Nitânis, who, in sharp contrast, is looking squarely at her friend and smiling intently. She touches Sara's arm before we walk away.

During our meanderings, Nitânis also tells me about an older man she befriended upon arrival at the hospital. She speaks slowly, halting between words. "No one wanted to go near him. He had these sores on his feet and I would take off his slippers so he could get air on his toes. And I read Beverly Cleary stories to him and played Elvis records in his room. He liked that. Nobody else was ever there. I wish I could have been with him when he died."

We end our tour in Nitânis's bedroom, located in a separate building, down a roadway that leads away from the main psychiatric complex. I step into the living quarters where her bed and few personal belongings are neatly arranged and look around. "Look how clean it is!" she exclaims with pride. As I scan the room, my eyes catch sight of 3 × 3-inch piece of square white paper taped to the middle of one of the four otherwise bare walls. Typed in lower case letters, it plainly reads, "I'm not telling you it is going to be easy, I'm telling you it is going to be worth it." Given everything I know about Nitânis's life, and the immense challenges she has encountered and insidious suffering she has endured, I am humbled by these words. The tenacity and determination she possesses, the will to simply "keep going," are a testament to her and her people's survival in the face of unthinkable odds – watermarks of humanity's strength.[5]

One thing is indisputably clear: the intergenerational and multifaceted impact of the colonial "founding" of Canada is ever present. The effects are material and discursive. They are social and political. And they live in the flesh and bones of young people like Nitânis.

## A Steady Pulse in the Colonial Space of Reckoning

Written from the standpoint of an advocate and ethnographer, this book provides an account of Indigenous–state relations and does so to incite a series of critical reflections about the changing face of settler colonialism in Canada.[6] To this end, I uncover how state agents, youth workers, and representatives from Indigenous and community organizations engage participatory politics in order to facilitate regimes of intervention in the lives of urban Indigenous youth living on the margins of Saskatoon, Saskatchewan's largest city. To be clear, this book is not about the personal suffering of Nitânis or the sensationalizing of her individual story – her reality speaks to that of many. In fact, to claim that Nitânis's life is a unique instance of marginalization is a gross misrepresentation both of the larger narrative and of statistical evidence that suggests quite the opposite.[7] Instead, I am interested in turning an analytic gaze towards the shifting logics of the Canadian government that seek to address lives like hers. While Nitânis has, without a doubt, been shaped by a long colonial history, it is equally true that her life is being managed and addressed through new state assemblages that coexist alongside powerful Indigenous political claims to self-determination and indictments over dispossession. Governance changes form; it reinvents itself in accordance with historically emergent contexts and ongoing colonial interactions. And in nation states with a lasting settler presence, where there is a deliberate intention to permanently displace Indigenous populations from territories to which they have an inherent right, the stakes are especially high when it comes to the maintenance of settler sovereignty.

A growing global Indigenous movement, accompanied by heightened international awareness of genocidal histories and political conflicts over self-determination (McConaghy 2000; Maaka and Fleras 2005; Coulthard 2007; Dei 2011; Povinelli 2011; Regan 2011; Ford and Rowse 2013), has forced a rethinking of Indigenous–state relations within Canada, Australia, New Zealand, and the United States (CANZUS) – archetypal settler states. Indeed, the unfinished business of settler societies involves a perpetual negotiation of settler jurisdiction over Indigenous peoples in terms of territory, law, culture, and identity. Moreover, these negotiations and their outcomes continue, as they always have, to produce material realities – this is not a rhetorical exercise. "Indigenous people don't experience colonialism as theories or analytic categories," writes Taiaiake Alfred (2009, 43). "Colonialism is made real in the lives of people when these things go from being a set of imposed externalities to becoming causes of harm to them as people and as communities, limitations placed on their freedom, and disturbing mentalities, psychologies, and behaviours." Governance, then, is lived in the everyday through power/knowledge systems and associated practices that frame possibilities for individual and collective action (Foucault 1982). Governance impacts Indigenous youth acutely and holistically, immediately and in the long term, for theirs is a future still in the making, a future that will be marked by ongoing settler self-articulation and the concomitant realities of an Indigenous resurgence that takes many shapes across many spaces (Dhillon and

Allooloo 2016). They are the lived connections among history, extant colonial realities, and the unfolding of what comes next.

Within the formal boundaries of Canadian geopolitical territory, social and legislative policies pertaining to Indigenous peoples, unapologetically marked by conquest and aggressive assimilation tactics of the past, have been under fire for the last four decades, largely due to the tenacity and unwavering dedication of numerous Indigenous activists, community leaders, and organizations (Cairns 2000, 2005; Coulthard 2014a). While this criticism has moderated some of the most egregiously unjust policies, a worthy gain in its own right, it has also presented an opportunity for Indigenous peoples and their allies to document and publicize present-day instances of inequality, scarcity, and political suppression that are bound up with colonial policies and racist governance approaches from the past. As I explain in detail in chapters 1 and 2, these instances of inequality take the form of longstanding and profoundly debilitating poverty; structural violence across the country's child welfare, health, criminal justice, and education systems; endemic violence against Indigenous women and girls; and unrelenting racism[8] that is, as Ann Stoler (1997, 172) puts it, "internal to the biopolitical state and woven into the web of the social body." Ongoing dispossession is also indexed by the ongoing seizure of Indigenous land and displacement of peoples for the purposes of capitalist development and "natural resource" extraction, which is carried out through "settler state policies aimed at explicitly undercutting Indigenous political economies and relations to and with land" (Coulthard 2014a, 4). Undeniably, territoriality remains one of settler colonialism's specific, irreducible elements (Wolfe 2006, 388; Asch 2014).[9]

As this colonial story continues to unfold and morph across the country, the Assembly of First Nations, Canada's largest and most prominent Indigenous organization, has placed the discourse of "mutual recognition" squarely within its vision for a different kind of arrangement between Indigenous peoples and the state while pushing demands for self-determination and treaty rights to the centre of a tenuous political stage. In his book *Red Skin, White Masks*, Dene scholar Glen Coulthard (2014a, 3) argues, in fact, that recognition has emerged as the hegemonic expression of self-determination within the Indigenous rights movement in Canada, and one that must be critically interrogated in terms of its ability to radically transform colonial power relations. Under a broad banner of liberal pluralism, recognition models of governance seek to reconcile Indigenous claims to nationhood, on the

one hand, with Crown sovereignty, on the other, via the accommodation of Indigenous identities and objectives,[10] ostensibly producing a
renewed relationship based on common ground and reciprocity (Day
2000). In concrete terms, this shift towards a liberal "politics of recognition" (Taylor 1994) has resulted in a proliferation of inclusionary modes
of political engagement that invite Indigenous peoples to partake in the
development of programs and policies affecting their communities and
that use the ethics of participation as a central organizing concept to
"shape the legal and political relationship so that it respects Indigenous
worldviews" (Turner 2006, 5).

Issues pertaining to urban Indigenous youth have been no exception
to this shift in state logic, especially in those cities deemed by Canada's
federal government to be "high risk" for problems associated with the
migration of Indigenous youth to urban centres. These cities, located
primarily in Western Canada, are marked by large concentrations of
Indigenous people, along with the greatest relative disparity in wealth
between First Nations and the settler population.[11] As recently as April
2014, municipal governments were deliberating about ways to address
the increasing urban Indigenous presence. The mayor of Edmonton,
one of the cities expected to encounter (along with Saskatoon) the largest rise in Indigenous urban migration, has been recorded speaking
publicly about confronting the fears of white settlers who are expressing concerns over the new demographic patterns ("Edmonton Mayor"
2014). The urban Indigenous population in Canada now numbers over
600,000, an all-time high, and more Aboriginal people live in urban
centres across Canada today than in Aboriginal territories and communities on reserves, in Métis settlements, or in Inuit communities (Environics Institute 2011).

Thus, with rising numbers of Indigenous children and youth every
year, educational and social services across Canadian cities with a high
concentration of Indigenous people coupled with notable wealth disparity, have experienced a growing number of state–Indigenous community alliances. Together, state and community actors have developed
and implemented social interventions to address the "Indigenous
youth crisis,"[12] a narrative that gains traction and sustenance through
the widespread, public elevation of life stories like that of Nitânis.
Truncated life stories, however, rarely, if ever, capture the complexity,
colonial histories, and constellation of contextual factors that produce
a "crisis" standing ready and waiting to be addressed. Instead, past
configurations of state control over the lives of Indigenous people, with

their vestiges of overt domination and civilizing undercurrents, give way to a "politics of inclusion" (Young 1990) imbued with the symbolic language and normative assertions of participation and "working together." In *Prairie Rising*, I show how these politics stand as a reconstructed version of colonial statecraft that transforms the texture and mediations of modern governing.

This sentiment of alliance building vis-à-vis a politics of recognition – and, in turn, inclusion – was clearly communicated by the federal government in a formal response to the *Sixth Report of the Standing Senate Committee on Aboriginal Peoples*. The Standing Senate Committee on Aboriginal Peoples was created in December 1989 with a specific mandate to "examine legislation and matters relating to Aboriginal Peoples of Canada" (Aboriginal Affairs and Northern Development Canada 2010). The *Sixth Report* specifically addresses the social issues that urban Indigenous youth face and lists their "needs" as identified by the committee. The formal response of the government speaks to "the conditions that challenge many urban Aboriginal youth" (Aboriginal Affairs and Northern Development Canada 2010) and contains 19 recommendations across the following four areas:

- Restructuring the current jurisdictional and policy framework with respect to federal government responsibility for Aboriginal people not living on reserve
- Enhancing the ways in which urban Aboriginal programming is conceived, designed, and delivered, including proposed principles for service delivery reform
- Strengthening the federal role in urban Aboriginal issues and facilitating intergovernmental mechanisms to address policy and program concerns of urban Aboriginal people and youth
- Providing support for Aboriginal youth living in, or coming into, cities.

My work here is especially attuned to the fifth recommendation emerging from these four central areas, which states, "[T]o the greatest extent possible, programs [will] be developed locally with a *high degree of Aboriginal involvement* and ownership" and that "urban Aboriginal youth or their appropriate representative organizations [will be involved] in the identification of needs, priority setting, and program design" in partnership with mainstream organizations and government agencies (Aboriginal Affairs and Northern Development Canada

2010, 4; emphasis added). I am interested in peering past the surface of the glossy coversheet offered by such governmental directives and improvement schemes (Li 2005) and looking closely, ethnographically as it were, at what lies underneath.

For the purposes of this book, "participation" is defined as both a discursive apparatus and a process that plays out in the concrete practices that inform the development of social interventions for urban Indigenous youth. As a discursive apparatus,[13] participation refers to a facet of liberal, multicultural ideology that challenges the notion that the state is solely responsible for determining the future and fate of Indigenous children and youth (Razack 1998; Schouls 2003; Coulthard 2007; Thobani 2007; Kowal 2008; Rifkin 2009).[14] Instead, aspirations for self-determination, recognition of past wrongs, a valorization of cultural difference, and imperatives for Indigenous subjects to produce new social imaginaries of pluralism within the frame of Canadian nationalism, all call for local Indigenous knowledge and expertise – sentiments that go hand in hand with a politics of recognition. As concrete action, participation encompasses the creation of those partnerships and/or collaborative entities that attempt to bring Indigenous subjects into the decision-making structures of social institutions, through the devolution and decentralization of state authority.

The heart of this book is located within a critical appraisal of participation itself as an ethnographic object, and I draw linkages between its discursive forms as a strategy of inclusionary governance and as a practice that produces action in everyday life (Smith 1988). Consequently, this analysis is grounded within the local conditions that make visible the contextually specific colonial ideologies and social formations through which the politics of the everyday for urban Indigenous youth are both imagined and lived. Indigenous–state alliances embody a distinct view of linear social progress and developmentalism and blur the lines between the state and civil society (Li 2007). They are predicated on the seductive notion that increased participation of Indigenous communities in the design and delivery of social programs will catalyse change in bureaucratic policies and programs by making these interventions more responsive to Indigenous desires[15] and by recognizing the distinct aspirations of First Nations for their children's futures. In turn, it is anticipated that these interventions will tackle longstanding issues of marginalization, even evisceration, and be a grounded step towards integrating the cultural practices and place-based knowledge (Marker 2000) of Indigenous peoples into the fabric of dominant social institutions like the education, child welfare, and criminal justice systems. In the most optimistic projection, the generation of Indigenous youth who have been "lost" as a result of the myopic social policies of the past will begin to rise above structural domination through new forms of youth programming destined to chart a different course.

I show throughout this book, however, that promoting alliances as symbolic and material evidence of Canada's recognition of Indigenous peoples' aspirations of sovereignty and control over the destiny of their children and youth is only a partial story, a one-sided account. I offer a crucial corrective to this normative view by demonstrating that participation does not exist in a neutral, suspended space, empty of power and history, nor are its benefits necessarily axiomatic or its implications readily predictable. I delineate how participation, as an instantiation of contemporary inclusionary governance, is fundamentally a reassertion of asymmetrical power relations, albeit in a new guise, because the terms and form of political engagement are mediated by a settler nation state that has been created through colonial dominance.[16] Throughout this book, I ask, what role does participation play in altering the terrain of domination framing Indigenous–state relations and what are the intended and unintended consequences of such political, and often ambiguous, engagements? what are the ways that the lives of Indigenous young people continue to be shaped by settler colonial practices of the state, even in the wake of these new governing logics? Participation, then, is also about the ostensible empowerment of marginalized Indigenous communities through dominant societal institutions and about the complex political, cultural, and bureaucratic practices that shape the categories, classification systems, and social norms for what it means to be Indigenous in Canada (Cannon 2011). Moreover, rival beliefs about what it means to be Indigenous in Canada (or not) – particularly the often troubling distinction between modernity (defined as progress and enlightenment) and tradition (read as backwardness and ignorance) – are critical in shaping narratives about the lives of urban Indigenous youth and the related meanings of "empowerment" that are ascribed to a participatory process (Marker 2000; Garcia 2005).

In line with these crucial questions, I argue that a participatory politics demands ethnographic study and analysis in some of the sites and spaces where its effects will be most profoundly and urgently experienced – the design and enactment of social interventions targeted at urban Indigenous youth who have inherited, by virtue of their ancestral history, a political standing in Canada as colonial subjects – and where its limits, constraints, and possibilities will be unveiled. Thus, the aims of this book are threefold:

1. To trace the logics of participation and politics of recognition as it relates to the history of Indigenous–state relations and to locate these politics within the invariably complex sociopolitical and economic terrains that inform the lived experiences of urban Indigenous youth
2. To show how a larger structure of dominance that characterizes Indigenous–state relations regulates the boundaries and parameters of participatory politics and includes gendered aspects of colonial violence that are fundamental to these politics
3. To document the political and social tensions surfacing in the extension of state power vis-à-vis participatory alliances by exposing how state agents, Indigenous community representatives, youth workers, and Indigenous leaders put this discursive apparatus into practice and how it is resisted and manipulated by state and non-state actors alike

I address these domains of inquiry in order to bring to light the network of power and persistent dispossession that overwhelmingly marks sociopolitical relations between Indigenous peoples and the Canadian state – a reflection on Indigenous politics without a related discussion of colonial power structures is either strategically reductionist or massively obtuse within the context of settler governance. Disturbingly, the exercise of power is consistently obfuscated in the design and delivery of improvement schemes for urban Indigenous youth. A case in point is one among many meetings I attended for a youth social program. The program's primary goal was to reduce the recidivism rate for urban Indigenous youth emerging from detention facilities and included an emphasis on school attendance. During this meeting, a higher level staff member at an Indigenous community organization turned to a youth worker and said, "Don't bring your fancy ideas about colonization into this program. It's not what these youth need and they will never understand what you are saying anyway. It's not what they need." The youth worker was trying to explain that teaching Indigenous youth about some of the political struggles facing Indigenous peoples was important to promote young people's understanding of their individual circumstances and to build a connection between herself and them, based on shared experience. In response to the remark by the senior staff member, she simply nodded her head in passive agreement. As we walked out of the meeting together, she turned to me and whispered, "It's my job, what can I do?"

Implicated in this example are two profound questions: what is the role of epistemology and power in determining the scope and hierarchy of the politics that frame social programming for urban Indigenous youth? how are knowledge and leadership constituted in order to guide these politics? The example also demonstrates an urgent need for a more nuanced set of understandings through which Indigenous communities and their allies can unveil, and subsequently challenge, the multiple articulations of power and structural, settler colonial violence as they continue to be practised by the Canadian state.

### Spotlighting Frames: Settler Colonialism, Anti-Racist and Indigenous Feminisms, and Colonial Governmentality

I engage three broad conceptual formulations when attending to the book's aims, formulations to which I have briefly alluded in the preceding pages.[17] The first, settler colonialism,[18] provides an overarching framework for discussing the characteristics and temporalities of the Canadian Indigenous experience and the legal and political legacies of colonial control that have a profound influence on contemporary negotiations involving urban Indigenous youth (Stasiulis and Yuval-Davis 1995; Wolfe 1999; Razack 2002; Elkins and Pedersen 2005; Belich 2009; Veracini 2011; A. Simpson 2014). Drawing on the work of scholars who have traced the itineraries of "the colonial present" (Gregory 2004, 4) in settler nation states (Bruyneel 2007; Coulthard 2007; A. Simpson 2007; Strakosch and Macoun 2012), I regard Canada first and foremost as a settler colony marked by the ongoing dynamics of colonialism.[19] In the tradition of this scholarship that ruptures the myth of the two founding fathers,[20] the emergence of Canada is configured as narrative of conquest (Mamdani 1998), based on the doctrine of *terra nullius* (empty lands), and no longer as a mystical migration story. The principle of "empty" lands served, historically, to unlock the ideological gates and secure the secular and religious rationalizations for the "legal" dispossession of Indigenous peoples from their original territories (Alfred 2009) and for the subsequent implementation of laws and social policies that institutionalized the forced assimilation of Indigenous peoples and elevated the cultural and social status of white settlers.

The goal of settler colonizers is to create a new social and political order with the ultimate aim of securing a permanent hold on specific, conquered locales. Structural decolonialization, as both a discursive and practical undertaking, exists entirely outside the purview of a colonial social order – there is no intention to return stolen territory.[21] To accomplish such a goal, however, settlers have a surreptitious, recurring need to disavow the presence of the Indigenous "other" and effectively repress, co-opt, and extinguish Indigenous alterities (Povinelli 2002; A. Simpson 2007). This, in fact, becomes the central agenda of the settler colonial nation state: to map the terrain of the conflict waged over tactics of epistemic violence and assimilation and assert authority over "authentic" Indigenous discourse and the terms under which political resistance takes place. The emergence of settler nation states, thus, has a distinctly sovereign charge and claims a "regenerative capacity" in relation to conquered territory (Veracini 2010) that aims to destroy, replace, rename, classify – to assimilate in all of the ways that mitigate threats or resistance to the process of growing settler dominance. Through this process, power is consolidated across social institutions and legal mechanisms that reorganize geography, access to land, cultural practices, family and kinship networks, spirituality, identity, and ultimately political subjectivity (Cannon 2011).

Patrick Wolfe's work is especially instructive in illuminating the staying power of the settler colonial present. Tracing the footsteps of colonial settlement through what he calls the "logic of elimination," Wolfe (2006, 387) argues that this logic, which seeks to contain and regulate all things Indigenous, may change in form but ultimately remains continuous through time. When explaining the variation in elimination strategies, he writes, "The positive outcome of the logic of elimination can include officially encouraged miscegenation, the breaking down of native title into inalienable individual freeholds, native citizenship, child abduction, religious conversion, resocialization in total institutions such as missions or boarding schools, and a whole range of cognate biocultural assimilations. All of these strategies, including frontier homicide, are characteristic of settler colonialism" (Wolfe 2006, 388). In a similar vein, Elizabeth Strakosch and Alissa Macoun (2012, 45) describe the myriad ways in which elimination can take place: through the physical elimination of people, by severing connections to land that lie at the heart of Indigenous political systems, by breaking down families and communities, by drawing Indigenous polities into the state and reforming them, and by entering into specific contractual agreements.

Accordingly, "invasion is a structure rather than an isolated event" (Wolfe 2006, 387) and the particular manner in which elimination takes place, both in terms of target and methods, changes with the specificity of the historical moment in which we find ourselves. At the heart of the matter, though, lies the following reality: the continued existence of Indigenous peoples in Canada constitutes a direct threat to settler control and the related political entitlements of settler governance. They have not been eliminated, nor wholly assimilated.

With respect to undertaking a critical appraisal of the politics of intervention in the lives of urban Indigenous youth, a lens of settler colonialism importantly serves to re-establish essential linkages between the everyday lives of these young people and the dynamics of colonial power and imperial navigation in which deliberations about social programs to assist them are deeply, and necessarily, enmeshed. In other words, while the lived realities of young people like Nitânis may be positioned by state agents, youth workers, and community representatives as outside the scope of the larger political questions of Indigenous sovereignty and self-determination (positioned instead as a matter of immediate crisis response, individual failure, and fragility; see chapter 2 of the present book), scholars of settler colonial studies enable us to collapse the distance between these seemingly disparate sets of issues and place them in direct conversation with one another. Nitânis and her peers, then, operate as young Indigenous people in a distinctly settler colonial space where their very resistance and survival stands in opposition to a fully consummated settler ownership and legitimacy. Part of my purpose in writing this book is to unpack how social interventions and policies targeted at these youth factor into these ever present problematics and to consider how discourses of participation and dispensations of reciprocity intertwine with the historiography of a Canadian settler state whose nationalist project continues to rest on stolen land.

The second broad formulation I draw upon, anti-racist and Indigenous feminism (Monture-Angus 1995; Jiwani 2006; Suzack et al. 2010), places gendered racial, colonial violence at the centre of my ethnographic investigation of the lives of urban Indigenous youth in Saskatoon. An equally strong thread throughout this book, then, is an unveiling of the ways that colonial relationships are themselves highly gendered and sexualized and so, as a result, are state encounters with urban Indigenous youth that build on a historical legacy of gender violence. For example, sexual violence as experienced by Indigenous women and girls, and their concomitant disempowerment, was an integral part of

nineteenth-century strategies of domination. Sexual violence continues into the present day through the foundational violence of the state
and the state's complicity in sanctioning the invisibility of gender violence against Indigenous women and girls.[22] The condoned invisibility
works in concert with individual acts of male violence and reinscribes
a dehumanized and racialized "other" (the Indigenous woman or girl)
who can be violated at will with minimal or no consequences.[23] Further,
the Canadian regulation of Indigenous identity through the gendered
notions of "Indianness" produced through the Indian Act has generated, as Bonita Lawrence (2003, 5) writes, "unimaginable levels of violence, which includes, but is not restricted to, sexist oppression."[24] This
legislation also eradicated traditional leadership in Indigenous communities through the creation of band governments, which, in turn,
systematically restricted Indigenous women's roles in politics and reinforced politics as a strictly male domain.[25]

In her book *Conquest: Sexual Violence and the American Indian Genocide*, Andrea Smith (2005, 3) expands on this argument, when she says,
"Putting native women at the centre of analysis compels us to look at
the role of the state in perpetrating both race-based and gender-based
violence. We cannot limit our conception of sexual violence to individual acts of rape – rather it encompasses a wide range of strategies
designed not only to destroy peoples, but to destroy their sense of being
a people." The project of colonial sexual violence, then, establishes, as
ideology, the belief that Indigenous bodies are inherently violable and
by extension, that Indigenous lands are available for the taking. In failing to respond to instances of abuse and in implementing social policies that conceal the layered realities of Indigenous women and girls,
the state continues to perpetrate instances of violence.[26] Therefore, any
assessment of social programming that targets urban Indigenous youth
should arguably interrogate forms of violence mapped onto the Indigenous body and, by extension, onto the land (Sterritt 2007).

Throughout this book, then, I purposefully write in opposition to
those who would de-race and de-gender the experience of what it
means to be an Indigenous youth living in a Canadian urban centre.[27]
Settler colonizers have inscribed hierarchy and domination on the bodies of Indigenous people through patriarchal gender violence, and the
day to day experiences of urban Indigenous girls are not exempt from
this practice. Moreover, as I reveal in numerous instances throughout
this book, Indigenous girls' experiences of colonial gender violence
continue to be strategically bypassed, or erased altogether, in dialogues

and debates regarding the regimes of intervention that are intended to alter and/or improve their everyday lives. These ongoing omissions speak volumes to the power of colonial gender violence that has, from the point of first contact, systematically subjugated Indigenous women and girls and symbolically positioned them as agents of a counter-imperial order and, consequently, a direct threat to colonial rule (Smith 2005).

Finally, in its conceptual preoccupations, this book finds common ground with Michel Foucault's theories of governmentality[28] and modern power and with the application of these analytics to the domain of colonial, settler nation states – a form of governing defined as "colonial governmentality" (Scott 1995; Crosby and Monaghan 2012). Within the framework of colonial governmentality – a distinctive form of political rationality – governmental power comes to be directed at the destruction and reconstruction of colonial space in order to produce, not so much extractive effects on colonial bodies, as governing effects on colonial conduct (for both the colonized and the colonizers).[29] In the persuasive words of David Scott (1995, 204),

> The point rather is that in order to understand the project of colonial power at any given historical moment one has to understand the character of the political rationality that constituted it. And what is crucial to such an understanding is not what the attitude of the colonizer was toward the colonized, nor whether colonialism excluded or included natives as such. Rather, what is crucial is trying to discern colonial power's point of application, its target, and the discursive and nondiscursive fields it sought to encompass.

Simply put, colonial power depends on the systematic redefinition and transformation of the terrain upon which the life of the colonized is lived. Historically, this statement rings particularly true for Indigenous peoples in Canada, given the settler state's mandate of forced removal of Indigenous children and youth from their communities and the related experiences of residential schooling, ostensibly rehabilitative incarceration, and the sexual regulation and legal mediation of kinship lines, political engagement, and identity through the Indian Act (Cannon 2011). Government, then, suggests a "contact point" where techniques of domination (or power) and techniques of the self "interact," where "technologies of domination of individuals over one another have recourse to processes by which the individual acts upon himself and, conversely, where techniques of the self are integrated into structures of coercion" (Foucault; quoted in Burchell 1996, 20). The critical purchase of this conceptual lens, thus, lies in its ability to move beyond the question of whether or not Indigenous peoples are merely included or excluded from formal governmental decisions and orders of social programming – this is not just a numbers game. Instead, the terms of the engagement between the state and Indigenous peoples, as well as the social mandates that serve to alter ethical and moral character and political subjectivity, become the critical points of interrogation for two reasons: first, they normalize specific kinds of desire and sensibilities about the Canadian state; and second, they sanction the forms of knowledge production and the methods used to elucidate the "needs" of urban Indigenous youth. Participation, as a vehicle for increasing Indigenous representation in youth directed social policy in urban centres, has, at a very fundamental level, been constructed by the state as a mechanism to recalibrate relations between the governing and the governed. This reconstruction, however, takes place within a context of settler colonialism that simultaneously distances the political and legal entity of Canada from its history of conquest while purposefully fostering a new national imaginary of the peaceful postcolonial. In turn, for Indigenous peoples to be actively involved in decisions regarding the future of their children and youth, they must be inserted into a political game already being played with a set of rules not of their own making.

The concept of "governmentality" has served as the foundation upon which a number of scholars working in this tradition have sought to develop optics for understanding the shifting and changing nature of modern governance in terms of its relationship with civil society (Ferguson 1994; Gupta 2006; Rose 1999; Hansen and Stepputat 2001).[30] These scholars have challenged the position of the state as the sole repository of power and have instead looked beyond the formal boundaries of the government to include a range of parties (e.g., NGOs, social reformists, and social scientists) that have become implicated in the work of governing. Drawing attention to the creation of multiple authorities that call for a rethinking of the state vs. civil society dichotomy,[31] one can assert that the links between the political apparatus and the activities of government are heterogeneous and dependent upon a range of knowledge frames and knowledgeable persons that are not necessarily formal state agents (Rose 2000; Li 2005).

In his article entitled "Governing Liberty," Nikolas Rose (2000, 111) works squarely within a Foucauldian framework to understand how everyday practices in population management have served the interests of the state, whose mission is to foster more and more automization, rationalization, and responsibility among the governed.[32] Treating governing as a methodology involving the "systemized conduct of conduct," Rose argues that people are governed by the methodology of government to imbue the populations to be governed with the norms, techniques, and values of civility. "Neo-liberalism," writes Rose (1996, 53), "does not abandon the 'will to govern': it maintains the view that failure of government to achieve its objectives is to be overcome by inventing new strategies of government that will succeed."[33] Contemporary theories of the state, then, lend insight into interpreting, analysing, and making sense of the plethora of policies, procedures, and competing discourses that have come to represent "the state" and the numerous processes through which the state comes into being in order to enact regulatory mechanisms.[34] Of equal importance, however, the conceptual frame of governmentality raises the question of how human populations across the globe are being governed in new and more coercive ways that may escape our common sense notions of the "relations of ruling,"[35] and of the unintended, intended, and multilayered effects of these new strategies and technologies in terms of the ostensible freedom, liberty, and political resistance that form the *basis of* liberal democracies. Rose (1996, 62) makes this point best when he says, "It is to say that the agonistic relation between liberty and government is an intrinsic part of what we have come to know as freedom." With respect to regimes of intervention in the lives of urban Indigenous youth, it behoves us to be thoughtful about the way modern forms of power become part and parcel of the social transformation advanced through the accommodation of difference. Thus, the gaze shifts towards looking more closely at a form of colonial statecraft camouflaged by a discursive landscape of recognition and reconciliation (Coulthard 2014a).

\* \* \*

Ultimately, I argue that this intersection of interests cohering around a regime of social intervention for urban Indigenous youth is far from a neutral and simple process. I assert, rather, that participatory alliances reflect a changing form of settler colonialism through which the very constitution of Indigenous resurgence, social location, and political resistance continues to be mediated by the state under the ambiguous guise of "Indigenous involvement" and collaborative social reform efforts – reforms taking place in a time of extensive and mounting political contestations over land and water, and of persistent, systemic violence both on and off reserves. In the chapters that follow, I expose how this intervention politics is a complex and contradictory venture, whose consequences include the preservation of social hierarchies, the manufacturing of inclusionary and exclusionary boundaries of what participation means and who is qualified to take part, and the potentialities for the state to reinvent itself through the auspices of Indigenous community organizing while simultaneously depoliticizing the lived realities of urban Indigenous youth. I also pay close attention to the strategies that youth workers draw upon, sometimes successfully and sometimes not, to subvert social programs in order to advance an alternative agenda; and to the constellation of actors who become engaged in problem solving around the nuanced realities of young peoples' everyday lives. Human interactions, after all, are dynamic and multifaceted – we do not always follow a script.

At stake, I believe, in undertaking this kind of close range scrutiny is making analytic inroads that are not limited to the impact of these collaborative efforts on the "materiality of the social" (Farmer 2004) as it relates to the everyday lives of Indigenous children and youth. An ethnographic investigation opens up a space to consider how these configurations shape and reshape the objectives, as well as the ambiguities and inconsistencies, of sovereignty and the fostering of new political relationships between Indigenous peoples and the settler state of Canada. Put another way, gesturing analytically towards the conception and enactment of a participatory politics – its problematics, strategies, and results and effects – elevates critical insight and awareness to a point where we can endeavour to imagine new possibilities for change that move beyond the (re)creation of hegemonic social formations. Techniques for the governing of Indigenous peoples, then, are always a story of aggressive and swarming state power, but also a reflection of how social and political conditions, while structured, are never fully determined (Ferguson 1994). The recent rise of the Indigenous social movement Idle No More, which I speak to at greater length in the final chapter, is evidence of the mobilization and potential for change that comes when we think critically and reflexively about contemporary settler colonial governance and highlights the possibility that some of our political strategies may need to be rethought or abandoned altogether. It is my hope that demonstrating how participatory politics are important reconfigurations of the shadow lines of settler colonialism to which urban Indigenous youth remain tethered (the work of the remainder of this book) is a worthy contribution to such efforts. Indeed, an ahistorical view of participation that valorizes it as a mark of progress towards the postcolonial and a dismissive view that rejects it without a nuanced understanding of its inherent logics both fall short of producing an informed social and political agenda that can strategically advance Indigenous sovereignty. I am fully aware, however, that this book enacts its own limitations and may also be considered, by some, an incomplete tale. My point in writing it is to contribute to a compendium of critical, public scholarship that demands ongoing reflexivity as we think about advancing movements for justice and decolonization in Canada. All of this is overshadowed, of course, by the grim reality that ongoing dispossession is largely made possible only if Indigenous children and youth continue to experience lives of social and economic marginalization and political containment.

### Territories of Knowing and Being Known: Place, Methods, and Notes

*Saskatoon: The Here and Now of a Place*

Treaty Six Cree Territory, Land of the Buffalo.[36] The stark blue sky and radiant sun provide an ideal backdrop for the aerial view out of my small, glass porthole, the Dash 8 swiftly descending through the frozen air towards the city's jet way. As the plane emerges from the white haze of floating clouds, it is easy to mark where rural ends and urban begins; a smattering of buildings, signage, paved roads, truncated alleys, and strip malls of commerce gives way to the immense, breathtaking horizon of "big sky country." In the middle of all this space, where land is as open as the sea, the earth itself holds rusty keys to unlocking tales of conquest and rebellion. While these tales may be buried in centuries of stately, revisionist history, they are not easily washed or written away. "History" can be backfilled with competing truth claims simply by digging deeper.[37]

The grand openness is due, in part, to the notoriously sparse population of the prairie provinces.[38] Long stretches of lush agricultural fields (replaced by blankets of shining snow in the winter), red wooden barns, the occasional solo tree, and majestic grain elevators connect one municipality to another in the southern section of these sprawling lands. To an outsider with little knowledge of this region, it could well seem as though the area were full of sleepy, quaint communities where nothing much happened and people simply lived their day to day lives in a way reminiscent of Coen and Coen's film *Fargo* set on the plains of the Midwest – a romanticized view of small town life, minus an awareness of the complex realities lived by generations who have emerged from a deeply unsettled past.

The geographical texture and spatial arrangement of the city is also clearly visible from the hovering aircraft. The South Saskatchewan

Figure 1. Big sky country at Wanuskewin Heritage Park, 2012
(Photo credit: Marcel Petit)

River partitions the city into its east and west sides, and this natural cleavage is integrated into the city's design. Eight bridges traverse the distance between opposing riverbanks and make it possible for residents to move, by means of physical transport, from one side of the city to the other. Depending on who you are, social movement between these zones is a more complicated story.

The expansive university grounds, occupying a substantial portion of the riverbank's eastern edge, signal one of the province's primary institutions of higher education, where future leaders are being made in sanctioned places of learning. The rapidly changing eastern and southern suburban perimeters, with their cookie cutter homes, dirt and bulldozers, and construction-style orange fences that shield the danger zones of development, are an obvious indication of Saskatoon's population boom over the last five years. This rise is partly attributable to the expansion of fossil fuel industries in the province's north, one of the lowest unemployment rates in the country until recently, and a substantial rise in the new immigrant population, bolstered in part by federal immigration policies (Statistics Canada 2011). Saskatoon is not yet a city of high rise office towers and never-ending suburban sprawl, but it is a city on the move. Growth, prosperity, and economic progress have become synonymous with Saskatchewan in recent years. Privileged property owners have revelled in large profits from home sales, and low vacancy rates have resulted in skyrocketing rental prices. Desirable portions of Saskatoon's waterfront property have received injections of beautifying funds from the municipal government to elicit interest in public spaces of gathering. Baroque structures are being erected to showcase the work of city's talented arts community. The view that "Saskatoon Shines" – as a large blue and yellow sign suggests to visitors and inhabitants departing the international airport on the only road leading into the city centre – holds true for some. Less obvious from the air, though, is another section of the city, where growth, prosperity, and economic progress have not emerged in the same way and where a different kind of transformation is being conceived and contested.

The ground I walk in this othered space is frozen, a pastiche of freshly fallen snow, footprints, and black ice. Late afternoon in a prairie winter is marked by rapidly fading sunlight and crisp arctic air, usually blowing. At the peak of winter, darkness falls under an endless, clear sky around 4:45 p.m. and sometimes earlier. The temperature hovers around −25°C, so cold that your breath leaves small clouds in the air. In a certain corridor of Saskatoon's Westside, signifiers that commonly mark struggling urban neighbourhoods abound: antiquated pawnshops, bingo halls, sporadic graffiti and gang tags, empty storefront windows, shoes hanging from power lines, and decrepit bars line the main artery of the Westside. This is considered the bad side of the city. On any given night, young women, sometimes scantily dressed even amidst the wind and snow, stand on alternating street corners of the stroll, shifting nervously to protect their domain while projecting an image of vacancy and ultimate loss – present and absent at the same time. Young people and children gather in groups, a few blocks away, outside the entrance of a youth service organization, some without proper winter clothing to protect them from the frigid cold – their extremities subject to the beginning stages of frostbite. Police cruisers officially sanctioned to increase public safety cast shadows of blue and red against the whiteness of snow as they attempt to keep criminality at bay and out of plain sight. An old church stands empty, waiting to open its doors on select days to those people willing to surrender to the benevolence of God. To the detached passer-by, the Westside has the potential to appear as a puzzled skein of tragic stories, a patchwork of individualized failure, where ravaging misfortunes are locally derived. The fretwork of entrenched social maladies obscures the historical and political tale of colonization, structural violence, and disinvestment of "these people" and instead foregrounds the vivid representations of poverty in the present – what is visible to the eye (Farmer 2004).

This particular zone of Saskatoon is commonly referred to as the "core neighbourhood" by social service workers, government agents, and local residents alike and is home to the majority of Indigenous people residing in this urban locale. Partitioned by a wide and frequently travelled main street that begins at the city's outer, industrial edge, the core neighbourhood abruptly ends when the zone rubs up against the lively, manicured thoroughfares of downtown. Here, social policy deals are brokered in impressive government buildings fitted with rows of neatly arranged management cubicles and boardrooms containing long wooden tables and swivel chairs. Downtown is also the commercial and tourist centre, where Indigenous cultural artefacts adorn public spaces and local parks, marking the outward acceptance of Indigenous difference and celebrating its richness as part of the city's social fabric. The Treaty Six flag has recently been erected in front of City Hall, to fly in tandem with city and provincial flags seen throughout the municipality. The city's official tourist website echoes these protestations of postcolonial calm. These public displays of Native endorsement, however, stand in sharp contrast to the high rates of poverty and suicide; sexual exploitation; limited access to education; lack of safe and affordable housing; compounding health concerns as a result of malnutrition, infectious disease, and drug addiction; and soaring rates of criminalization for urban Indigenous children, youth, and families living in the blocks immediately to the west. In the core, one must always walk with bodily senses alert to the immediate surroundings, especially if turning onto one of the dimly lit residential streets flanking the primary road. Clusters of small, rundown homes, some boarded up, a whiff of smoke and car engines endlessly running, and suspect social transactions are almost a certainty. The cheap rental accommodations have changed little since the 1960s, when a steady stream of Indigenous people migrated from reserves to urban spaces, spawning a deeply entrenched, spatially concentrated, and racialized poverty in the Westside. If you look up from the ground, your blinking eyes will likely be met with a partially crumpled flyer stapled to a streetlight post, revealing photographic and related details about the disappearance of another Indigenous young woman.[39]

Figure 2. Remembrance rally for murdered and missing Indigenous women, Saskatoon, 2014 (Photo credit: Jaskiran Dhillon)

Latent hostilities simmer beneath the surface of municipal, provincial, and federal debates about the social interventions, state policies, and systems of regulation that intersect with the lives of Indigenous peoples living in Saskatoon's core neighbourhood. Political standoff always threatens to come forth. One only has to read the local newspaper or listen to local radio stations[40] to come face to face with the latest allegations of systemic discrimination in state systems and the concomitant public contestation of the demands for self-determination asserted by Indigenous peoples. Widespread public outcry over what is often represented as "special treatment" or "citizen-plus or race-based privileges"[41] afforded Natives through ostensible tax breaks, tuition relief in higher education, and various social service supports – can be found in all corners.[42] Lived expressions of racism, both obvious and subtle, have long tainted relations between Indigenous and non-Indigenous residents in Saskatoon.

Historically, Indigenous migration to Canadian cities was viewed with resentment and fear, solidifying the belief that their rightful place

Figure 3. South Saskatchewan River Park, 2014 (Photo credit: Marcel Petit)

was on the reserve. The Saskatchewan government's 1960 submission to the Joint Committee of the Senate and House of Commons on Indian Affairs issued the following grave warning: "The day is not distant when the burgeoning Indian population, now largely confined to reservations, will explode into white communities and present a serious problem indeed" (Saskatchewan 1960). Even now, despite provincial and federal initiatives to address the specific social conditions facing Indigenous peoples, the degree of marginalization remains severe.

Indigenous youth have told me about the palpability of this hostility when they describe their experiences of moving from the Westside to the Eastside of Saskatoon across the South Saskatchewan River over one of the city's eight bridges. They have told me about the way business owners stare at them when they enter restaurants, bars, and clothing stores they are not expected to enter, when they break the informal codes of conduct in an overtly segregated city. They have told me about the whispered comments they overhear on the street and the derogatory references to Indigenous peoples that move through the city like an infectious wind. They have told me about the endemic racism that has become part of their day to day existence in the city's schools, parks, and shopping malls. And they have told me stories of how they are treated by social service agents – from hospital staff and doctors to teachers, social workers, and police probation officers – who pass judgment on their appearance and lived experience, making them extremely cautious about seeking assistance with the many harsh realities they face. Few have formally or explicitly evaluated their social position as a denial of Indigenous sovereignty. The time to discuss "these things," they say, is a privilege granted to those who have a place to sleep at night and a steady supply of food, to those not fleeing the brutality of the street. Notions of empowerment seem to exist somewhere else, in another time and place, where systemic colonial violence has not gained so much ground.

Adding to this scene, a recent government inquiry into issues of police violence in Saskatchewan, through the investigation of the murder of Neil Stonechild (Saskatchewan 2004) and the Missing Women Commission of Inquiry in British Columbia, has only served to highlight the ongoing struggles between Indigenous peoples and the Canadian state in the areas of social justice and political emancipation – calling attention to the contradictions within the concept of self-determination itself. Pushing beyond the boundaries of Canadian domestic territory, the United Nations Committee on the Elimination of Discrimination against Women has also brought Canada's colonial history to centre stage and put it under

Figure 4. Twentieth Street, 2012 (Photo credit: Marcel Petit)

close international scrutiny, by drawing attention to the Canadian government's failure to investigate the murder and disappearances of Indigenous women and girls (and related experiences of violence) and to the implications for Indigenous communities and families that go hand in hand with these violations. Feelings of distrust towards government mechanisms seeking to "involve" Indigenous people in state machinery occasionally surface in splashy news stories sensationalizing long-time disputes over land, momentarily bringing contentious questions about the nation's confederation into the purview of the country's myopic eye. Indigenous resistance since the advent of colonization provides us with some insight into the cultural and political cachet from which they draw to meet the many exigencies of living in Saskatoon's Westside. They have been navigating scarce resources and suppression since the bloody beginning of Kanata.[43]

## The Writer and Her Methods[44]

While the currents of my day to day now circle around my role as a university professor at The New School and an advocate and ally with a number of community organizations, my interest and passion for the work that forms the heart of this book originated in a place far from New York City. I am the daughter of immigrant parents from Northern India, who settled on the Saskatchewan prairie in a town approximately 200 km west of Saskatoon – a landscape that has been etched on my psyche since the time I was very young. One only needs to spend a short amount of time on the plains of Western Canada to realize that rural Saskatchewan is a far cry from the hustling, and rather aggressive, streets of New York City – especially considering that there, land and sky are visible as far as the eye can see, while New York blocks one's line of vision with one building after another, both horizontally and vertically.

Not unlike many first generation kids, with multilingual households and dinner table discussions where views from around the world collide, occasionally in volcanic-like eruptions, I developed somewhat of an innate curiosity about and awareness of difference and power by virtue of the complex cultural terrain on which I grew up. My father was an atheist, immigrant principal in a small, almost entirely homogeneous, farming community of approximately 300 people. I lived alongside him, my mother, and my two sisters as we tried to make sense of the dislocation, contradictions, and tensions we encountered, both personally and institutionally, as individuals positioned on the borderlands of Canadian nationalism. I always felt lodged in an invisible seam between two worlds and grew up accustomed to being asked where I was from (even by those who considered themselves to be the most enlightened), despite my being born in Canada. There was an unspoken, consistent, and unsolicited reminder that – even though my family and I had made Canada the place to live our lives, either by personal design or cosmic accident – we were pioneering our way in a new land and culture to which we were not always welcome. Somewhere else, in this case, was deemed home, regardless of my birth right.

Being raised in this geographically and socially isolated environment, however, also afforded me an opportunity to bear witness to ruptures in the dominant trope regarding Canada's peaceful history and formal consolidation as a nation. I began to notice first-hand how discussions about Indigenous and non-Indigenous (or largely white) relations seemed to pervade local newspapers, educational debates, questions of employment and labour, and federal concerns over place, land, and belonging. Over the years, I watched my father, the principal of the K-12 school where I received my formal education until I graduated from high school (a school of only 100 students in total), struggle to support the few Indigenous students who attended our school, youth who were placed in foster homes in farms close to the town. I also remember visiting small prairie cities like North Battleford, Prince Albert, and Moose Jaw, where there was a significant urban Indigenous presence, and witnessing my father's respectful and inquisitive interactions wherever we travelled – positioned as alien himself, he always seemed to be seeking answers. I would often ask questions on these excursions, wondering why the perceived difference of Indigenous peoples, and us, seemed to matter so much and how their history was tied to the land where he and my mother chose to live. I was also able to detect that there were levels and nuances in this hierarchy of difference and that my family's experiences were qualitatively distinct from what I was witnessing with Indigenous peoples, since their relationship with the land predated the colonial founding of the country that I called home.

I remember one instance, in particular, when my family and I had travelled to North Battleford to purchase a few things we could not get in the small town where we were living; North Battleford was the closest thing we had to a bustling urban centre, where consumer wants could be more easily met. At one point during this outing, I found myself standing in a department store, face to face with a series of gumball toy machines – the kind into which you insert coins and turn a metal knob. I am sure I was looking longingly and wishing my parents would satisfy my desire to deposit the required change and receive whatever magical prize the machine would yield. To my surprise, an elderly man with stunning long braids and a beautiful, intricately beaded leather jacket approached me a few moments later. He reached into his pocket and pulled out a series of coins and carefully placed them in my hands, encouraging me to fulfil my wish. My father, standing only a few feet away, came over and introduced himself to the man, thanking him, and they began a short conversation about the weather and related chitchat. After we parted ways, and I had my prize, my father turned to me and said, "If you ever grow up to fight for something, fight alongside the people in this country who have had so much taken from them."[45]

These cumulative experiences, however unintentional, assisted in the development of my political awareness of the dirty business involved in "the making of Canada," both as an "imagined community" (B. Anderson 1991) and as a formal state entity. These experiences also brought to the fore the history of disinvestment and violence between Indigenous peoples and the Canadian state through a constellation of social, economic, political, and cultural practices that were conveniently absent or erased altogether from most of the history and social studies textbooks included in my formal school curriculum. In his work on structural violence, medical anthropologist Paul Farmer (2004, 308) calls attention to the importance of erasing history in the enactment of social and political marginalization by explaining, "[E]rasing history is perhaps the most common explanatory sleight-of-hand relied upon by the architects of structural violence. Erasure or distortion of history is part of the process of desocialization necessary for the emergence of hegemonic accounts of what happened and why." And for Frantz Fanon (1963, 199), "Colonialism is not satisfied merely with holding a people in its grip and emptying the native's brain of all form and content. By a kind of perverted logic, it turns to the past of an oppressed people, and distorts, disfigures, and destroys it." It is therefore imperative that one pay attention to the role that the erasure of historical memory plays in order to ask what social and political conditions the erasure enables – conditions that ostensibly are "nobody's fault," although massively unjust (Farmer 2004, 307).

Not surprisingly, my personal and professional journey thus far has been intimately linked to these day to day experiences of growing up and a subsequent desire to bridge the gap between the visible and material manifestations of marginality and deprivation, on the one hand, and the history and politics from which these social conditions grow, gain strength, and through which they are ultimately sustained, on the other. I am interested in contributing to a contextual, critical understanding of the interlocking and overlapping social systems that produce the widely quoted statistics around Indigenous youth suicide, drop out, and criminalization in Canada[46] – this is not a story without origins or roots. This book has also emerged out of years of advocating alongside colleagues for community programs for youth who embody the history of their ancestors in both the public and private domains of social life. I have encountered numerous young people in Saskatchewan and British Columbia, and in various other locations in Canada and the United States, through my role as program developer for "homeless and street-involved" youth and researcher of youth issues – as mentor, and advocate. The youth I encountered struggled to find ways to have their basic needs met and to move beyond the legacy of intergenerational poverty and violence, both institutional and interpersonal, that had become normalized and entrenched in their daily existence. I can attest to an endless stream of stories from Indigenous youth, who recounted experiences of sexual exploitation, racism, gendered violence; deprivation of housing, food, and medical care; and numerous forms of institutional malaise and neglect. These stories underscore a tremendous sense of urgency with respect to the need for political change and related discussions about how that change will happen and what it will look like. I also made note of the ways in which the life trajectories of youth were repeatedly being shaped by forces outside the realms of "personal choice" and "individual accountability" – slogans that have become synonymous with many recent governmental initiatives marked by the structural violence of disinvestment characteristic of neoliberal regimes (Dhillon 2011).

Over the years, I wove my way through the multiple locations where governmental officials, non-profit workers, and community representatives were, theoretically, cooperating to think about how to address better the longstanding issues these youth were facing. Across the various settings, it became clear to me that the creation of social programs was embedded with particular assumptions, ideas, and stories about who these youth were, the communities they came from, and the skills and forms of knowledge that would be required to move them to some magical state of "empowerment."[47] It seemed as though the fight for land, justice, and self-determination had been replaced by the ambiguous goal of personal empowerment – a notion that, in many instances, seemed to suggest that the individual alone could be (and was) the locus of action and change. Entangled in the network, language, and culture of social program development, it took me a moment to step back from this scene and reconsider what I was observing. The distance helped me to think critically about how the category of youth had become homogenized through these spaces of policy and program creation and about the potential challenges and incongruities the absence of competing constructions of "youth" or of the multiple communities from which they came presented. Knowing that many of the youth self-identified as Indigenous or were ascribed this designation, the absence of a more nuanced understanding of youth became a particularly salient concern, and I began to consider the political implications of social intervention strategies within the greater context of Indigenous sovereignty and decolonization.

For instance, I recall being at a meeting of youth service workers who were attempting to develop a life skills program for "at-risk" youth in a particular section of one of the cities in Western Canada where I had been working. Becoming increasingly conscious of the paternalistic and deficit-oriented language being used to describe these young people and their life circumstances, and knowing that almost all of the youth who would be participating in this program would be Indigenous given the specific location of the program, I asked if the objectives of the program were being created in dialogue with Indigenous leaders in the city. I was fed the old adage of, "Oh, they have their own programs they are working on"; or "We have invited them but they never come – what does that demonstrate about their commitment to these kids!" The sentiment of developing empowerment programs centred on capacitating individuals and communities to "take care of themselves" came across loud and clear at this meeting, without any consideration of who these youth were beyond their being "at risk."

I began having conversations with some of my colleagues both in the non-profit sector as well as in the academy (because these worlds, not surprisingly, often offer very different perspectives) about my concerns, trying to make sense of how all of us became implicated in this increasingly messy and multilayered story of attempted social change that was likely perpetuating colonial relations of power (however well intentioned these efforts might be). These critical discussions ultimately led me to three important realizations that provided the impetus for the ethnographic research I undertook in Saskatoon:

1. Both federal and provincial governments were spending significant energy contemplating the social issues confronting urban Indigenous youth, and state–community collaborative initiatives for social reform had begun emerging as a desirable approach for balancing state interests against Indigenous political demands for self-determination – hence, the focus on a new approach towards governing.
2. The erasure or undermining of an anti-colonial framework in the area of social and educational program development held particular significance for Indigenous peoples who were attempting to assert a political status distinct from other minority groups; thus, while I was interested in supporting and advocating for youth generally, I needed to pay careful attention to the specific backdrop against which my interests in supporting Indigenous youth[48] existed. In other words, this signalled the necessity of decolonizing youth studies in order to speak to the settler colonial realities facing Indigenous youth, a proposition I take up comprehensively in the conclusion.

3. My position as a university researcher and advocate for marginalized youth through my work in various capacities afforded me a unique opportunity to leverage the skills and knowledge I have acquired both inside and outside the walls of the academy to explore these issues further and to interrogate the conception and political implications of social intervention strategies for Indigenous youth through the frame of a participatory politics based on the ambiguous notion of collaboration.

Western Canada seemed an obvious choice in thinking about a place to locate my research on social reforms targeting urban Indigenous youth at its intersection with larger questions of Indigenous resurgence. Having grown up in and lived in Saskatchewan for a long time, in both rural and urban settings, I had an experiential connection to the political questions that are at the centre of this book and that surface repeatedly, not only in this province, but also across the country. I also had the benefit of distance from the daily realities of life and politics on the prairies that allowed me to return with a pair of fresh eyes and the ability to make connections between what I was encountering and engaging on the streets of Saskatoon and larger questions of Indigenous political claims within the context of Canadian nationalism and calls for a multicultural, social integration of Indigenous people on a global scale. My long-standing relationships with people in numerous community organizations through my work in the city over many years also facilitated relative ease of access to the various sites in which this research takes hold.

Further, Saskatoon boasts the second largest urban Indigenous population in Canada, second only to Winnipeg – according to the 2006 census, accounting for 9.3 per cent (Saskatoon) and 10 per cent (Winnipeg) of the total population respectively. Consistent with demographics in other urban centres, this population is also relatively young and is growing (Environics Institute 2011). The stories this city has to tell, however, stretch far past the compass coordinates of the place from which they emerge – it is a case in point of a much broader dynamic that weaves its way through the country.[49]

The formal field research was conducted between the years of 2006 and 2009, with brief follow up research on the emergence of Idle No More in 2012 and 2013, although, importantly, it also draws on my cumulative work in this area that spans over a decade. While reading and reviewing government and community documents about

the importance of participatory politics for social programming that
intends to alter the lives of urban Indigenous youth was a useful starting point for building my critical inquiry, I needed to witness how participation hit the ground through micro-level interactions between the
various players in the city who were implicated in these attempts at
political inclusion – both in terms of conceptual design and through the
creation of specific boundaries and types of programming. The underlying contradictions and tensions inherent in this governing strategy
were certainly not formally written into the documents, which emphasized the importance of "Indigenous perspective and voice"; nor did
they raise the possibility that there might be unintended outcomes of
such efforts that could have serious implications within a broader discussion of Indigenous political demands for sovereignty. In fact, most
of the discourse was written in a form considered to be as "apolitical"
as possible, or in a manner that positioned Canada as having ended its
colonial rule.

Two sets of fieldwork sites and methods of ethnographic research
enabled me to take a much closer look at what was happening and,
ultimately, allowed such implications to come to light over time and
across locations.[50] I consider the first set of field sites as avenues where
I was actively and directly "engaged" with collectives, associations,
and networks concentrated on addressing the social issues facing
urban Indigenous youth. Operating from within feminist and Indigenous methodologies of solidarity that highlight co-responsibility and
the relational nature of knowledge production (Tuhiwai Smith 1999),
I worked alongside youth advocates and front line service providers
who were engaged in social reform projects converging around participation. This included working with many different types of entities,
including government agencies, schools, Indigenous organizations and
community spaces, and a collection of non-profits. While I intersected
with many of these entities, I found myself spending the majority of
my time with a collective I refer to in this book as the "Indigenous
Peoples Collective." To meet their social programming goals, the collective interacted directly with a range of youth service organizations
with which the lives of young people were enmeshed. Young people
came into contact with the Indigenous Peoples Collective via teachers,
social workers, and community advocates, and word of mouth; and the
collective itself supported a number of programs targeted at improving the social experiences and, in turn, the broader material reality for
urban Indigenous youth. While these interventions occurred across a

host of institutional arrangements, the ones I focus on this book are primarily related to the arenas of education and criminal justice, which are particularly relevant for Indigenous youth.

The second set of field sites involved both the Canadian state, at the municipal, provincial, and federal levels, and those directly involved in the production of "expert" knowledge about urban Indigenous youth. Through these sites, I carried out participant observation and conducted interviews with a range of state officials – teachers, social workers, official government representatives, and others who were charged, in some form of another, with designing and implementing programs for urban Indigenous youth in Saskatoon. These sites provided a window into the competing vernacular representations of participatory politics and the attendant social constructions of the "problems" facing urban Indigenous youth.

I also wish to be clear that the point of this book was never to create a series of vignettes that showcased one sad story of Indigenous youth after another. In the telling words of Indigenous scholar and activist Vine Deloria (Deloria and Wildcat 2001, 161), "Indian education does not need another shallow report." Beginning from this premise, one of the central tenets of this book was to replace facile analysis with deep ethnographic inquiry situated within place, history, and politics. Scholars have already spilled much ink reciting, in very general terms, the crisis of disengagement and despair confronting Indigenous youth (Schissel and Wotherspoon 1998). This book moves away from this trend and instead acts as a porthole for unpacking the metrics of regulatory social projects intended to alter their lives. In concrete terms, this means that the writing contained in the following pages is not replete with exposing details about the lives of Indigenous youth but rather relays their compelling narratives and articulations of experience when it makes sense to do so and not simply for the sake of sensationalized revelation. Saskatoon is also a small city where people operate in close quarters and intimate proximity to one another, and I wanted to be as careful as possible to protect the privacy and safety of the young people whom I encountered throughout my research. Since the book, in the end, is about the institutional systems these youth navigate and their attempts at social integration through the mechanism of participatory citizenship, the young people are indeed an essential part of the way this narrative is constructed. However, the book deliberately avoids offering nuanced details or personal descriptors that could increase the risk of vulnerability to public exposure.

The presentation of the various narratives and ethnographic vignettes interwoven throughout the book also does not rest on the assumption that there is an opaque boundary between "theory" and "ethnography" – my theoretical questions, political orientations, and analysis undeniably shaped the research and the resulting account. Following the lead of Marker (2003, 368), "the categories for what counts as true, significant, and even interesting are constructed by the researchers as they apply their own hierarchies of concepts to the inquiry process." In accordance with the growing inclination in ethnographic writing (Caplan 1993) to expose the ways in which ethnographers co-produce the research context and make more explicit the politics and scaffolding of doing ethnographic research, the forms of writing I have chosen, including the self-reflective ethnographic musings, reflect this move to challenge the notion of transparently objective knowledge and "pure" lived experience. I am present in the telling and recuperation of these stories – it would be misleading to insist otherwise, as feminist methodology has pointed out (Lather 1993; Wolf 1996). In this book, then, I walk the careful line between rejecting the idea of objective, "absolute facts" and condoning the notion, as Sunaina Maira says (2009), that there is no truth.

It also merits stating that, while I have attempted to be cognizant of my own orientation to these issues throughout the entire research process, my own location as a researcher is rife with contradictions – a condition made startling clear through the work of Indigenous methodologists (Innes 2004; Marker 2003; Tuhiwai Smith 1999). I am a non-Indigenous, Ivy League–educated scholar studying social interventions in the lives of Indigenous youth. When I first began to think about conceptualizing this research project, I was immediately confronted with numerous images of the academic researcher entering Indigenous communities to gather evidence on the "other." That is to say, that the legacy of research on Indigenous communities throughout the world is a history we all must attend to with a heightened degree of self-reflexivity. In her book *Decolonizing Methodologies*, Linda Tuhiwai Smith (1999, 1) addresses this history when she says, "From the vantage point of the colonized, a position from which I write and choose to privilege, the term 'research' is inextricably linked to European imperialism and colonialism. The word itself, 'research,' is probably one of the dirtiest words in the Indigenous world's vocabulary." Given this historical context, questions of how to work respectfully and responsibly within Indigenous communities was something of paramount concern.[51]

## A Note on Names and Terminology

Consistent with standard ethnographic practice, pseudonyms are used for all of the people I encountered during my research, with the exception of state officials or leaders whose prominence in the public sphere necessitates the disclosure of identity. I also wish to add a few notes about the terms that I use throughout this book. Specifically, "Indigenous," "Aboriginal," "First Nations," and "Native" are used to refer to the original inhabitants who occupied the land of Turtle Island (North America) prior to colonization. I am fully aware that these terms do not signify a singular common identity or lived experience among people who are marked or self-identify as such. Rather, I am using Gayatri Spivak's (1990) notion of strategic essentialism to draw attention to the material reality and abhorrent marginalization faced by many Indigenous peoples throughout North America. As Alice Feldman (2001, 149–50) observes of the international Indigenous movement:

> [I]n international contexts, Indigenous peoples have sought to articulate a unifying and politically operational identity emanating from their shared experiences of colonialism and goals of self-determination, as well as the diversity of their localized experiences and immediate needs. They have drawn upon cultural traditions, both intact and fragmented, to construct and empower an overarching "Indigenousness" that is simultaneously hybrid. Recognition of their identity as peoples and nations who have legitimate claims to the rights and means of sovereignty and self-determination constitutes the foundation of this collective consciousness and the claims it animates, and serves as a central vehicle for change.

In order to formally establish a broad set of descriptors that could provide consistency around advocacy discourses in the international realm, UN special rapporteur José Martínez Cobo (1981, 1) set forth the following working definition of "Indigenous" people:

> Indigenous communities, peoples and nations are those which, having a historical continuity with preinvasion and precolonial societies that developed on their territories, consider themselves distinct from other sections of societies once prevailing in those territories or parts of them. They form at present nondominant sectors of society and are determined to preserve,

develop and transmit to future generations their ancestral territories, and their ethnic identity, as the basis of their continued existence as peoples, in accordance with their own cultural patterns, social institutions, and legal systems.

It is worth noting that Indigenous politics around questions of land, place, and culture in Canada is also informed by this definition.

## A Map of What Follows

This book is divided into three parts. Part 1, "A World of Invisible Things: History and Politics in the Context of Settler Colonial Encounters," sets the stage for the unfolding of the ethnographic chapters. Chapter 1 demonstrates how the logics of participation surface as part of contemporary Indigenous politics and of related debates over rights and claims to self-determination in Canada. I position this governing mode within a recent history of Indigenous–state relations that reveals how Indigenous peoples' engagement with participatory state programs is part of this broader political landscape, even though rights claims and participatory programs may appear as disparate projects. Thus, current aspirations of the state to "work together" do not simply materialize out of nowhere. Rather, I show that these gestures are lodged within a nexus of state moves to "manage" the "Indigenous problem" as part of the continued social, political, and economic development of the Canadian nation. I argue that both the historical and contemporary status of Indigenous people is animated by the interplay of the competing forces of nation building and Indigenous models of self-determined autonomy, epistemology, and politics since the colonization of the Americas.[52] In chapter 2, I ground the emphasis on the "crisis" for urban Indigenous youth by providing an overview of the scholarship documenting the experiences of Indigenous youth in Canada, including high school completion rates, engagements with teachers and students, criminalization, sexual exploitation, and poverty. By drawing on fieldwork in youth organizations and community spaces in the city, the chapter also paints a broader, ethnographically driven picture of the lived realities of urban Indigenous youth across the prairies and illuminates the variations in this experience across class and gender lines. What becomes alarmingly clear as this chapter unfolds is the paucity of research in this area and the lack of a materially anchored interrogation of social programming targeted at urban

Indigenous youth. By beginning to fill this gap, this chapter establishes important links between education and a range of other social institutions (social welfare, criminal justice, health, etc.) with which the lives of urban Indigenous youth are deeply enmeshed (Dhillon 2011).

Part 2, "The Space That Lies In Between: Ethnographic Encounters with the Land of Living Skies," and Part 3, "Pushback on the Plains: Tensions and Trials of Participation," contain major organizing themes that telescope between these ethnographic chapters. In chapter 3, I trace and document the underlying logics of participatory politics for Indigenous peoples in Canada through the work of an entity I call the "Indigenous Alliance" operating through the Indigenous Peoples Collective. To this end, I analyse official government documents, forums, and recommendations that coalesce around collaborative social intervention and draw on my fieldwork across numerous sites in the city in order to highlight the competing vernacular representations of "participation" set forth by state agents and representatives from the urban Indigenous community alike. I ask how the social aims of participatory politics are articulated through discourses of collective obligation, cultural recognition, and hope for change. Further, I explore how a range of actors understand these discourses and how they envision them, or not, as an avenue for social transformation in the lives of urban Indigenous youth. Chapter 4 sets forth an ethnographic account of the way the boundaries between the state and urban Indigenous peoples in the city are taken up through the Indigenous Alliance. Here, my research shows how the state facilitates a socially constructed consensus between the governed and the governing in order for participatory projects to take shape and how, in turn, this consensus functions to partition Indigenous political subjectivity and lived experience. Colonial gender violence, as experienced by young Indigenous women and girls in urban contexts, frames much of this discussion.

In chapter 5, the ethnographic focus shifts to a critical appraisal of how "culture" operates under the umbrella of participatory politics (Cooke and Kothari 2001; Popkewitz 1991). I examine the way particular social constructions of culture become privileged through a number of the collaborative projects of the Indigenous Alliance that bring state agents and Indigenous and non-Indigenous actors to the same table to work on social issues. Chapter 6, the last ethnographic chapter, moves to connect a number of the conceptual themes I have explored throughout the book, by inviting the reader to an intimate engagement with a criminal justice program of the Indigenous Peoples Collective targeted at urban Indigenous youth. My aim in this chapter is to provide a window for discerning how social reform projects formulated through participatory politics, such as the one described here, are not simply suspended in the city's air but enter into the daily lives of urban Indigenous youth. I argue that the tensions emerging through this exposition signal larger frictions experienced in the city around the containment of Indigenous political claims, resistance to an ongoing settler colonial enterprise, and demands for social programs that address the material deprivation facing Indigenous youth. Struggling to make connections with urban Indigenous youth, youth workers are repeatedly confronted with discourses of risk, the salvation narrative of education that views access to formal schooling as "the way out," and the use of social science expert knowledge (Cruikshank 1996) to produce a singular epistemological framework for assessing lived reality and cultivating a new urban Indigenous youth subjectivity (Foucault 1982; 1991).

The book concludes with a final chapter that finds a common thread of contradiction and ambiguity woven through the politics of participation as explored throughout the book. I offer the reader a reflexive discussion of power that captures the multilayered nature of inclusionary governance (both discursive and practical) and highlight a number of the ways such politics may undermine an assertion of Indigenous rights and political goals of self-determination. In the final part of the conclusion, I bring to the fore a discussion of the critical considerations that I draw from this work and address the range of circumstances we will need to pay close attention to as we, in our allied efforts, collectively engage in the process of change. Indeed, this book does not seek to reinforce a separation between the discursive and material stakes of what it means to engage in social reform through the politics of recognition. Rather, and perhaps more importantly, the analytic revelations of this work sequester an alternative framework for thinking through an agenda of research and action that is more deeply anchored in the aspirations and aims of a resurgent Indigenous politics.

# PART ONE

## A World of Invisible Things: History and Politics in the Context of Settler Colonial Encounters

# Breakage: Colonization, Violence, and the Possibility (Still) of a Self-Determined Destiny

Our objective is to continue until there is not a single Indian in Canada that has not been absorbed into the body politic and there is no Indian question, and no Indian Department.

– Duncan Campbell Scott (1862–1947), Deputy Superintendent
General, Indian Affairs

When we consider the resources deployed to achieve the cultural alienation so typical of the colonial period, we realize that nothing was left to chance and that the final aim of colonization was to convince the Indigenous population it would save them from darkness.

– Frantz Fanon, *Wretched of the Earth*

On 17 October 2013, members of the Elsipogtog and Mi'kmaq First Nations blocked Highway 134 in the province of New Brunswick to stop Texas-based shale gas company, SWN Resources, from continuing to explore sites for fossil fuel extraction in the area. Hundreds of people, including children, youth, and elders, turned out to support the anti-fracking rally and call attention to the environmental impact of shale gas exploration and related infringements on traditional Indigenous land and lifeways. A large white banner with black and red block lettering hung in the background and read: "SWN TOXIC INVESTMENT."

Canada's national police force, the Royal Canadian Mounted Police, arrived in three busloads[1] and subsequently infiltrated the area, attempting to disperse the group with dogs, pepper spray, fire hoses, tear gas, rubber bullets, and snipers. Protectors[2] persisted in keeping the road blocked. At one point, six RCMP officers, all armed, were caught on video holding a man down on the ground, with the gathered crowd demanding his release, chanting "free Roger." In the same video that captures how Roger is violently dragged off by police, an older Indigenous person can be heard telling the police officers that they should be ashamed of treating the young man this way.

Roger, however, was only one of many arrested by the police that day; by the end of the confrontation, the RCMP had charged at least forty protectors, including a number of youth. Several police cars were set ablaze in retaliation. A peaceful demonstration was turned violent by institutions of the state, signalling yet another example of how jurisdiction over seized territory is a central feature of settler sovereignty. "In situations where sovereignties are nested and embedded," writes Mohawk anthropologist Audra Simpson (2014, 12), "one proliferates at the other's expense; the United States and Canada can only come into political being because of Indigenous dispossession." In other words, geography is arguably a social landscape as much as it is geopolitical topography. Sovereignty is understood to mean supreme and indivisible authority over all within a territory whose "legal" existence within that territory has come into being through an exercise of power (Hindess 2005).

The strategies for exercising settler state authority over land in New Brunswick that day were captured through the wondrous communication capabilities of handheld recording devices. Today, social media opens everything that happens in public spaces to unsolicited documentation, to the thorny and immediate grip of mass consumption. News quite literally spreads like wildfire. Even as the standoff was unfolding, images and video recordings were being uploaded to YouTube, Twitter, and Facebook – a viral spectacle teeming with the unedited imagery and sounds of violent state power and Indigenous pushback. The photograph below was taken by freelance journalist Ossie Michelin at the height of the resistance efforts in Elsipogtog and became one of the most popular symbols associated with the blockade. It has since been modified, adapted, and used in a range of capacities by Indigenous resistance movements in North America.

Across Canada, Indigenous communities and their allies mobilized in support of the members of the Elsipogtog and Mi'kmaq First Nations. Many flew to New Brunswick to join the ongoing blockade efforts and offer support in the front line resistance camps. As acts of solidarity across this vast land, sister rallies were organized in numerous

Figure 5. Protest against SWN Resources, New Brunswick, 2013 (Photo credit: Ossie Michelin, Aboriginal Peoples Television Network [APTN])

cities in the days following 17 October. Some even called the events in New Brunswick "Harper's Oka," drawing parallels between the 1990 Mohawk standoff to protect Indigenous land, including burial grounds, in Quebec and this most recent attempt at encroachment on Indigenous territory sanctioned by the Canadian state. In the case of Elsipogtog, the land in question had not been handed over by treaty and Canada's highest court upheld the Mikmaq's right to continue to use the lands and waters – rights the protectors said would be rendered meaningless if the territory were poisoned by fracking toxins (Klein 2014a, 299).

In a courtroom in Fredericton, New Brunswick, on 22 November 2013, several weeks into the roadblock, Judge Paulette Garnett ruled to continue an injunction granted to SWN Resources to keep protectors from interfering with seismic testing work (see "RCMP, Protesters" 2013). During the hearing, the court was told that SWN Resources was losing C$60,000 for every day its seismic exploration trucks remained blockaded in the compound off Highway 134. The injunction required that demonstrators remain at least 250 yards in front of or behind contractors and their vehicles and 20 yards to the side – a direct attempt to curtail the resistance to fossil fuel exploration and subsequent extraction that was likely to ensue. The injunction, however, did not deter the anti-fracking alliance of Indigenous people and members of New Brunswick's settler communities. Protectors continue to confront the police in efforts to stunt the seismic testing operation. They are still pushing back against the powerful and widespread structures of settlement across Canada. SWN Resources has not agreed to stop shale seismic testing. The struggle continues despite mounting dissent that falls on selectively deaf ears.[3]

The fight over land, water, and place, as evidenced in this most recent uprising in Elsipogtog, is not a novel occurrence. Indeed, in a country "overlaid with settler regimes" (A. Simpson 2014, 7), where Indigenous life is circumscribed and constrained by an ever present intention to keep colonization alive, albeit in a different form, the struggle over occupation is more commonplace than one would think. Not all stories of resistance, or those Simpson terms stories of "refusal," however, make for flashy headlines.

The stark words of Duncan Campbell Scott, Chief Administrator of Indian Affairs from 1913 to 1931, which open this chapter, speak succinctly to the reverberating logics of elimination that are the backbone and lifeblood of the Canadian settler nation state. Scott pursued an aggressive agenda of intermarriage, colonial education, religious conversion, and agricultural labour to forcibly "encourage" Indigenous peoples to relinquish their identity and epistemology – the essence of who they were (Salem-Wiseman 1996). The notion of absorption via assimilation[4] set forth by Scott, as a basis for analysis and its concomitant set of settler colonial social practices seeking to undermine, consume, and ultimately erase Indigenous forms of knowing and being, are indicative of the colonial residue and recalcitrant historical attitude from which the contestations in New Brunswick emerged and sustain themselves. The events in New Brunswick, however, also importantly illustrate that, despite virulent techniques aimed at eradication, coupled with a variety of disciplining regimes that I describe throughout this chapter, Indigenous communities have not been vanquished. They continue to fight for their bodies and by extension their land, and for their histories, which have been muzzled by centuries of broad-reaching repudiation (A. Simpson 2014). They continue to fight for their inherent political "difference" within the legal boundaries that mark Canada as Canada and also beyond its borders. They continue to fight through youth like Nitânis who are still standing.

In the contemporary context, Canada is often cited as a paradox in the international arena of Indigenous rights and emancipation. In one respect, there is global admiration for the "Canadian way" of exploring models for living together that balance a universal humanity with a commitment to personal autonomy and cultural rights (Kallen 2003; Maaka and Fleras 2005, 155).[5] On the other hand, Canada is criticized for failing to match theoretical ideals with changes in the material conditions facing Indigenous peoples and for the persistence of state power that grounds questions of belonging, identity, and rights for Indigenous peoples in a network of historical and current processes of dispossession.[6]

Augmenting this critique, Woolford, Benvenuto, and Hinton's (2014) recent co-edited volume, *Colonial Genocide in Indigenous North America*, offers a series of insightful reflections about the applicability of the analytical concept of genocide to settler state–Indigenous relations in Canada. Citing the definition of genocide set forth in 1948 by the United Nations Convention on the Prevention and Punishment of the Crime of Genocide (United Nations 1948) to which most nations are now signatories, the essays provide a much needed entry point to thinking through how settler nation states such as Canada demonstrated an "intent to destroy" Indigenous families and communities through the various structural realities of settler colonialism. The chair of the Truth and Reconciliation Commission of Canada, Justice Sinclair, used the term "genocide" when he delivered his keynote address on Canadian residential schools in September 2012 at the University of Manitoba (quoted in Woolford, Benvenuto, and Hinton 2014, 1). While some scholars demonstrate a reluctance to use "genocide" to describe the lethal processes entailed in conquest and seizure for the purpose of securing settler sovereignty (see Joseph Gone's work, for instance), these debates, nonetheless, make clear the extreme levels of violence endured by Indigenous peoples across Turtle Island.

Most recently, this "intent to destroy" was acutely witnessed in the disappearance of Indigenous young women and girls along the Highway of Tears in Northern British Columbia and in many communities across Canada, which I address later in this chapter, and in the horrific, decade-long serial murders by Robert Pickton of women in the Downtown Eastside of Vancouver, many of whom were Indigenous. The abhorrent actions (and inaction) of the Vancouver Police Department and the Royal Canadian Mounted Police in launching an investigation into the disappearances and murders is indicative of the way power functions to create spaces of invisibility and suffering for those who exist on the edges of a grossly unjust world.[7] The grounds for this two-way mirror are nestled in a history of colonization, racialized violence (institutional, symbolic, and interpersonal), and nation building that spurns contestations in many areas of social life (Dua, Razack, and Warner 2005).

In this chapter, I take up this paradox of Canada as a more "gentle colonizer" by demonstrating how the politics of participation surfaces as part of settler colonial governing through recognition and related debates over reconciliation and claims for self-determination. To this end, I position this governing mode within a recent history of Indigenous–settler state relations that reveals how Indigenous peoples' engagement with participatory state programs is part of this broader political landscape even though they may appear as disparate projects. The current aspirations of the state to bring Indigenous peoples into the bureaucratic folds of government with respect to social programming for urban Indigenous youth do not simply materialize out of nowhere. Rather, I show that these gestures are lodged within a nexus of state moves to "manage the Indian problem" – an intricate social web that connects the past with the present and raises essential questions about the future. I argue that both the historical and present-day status of Indigenous people is and has been animated by the interplay of the competing forces of nation building and of Indigenous models of self-determined autonomy, epistemology, and politics since the colonization of the Americas. I also set forth a related discussion that situates the inconsistencies and tensions framing the specific case of Canada within a panoramic view of a transnational Indigenous movement. Such an exploration makes crucial connections between the lived experience on the prairies of Western Canada, the story that makes up the majority of this book, with specific theoretical and normative questions prompted by worldwide debates over Indigenous rights and issues of social and political emancipation (McConaghy 2000; Povinelli 2002; Garcia 2005; Postero 2006; Cattelino 2008).

## The Paradox of "Just" Settlement in a Land with No Justice

For heuristic purposes, I am speaking quite generally here both about the experiences of Indigenous peoples in Canada with the advent of colonization and about the various approaches/stages I identify.[8] Obviously, there are substantial differences between various communities in terms of their specific encounters. My point here is to establish central tendencies rather than offer an intricate rendering of the complexities and nuances of colonization as they relate to specific communities from the point of first contact and onward.[9] In other words, while this chapter is not intended to offer an exhaustive account of hundreds of years of settler colonial history, understanding the changing landscape of Indigenous–state relations goes some way in establishing a context for the rise of the state's emphasis on restoring damaged social and political relationships with Indigenous peoples through a material and discursive shift to recognition and reconciliation.

Numerous events and critical historical periods have shaped the relationship between Indigenous peoples and what is now known as "the Canadian nation" since the first point of contact. Accordingly, there have been shifts in the political formations used by the Canadian state, each with its own temporal narrative encoded in specific social policy frameworks that dictate the rules by which Indigenous lives will be lived (Strakosch and Macoun 2012). Stated otherwise, each political formation sets forth its own story about how settler colonialism unfolds through time. The range of actors taking part in this story has also changed, depending on the specific historical moment. In the two sections that follow, I briefly trace the stages of Indigenous–state relations and emphasize how the idea of working in alliance with Indigenous communities, the most recent governing mode, is reflective of an inclusionary politics of recognition that boasts reciprocity and mutual exchange as a signifier of ostensible postcolonial arrival. Participation, then, requires a particular approach to governing that is ensconced in the work of recalibrating the relationship between the governing and governed. Thus, it requires a very specific kind of dynamic between Indigenous peoples and the state through which concealed power can continue to flow.

### Colonial Trespassing, Temporality, and the Political Formations of Indigenous–State Relations

Formal government policy on Indigenous status, broadly speaking, can be seen as evolving through a series of overlapping phases that begins with an initial period of cooperation between First Nations and the fur traders in the fifteenth and sixteenth centuries. In his book *Skyscrapers Hide the Heavens: A History of Indian-White Relations in Canada*, James R. Miller (2000, 393) describes how Europeans came to Turtle Island primarily for fish, fur, exploration, and evangelization. Up until the seventeenth century, Miller argues, "Indians" were indispensable in the process of "exploration"; fishing and fur trading would have been impossible without the knowledge, methods, and transportation skills of Indigenous peoples. In explaining this initial phase Miller (2000, 394) remarks that "Europeans found themselves dependent on the Indians' knowledge and transportation technology when probing the continent in search of a passage to Asia. For the missionary, too, Indian cooperation, food, transportation and toleration of his presence were essential if the black rode was to win souls for Christ." According to Miller, the Europeans regarded the Indigenous people they encountered along a frontier of commerce and faith as a means rather than as an impediment to the realization of settlement objectives in the initial stage.[10]

This period of relative accommodation was also signified by the passage of the Royal Proclamation in 1763, which was intended to establish the primacy of Crown sovereignty over unexplored territory in the Americas and chart the course for more aggressive "settlement" (Slattery 1997, 76). The 1763 Proclamation became the imperial framework for addressing the Indigenous people of "British North America," but also importantly acknowledged Aboriginal title to land. By force of the Royal Proclamation, Aboriginal interest in land was acknowledged as a pre-existing right rather than a right granted by the Crown, and in order to prevent the "pre-emptive purchase" of such lands, purchase and exploration of "Indian lands" were closed to European trespass or individual purchase without the approval of the Crown (Slattery 1997; Miller 2000; Maaka and Fleras 2005). The Proclamation, however, should also be seen as a strategic attempt on the part of the Crown to garner support from the Indigenous nations for the settlement of Upper Canada against the interests of French imperialism – multiple agendas are always at play.[11] Of this strategic alliance between the Crown and Indigenous nations, Maaka and Fleras (2005, 182) document, "from 1755–1812, the British Indian Department (forerunner of the Department of Indian Affairs) implemented the key tenet of British policy, namely to blunt American and French imperialists by fostering Aboriginal alliances." Moreover, this tactic for contending with Indigenous communities and their lands, as articulated by the Crown, assumed a de facto sovereign–subject relationship where indigeneity was no longer considered self-determining but reliant on the Crown for its continued existence (Shewell 2004, 7). Thus began the modern Indigenous administration in Canada and a host of self-authorizing techniques and frameworks that would lay the foundation for long-term dispossession and occupation.

The post-Proclamation relationship between Indigenous peoples and French and British explorers, missionaries, and traders was characterized by an initial period of cooperation (Miller 2000). Although, once the British assumed primacy as the major European power in Canada, this relationship began to alter and British policies paid lip service to the more accommodating policies of diplomacy, negotiation, and treaty making (Maaka and Fleras 2005). In fact, the Crown moved to assert unilateral sovereignty over the people and lands. Indigenous consent was simply assumed or deemed irrelevant. Seeking permission was not possible within the purview of takeover (Jhappan 1990) because built into "sovereignty" is a notion of a singular law, a singular authority (A. Simpson 2014, 12).

Furthermore, the end of the 1812 war with the United States eliminated the need for Indigenous allies. This rendered Indigenous people more expendable and subject to the expedient actions of the Crown and the quickly growing settler population.[12] To this end, Frideres and Gadacz (2001, 16) assert that "by 1830, the federal government was questioning the value of the Aboriginal person for Canada's future. Although it remained a concern for some time, invasion from the south by the United States was no longer an immediate and direct threat ...

without their status as military allies, the Indians had no value for 'White Canada.'"

The 1867 Constitution Act acknowledged state responsibility for Indigenous nations (thus configuring them as "peoples" or a population to be managed under Canadian governmental rule) by conferring federal jurisdiction over federal lands and affairs. At the same time, the 1867 Act formally put Indigenous nations under Dominion jurisdiction without their consent (Ponting and Gibbins 1980). Subsequent to Canadian Confederation in 1867, the Indian Act of 1876 consolidated past colonial and federal legislative works relating to the status and treatment of Indigenous peoples. Thus, the 1876 Act became the hallmark instrument for assimilationist policies, strategies, and nation-building projects targeting Indigenous communities for nearly a century.[13] When commenting on this legislation, historian John Tobias (1976) writes, "What becomes clearer is the Government's determination to make the Indians into *imitation Europeans* ... to eradicate the old Indian values through education, religion, new economic and political systems, and a new concept of property" (15; emphasis added). This approach is readily witnessed in the haunting words of the first Prime Minister of Canada, Sir John A. MacDonald, whom Miller (1989, 203) quotes as stating that "[t]he great aim of our civilization has been to do away with the tribal system and assimilate the Indian people in all respects with the inhabitants of the Dominion, as speedily as they are fit for change." Given that the appropriation of Indigenous land was reimagined by the newly developing Canadian state as an acquisition (as opposed to seizure) obtained through the more benign designations of "purchase or surrender," protection and assimilation became the only alternative for the peoples who were conquered. In short, Indigenous progress lay in embracing western civilization, and in the loss of Indigenous culture lay the ultimate loss of difference with respect to entitlement to land itself.[14]

Assimilationist policies were predicated on the notion that nation building was the embodiment of western progress and modernism; a liberal state provided the foundation for a market society – that is, a society of "choice" where people were free to pursue private self-interest.[15] From this perspective, Indigenous people, by virtue of their band and tribal groupings, were understood as primitive, uncivilized, and savage. The paternalism of the Canadian state assumed that the only hope for the survival and advancement of "primitives" lay in their casting off their past and accepting the "progress" engendered in the creation of the settler nation state. As Comaroff and Comaroff (1992, 289) remark of nineteenth-century British imperialism, the sacred task of the colonizing mission was to reconstruct the lives of the "uncivilized and immoral" by inculcating in their daily lives the bourgeois values of "modern domesticity." Shewell (2004, 11) also makes this point at length when he states:

> Yet we cannot separate nation building and other, more practical bases of assimilation policy from the perceptions of the Indian "other" that prevailed in colonial and post-Confederation times. These perspectives were held by settlers, by their colonial governments, and in less virulent form by the colonial office in London. These perceptions were racist, but they were also more than that; they reflected and expressed the imperial materialism and liberal culture that supported racism. Liberal culture and values, in all their glory, emphasized property, individualism, and the virtues of work, science, and progress. English perceptions about Indians revealed more about the liberal bias than they did about the true nature of First Nations people.

Thus, echoing the sentiments of John Stuart Mill, who saw liberal democracy as an agent of moral purpose and the rights of citizenship, the Canadian state moved to the model of equal opportunity and citizenship for the "individual development" of Indigenous peoples. State power was to be made real through the granting of citizenship and the attendant benefits acquired for the individual as a result of this designation (A. Simpson 2014; Berlant 1997).

The material manifestations of the assimilationist agenda targeted at absorbing Indigenous people into a "progressive Canadian society" and usurping Indigenous authority are numerous and deeply troubling, to say the least. These include, but are not limited to, specific policies relating to local governance on Indigenous land; the creation of the "reserve" system[16] (makeshift laboratories to teach the ways of European civilization, where Indigenous peoples could be isolated and contained geographically with relative ease); the curtailment of economic development and opportunities; and the forced removal of First Nations children from their home communities and their placement within the residential school system. In describing the range of practices associated with the logics of elimination coded as assimilation, Shewell (2004, 15) explains:

> The government banned religious and cultural rites such as potlatching, dancing, and traditional funerals and burials. New forms of political

organization were imposed on bands; these supplanted traditional decision making with liberal, parliamentary rules of conduct. Very often,
bands were formed by uniting unrelated and even hostile peoples. Criminal and civil law were declared applicable on reserves. Indian children
were removed from their homes, placed in residential schools, forbidden
to speak their native language, and systematically taught white ways.
Industrial training schools were established to teach young Indians basic
labouring skills. Housing was built according to European design.

In brief, through this gendered and racialized piece of legislation,
the state gained sweeping and broad-reaching powers to invade and
regulate the smallest aspects of Indigenous life, dictate the terms under
which local communities would operate, and determine what would
be done with reserve lands and resources. This process of "othering"
further served to justify colonial actions and to deny the historical and
contemporary completeness of Indigenous existence in Canada (Green
1995). Activist and scholar Sunera Thobani (2007, 48) reminds us that
the Indian Act has been described as representing the "Euro-Canadian
government's apartheid system" and the "bureaucratized hatred" of
Native peoples.[17] The creation of the Department of Indian Affairs in
1880 further institutionalized the relationship between Canada and
the Indigenous peoples by creating a "miniature government," whose
sole responsibility was "Indian affairs" and which operated in isolation from other governmental departments (Shewell 2004, 14). During
this period, Indigenous peoples were infantilized as wards of the state,
subjected to a racialized "coercive tutelage" of the nation state that
assumed the form of arbitrary restraint or guardianship exercised by
one power over another (Thobani 2007).
    This is not to say that there was no social and political resistance to
such governmental efforts. Indigenous peoples began to organize themselves formally in the early part of the twentieth century. By the last
third of the century, Ottawa bureaucrats had come to recognize that the
direct changes they were hoping for through forced assimilation and
absorption were not happening.[18] This failure of the nineteenth-century
policies, then, together with a growing Indigenous demographic, made
attempts to (re)craft social policies that spoke directly to the lives of
Indigenous peoples unavoidable (Miller 2000, 311). In addition, during the resource-based boom that fuelled much of the prosperity that
Canada enjoyed until the recession of 1957, Euro-Canadian enterprises
began to penetrate what was known as "Indian country" in a way that

had not been seen since the agricultural expansion of the Western provinces in the previous century. A renewed interest in exploration for raw materials and energy heightened attraction to areas of the country (read "the North") that had previously been considered economically marginal. For example, Miller (2000, 327) observes that when Canada's Crown uranium corporation (Eldorado) expanded its operations in northern Saskatchewan, it encountered large numbers of Indigenous peoples who were still participating in a traditional economy. The expansion to "Indian country" put Canada's international reputation at stake, especially after World War II, when the contradiction of fighting for freedom overseas with infringements of fundamental rights at home became painfully obvious. Hence began the next stage, which was predicated on the concept of "integration" as a way to pacify Indigenous concerns and normalize relations between them and the federal government.[19]

The Trudeau government, an epitome of the universalist, integrationist model of settling Indigenous concerns, was elected in 1968 under the now famous slogans of "Just Society" and "participatory democracy." Its prime minister, Pierre Trudeau, championed the idea that it was time for fairer treatment of a "variety of disadvantaged groups" (Weaver 1981; Miller 2000). The sentiment of the time is best expressed in the words of Trudeau himself, who is quoted in Miller (2000, 329) stating, "It's inconceivable I think that in a given society, one section of the society have a treaty with the other section of that society. We must all be equal under the laws and we must not sign treaties amongst ourselves ... We can't recognize Aboriginal rights because no society can be built on historical might-have-beens." Simply put, for Trudeau, there could not be more than one sovereignty that governed Canada with legal and political authority. Trudeau's commitment to popular participation in policy making, however, ensured that policy makers were enlisted to stage consultation with Aboriginal organizations and peoples about matters that affected them – at least on the surface.

Not surprisingly, Trudeau's emphasis on the idea of a participatory inclusion developed alongside the international community's questioning of the western assumptions of racial and cultural superiority of the Canadian government. Canada's domestic policies and practices were coming under the scrutiny of critical international eyes.[20] Knowledge of the massive scale of the violence used against Indigenous peoples and their communities could no longer be denied or fully avoided by Canadian nationals. Indigenous peoples were excelling in their organizing at the international level and were turning (with greater visibility) to the Canadian courts to assert claims to land and sovereignty. As articulated by Thobani (2007, 151):

> The on-going Aboriginal presence in Canada pointed to the implausibility of the national fantasy of benevolent, innocent, and liberal origins. With the worldwide struggles of Aboriginal peoples having received increased legitimacy in the international arena through their petitioning of the United Nations, the realities of the nation's genocidal practices against these peoples were being named as such by increasingly vocal and powerful forces. The growing strength of anti-colonial movements in other parts of the world increased the visibility of these struggles of Aboriginal peoples in North America: the destructiveness of colonial policies could no longer be cloaked as effectively by platitudes of civilizational and moral superiority as had once been the case.

Perhaps the most notable indication of this era is an act by Jean Chrétien, Minister of Indian Affairs, who, in 1969, tabled a discussion paper that sought to deal with the "Indian problem" by abolishing Aboriginal peoples as a legal construct. The infamous White Paper proposed to terminate the "special" relation between Indigenous peoples and the Crown, thus eliminating the status of First Nations peoples as a collective and politically distinct entity (Weaver 1981; Miller 2000; Maaka and Fleras 2005). In material terms, this discussion advocated dismantling the Department of Indian Affairs, transferring federal responsibility over Indigenous peoples to the provinces, and repealing the Indian Act. "Canada is made up of many people with many cultures" intoned the White Paper, where "each has its own manner of relating to the other; each makes its own adjustments to the larger society" (quoted in Miller 2000, 332). As consequence of this paper, the first seeds of multiculturalism were planted in the social imaginary of Canada, with Canada depicted as a mosaic of cultures and histories, each worthy in its own right, yet each residing in and mediated by the greater nation of Canada. According to Trudeau and his Parliament, the legal status of Indigenous difference had proven its exclusionary effect: the legal and social isolation of Aboriginal peoples had contributed to their inequality and marginalization in Canadian society. The White Paper, for Trudeau's form of colonial government, was a way to "reintegrate" Indigenous people by providing them with universal citizenship rights and a level of political participation like that of all other citizens of the nation.

In practice, the White Paper ended up having the opposite effect. The tabling of this integrative policy dressed up in multicultural liberalism proved to be an extreme miscalculation on the part of the Canadian government. In response, Aboriginal peoples across the country roared into political dissent, and Red Power activism spotlighted the racist, colonial underpinnings of the Canadian settler state. The National Indian Brotherhood (predecessor to the Assembly of First Nations), the Indian Association of Alberta, the Union of Ontario Indians, among many other provincial federations, lobbied the government to shelve the White Paper in exchange for a new "Indian" agenda that embraced Aboriginal demands for control over their own destiny, lands, and political status (Miller 2000). The solidarity and collective strength of this movement chastened Ottawa, and the federal government was left with no alternative but to discuss a new policy agenda, embracing principles of devolution and self-administration through a vague notion of "power sharing."

The White Paper of 1969 was also symbolically important because it marked the first formally recognized and unified political protest by Indigenous peoples in Canada against the federal government. Putting political action to the test by expressing resistance to the White Paper, the National Indian Brotherhood saw "that unified and militant action worked" (Miller 2000, 339). In the decade that followed, the National Indian Brotherhood would undertake a series of policy initiatives that concerned social services and education. The 1973 Indian Control of Indian Education Act, lobbied for by the National Indian Brotherhood, was the consequence of the abject failure of the government and church-controlled residential school system to assimilate Indigenous children, which Ottawa viewed as an enormous cost.[21] The birth and acceptance of this policy paper by the federal government in Canada "rescinded the proposal to turn over education to the provinces and acknowledged the right of national Aboriginal leaders to assume jurisdictional control and parental responsibility for Indian education" (Battiste 1995, 10).

With the *Calder* decision of 1973, the Supreme Court of Canada provided further support for the idea that Aboriginal peoples lived in societies before European arrival, thus implying that their institutions and practices continued to exist despite the presumption of Canadian sovereignty. The ruling also implied that the principle of Aboriginal title and rights challenged the foundational myths of the rights of first discovery and entertained the possibility of reimagining a Canada outside of a colonial constitutional order (Asch 2014). This decision laid the foundation for Indigenous peoples to shift the federal policy agenda in a manner that aimed to enhance Aboriginal autonomy with respect to land, representation, and political voice. As a result, there was an expansion of government initiatives to extend Aboriginal jurisdiction over domains of relevance to Indigenous peoples by devolving responsibility (as witnessed in the case of education) from "the centre" to "the community" (Maaka and Fleras 2005). Consequently, Maaka and Fleras (2005, 19) justly conclude, "The government continued to explore avenues through which to devolve its administrative burden by increasing ways for Aboriginal communities to assume greater control over and accountability of their local affairs, including a devolutionary program for community self-sufficiency."[22] How this devolution played out on the ground, however, raised a whole other set of questions.

The federal government's focus on devolution also created an impetus for change in the Department of Indian Affairs. There were three devolutionary assumptions that inspired the reorganization of this federal department: (1) the need to establish Aboriginal rather than federal control over local Indigenous affairs, (2) the perception that properly resourced communities were better equipped to solve local problems, and (3) the suspicion that centralized structures were ineffective for problem solving when dealing with a geographically dispersed and culturally diverse people (Frideres 1998; Maaka and Fleras 2005). The department was said to reposition itself from an agency of containment to one of "advocacy and advising." The focus on self-determination and devolution spearheaded the entrenchment of Indigenous self-government in Canada's Constitution. The aim of this engineered transformation was to dissolve the problematic relations of colonialism through an approach to governing that placed "recognition" at the centre of Indigenous–state social exchange.

## "Postcolonial" Machinations: Recognition and Reconciliation in the Present

Centred on recognition and reconciliation, the most recent developments in the relations between Indigenous peoples and the Canadian state continue to evolve around a direct political repositioning of Indigenous peoples within the constitutional framework of Canada. In 1982, Aboriginal and treaty rights became constitutionally entrenched, making Canada the first country to officially embark on this path of conditional autonomy (Schouls 2003). At the core of this policy commitment towards conditional autonomy was a violent seventy-eight-day stand-off at Oka in 1990, where Mohawk occupied a sacred burial ground slated for golf course expansion and residential development. In response to the standoff, the Canadian government introduced a four-pillars policy commitment to accelerate land claims settlements, improve the socio-economic status on reserves, reconstruct Indigenous–state relations (loosely defined), and meet Aboriginal concerns (Miller 2000; Maaka and Fleras 2005). Subsequently, the federal government endorsed a commitment to negotiate the working arrangements and principle of the inherent right to self-government. Taking up the role of mediator, the federal government overtly embraced the notion of "working alongside" Indigenous communities to address some of the longstanding issues relating to their social and political marginalization. Negotiations were legitimized with the goal of creating a Canada where everyone could coexist. This approach embodied a move towards "partnership" and "shared responsibility."

Consider, for example, the federal government's launching of a five-year process to review nearly every aspect of Indigenous life in Canada through the Royal Commission on Aboriginal Peoples (RCAP) in the early 1990s. The 1997 report, entitled *Gathering Strength: Canada's Aboriginal Action Plan* (Minister of Indian Affairs and Northern Development 1997), reaffirmed the Canadian state's ostensible commitment to the inherent right to self-government, albeit through the framework of the Canadian Constitution, and was couched in the language of recognizing the distinct needs and aspirations of Indigenous peoples. Released in 1996, the report was also said to capture the view of Indigenous "grassroots" in Canada, the RCAP having elicited the opinions, ideas, and stories of everyday Indigenous people in Canada. Indeed, it was the mandate of RCAP to "travel extensively to Aboriginal communities and let Aboriginal persons tell their stories in person" (Schouls 2003, 62). This massive effort launched by the Canadian government was said to serve as a national model through which the harnessing of "Indigenous voices" in local planning and decision making could come to fruition.

Changes were also afoot in the country's largest Indigenous political organization. In a 2005 policy position on self-determination, the Assembly of First Nations asserted that they had reached consensus around re-envisioning the relationship between First Nations and Canada, which would lead to strengthening recognition and the implementation of First Nations governments (Coulthard 2007, 438). They went on to state that this vision would be grounded in the core principles outlined in the RCAP's 1996 report; namely, recognition of the nation to nation relationship between First Nations and the Crown, recognition of the equal right of First Nations to self-determination, recognition of the Crown's fiduciary obligation to protect Aboriginal treaty rights, recognition of First Nations' inherent right to self-government, and recognition of the right of First Nations to economically benefit from the use of their lands and resources (Assembly of First Nations 2005, 18–19). Several years later, moves towards a recognition-based politics were augmented with an official apology from the Canadian federal government in 2008 regarding the atrocities associated with Indigenous experiences of residential schooling.[23] In his "Statement of Apology" from 11 June 2008, Prime Minister Stephen Harper professed the following to the country, and to Indigenous communities specifically:

> To the approximately 80,000 living former students, and all family members and communities, the Government of Canada now recognizes that it was wrong to forcibly remove children from their homes and we apologize for having done this. We now recognize that it was wrong to separate children from rich and vibrant cultures and traditions that it created a void in many lives and communities, and we apologize for having done this. We now recognize that, in separating children from their families, we undermined the ability of many to adequately parent their own children and sowed the seeds for generations to follow, and we apologize for having done this. We now recognize that, far too often, these institutions gave rise to abuse or neglect and were inadequately controlled, and we apologize for failing to protect you. Not only did you suffer these abuses as children, but as you became parents, you were powerless to protect your own children from suffering the same experience, and for this we are sorry.
>
> The burden of this experience has been on your shoulders for far too long. The burden is properly ours as a Government, and as a country. There is no place in Canada for the attitudes that inspired the Indian Residential Schools system to ever prevail again. You have been working on recovering from this experience for a long time and in a very real sense, we are now joining you on this journey. The Government of Canada sincerely apologizes and asks the forgiveness of the Aboriginal peoples of this country for failing them so profoundly.
>
> *Nous le regrettons*
> We are sorry
> *Nimitataynan*

*Niminchinowesamin*
*Mamiattugut*

In moving towards healing, reconciliation and resolution of the sad legacy of Indian Residential Schools, implementation of the Indian Residential Schools Settlement Agreement began on September 19, 2007. Years of work by survivors, communities, and Aboriginal organizations culminated in an agreement that gives us a new beginning and an opportunity to *move forward together in partnership.*

A cornerstone of the Settlement Agreement is the Indian Residential Schools Truth and Reconciliation Commission. This Commission presents a unique opportunity to educate all Canadians on the Indian Residential Schools system. It will be a positive step in forging a new relationship between Aboriginal peoples and other Canadians, a relationship based on the knowledge of our shared history, a respect for each other and a desire to move forward together with a renewed understanding that strong families, strong communities and vibrant cultures and traditions will contribute to a stronger Canada for all of us. (Aboriginal Affairs and Northern Development Canada 2008; emphasis added)

While Indigenous communities across Canada have been waiting for a long time for such a speech to be offered by Canada, and understandably the apology carried emotional weight for the survivors of residential schools, this performative address was much more than just an overdue admission of wrongdoing. Laced between, through, and underneath the official and repeated renditions of "We are sorry," is a subtext about the settler colonial imaginary of Canada and the essential role the government should play in transitioning the association between Indigenous peoples and the state from a relationship of damage and mistrust to one of compatibility and agreement (Coulthard 2014a, 107). For example, in Harper's assertion of "failure to protect," the state effectively reinforces its paternalistic roots as opposed to suspending them. The implicit suggestion that the state could have, in fact, "protected" Indigenous children and their families from the harm and horror of residential schooling is simply ludicrous when we acknowledge that it was the very same state that created the mandate of these institutions, in partnership with the churches, and denied this intergenerational and living legacy for years to come.[24] How could the state have protected Indigenous people from the forcible removal of babies, toddlers, and youth from the arms of their parents and grandparents when that would have required protection from the settler colonial laws and social policies that were created and enforced by the state itself?

Further, in the declaration that we would "move forward in partner-ship" with the communities who were living on this land before Can-ada became Canada, Harper's speech symbolically aligns Indigenous peoples with the federal government and breathes life into the assump-tion that there is a shared desire, between Indigenous nations and the settler society, to build a "stronger Canada for all of us." In other words, both Indigenous peoples and Canadians are constrained and dimin-ished in their efforts to build a stronger Canada by being trapped in an unjust history – the time has come to confront these constraining condi-tions rationally and choose to enter a unified future together. The basic idea is this: if we all work together, we can share the riches and benefits of living off (and I mean this literally, given Canada's reliance on fossil fuels as a major component of its economic prowess) this vast territory. Yet, it only takes a quick glance into the yearly income levels of Indig-enous people compared to those of settler Canadians, not to mention the incarceration rates, to see that these riches and attendant benefits of citizenship have not been materially granted; the comparison is not even close.[25] When writing about anti-blackness in the United States in an editorial published 23 June 2015, Kiese Laymon (2015) gestures towards this kind of settler-driven futurism when remarking, "Like good Americans, I told Grandma, we will remember to drink ourselves drunk on the antiquated poison of progress. We will long for shall's and will be's and 'hopes' for tomorrow. We will heavy-handedly help in our own deception and moral obliteration. We will forget how much easier it is to talk about gun control, mental illness and riots than it is to talk about the moral and material consequences of manufactured white American innocence." Similarly, Indigenous peoples exist in the sus-pended space of "what could be," the allure of a not too distant future where justice and equality is the order of the day.

Such an assertion that this is a joint vision also assumes consent from an a priori Indigenous community via the Assembly of First Nations and other formal political organizations created by the colonial state – organizations imbibing "official" power sanctioned by the state. The burden to ensure that these political bodies are representative of a diverse and heterogeneous set of realities falls to the Indigenous nations themselves. The communities, however, are constrained by a formula for inclusion that has been created on their behalf – a palatable solution to their political difference and hence an inherent challenge to settler dominance. Moreover, I would argue that heterogeneous representa-tion is a near impossibility, given the homogeneity that characterizes all enterprises of nation building; nationalism begets the loyalty of its citizenry through a range of techniques that quell difference and foster and reward allegiance to an ideal citizen subject (B. Anderson 1991; Jiwani 2006). Indigenous communities, then, must shift and distort themselves to fit within the boundaries of participation that are set forth by the state through the very politics of recognition that are said to include them.[26]

In his recent book deconstructing the colonial politics of recognition, *Red Skin, White Masks*, Glen Coulthard (2014a) challenges forcefully the proposition that a governing approach founded on recognition and reconciliation can significantly transform the asymmetrical relationship between Indigenous peoples and the Canadian state. Indeed, through a careful and systematic analysis of mediated forms of state recognition and accommodation, Coulthard (2007) asserts that this colonial governing mode recreates the very same political conditions that sustain Indigenous dispossession – conditions that government officials and members of the Assembly of First Nations claim an explicit interest in dismantling. Through a deft and sustained engagement with the work of anti-colonial theorist, revolutionary, and psychiatrist Frantz Fanon, Coulthard (2007, 439) argues that the reproduction of the colonial structure of dominance upon which Canada rests is dependent on the state's ability to entice Indigenous peoples to "come to identify, either implicitly or explicitly, with the profound asymmetrical and non-reciprocal forms of recognition imposed on or granted to them by the colonial-state and society."[27] On this point, Coulthard (2007, 16) writes, "Fanon's analysis suggests that in contexts where colonial rule is not reproduced through force alone, the maintenance of settler-state hegemony requires the production of what he liked to call 'colonized subjects': namely the production of the specific modes of colonial thought, desire and behaviour that implicitly commit the colonized to a types of practices and subject positions that are required for their continued domination." In other words, "recognition" by a settler colonial state cannot be understood as a source of freedom and dignity, but should be seen rather "as the field of power through which colonial relations are produced and maintained" (17). Within this matrix of settler colonial smoke and mirrors, Indigenous subjects, as mediated by and through state policies and processes, come to associate with "white liberty and white justice" and come to see the forms of structurally limited and constrained recognition conferred on them by the state as their own and as "a political antidote to historical wrongdoing" (A. Simpson 2014, 20). The locus of imperial control, then, extends beyond political and economic institutions to meaning making in the world as understood and propagated by the consciousness and self-reflective capabilities of the colonized (Axel 2002, Biehl 2005). On the mediation of subjectivity, Fanon (1963, 250) reminds us that "because it is a systematic negation of the other person and a furious determination to deny the other person all attributes of humanity, colonialism forces people it dominated to ask themselves constantly the question, 'In reality, who am I?'" In settler nation states, acquiring a political subjectivity that exists outside the rationales of the state, when one is enmeshed in all of its institutions and is required so to be as a result of the impress of economic pressures, is a tall order, although not an impossibility.[28] How does a person resist internalizing the everyday social practices and sensibilities of the social world contained in the political spaces she occupies?

Audra Simpson (2014, 20) cautions that, while this recognition, an outwardly less coercive form of managing Indigenous political difference, may seem a virtuous and celebratory multicultural performance, [29]"the trick of tolerance" or of beneficence with no strings attached may actually extend the power of settlement through the language and practices of democratic inclusion.[30] As witnessed in the recent Indigenous resistance to state-sanctioned resource extraction in Elsipogtog, a politics of recognition does, very much, come with a series of interconnected gendered, raced, and classed strings that extend out from the beginnings of this settler colonial story. Hence, when the "problem" of difference and alterity is too much of an affront to settler society – that is, when it poses a direct threat to settler desires, to the rules of governing that are enshrined in the laws and policies of the social institutions that circumscribe everyday life (law, economics, health, justice, education) in Canada – then that difference is contained with whatever means are deemed necessary to reinstate settler order, norms, and secure access to, and ownership of, land. Guns, beatings, unlawful arrests, lock-up, intimidation, and legal instruments are all fair and legitimate in the processes of reinstatement.[31] Periods of democratic inclusion, then, are interrupted by fits and bursts of settler colonial violence that work to reinforce the illusion of geopolitical stability and the seemingly indomitable power dynamic reflected in this social order. It is another way of communicating, "You may play this game of inclusion, but you will play it on my terms. I reserve the right to pull out of the game at any time, without warning. And in case you didn't know this already, I hold the key to restarting the game."[32]

Within the context of an ongoing settler colonial project, it is essential that we be vigilant about closely examining what Carmela Murdocca (2013) refers to as state-led "reparative justice"[33] projects that ostensibly aim to rectify historical wrongs. Through a critical analysis of section 718.2(e) of the Criminal Code in *To Right Historical Wrongs*, a section she positions as part of a constellation of reparative projects associated with the post–World War II trend of amending historical injustices in liberal nation states, Murdocca outlines how race-based and restorative approaches to sentencing work to *entrench* rather than alleviate certain forms of racism and sexism (and there are severe implications for Indigenous women in this regard), especially when they are structured as appeals to culture difference. In other words, even though it may appear that the Canadian state is progressively tackling the mass incarceration of Indigenous peoples by requiring judges to consider "contextual factors" such as colonialism, displacement, and residential schools when determining sentencing for Indigenous offenders, such provisions prevent a focus on present-day systemic injustice that arguably produces the conditions for the invention of criminality and subsequent arrest of Indigenous peoples (which I take up in chapter 2); and the provisions support as well a persistent colonial management of racialized and Indigenous people through a social institution that is very much *still* caught up in the production of Indigenous and racialized subjects. On this point, Murdocca (2013, 63) writes, "This obscurity highlights the realization that even as the state attempts to address national responsibility in law through this sentencing provision, the state remains committed to an understanding of overincarceration rates in which it officially severs the relationship between colonial injustice and contemporary incarceration rates. This result reveals the limitations in the ability of the criminal justice process to attend to forms of marginalization and structural violence." Things, in other words, are not always what they seem.

It also merits stating that the Canadian state's preoccupation with identifying ways to "improve" the social conditions of Indigenous peoples, one of the most salient rationales for engaging recognition-based forms of governing, can be read as a quintessential colonial move linked to the settler state's need to legitimate itself as benevolent, as exercising a form of colonial care bent on saving a dying race. In *Dying from Improvement: Inquests and Inquiries into Indigenous Deaths in Custody*, Sherene Razack (2015) deftly argues that, through the legal performance of inquests and inquiries, the settler state continues to depict Indigenous people as fundamentally incapable of integrating into the modern capitalist world – a cross-institutional strategy which legitimates a form of liberal humanitarianism to "save." She attests, "Through a legal performance of Indigenous people as a dying race who are simply pathologically unable to cope with the demands of modern life, the settler subject is formed and his or her entitlement to the land secured. The settler and the settler state are both constituted as modern and as exemplary in their efforts to assist Indigenous people's entry into modernity" (Razack 2015, 6). The mark of the racial, then, is always to need assistance into modernity. And when the racial is cast as such, the settler state must become adept at producing portraits of Indigenous self-destruction and dysfunction – as remnants always living on the edge, on the brink of death; colonial subjects in need of settler state rescue (Razack 2015, 17).

Finally, under the lens of critical scrutiny, it is clear that this latest approach to the governing of Indigenous peoples produces yet another tangible consequence: it positions Canada in the temporal space of the postcolonial. That is, in its move towards a space of "common goals" and "mutual respect and recognition," Canada claims to have shed the skeletons of its imperialist roots and entered a fresh era with respect to its approach towards Indigenous nations. This new era was ushered in, concretely, by adopting a mode of governing that claims to place value on Indigenous knowledge and cultural practices and by apologizing for its historic mistreatment of Indigenous peoples.[34] The attempted creation of this Lockean *tabula rasa* also functions to obscure and circumvent a distinct focus on Indigenous sovereignty and Indigenous resurgence that aims to transcend the very existence of the Canadian settler state. A settler colonial politics of recognition works to cover this up when elevated to a conceptual means for comprehending the stakes of political contestations over identity and difference in this colonial context. In obscuring the consequences of this new logic of governing, Canada's illusion of postcolonial arrival legitimizes its own existence as a nation and reroutes questions of land rights, identity, culture, and place within and through this newly granted legitimacy. Perhaps the most glaring example of the promotion of this postcolonial status was witnessed in a news conference at the end of the G20 summit in Pittsburgh, Pennsylvania on 25 September 2009, when, with notable temerity, Prime Minister Stephen Harper commented on his version of Canada's history, having just apologized for residential schooling one year prior: "We also have no history of colonialism. So we have all of the things that many people admire about the great powers but none of the things that threaten or bother them."[35] Apparently, colonialism has transcended its own history and is now consigned to a coffin lodged somewhere deep between layers of the earth, if it existed at all.[36]

It is my contention that urban Indigenous youth are entangled in this messy terrain of recognition that has gained a material foothold through the participatory endeavours I explore in this book. The regulatory programs that dictate the rules under which these young people live and that consequently make only certain ways of being in the world possible are clear examples of how the destinies of young people are being determined by a constellation of factors outside of their immediate control. Recognition politics work to recode the logics of settler colonial social policy through the discourse and practice of an ambiguous apparatus of participation that does little to shift dynamics of power. And, as I explain in the following chapters, it is not an accident that the lives of urban Indigenous youth are so heavily constrained by the state; the Canadian government (both federally and provincially) has a vested interest in curtailing the political, critical consciousness of these youth, as well as of the generations of Indigenous descendants yet to come, in order to maintain the sanctity of the Canadian nation and to keep the possibility of large scale Indigenous resistance at bay – in nations where settlement has yet to reach its final stage of completion, possibility is enough of a threat. To clarify, I am not suggesting that all state agents are deliberately trying to engage in acts of subjugation and suppression. Instead, I contend that the systems in which state agents work and the power/knowledge nexus (Foucault 1982) which informs their work are linked to an overarching set of beliefs about who these young people are and what they should become. Indeed, the severe marginalization experienced by these young people and the material dispossession and suffering that continues unabated under such regimes of governing remain so great that they now occupy a place in global deliberations over Canada's compliance with international treaties and several conventions to which it is a signatory.

In the remaining portion of this chapter, I explore more fully Canada's relationship to Indigenous children and youth by offering an experiential account of advocacy that takes this notion of a "recognition that dispossesses" to an international stage. I conclude with a related and more general discussion of transnational Indigenous organizing, which I argue holds merit when considering questions of Indigenous collectives organizing across Turtle Island.

## Canada within the Context of a Worldwide Indigenous Movement

September 17, 2012, marked the beginning of the Sixty-First Session of the United Nations, Committee on the Rights of the Child. Canada's adherence to the United Nations Convention on the Rights of Child, after its ratification by Parliament in 1991, was being systematically reviewed in this session. My colleagues from Justice for Girls, a Vancouver-based NGO, and I flew to Geneva, Switzerland to be present for the proceedings.[37] We were scheduled to meet with several rapporteurs to discuss the grim realities facing young women and girls living in poverty in Canada and to speak out about the ongoing forms of structural colonial violence experienced by Indigenous girls.[38] To get into the proceedings required a series of lengthy bureaucratic and security procedures. Justice for Girls has official accreditation status with the United Nations so we were permitted observational attendance, but we were still required to submit clearance forms and passport information and acquire special visitor IDs in order to obtain access to the premises.

The proceedings were held in a very large, chamber-like room in one of the many historic buildings that make up the sprawling complex of this international assembly with post–World War II roots. An elevated stage with tables and microphones stood at the front of the room, where members of the Canadian government delegation were positioned to provide summative evidence of Canada's adherence to the convention. Official members of the UN committee sat surrounding the stage; if you can imagine a rectangle, with the front of the stage being the top side of the rectangle and then rows of UN representatives making up the remaining three sides, you can get a sense of the formality and physical arrangement of the space – it conjures up the sensation of tiptoeing through a very quiet and delicate crystal shop where one must walk cautiously between the aisles, careful not to bump into anything. Everything had its place. Translation was available in multiple languages through handset devices. Headphones and seating were available for representatives from NGOs (there were advocates from all across Canada representing myriad social issues), all located on the periphery of the central area.

Members of the NGO delegation were not allowed to speak during the formal proceedings. Instead, our participation was restricted to advocacy meetings with members of the committee conducting the formal review. In these closed meetings before, during, and after the proceedings (and arranging these meetings required its own set of strategic alliances and political manoeuvring), we presented a series of well-honed points about the lived realities facing Indigenous young women and girls. We provided as much detail as possible about the high degree of sexual exploitation, disproportionate criminalization and incarceration, police violence, endemic poverty, environmental degradation and accompanying health impacts, institutional violence in housing and education policy, and abhorrent child welfare stories.[39] The idea was to get this committee to consider these conditions as direct violations of Canada's ostensible agreement with the tenets of the UN Convention on the Rights of the Child. In turn, we hoped the committee would pressure the Canadian government into compliance before the next formal review. It is important to note that, while the mandate of this convention is not restricted to the experiences of Indigenous children and youth and their communities, it provides a framework and international mechanism for outlining Canada's failure to support, both materially and institutionally, Indigenous children and youth and to make clear their specific relationship to the settler state. Moreover, our research and advocacy exposed the Canadian state as a consistent perpetrator of gendered colonial violence against them.

At the end of the review, "Concluding Observations" (United Nations 2012) were released to the public. They contained an explicit overview of the committee's observations and follow-up recommendations. Not surprisingly, embedded in the pages of this report were numerous references to the gross marginalization and disinvestment experienced by Indigenous children and youth, with several direct citations of the lived realities facing Indigenous young women and girls. Given the repeated failure of Canada to create the social and political conditions for these young women and girls to grow and prosper, combined with the state's own propensity for foundational violence, we viewed the space of international advocacy as offering a possibility for pushing in from the outside, or at least consolidating ties with other communities around the world seeking similar kinds of justice in order to determine what could collectively be done to support social change efforts at home.[40]

Our engagement with this international legal and political constituency, as explored above, is not the first of its kind. It builds on a history of global advocacy and mobilization by Indigenous communities with respect to shared histories of oppression as well as current infringements on territory and related political insurrections.[41] Despite the Canadian state's decision to decline signatory status in the United Nations Declaration on the Rights of Indigenous Peoples up until 2013 (see "Canada Endorses" 2016), and even then only acquiring that status with grudging approval, Indigenous communities from Turtle Island have, since long ago, taken part in international activism, including, most recently, the UN Working Group on Indigenous Peoples. As far back as 1923, the Iroquois Six Nations travelled to Geneva as part of a small delegation to present their grievances to the League of Nations regarding Canada's failure to respect the assertion of Indigenous sovereignty.[42] In a post–World War II historical moment, the struggle against fascism contributed to an increased receptiveness at the international level towards measures for the protection of minorities (and standards to resist racism and discrimination). Moreover, the experiences of World War II illuminated the fact that states could not always be relied upon to protect their own citizens. The dismantling of the European colonies further highlighted the power of political hegemony and raised global awareness about the range of cultural suppression tactics that were being used in "civilizing" processes. How could colonial governments be trusted to safeguard human rights?[43]

Connected to this important question were international lobbying efforts that coalesced around anti-assimilation campaigns. These campaigns, launched by "pan-Indigenous" minority groups, made clear that the tools of "re-education" that were used through boarding schools in settler states like Canada, the United States, and Australia had failed in their goal of eliminating all vestiges of Indigenous life. In doing so, the campaigners painted a sobering picture of the massive human rights violations taking place within major democracies claiming liberty, freedom, and justice for all.

In 1975, the formation of the World Council of Indigenous Peoples marked the creation of an Indigenous organization aimed at linking together existing national and international alliances within a global framework (Wright 1988, 376). Indigenous cultural politics were crucial to this formation, and in the hundreds of Indigenous interventions, there was a striking unity in the cultural political arguments set forth, reflecting a carefully crafted discourse developed over time. Fast-forward to 2015 – this activism has grown by leaps and bounds and stands as a powerful transnational Indigenous political practice.

### The United Nations Working Group on Indigenous Populations: Seeking Change beyond Geopolitical Boundaries

To explain the prowess of the current global forum, it is useful to turn to the work of Andrea Muehlebach and her essay "Making Place at the

United Nations: Indigenous Cultural Politics at the UN Working Group on Indigenous Populations."[44] Muehlebach (2001) closely examines the UN Working Group on Indigenous Populations (WGIP) as a particularly dense discursive space enabling a substantive and diverse group of activists to engage in a number of battles on a number of fronts while retaining consistent political messaging through the deployment of the notion of "Indigenous place." As a conceptual tool, "Indigenous place" articulates a specific and meaningful relationship between Indigenous peoples, culture, and their territories that enables Indigenous delegates to explicate a distinct way of being in the world and to assert having a particular position in it (Muehlebach 2001, 432). Indigenous difference, then, is the dictum of the WGIP, and in their assertion of sovereignty, Indigenous activists claim that the right of a people to determine their own political and economic development does not belong exclusively to nation states emulating the European liberal model of equal rights and freedoms (Wilmer 1993).

In particular, Muehlebach (2001) has argued that the discourse of "Indigenous place" has integrated a broad set of issues and tensions regarding the worldwide social and political emancipation of Indigenous peoples and the concrete realization of justice and equality.[45] "Place" symbolizes a "source of life and a reference point which people may identify with from their particular position in the more global network of human relations" and effectively explains what Indigenous activism is always about – territory (Hastrup and Olwig 1997, 12). Further, the critiques Indigenous delegates have levied against dominant conceptions of human rights illustrate three basic tenets that form the basis of their international activism; namely:

1. Indigenous cultural communities are invested in and live off a specific place, the land, and without unwanted interference.
2. The places with which Indigenous delegates portray themselves as being meaningfully intertwined are either already or on the verge of being destroyed and/or polluted.
3. In claiming rights for "those who cannot speak," delegates assert that the natural world embodies and means more to Indigenous peoples than merely as the basis for the economic sustenance of the community.

The relationship to territory, then, is not just a political or economic matter but also a moral and spiritual one. The heart of this combination of ethnicity and ecology that runs up against a "whole civilization design based on modern reason" (Escobar 1992, 41) is well captured in Muehlebach's (2001, 425) assertion that "place, then, is infused with culture and vice versa, so that all Indigenous cultural politics are always also a politics of land, and a politics of rights to land. By implication, all struggles for and about land are always also struggles about identity and culture." In this regard, the eco-political framework positions territory as a "fundamental and multidimensional space for the creation of and recreation of the ecological, economic, and cultural practices of community" (Escobar 1998, 69). Place is not just place. It is everything.[46]

My inclusion of a section, albeit brief, on a growing transnational Indigenous movement is relevant for a number of reasons. First, from an advocacy perspective, there has been some recognized advantage in cutting across state interests under the gaze of the international community.[47] In December 2011, the United Nations Committee on the Elimination of Discrimination[48] against Women announced its decision to conduct an inquiry into the murders and disappearances of Indigenous women and girls across Canada. Importantly, these murders and disappearances are being analysed through the lens of systemic discrimination, social exclusion, and the denial of basic social and economic rights. The decision to undertake this investigation is also being positioned as a response to the state's complicity in maintaining colonial, gender violence and to its failure to respond to acts of racialized male violence directed towards Indigenous women and girls. This claim was recently substantiated by a Human Rights Watch (2013) investigation, in partnership with Justice for Girls – the first ever to be conducted on Canadian soil – in ten towns across Northern British Columbia. The subsequent report revealed numerous instances of police neglect, abuse, and failure when providing legal protective measures in cases of reported domestic violence: a twelve-year-old girl attacked by a police dog, a seventeen-year-old punched repeatedly by a police officer who had been called to help her, women strip-searched by male officers, and women injured due to excessive force during arrest, to name a few (Human Rights Watch 2013, 8).[49] The murder and disappearance of Indigenous women and girls along British Columbia's Highway of Tears served as the basis for this investigation, although the findings from the inquiry produced through the report resonate across communities in Canada.[50] The Canadian federal government has repeatedly denied requests by the Native Women's Association of Canada (NWAC) and numerous anti-violence non-governmental organizations for a national public inquiry into violence against Indigenous women and girls.

Second, the discourse of international Indigenous activism is politically instrumental in its ability to redirect mobilizing efforts away from the limited, myopic conversations about service delivery that inform much of the discursive space of Indigenous–settler state relations in Canada and certainly speak to the context of discussions pertaining to urban Indigenous youth. Longstanding notions of "help" and "salvation" underlie many of these deliberations that are preoccupied with creating reactionary solutions to the complex social problems that have emerged from a host of legislation and social policy aimed at eradicating Indigenous life. These "solutions" are often based in concepts of healing and reconciliation, or more recently, in the trope of "capacity-building," as will be seen in the following chapters, concepts that problematize individual people and communities and direct the focus away from state complicity. Such critiques are already gaining ground. For example, in his work on Indigenous peoples and state dependency, Mohawk scholar Taiaiake Alfred (2009, 49) passionately argues that "denial of access to land-based cultural practices leading to the loss of freedom on both the individual and collective levels equates to the psychological effect of anomie, or the state of profound alienation that results from experiencing serious cultural dissolution, which is then the direct cause of serious substance abuse problems, suicide and interpersonal violence." In the same vein, international Indigenous organizing places the history and actions of the state within the purview, if not at the centre, of claims to "Indigenous place" and strategically links the dispossession materialized on Indigenous bodies and in larger communities with the occupation of Indigenous land.

Third, even though the deliberations happening in these dynamic and complex spaces are far removed from the streets of Saskatoon and the lives of the urban Indigenous youth around which this book unfolds, there is nonetheless a powerful set of connections being forged across national boundaries that merit attention. Among these connections is the newly emerging Indigenous People's Biodiversity Network and the Indigenous Knowledge Program, a transnational Indigenous organization fostering much needed links between environmental activism and Indigenous politics, including those that focus on youth. Further, these international networks, at least in terms of potential, create a mechanism to bypass some of the domestic detritus that constrains our ability to even imagine that some other global reality is possible with respect to ecological preservation. Indeed, in offering an alternative to the widespread western epistemologies of modernity and development, progress and profit, Indigenous delegates, alongside numerous activist allies and public intellectuals, are proposing alternative values and ways of being in the world that reposition our relationship to the natural world and taking on some of the problems arising out of transnational capital and the short-sightedness of state officials when considering crimes against future generations. The recuperation of origin stories, the evocation of ancestors, and the responsibility voiced towards those who have yet to live on the land are strategies used by Indigenous delegates to "effectively convey concepts of interconnectedness, notions of morality, and respect, as well as what is lost once the interconnectedness is forcibly destroyed" (Muehlebach 2001, 429). Such an emphasis seems more urgent than ever before, as the largest industrial development project in the world, the tar sands in Northern Alberta, and a spectrum of other extractive fossil fuel projects continue in Canada, with widespread provincial, federal, and corporate involvement (Klein 2014a). What the role of Indigenous youth in Canada will be against such a backdrop remains to be seen.

\* \* \*

After several applications had been denied, the United Nations Special Rapporteur on the Rights of Indigenous Peoples, James Anaya, was finally granted permission by the Harper government to enter Canada in October 2013. His concluding statement lays bare the deprivation, neglect, and continued colonialism that is interwoven into the dynamics of the everyday for many urban Indigenous youth. Mapping the possibilities for social life that are claimed to exist against those that actually do exist is essential when trying to make sense of the regimes of intervention that circumscribe the lives of these young people. Such dynamics and their consequences are made even clearer by moving closer to the lived realities on the ground.

## Chapter Two

# The Making of Crisis Stories

All of us have to learn how to invent our lives, make them up, imagine them. We need to be taught these skills; we need guides to show us how. If we don't, our lives get made up for us by other people.

– Ursula Le Guin, *The Wave in the Mind: Talks and Essays on the Writer, the Reader and the Imagination*

We live in a reality now where I would say to anyone: protect your spirit, protect your spirit because you're in the space where spirits get eaten.

– John Trudell; qtd. In Red Skin, *2Hours*

When I look back to 2000 and the beginning of my advocacy and research on issues of youth marginalization, this is what I remember most: She was crouched down on a street corner. One of her knees was pointed up towards the sky and the other was resting against the cracked cement. Long brown hair from a high ponytail fell against one side of her small face. A string of cheap gold beads graced the deep neckline of an ivory sleeveless tank, her short skirt leaving thin legs mostly exposed. Her lips were accentuated with a bright shade of red mixed with just the slightest bit of purple. I could not see her eyes when I first approached. She was looking down at a teen magazine lying close to her feet, flipping the pages in the dim light of an abandoned corner of the city in the late hours of the night. The road was deserted except for the intermittent flash of headlights from a vehicle driven by someone seeking to violently exploit a young Indigenous girl living on the margins of a big city; a city where she has lived in poverty[1] and been unable to stay in school or find a safe place to live, a municipality whose existence relies on the theft of land. "The roots of sexual violence in Canada are as deep as colonialism itself," argues Sarah Hunt (2010, 27), writer and activist from the Kwakwaka'wakw Nation. Elsewhere I have written that these mephitic roots strangle life and sanction the invisibility of violence if you are an Indigenous girl.[2] It is structural exploitation offered up in plain sight yet systematically denied.[3]

I was out on the streets of Vancouver[4] that summer night as part of my work for the province of British Columbia, where I was tasked with creating programs for youth experiencing sexual exploitation and developing policy standards for safe housing across the province.[5] Two outreach workers from the Adolescent Services Unit, a youth agency operating under the auspices of the Ministry of Children and Families, and I had driven to the far east corridor of Vancouver to a section of the city where desecrated buildings, deserted warehouses, and old factories made up most of the urban landscape. On our way there, I asked the youth workers who we could expect to encounter on the streets, in terms of broad demographics, since up until this point I had been restricted to learning about these issues by scouring the few government summaries and academic articles I could find, and information was rather limited. They explained that this place was an extension of the "low track" in the hierarchy of prostitution in Vancouver. Here we would find mostly Indigenous girls who had left their reserves, for numerous reasons, and ended up on the street. Among the officers of the Vancouver city police, this area was also known as the "kiddie stroll"[6] for the notable preponderance of young women and girls walking the streets and experiencing sexual exploitation. The mainstream media had taken up this phrase in earnest when reporting on issues of prostitution in the Lower Mainland of British Columbia.

Our aim that night was to identify "new girls" who had not previously been seen by the outreach team in order to begin developing relationships with them and identifying "service needs." In addition, we were to employ harm reduction strategies, such as the distribution of condoms, food, and first aid supplies. This was my first night working alongside the outreach team. I was nervous – talking and doing are often two totally different sets of experiences. Things are rarely as you expect them to be.

We parked our vehicle on Commercial Drive and began walking. None of the bustling night time activity that one might find in other neighbourhoods – mini-marts or 7-elevens, gas stations or coffee shops – surrounded us. Where would someone go for help in such a place? The desolation was visceral as much as it was visual; the notion of safety destroyed, an illusion at best.

At the sight of the girl, we crossed the street to offer her a handful of condoms and a card with a list of the names of youth organizations (and phone numbers) in the city. She stood up and stared right through me after I said "hello." Her light-brown sunken eyes were expressionless, her mouth in a straight line. I reached out my hand towards her and she took the condoms before quietly uttering "thanks" and crouching back down. I was struck by how young she appeared. The queasiness in my stomach began to grow. The outreach worker who was standing beside me – mid-twenties, blondish hair, and light skin – attempted to engage the girl in a conversation about youth agencies in the city that could offer housing assistance, but she declined with silence. After a couple of minutes, the youth worker stopped trying. I was perplexed at the thought of leaving this girl out on the streets alone. When I voiced my concerns, the outreach worker shrugged her shoulders and said that it was the girl's decision to remain there. The most we could do, she asserted, was to provide information that she might one day choose to draw upon. In other words, this girl had gotten herself into this situation and she would get herself out. I glanced back at her as we stepped away, wanting to say something, but I had no idea what to say. I walked away without saying anything at all.

The outreach worker's intimation about the intricacies of "personal decision making" had also surfaced the day prior at a "hard target" meeting. These meetings were organized around the case files of "targeted high risk" youth living on the streets. In a small room at the community policing station in Vancouver's Downtown Eastside, I sat with social service providers from across child protection, criminal justice, addiction services, and youth outreach while they deliberated how best to intervene in the lives of youth deemed the most likely to be taking part in dangerous street activity and, in turn, most susceptible to street violence. Many of the youth were Indigenous girls who the service providers argued were in need of state protection because of the "bad decisions" (running away from group homes, dropping out of school, breaching probation orders, to name a few) they had made. "They just keep running and running. Sometimes we just have to force them to accept help," one worker boldly exclaimed at the meeting. Witnessing this Indigenous girl's refusal to engage state assistance vis-à-vis the outreach worker, however, it was obvious that her "decision" was bound up in layers of lived experience.

This young woman was not the only one we encountered that night. Up and down the shadowed, dark streets we ambled (there were only a few streetlights) and more girls kept surfacing at corners, leaning against buildings and bus stops, sitting on the pavement. Some held to small groups of two or three. Most were alone. Watching for the headlights.

Up until this point, I thought I knew Canada. It is a country where manufactured notions of freedom and opportunity pervade the dominant discourses of nationalism and civic pride. It ranks eleventh overall in the United Nations Human Development Index and among the highest in international measurements of education, (ostensible) government transparency, civil liberties, quality of life, and economic freedom (see United Nations Development Program 2014). Even still, I knew that, as a nation allegedly concerned with questions of justice, yet increasingly the focus of international inquisitions into the denial of human rights on Canadian soil, we had a substantial distance yet to travel. After all, I had a critical awareness of the history of colonization and the social suffering that emerges from reconfigured forms of settler colonialism. I was taught about these things, in some measure, throughout my undergraduate and graduate careers. I sought out information about social issues from community organizations, attended talks and political protests. I facilitated workshops on anti-racism strategies and eradicating gender violence. For better or worse, I considered myself to be a knowledgeable person with a social conscience who was willing to act.

None of that, however, prepared me for the vexing gravity of dispossession I came face to face with that night. These were human beings; Indigenous girls with social histories, families, gifts, imaginations, and dreams. Somehow, though, all of that had been reduced to destitution. These girls were living a life of brutal settler colonial dead ends right in front of me.

I wish to clarify my intent in sharing this encounter. My purpose is not to suggest that Indigenous young women and girls, and Indigenous youth more generally, are incapable of developing complex and multiple resistance strategies and survivance[7] within the context of the immense difficulty they endure living on the street. Such an exploration is an important and worthy endeavour, withholding the "sanitization of painful realities" of course (Bourgois 1996, 250).[8] Cherry Smiley (2012, 2), an Indigenous feminist from the Navajo and Thompson Nations, intimates this when writing, "Colonial policies, practices and attitudes have and continue to impact every aspect of an Indigenous girl's life, limiting her options and constraining her opportunities from birth. However, despite these difficult realities, Indigenous girls continue to resist these impacts, as they work to create safe and meaningful lives for themselves and their loved ones."[9] Nor is it my desire to create reductionist portraits of victimization that strip bare the nuances of social life that are undoubtedly present in the turbulent dynamics of an everyday existence set against the trenchant features of an unwelcoming and hostile society. My interest throughout this chapter, rather, is in prioritizing the state's ongoing and manifold strands of assault on Indigenous youth in order to make visible the profound restrictions and harm that comes from the everyday, routinized violence inherent in particular social, economic, and political formations, and in this case, specifically settler colonial ones.[10] Inequality and dispossession in settler states are purposefully consequential. They are knitted together with race, class, gender, sexuality, and other social categories laden with power to form multiple and interconnected axes of subjugation (Collins 1990; Razack 1998; Crenshaw 1991; Mohanty 2003; Lugones 2007; Driskill 2010) that work to "structure possible fields of action" (Li 2007, 16). They authorize and naturalize violence in the everyday through the dehumanizing controlling processes (Nader 1972) inherent in racialization and the attendant forms of settler colonization manifested in the corporeality of the body (Scheper-Hughes 1992), and by cultivating psychological states of self-negation (Coulthard 2014a).[11] Colonial violence, then, is always deliberately attached to an agenda of individual subjectification that functions to sublimate collective resistance and reinforce self-rule in the name of settler sovereignty.

## The Trickery of Choice

I turn now to a related but distinct point. My rendering of this encounter inevitably raises the complicated and slippery question of "choice" that itself calls into view longstanding sociological and anthropological deliberations over the binary relationship between structure[12] and agency and the debates of duality they entail (Giddens 1984; Sewell 1992; Wacquant 1989; Ortner 1984; Lévi-Strauss 1963). Stated otherwise, gesturing towards the "socio-culturally mediated capacity to act" (Ahearn 2011, 112) opens the floodgates to polemics concerning the interlinkages among agency, oppression, personhood, and resistance – the tension that exists between the idea that human action is constrained by a given social and cultural order and the idea that human action also cre-ates structure in ways that reproduce or transform that order (Bourdieu 1977; Willis 1977). Sherry Ortner (2001, 77) argues that agency concerns the mediation "between conscious intention and embodied habituses, between conscious motives and unexpected outcomes, between histori-cally marked individuals on the one hand, and the cumulative repro-ductions and transformations that are a result of everyday practices on the other." She uses the image of "serious games" ("serious" is used to emphasize the idea that power and inequality pervade the games in multiple ways and that the stakes are high) to flesh out the rules and goals that make up social life and the networks of social relationships and interpersonal dynamics as well as multiple subject positions that inform everyday action.

While I undoubtedly see merit in understanding how urban Indig-enous youth who are living lives of extreme marginalization navigate deprivation (and some scholars refer to this as the "bounded circle" of agency), I am concerned that a romanticizing of agency, coupled with the downplaying of an anti-colonial analysis of the institutional undercurrents that foster the circumstances in which they these young people find themselves, may do little to alter the material realities they face or the broader asymmetrical power dynamics that scaffold their lives.[13] Moreover, in this book, I am interested in shining a spotlight on (indicting, in fact) the ways that settler colonial state logics continue to actively produce conditions of neglect, deprivation, and symbolic violence (Bourdieu 1977) while simultaneously claiming to recognize Indigenous self-determination through discourses of reconciliation and recognition – to perform the work, in other words, of (re)storying the narrative of a benevolent Canada (McLean 2014). This (re)storying requires reorienting an anti-colonial analysis towards an examination of statecraft itself and the "practical technicians of everyday violence" (Scheper-Hughes and Bourgois 2004) who are instrumental in concep-tualizing and enacting the inherited social fields in which these young people must act. The idea of "choice" within the context of ongoing structural dispossession, then, demands deep politicization as much as it demands (re)engagement with the collective denial and misrecogni-tion of settler colonial state violence in all its forms.

Indeed, I contend that what I witnessed that evening was the clearest manifestation of what happens when only certain kinds of living are made possible in a settler colonial reality Patrick Wolfe describes as a "winner takes all project" (Kauanui and Wolfe 2012, 248) – the reality that arises when choice is no longer choice because it is so grossly overdetermined by social forces outside of one's immediate control. It is what happens when life becomes predominantly about survival – materially and socially – and the available avenues for meeting the most basic needs also egregiously violate human dignity (even though they may represent a creative response to social exclusion), inflict immense emotional and spiritual harm, and collapse the complexity of human experience into portraits of pathology and blame. These young girls on the street were no longer registered by the state social workers whom I was accompanying as young women with particular political identities or claims to stolen land, much less as embodying the possibility of Indigenous resurgence (which in my own work with youth I had encountered frequently). Instead, they were socially (re)constituted by the state as racialized citizen subjects in desperate need of saving, a group of lost and misguided souls who had not yet capitalized on what their country had to offer.

One need not look far into the landscape of youth programming to see how the notion of "choice" together with "risk" mediates portrayals of Indigenous youth, thereby negating the macrolevel sociopolitical and economic dimensions of ongoing settler colonialism that are central to the micro-interactions of everyday life. The StreetGraphix project, created through the Saskatoon Health Region in partnership with Saskatoon Community Youth Arts Programming and a number of other government agencies, is an exemplary case in point. Claiming to "make art relevant and make relevant art" by offering an "incisive truth" about street life in Saskatoon, StreetGraphix uses graphic comics to showcase the "life stories" of four young people who have been marked as "at risk" because of their experiences with "poverty, domestic abuse, problematic relationships with parents, and violence literal and implicit" and to demonstrate "how choices always have repercussions."[14] The underlying premise is preventative: other street youth will engage with these stories and learn from them and the decisions they make in their own lives may be affected.

To facilitate this process, an online platform creates an interactive space where the reader may decide which direction to take in terms of life events (you could, for example, continue to take drugs or opt to contact an addictions resource centre and depending on which "choice" you make, the resulting story unfolds accordingly). "Tala's Story," one of the four narratives presented, is the story of a young Indigenous woman who has struggled with many of the above issues. The opening lines of her account read, "Every choice has a consequence. Good or bad, you have to live with your choices" ("Tala's Story" 2016). Interspersed throughout the framing of her "choices" are links to city resources (phone numbers for Alcoholics Anonymous, short-term emergency shelters, and domestic abuse services among others), so that, if a young person reading this account recognizes similar tendencies in herself, she could consider contacting these organizations for help, thereby exercising her ostensible agency.

Not surprisingly, while the graphic depictions of Tala's life contain visual imagery that gestures towards her Indigenous ancestry (she is smudging in one frame, for instance), there is nothing in the presentation that explicitly posits her political status as an Indigenous youth, or the historical and contemporary struggles inherent in settler colonialism that arguably have something to do with her life story, as part of her narrative script. What is left open to public scrutiny is a decontextualized individual, stripped bare of her political embodiment and the intergenerational social histories that comprise the foundation of her lived reality. Implicit here is the idea that if Tala could only exercise her personal agency to access state services (and there is no discussion of the problematics associated with the social services outlined either), her life would be magically, and quite easily, transformed.[15]

Sandy Grande (2004, 69), a Quechua scholar of Indigenous social and political thought, points to the pervasiveness of ontological individualism running through the deep structures of colonial consciousness. She reminds us that "this assumption [of ontological individualism] is most often linked to the Cartesian idea of the self-constituting individual whereby the self is viewed as the basic social unit. Individuals in possession of high degrees of independence and autonomy are considered to be the ideals of 'health,' and concepts such as self-governance, self-determination, and self-actualization are viewed as goals towards which individuals are encouraged to strive." Read through this lens, the choices Tala makes are hers and hers alone.

Let me be crystal clear. In all of my years working with youth I have never come across a single young person who has told me that they aspired to a life of gross marginalization – that this is the existence they imagined for themselves, the life, as Ursula Le Guin (2004) writes, they wished to invent. This is not a simple matter of choice. These are the lives that are partly made up for urban Indigenous youth through numerous social policies and institutional practices constructed and carried out by the settler state, often in partnership with non-governmental organizations, as I explain throughout the rest of this book. Everyday acts of racialized and gendered violence that augment and legitimize these policies and are inherent in Canada's social institutions constrain their lives in immeasurable ways.[16] These are the lives that are generated when paternalistic, rescuing social interventions are enacted in a "crisis" that has been created by the state in order to maintain the power and politics of the settler colonial status quo.

Canada, then, is also a variegated space, where the prospect of opportunity and the absence of choice, despite the meritocratic ideology of liberal democracy, exist side by side. A combination of hierarchical social categories, constrained political subjectivity, and differential access to semiotic and material "rules and resources" (Giddens 1984, 26), is part of what determines the line between opportunity and scarcity. It is a country in which notions of freedom and liberty pulsate through the social veins of national museums and mainstream media, and a country in which disavowal of lethal settler colonial violence happens every single day. Like Nitânis, whose life story, albeit in abbreviated form, opens this book, this young woman squatting down on a street corner next to a chicken factory in the east end of Vancouver has come from somewhere. A strategically insidious way to avoid accountability in this scenario is to create frameworks of pathology (criminal, drop out, hooker, troubled youth)[17] that position her as solely responsible for the "choices" she has made leading up to her arrival on the street that night. A "blame the victim" inferiorizing fantasy narrative works wonders in the service of abdicating societal culpability and negating an analysis of settler colonial power (Palmater 2011).[18]

In the pages that follow, I provide an overview of the strangulating web of colonial institutions that mediates the lives of urban Indigenous youth and trace the relational dynamics between their experience and the settler colonial scripting that informs them. While there are numerous institutional spaces that govern their lives, the majority of social regulatory projects reflect a constant concern with education as a panacea for severe social deprivation, and this is also reflected in the foci of the participatory alliances with the Indigenous Peoples Collective that I address in subsequent chapters. Hence, I have chosen to highlight the experiences of Indigenous youth within this institution, both historically and within the contemporary moment, in order to trace the linkages between educational experience and the larger sociopolitical realities in which education takes place.[19] To speak to these larger sociopolitical realities, I have integrated ethnographic episodes and discussions of the criminal justice and child welfare systems and related issues of gang involvement and violence against Indigenous women and girls – all of these social experiences cumulatively work together to produce the crisis narrative that has come to publicly mark urban Indigenous youth in Canada. By offering this portrayal, I aim to (re)position the experiences of these young people directly within a settler colonial social context, as well as move beyond simplistic explanations of individual choice and personal responsibility when considering the endemic human destiny charted by their experiences of marginalization.

**Restricting Breath: The Institutional Traps of Settler Colonial Rule**

*The Power of Education and Education as Power*[20]

I entered the room and the walls were adorned with posters lauding education as "the future that lies within us." Glossy leaflets laying on the conference table were decorated with the smiling brown faces of Indigenous children and youth who were grouped together on well-equipped school playgrounds or seated in typically arranged western classrooms, their faces attentively pointed upward towards the educator at the front of the class. In some pictures, children were depicted outside, at a pow-wow or community event of some sort, dressed in "traditional" Indigenous clothing and participating in cultural practice, with a Canadian flag forming a silhouette in the background. I stepped into this space in 2005 when I was asked to participate in a youth conference on homelessness in Saskatoon. I was directed by the conference organizers to take part in a roundtable discussion of the "promising practices"[21] identified to engage Indigenous youth in school. The sight of these images as I entered, however, sent a ripple of apprehension through me. Indeed, the subtle message portrayed by these pictures of subsuming Indigenous "culture" into the public system of education in Canada, coupled with the essentializing depictions of Indigenous children and youth, seemed especially troubling. I was left wondering how the underlying messages about the power and role of education embedded in these posters was going to be translated into concrete reality, given the tumultuous record of Indigenous education provision in Canada.

Educational programming for Indigenous nations resides at the critical intersection of settler nation building, citizen development, and societal prosperity.[22] On the one hand, socially manufacturing educational programs for Indigenous peoples has been considered one of the primary vehicles of forced assimilation and integration by the Canadian state (Milloy 1999; Maaka and Fleras 2005). In contrast, educational development has also been envisioned as a potential means of political mobilization and reparation – a view that considers how Indigenous peoples decolonize from within, forcing the government to begin disassembling the most demeaning and debilitating aspects of colonial tutelage. Moreover, existing against a backdrop of high levels of poverty, education is often posited by the settler colonial state as the doorway to access for Indigenous peoples, the key to social mobility, and the pathway to the shedding of their status as colonial subjects thereby repositioning them as "equal citizens" within the country – the trope of opportunity. Numerous provincial and federal documents concerning the place of Indigenous peoples in Canadian society echo these sentiments, arguing that "we believe a greater effort must be made to educate urban Aboriginal youth, their families and communities about the importance of education, the ways in which higher education will improve the quality of their life, and more importantly, how it can help youth achieve a sense of accomplishment, self-worth, and esteem" (Canada, Standing Senate Committee on Aboriginal Peoples 2003, 68).

The "salvation project" of education, created first as a solution to the "Indian problem" in the early days of settler nation building and later as a response to Indigenous critiques of the structural violence inherent in colonialism, is not a novel or recent phenomenon. Rather, contemporary appeals to the miraculous, almost magical, power of education are nestled within a history of state preoccupation with the potential utility of education as an avenue to (re)invent the social location of Indigenous peoples in Canada and ultimately socially engineer them out of existence. In the contemporary moment, state logic to address the Indigenous crisis in education has reflected an array of interventions, mostly resulting in substantial amounts of public funds being spent on the development of "how-to" kits for teachers to draw upon when attempting to engage Indigenous students in school, more control for Indigenous communities over the education of their children and youth, and the resurrection and celebration of "Indigenous culture" within Canadian classrooms across the country.[23] A focus on the recruitment of Indigenous educators has also been part of this process, although with limited success, and Indigenous youth in Canada continue to fall behind their white counterparts in areas of high school completion and post-secondary training.

This continued legacy of educational adversity (Miller 1989; Haig-Brown 1993; Battiste 2000; Marker 2000; Ponting 1997)[24] has induced federal and provincial educational jurisdictions to move towards the creation of participatory alliances, as I mention in the introduction, between local state agencies and Indigenous groups as a way to work together to solve the "educational crisis"[25] facing Indigenous communities. Formulated under a federal and provincial discourse of "common vision," these state–Indigenous alliances are imagined as an avenue to recalibrate the relationship between the state and Indigenous peoples in the educational arena, particularly within the context of urban sites where many Indigenous students attend school.

In some respect, state–Indigenous alliances also reflect an imperialist preoccupation with social reform that is increasingly focused on the strengthening of individual capacities and democratic spaces of liberal inclusion. The focus on individual betterment marks a turn towards the social economy as a way to bridge the divide between the state and civil society. Such an approach of capacitating individuals can readily be seen in the action plans for change advanced by Indian and Northern Affairs Canada (INAC). For instance, one of INAC's plans suggests:

> Building relationships and forming partnerships is a key theme of the Roundtable process and INAC's education initiatives. Progress in First Nation education cannot be accomplished by one federal department working in isolation, nor can it be achieved by federal efforts alone. Launching effective responses to complex challenges and policy issues will require the ongoing concerted effort of the federal government working with First Nations, provinces, territories and other key parties to ensure that First Nations learners enjoy, at minimum, the same educational opportunities and outcomes as other Canadian students. (INAC 2005)

The two sets of discourses – the construction of education as an emancipatory and transformative tool and the portrayal of the educational failure of Indigenous students as a problem of the state – rely on the construction of "participation" as a key factor in promoting educational success and improving the social and material conditions for Indigenous peoples. To reiterate, although not entirely new, the emphasis on the power of education is tied to a history of conquest and colonization that serves as a fundamental backdrop for any discussions pertaining to urban Indigenous youth, in education or elsewhere. In the next two parts, I briefly trace state interventions in the lives of Indigenous peoples through the institution of education, both historically and in the present day. I maintain that in order to understand the current politics of participation and how it relates to social interventions in education and other institutions linked to education, such as the criminal justice system, it is necessary to map how this politics grows from and in reaction to the patterns of the past. Asserting a history of memory enables us, then, to recollect the place of education as one of the principal mechanisms through which the Canadian settler state attempted to violently shape Indigenous peoples into a particular type of state subject. This is an institution with a long and powerful history.

## Clash Zones: Education as Elimination

Prior to commencing a discussion of the deployment of educational institutions as an instrument of settler colonial logics geared towards elimination, I briefly turn to a discussion that marks some of the ways that Indigenous education prior to contact differed from western models of teaching and learning.[26] This is important for two reasons. First, it dispels the myth that education was a gift bestowed by settlers upon Indigenous communities – a sentiment that feeds into the representation of Indigenous peoples as primitive and underdeveloped. As Cardinal (1999, 9) attests, "Prior to the arrival of the Europeans, each First Nation had its own traditional forms of education." This is not meant to suggest that there was one set of purposes and goals of education for all Indigenous communities, and that there was not marked diversity within them. What I am underscoring here are the different ways Indigenous education was organized before the advent of settler colonization – and it is crucial to acknowledge that these forms of Indigenous learning and intelligence have continued as an ongoing resistance to linear thinking, despite settler attempts to extinguish them (Simpson 2014b). And second, a rendering of Indigenous approaches to education prompts recognition of the direct conflict between the sociocultural composition of Indigenous epistemology – knowledge systems, as Simpson (2014b) says, that were designed to promote and generate life – and contemporary instantiations of settler belief systems that came alongside the process of colonization and industrialization – designed to promote capitalism and individualism (Partridge 2010). Indigenous scholar Michael Marker (2000) describes the "clash zone" that characterizes educational debates and unveils the colonial underpinnings and political dimensions of educational initiatives advanced by the state.

He argues that "it is a complex landscape of colliding interpretations and fundamental goals and purposes across cultural barricades. In short, Indian education is about Indian–White relations. It has been, and remains, the central arena for negotiating identities and for translating the goals and purposes of the cultural 'Other'" (Marker 2000, 31).

Central to the Indigenous way of life, education served as a way to enhance spirituality, reinforce holistic ways of living, and emphasize notions of collectivity and community (Hampton 1995, 10). Character-ized most widely by storytelling, ceremonies, teaching stories, learning games, and teaching through example, the community became the edu-cational classroom through which the skills and lessons of living in a viable culture with the sense of a total being were imparted to children and youth (Kirkness 1999, 15). As Cardinal (1999, 10) puts it, "teaching occurred within Aboriginal cultural settings, which provided meaning and direction for young people to become positive, participating, and contributing members of society." Scholars of Indigenous education Kawagley and Barnhardt (1999, 118) have outlined how this pedagogy was sustained through a particular Indigenous knowledge system dependent on the notion of everyday survival and intimately informed by concepts of place, systems of governance with respect to nations, and ancestral knowledge of the land. It was only after contact with European colonizers, they argue, that this philosophical, epistemologi-cal, and culturally oriented approach to education began to shift; that it became positioned more as an extension of the imperial project, and consequently, of the control, assimilation, and regulation of political subjectivity and civic identity that sanctioned white settler dominion over social institutions and, in turn, over territory.

Given this rendition of history, any contemporary focus on educa-tional initiatives as a form of social intervention to improve the lives of Indigenous children and youth must first and foremost be understood as attached to an institution instrumental in domination since the begin-ning of the colonization of the Americas. For Mi'kmaw scholar Marie Battiste (2000, 193), "no force has been more effective at oppressing First Nations cultures than the education system." Intent on eradicating all things Indigenous, education was used as a tool to break perceived patterns of difference of the "other" that were viewed as oppositional to the consolidation of Canada as a sovereign, settler nation state.[27] There have been numerous and varied attempts by the Canadian settler state to violently regiment and discipline the lives of Indigenous peoples. These tactics actively instigated the cultural genocide required as part of a Eurocentric nation building project. In this regard, Battiste (1995) observes, "Various boarding schools, industrial schools, day schools, and Eurocentric educational practices ignored or rejected the world-views, languages, and value of Aboriginal parents in the education of their children. The outcome was the gradual loss of these world-views, languages, and cultures and the creation of widespread social and psychological upheaval in Aboriginal communities" (8).

Two significant strategies of colonial governance deserve mentioning within the settler–Indigenous history of education: missionary day schools and residential schools.[28] These technologies of colonial rule, particularly the residential schools that grew out of missionary day schools, hold special significance within the landscape of Indigenous–state relations because of the intergenerational passing on of trauma initiated by their inception and implementation in Indigenous communities across Turtle Island – an insidious and violent solution to the "Indian problem" in Canada's runaway expansion efforts. As Métis scholar Jeremy Patzer (2014, 168) argues, residential schools were particularly remarkable in that they represented a rationally planned form of social engineering that envisaged the elimination of Indigenous difference itself. Moreover, the dispossession of land and subjugation was necessary for something so acutely interventionist as residential schooling to take place (Patzer 2014, 176).

From the 1600s onwards, day schools, established by European missionaries to break the Indigenous spirit and ways of living, aimed to move First Nations peoples closer to a "civilized and western" way of life and were a major force that acted to destroy the identity and culture of Turtle Island (Jordon 1988, 190). Indigenous children and youth were subjected to religious indoctrination that encouraged them to "abandon their wandering life and to build homes, cultivate fields and practice the elementary crafts of civilized life" (Haig-Brown 1993, 33). Although, possibly, the missionaries may have held out some notion of literacy, conceived in the traditional sense of western ways of knowing, reading, and writing skills that were considered to demarcate the classification "literate," one must ask whether they were more interested in "saving souls" and destroying the "heathen practices" of the Indigenous peoples' traditions than in imparting western knowledge. The premise of missionary schools was, after all, undergirded by an assumption of cultural, moral, and religious superiority and directly linked to an unquestioned notion of evolutionary progress (Cardinal 1999, 13).

Abandoning the concept of day schools and linking hands with the newly forming Canadian state, churches developed a church–state partnership that further consolidated and buttressed the institutionally based cultural genocide of Aboriginal peoples through education (Milloy 1999, 13). Based on the premise that they could only be assimilated if they were removed from the influence of their families and communities, which were inculcating opposing epistemologies and worldviews, Indigenous children and youth were forcibly separated from their parents and their greater communities. Li (2005, 391) starkly refers to the simultaneous process of "undoing" Indigenous culture in order to facilitate the "remaking" of a Canadian citizen subject when he states that "the practice of tearing Native children from their families and sending them to residential schools was deliberately designed to 'undo' them and then remake them, minus the presumed pathologies of their 'Nativeness.'" The essential social structures of family and community, then, were assumed to imbibe "backward" language, values, and cultural practices, as well as give social identity and meaning to Indigenous nations (Hare and Barman 2000, 332). Residential schools were constructed as the means through which the isolation and subsequent "re-education" of the Indigenous child could be carried out. In her historical work on the intersection of colonization and education in Canada, Cree scholar Verna Kirkness (1999, 15) refers to the grave words of one government inspector from the Indian Affairs Branch, whom she quotes stating, "Little can be done with him (the Indian child). He can be taught to do a little farming, and stock raising, and to dress in a more civilized manner, but that is all. The child who goes to a day school learns little while his tastes are fashioned at home, and his inherited aversion to toil is in no way combated." This pattern of domination and reconstruction, the desire to break down before you build up, became further entrenched through the Indian Acts of 1876 and 1880 and the Indian Advancement Act of 1884 (Milloy 1999; also Haig-Brown 1993). This legislation made the power of the settler state all-encompassing by providing a legal mandate to create whatever infrastructure was necessary to clear the path for aggressive assimilation and the eventual disappearance of Indigenous epistemologies and of ways of life that were seen as antithetical to the advancement of Canada as a stable geopolitical sovereign entity.

The establishment of residential schools, then, hastened the destruction of Indigenous communities and, more importantly, served to disconnect Indigenous children and youth from intermediaries that could disrupt this state-sanctioned violence; namely, their kinship networks.[29] Formal education via residential schools replaced traditional education and undermined, or attempted to eliminate altogether, any influence of the family and community in shaping the sensibility and identity of Indigenous children and youth (Hare and Barman 2000, 332). The treatment of students within these schools was greatly oppressive and violent, and had devastating and long-lasting impacts on Indigenous peoples and communities.[30]

Forbidden to speak their language and receiving harsh punishments if they did so, Indigenous children and youth, who ranged in age from three to eighteen, were taken from their families and separated from their siblings while at school.[31] They were forced to embrace a Christian way of life that involved learning the domestic skills of cleaning and keeping house, mostly for the girls, as well as cleaning stables and working in the fields, primarily for the boys (Kirkness 1999, 15). In this regard, the residential schools did not even equip Indigenous students with the requisite tools and skills to participate in Canadian society as they claimed to be intending to do, but rather solidified Indigenous children and youth's status as second class citizens (Sangster 2002). The "remaking" they received through residential schooling ensured their social and economic exclusion from the dominant Canadian society and also served as a severe impediment to returning to traditional ways of life (Hare and Barman 2000, 333).

Many children suffered sexual and physical abuse while attending residential schools and a number of these oppressive facilities even had formal graveyards on the grounds. In a report by the Truth and Reconciliation Commission of Canada (2012, 17) it was revealed that some graveyards were unmarked but contained the bodies of Indigenous children who had attended residential school. At least 4,100 Indigenous children died in 130 residential schools across the country.[32] Detailing government-sponsored biomedical and nutritional experiments on malnourished Indigenous children within residential schools, Ian Mosby's (2013) postdoctoral research has added another horrific dimension to this acutely social interventionist settler colonial project.

The legacy of missionary and residential schooling and its impact on the current "crisis" facing Indigenous children youth, and Indigenous communities more generally, is not one that can be underestimated.[33] In fact, it is vital for scholars, educators, policy makers, and advocates researching and creating social interventions for Indigenous children and youth to recognize that Indigenous peoples in Canada, and in other settler nation states, have never reached a postcolonial state (Tuhiwai Smith 1999, 8).[34] Indigenous children and youth continue to wrestle with the ongoing impact of these experiences through direct engagement with their parents and grandparents, aunties and uncles, who are survivors of residential school trauma, and through the devastation that mediates the experience of Indigenous reserve and urban communities throughout Indigenous North America. This sentiment is captured succinctly by Patzer (2014, 182) who argues that "one of the ultimate lessons to be drawn from the history of residential schooling is that Aboriginal demands surrounding the restoration of land and self-determination are not just lofty, begrudging demands of principle." Patzer (2014, 182) insists, rather, that the demand for stolen land and Indigenous sovereignty itself are intertwined with this history "precisely because being subjected to genocidal institutional arrangements such as Indian residential school represents, par excellence, the disempowerment, dispossession, and loss of self-determination of people."

In order to further an understanding of how settler colonial power continues to articulate itself, I now shift my focus to present-day educational realities that mirror a colonial governing of Indigenous alterity and reinscribe the presumed political homogeneity of the state.

*Past Meets Present: Settler Colonial Markings in Contemporary Educational Experience*

In an article entitled "Land as Pedagogy: Nishnaabeg Intelligence and Rebellious Transformation," Leanne Simpson (2014, 6) recounts her experience as an Indigenous person in the Canadian system of public education:

[E]ducation, from kindergarten to graduate school, was one of coping with someone else's agenda, curriculum, and pedagogy, someone who was neither interested in my well-being as a Kwezens, nor interested in my connection to my homeland, my language or history, nor my Nishnaabeg intelligence. No one ever asked me what I was interested in nor did they ask for my consent to participate in their system. My experience of education was one of continually being measured against a set of principles that required surrender to an assimilative colonial agenda in order to fulfill those principles. I distinctly remember being in grade 3, at a class trip to the sugar bush, and the teacher showing us two methods of making maple syrup – the pioneer method which involved a black pot over an open fire and clean sap, and the "Indian method" – which involved a hollowed out log in an unlit fire, with large rocks in the log to heat the sap up – sap which had bark, insects, dirt and scum over it. The teacher asked us which method we would use – being the only native kid in the class, I was the only one that chose the "Indian method."

Simpson's recollection is an essential reminder that learning in formal institutions of education is a profoundly political enterprise. Education, even in democratic nation states, is one of the most critical sites for imagining national futures and creating ideal citizens (Hall 2002, 87). This continues to hold particular significance for Indigenous youth across Turtle Island, who are consistently bombarded with teaching and learning experiences that inflict dehumanizing processes of self- and collective negation and profound alienation.[35]

While undertaking fieldwork and advocacy in Saskatoon, I had numerous opportunities to witness settler colonial assaults on Indigenous students. Perhaps one of the clearest examples of these ongoing attacks came during a presentation given by Indigenous students to a city-wide working group, Keeping Kids in School, tasked with understanding the reasons behind the high dropout rates in the city. The committee was comprised of representatives from a number of youth organizations, a city councillor developing a gang strategy, a retired teacher, and government representatives from across education, child welfare, and corrections and public safety. While the group was not officially mandated to tackle Indigenous youth drop out specifically, they inevitably came up against this issue because the majority of youth dropping out of schools in Saskatoon were also Indigenous. The working group held monthly meetings and on one such occasion, in early 2006, after some debate at a previous meeting about why it was important to hear from Indigenous students because of the disproportionate dropout rates, two Indigenous girls stepped into a small boardroom in a downtown office building to share their experiences of public schooling in Saskatoon. Seated around a rectangular table, we waited for the girls to get comfortable. After short introductions, the chair of the meeting, a bubbly woman in her fifties who had been doing youth advocacy in Saskatoon for twenty years, asked them to share their stories.

The room was cloaked in nervous energy. The two students were looking at each other, trying to decide which one would break the silence and begin speaking first. I was surprised that the two of them had agreed to do this at all, given how intimidating it would be to sit in front of an almost all white working group committee and narrate experiences about the problems in the education system. Once they got started, however, they were surprisingly forthcoming with their concerns. They spoke of how they felt physically unsafe in some of the "Eastside white schools" because of rampant racism, how white students feared Aboriginal kids because "they [white students] think all of us are in gangs," and how they felt as though white school personnel, because of the stereotypes attached to Indigenous peoples, were judging them. Shifting her eyes back and forth between the committee and other young woman, one of the girls spoke: "They [school personnel] sit there and are prejudging us without even knowing what we are gonna be. How can you sit there and judge? Like judge an Aboriginal girl for instance, and say that in five years from now you are either going to overdose or you are going to be a prostitute. They are setting our goals for us already." After the girls had left the meeting room, the chair of the committee turned to the group and bluntly said, "We need to do a better a job of involving our Aboriginal partners in these meetings."

Hand in hand with the experiences of alienation voiced by these students at the meeting outlined above, Indigenous youth have commented on their estrangement from mainstream schooling by drawing attention to racist depictions in the formal curriculum[36] or their complete erasure altogether as Indigenous people and to the chasm that exists between Indigenous and Euro-American thought (Hampton 1995; Kawagley and Barnhardt 1999; St. Denis 2011).[37] This point is consistent with prior research I have conducted with Indigenous young women living in poverty about their experiences in school. In this study, for example, one young Indigenous woman commented that she would feel "dirty" when she went to school, to a point where she stopped attending altogether. She explained, "I wouldn't like anyone to take their kids to go there ... an awful school, they are so racist ... I felt dirty, basically I felt like people can just walk all over you ... so I stopped school for a year ... I didn't want to go back to school" (Dhillon 2011, 125).

Systemic racism and whiteness, then, infiltrate the cement and steel of the school building as well as the social and cultural dimensions of the educative encounter, giving enormous privilege to those whose histories, ethnic backgrounds, social class, family assumptions, and personal knowledges are in line with dominant social practices (Said 1993; Schick and St. Denis 2005). Leading scholars of Indigenous education

Verna St. Denis and Eber Hampton speak to this point in a recent report on the state of education for Indigenous students. They remark:

> Racism was present and active at all levels of public and post-secondary education, including the Aboriginal teaching workforce. The racism experienced on an everyday basis took multiple forms, including verbal and psychological abuse, low expectations of teachers and administrators, marginalization and isolation within the school community, a denial of professional support and attention, the unfair and discriminatory practices of rules and procedures, and the denial of Aboriginal experience, human rights, and history. The several ways in which racism is denied is in itself constituted racist practice because the issue could not then be considered for its contribution(s) to a lack of academic success. (quoted in Hesch 2010, 258)

In the concrete reality of student life, this arrangement results in students' distancing themselves from school altogether and in isolation and vulnerability in the classroom, which directly links with the limiting of future educational and career opportunities and the continued disintegration of Indigenous cultural identity and political mobilization.[38] When institutional pedagogies and curriculums centre on canonical norms to which Indigenous students must conform, either through their mastery of the norm or through their failure to master the norm, these pedagogies necessarily reinforce hegemonic subjectivities and the exclusion of those forms of subjectivity that resist dominant modes of social existence (McGee 1993, 284).

Thus, there is wide acknowledgment that Indigenous peoples are underrepresented across educational institutions, including schools, colleges and universities, and that the education system continues to operate as a colonial enterprise that fails Indigenous students (Dei 1996, 303). Indigenous youth across Canada have a dropout rate that is three times the national average. In Saskatchewan in 2013, 33 per cent of Indigenous peoples between the ages of 25–64 had not completed high school (Parkouda 2013, 8).

For the most part, social science research undertaken to examine Indigenous education in Canada is indexed by a failure of the public education system to address "the needs" of Indigenous students and by the creation of "quick fix" prescriptions for reform rather than in-depth investigations of the social and political context in which reform efforts have taken place (Schissel and Wotherspoon 1998, Hare and

Barman 2000, Hampton 1995). As Morrow and Torres (1999) point out, "Histories of education typically present the celebratory history of policy making as a progressive process based on 'reforms' culminating in the present" (92). Reform-based efforts, then, can often conceal the tensions, contradictions, and conflicts that inform the impetus for change in the first place and downplay the scope and power of hegemonic state interests in education development. Benton and Craib (2001, 48) highlight this point well when they comment, "Any particular policy intervention is likely to be modified in its effects by complex interactions between social processes, and unless there is some means of taking these into account, reform strategies are liable to generate unintended and possibly unwanted consequences." Pushing us one step further, Battiste (2000, 194) draws our attention to the implications of this legacy when she asserts that:

> After nearly a century of public schooling for tribal peoples in Canada, the most serious problem with the current system of education lies not in its failure to liberate the human potential among Aboriginal peoples but in its quest to limit thought to cognitive imperialistic policies and practices. This quest denies Aboriginal people access to and participation in the formulation of government policy, constrains the use and development of Aboriginal cultures in schools, and confines education to a narrow and scientific view of the world that threatens the global future.

Battiste highlights, then, the value of locating current social reform directed at Indigenous youth against the historical and contemporary backdrop of Indigenous youth educational experience.

Contemporary exploration of Indigenous youth experiences of education must also question the growing linkages between educational disconnection and criminalization and incarceration. In scholarly and advocacy circles, the linkage is known as the "school-to-prison-nexus" and has been defined by Sandler (2010, 4) as "systemic setbacks that gradually shepherd students away from positive school connections and academic success into increasing criminal activity." Critics of the school-to-prison-nexus have begun mapping the "punitive threads" (Simmons 2005, 265) between a disciplinary culture within schools and well-cited statistics characterizing the over-representation of racialized youth in prison (Noguera 2003). In the United States, the phenomenon has been well documented, particularly through the lens of inner-city, racialized youth and their experiences of public education and criminalization across major urban centres throughout America (Salt-man and Gabbard 2003). Yet, it has received much less attention north of the 49th parallel. In Canada, while statistics reciting the low levels of educational attainment of "inmates" litter government reports, there is very little critical research that goes beyond a facile depiction of the intersectional dynamics of these two institutions in the lives of urban Indigenous youth.

New research in this area has begun to outline the contours of these under-examined links between the educational experiences of Indig-enous youth and their high rates in youth custody. Amanda Gebhard (2012, 3) traces the heightened surveillance of Indigenous students in the public education system. She reveals the way Indigenous youth become positioned as incompetent, even dangerous and unwanted, stu-dents and how this approach contributes to their conflicts with school officials and peers and to the prevalence of truancy that, in turn, results in an increase in policing efforts within schools. Instead of resolving conflicts within the confines of the school walls, however problematic they may be, school administrators and educators, she argues, are now calling upon law enforcement agents to deal with youth who have been categorized as troubled or deviant for not abiding by standards of nor-mative behaviour within schools – or for what might be conceived of as pushback against school-based settler colonial alienation. Context-blind zero tolerance policies[39] have further exacerbated this problem, criminalizing youth for relatively minor schoolyard altercations.

The persistence of the hidden curriculum and the sustained privi-leges associated with whiteness (Roman 1993), in conjunction with a lack of diversity in a predominantly white teaching force with little to no critical understanding of the history of abuse and subjugation of Indigenous peoples by white Europeans,[40] has enabled a saviour-like mentality towards Indigenous children and youth to carry on unabated. According to Amanda Gebhard (2012, 6), "in a school setting, the con-struction of the Aboriginal child as in need or at risk is also dependent on the construction of the White settler as benevolent saviour." Stated differently, the heroic tales of successful occupation by white settlers (Schick 2002) fuel an ongoing disconnection between white educators and the Indigenous students who land in their classrooms as well as reinforcing the old settler colonial trope that Indigenous peoples are dis-appearing. "Through it," writes Sherene Razack (2015, 5), "settlers are able to feel Indigenous disappearance and to imagine their own superi-ority." This once again reproduces settler colonial power dynamics that have been endemic since the inception of educational institutions in Canada, as I outlined earlier in this chapter, including the ability to call upon the criminal justice system to respond to the "deviant" behaviour of Indigenous students who may be resisting their dehumanization through overt expressions of "anger" or by dropping out altogether. In this regard, schools have become sites for the increased policing of Indigenous students and thus intensified interaction with the criminal justice system, an institution to which I now turn my attention.

## Criminalization, Caging, and Toxic Care

One morning in 2007, I was meeting the director of a youth agency in Saskatoon to discuss the possibility of designing a program for young women and girls living in poverty. I arrived in the core neighbour-hood and was waiting at the entrance of the organization. Not long after I arrived, an Indigenous young man came in, opening the front door with such force that it rebounded from the wall and slammed shut behind him. His forehead was crinkled, his eyes narrowed. He was visibly upset. He had a small black bag slung over one of his arms and was dressed in jeans, a simple white t-shirt, and high-tops. Mid-night black hair and coffee-coloured skin. There were no other visual marks on his body. By this time, the director, Thomas, a white man in his early thirties, had arrived at the front of the building and asked the young man what was wrong. Speaking loudly, and pointing his finger in the direction of the doorway, as if motioning to the street beyond, the Indigenous young man responded, "It's the fuckin' cops. They keep stoppin' me for no reason. They're just waiting around to fuck with us Native kids. I didn't do nothing wrong! I was just walkin' down the street and they fuckin' stopped me. Asking me what I am doin' and shit. Lookin' through all my stuff. Chasin' me around. For no reason." Thomas shook his head, dismissively mumbled "I'm sorry," and told the young man to "calm down" and join his class. As the young man moved to walk towards the back of the building, presumably to his class, I asked Thomas if there was something we should be doing to address his experience. He plainly told me that this was just the way the system worked and that his job was to help these kids get school credits. Nothing more. Nothing less.

I had a similar experience in a different youth organization in Saska-toon, this one run by the Indigenous Peoples Collective. I was sched-uled to meet up with a couple of youth workers when I came across a young Indigenous woman named Sherry. I had seen Sherry a few times before, but on this day, she looked visibly different. There was a blackish bruise on her face, although her long brown hair concealed a part of it, and her arm was in a sling. She was dressed in jeans and a summer tank top; some kind of mobile device was clutched in her hand. She wasn't speaking. Sherry's caseworker, Pauline, was sitting behind her desk sipping coffee and typing on her keyboard.

When I saw Sherry, I immediately, of course, asked what happened. Pauline responded in a matter of fact tone, "Oh, it's the cops. They are harassing her again. It happens all the time once you get involved with corrections and public safety." I learned that Sherry had been out walking in the Westside, later in the afternoon the previous day, when she was stopped by two male police officers and accused of breaching her probation orders. According to Pauline, Sherry had tried to explain that she was not in breach of her probation orders but the cops didn't believe her and started accusing her of lying. The situation "escalated," that is how Pauline described it, and Sherry eventually contacted Pauline from St. Paul's Hospital, where she ended up to get her arm and face examined after the altercation with the police. "They let her go, but they roughed her up before they did," Pauline told me. When I asked Pauline what she was going to do to take this matter up, she told me that the only recourse she had was to go to the police station and file a formal complaint. But that, she said, would be very time consuming and often didn't result in anything being done. During this conversation Sherry simply sat still. Dead silent.

For both Pauline and Thomas, the experiences of these youth had become entirely normalized to the point that they did not warrant additional time or attention. Even when I pressed the issue further, asserting that this was happening to other Indigenous youth too, neither of them seemed to think that the incident was especially problematic. They offered no explanation beyond acknowledging that this was "the way things were," nor did they consider the possibility that their own actions of turning a blind eye to these youth's experiences might, in some way, be contributing to a lack of police accountability and, in turn, to the relentless and overly vigilant policing of Indigenous youth in the Westside. At best, the underlying message communicated to these youth was: exercise fortitude when challenged by the onslaught of racist police provocation and coercive force. Suppress your feelings of anger and vulnerability. Keep your head down. Stay out of trouble.

   The violation of personal liberty and insidious debasement of human dignity recounted by these Indigenous youth, in addition to their experiences of racism and public humiliation, was not news to me. Having done research and advocacy in Saskatoon for years, I found this story, while stunning in its level of injustice, also stunningly prosaic in its repeated occurrence as an act of settler colonial surveillance. On numerous occasions, I have been met with the following scene: a Saskatoon City Police cruiser pulled over on the side of 20th Street (or on more isolated roads, in back alleys, next to forsaken train tracks) with an Indigenous youth standing in the shadow of circulating red and blue lights, arms raised above the head or clasped behind the back. Personal belongings, sometimes broken, have been strewn about the unforgiving ground. One or two police officers are usually engaged in some form of rough "questioning"; voices are often raised. The interminable power of the criminal justice system is well evidenced by the material presence of guns, slash resistant gloves, bulletproof vests, handcuffs, batons, and split second radio backup. Sometimes there are dogs. The potential use of deadly force by these public safety sentries, in instances of perceived threat, imagined or otherwise, looms large. They have the authority to trigger the deployment of lethal violence to maintain the safety and protection of a (white) Canadian citizenry, to shut down by any means necessary those whose very presence threatens the social, political, and economic structures that have birthed white power and privilege.[41] They are the city's front line drones of white settler defence. And in moments like these, time becomes dilated. Anything can happen.

   Numerous youth workers have corroborated the high incidence of racial profiling and surveillance by city police that has been revealed, anecdotally, by Indigenous youth in Saskatoon. When I interviewed a youth worker involved in counselling Indigenous youth, a program I return to in greater detail in chapter 6, he told me it was commonplace for Indigenous youth to recount instances of being stopped by the police to the point of feeling deeply harassed because of the style of their clothing and the colour of their skin. He revealed, "If you live in the core, it's almost a certainty. They [Indigenous youth] always seem to be conscious of the presence of police. It doesn't matter where we go in the city, they are always looking out for them."

   The reference this youth worker made to the geographical specificity of heightened police surveillance also signals the way that the "core neighbourhood" in Saskatoon has become coded as "Indigenous space." Idylwyld Drive is the borderline that cuts the city longitudinally, bisecting Saskatoon into the east, associated with prosperity and wealth, and the west (also known as Alphabet City because the Westside avenues have no names, just letters), associated with poverty, crime, and suffering – ghetto territory. "This spatialized relationship," remarks Joyce Green (2011, 238), "maintains the focus on the Indigenous as needing to be controlled, for racism suggests they are ultimately not fit for civilized society." The targeting of Indigenous youth by police, then, is interlinked with a criminalization of the neighbourhoods where Indigenous families live and a deliberate categorization of these communities as simultaneously "native and degenerate" (Razack 2002, 126). Whiteness is able to move freely into these "projected crime zones" as a matter of exercising power over "Indigenous deviance" and ensuring the quarantining of Indigenous bodies.[42] On the containment of white city space, Razack (2015, 24) remarks that "to mark and maintain their own emplacement on stolen land, settlers must repeatedly enact the most enduring colonial truth: the land belongs to the settler, and Indigenous people who are in the city are not of the city. Marked as surplus and subjected to repeated evictions, Indigenous people are considered by settler society as the waste or excess that must be expelled." In Saskatoon, the processes of gentrification, the spatial politics of safety, and the ongoing displacement of Indigenous peoples on Cree territory within the city, have further fuelled white invasion into Indigenous urban space.[43] Indigenous peoples, thus, experience policing itself as a colonial force, an apparatus of capture *imposed externally* by a government they have not authorized and do not have effective participation in – one of the indicators of militarized surveillance and discipline (Nichols 2014, 446).

Bringing the propensity of this ongoing domination into razor sharp focus, a Métis youth worker and activist disclosed the following during one of our conversations in 2007 about the magnitude and range of social issues facing urban Indigenous youth. His account of how the criminal justice system works as a mechanism of settler state control and of the way Indigenous youth are particularly vulnerable to this system, warrants being quoted at length:

> When it comes to the city police and the Aboriginal youth I have worked with for close to fifteen years, or even longer, … well, I have seen the abuse from city police. I've seen the ego, the attitudes, the complete injustice. I understand why young Indigenous people don't trust the police. I am 46 years old and I still don't trust police. I see a cop car go by and … and I get

worried and I get scared and I get angry. I also remember the experiences of my sisters who used to work on the streets and them being picked up by cops and having to give oral sex so they wouldn't be arrested. Cops have even come into my own house and ransacked the place, picked up friends of mine and either beat them up or dropped them off outside of the city. A story that I always remember was when I was the Executive Director of Ground Up, we were taking Indigenous youth to a restaurant nearby to celebrate an end of term and all of these kids getting school credits. We were happy, we were joyful, and we were enjoying our day. We had just ordered our food from the server and it was a full house at this restaurant. There were a lot of people there. And all of a sudden two policemen burst into the restaurant and without any hesitation they came over to us and looked at our table and said to a few of the youth, "Where were you an hour ago?" And they said it loudly so they could show off and beat their chests. And, I stood up and said, "What do you want? They have been with us." And I argued with them and he [one of the cops] asked who I was and I told him who I was and he asked where these kids were and I said they have been with me. But as soon as they left … anyway, the excitement was gone. The kids started talking about how the cops were pigs and disgusting and assholes and that was the end of the celebration. The cops embarrassed the heck out of these amazing kids and pissed everybody off. And it made me realize that this is what is wrong with the city police. You give somebody a gun and you give somebody a badge and it's their right to treat people like shit. To treat people like crap and it's alright to choke somebody to death. It's alright to beat someone with a baton. It's alright to taser somebody. It's all right to take some Aboriginal girl into a back alley and get a blowjob from her because what is she going to do? Because with most of these kids it's always us against them, it's us against the system. The judges don't care. The cops don't care. The majority of the justice system in this province, in this city, is broken. I would love to see what would happen if a fourteen-year-old Aboriginal girl told a white judge that it was me against the white cop. The cop is always going to win.

The persistent sensation of being hunted, of monitored movement, of freedom being truncated through institutional caging is central to the daily reality of being an Indigenous youth in Saskatoon. It is not an anomaly. It is not the fictitious creation of a youthful imagination on overdrive. Through their existence as Indigenous youth, these young people constitute a direct threat to an already existing settler social order. A large part of the way this threat becomes contained is through state mechanisms of criminalization, policing, and incarceration that function as both regulators and producers of socially constructed notions of normativity and deviance against which Indigenous youth sociality can be measured. Scholar Judith Butler (2015, 7) argues, within the context of black conquest in the United States, that "one way that this [white dominance] happens is by establishing whiteness as the norm for the human, and blackness as a deviation from the human or even as a threat to the human, or as something not quite human." Similarly, young Indigenous lives have been constituted by the Canadian state as the "throwaways," the lives that are expendable in the quest to maintain settler control, the subaltern lives that represent everything Canada does not want to become. Racism's ratification as a way of seeing, as a mode of "dominant public perception" (Butler 2015, 3) that is both recurrent and customary, everyday and systemic, gendered and sexualized (Jiwani 2006), fuels the construction of these binaries of the value of human life and, in turn, standardizes heinous state techniques of subjugation. Settler colonies are heavily reliant on the reproduction of this age-old controlling technology because of their need to consistently extinguish Indigenous alterity – to stand firm in the march towards the endpoint of successful "elimination."

Hence, it comes as no surprise to anyone working with Indigenous youth that incidents of "conflict" with law enforcement agents are common markers of lived experience. In urban centres where Indigenous youth come into more direct and frequent contact with state institutions, clashes with the criminal justice system take on heightened levels. According to a report presented to the Commission on First Nations and Métis Peoples and Justice Reform:

> For Saskatchewan Aboriginal youth, conflict with the justice system was primarily urban. Similar to the Canadian data, most Aboriginal youth in Saskatchewan committed their offence or alleged offence in a city, and most planned on relocating to a city upon release. Many of the Aboriginal youth experienced conflict with the justice system in the city even though they lived on reserve. (Findlay and Weir 2004, 104)

Incarceration rates mirror the intensity of settler colonial confrontation between Indigenous youth and the criminal justice system, although it is important to reinforce that incarceration is part of a continuum of violence in the criminal justice system as whole that begins with initial police "contact," followed by arrest, detainment, court proceedings, sentencing, jail time, and eventually, probation orders.[44] In 2004, the Canadian Department of Justice conducted a snapshot study of Indigenous youth in custody (both open and secure). The report confirmed the disproportionate representation of Indigenous youth in prison, although scholars and youth advocates have been reporting this phenomenon for some time (Dean 2005; Justice for Girls 2015; Corrado et al. 2011). While they comprise only 5 per cent of the population, Indigenous youth make up 33 per cent of young people in custody. The highest rates of incarceration are in northern and central Canada, and Saskatchewan is among the most punitive provinces, second only to the Northwest Territories. In Saskatchewan, an astounding 88 per cent of youth in custody are Indigenous,[45] and *young Indigenous men are more likely to go to prison than to finish high school* (Therein 2011). The captivity of Indigenous young women and girls is equally distressing. Neve and Pate (2005, 27) argue, in fact, that the prairie provinces have witnessed some of the most egregious examples of criminalization of Indigenous women and girls. They note, "Aboriginal women continue to suffer the devastating impact of colonization. From residential school and child welfare seizure, to juvenile and adult detention, Aboriginal women and girls are vastly over-represented in institutions under state control ... in the Prairie Region most of the women and girls in prison are Aboriginal." The concluding remarks emerging from Canada's 2011 periodic review, with regards to the country's adherence to the United Nations Convention on the Rights of the Child, also noted the "criminal justice crisis" signalled by the over-representation of Indigenous youth in Canadian jails.

As explained above, statistics confirm that Indigenous youth are over-represented in detention facilities across Canada. Yet, the severity and scope of their entanglement with the criminal justice system warrants a degree of analytic clarity, particularly within the context of a book deconstructing the ways the state conceives and implements interventions aimed at assisting them. Robert Nichols (2014, 444) captures this succinctly when he says, "When the critique of incarceration rests upon over-representation of racialized bodies within penal institutions, this tactically renders carcerality as a dehistoricized tool of state power – even if distorted by the pathological effects of a racist society – displacing an account of the continuity and linkages between carcerality, state formation, and territorialized sovereignty." The persistent recitation of statistics demarcating the "crisis" of Indigenous youth in prisons, then, must be accompanied by an analysis that, once again, positions these numbers in the stark light of settler colonial rule – there is a backstory that produces this "crisis." As a point of departure for this analysis, three important arguments should be emphasized: the myth of justice, the invention of criminality, and intersections with toxic child welfare care. These arguments serve as a critical framework for considering the salience of the criminal justice system in the lives of Indigenous youth and for clearly articulating how their experiences are fundamentally tied to the larger political and historical milieu in which this institution operates, despite the denial of this context by everyday law enforcement officers.

## *The Myth of Justice*

To understand the ways that the criminal justice system plays an active role in the social containment of Indigenous children and youth requires revisiting the colonial foundation upon which this institution rests, a story that is almost always erased from public discourse on this issue. In the evocative words of the late legal scholar Patricia Monture-Angus (1995), who refers to the long history of the battle between the Canadian legal system and Indigenous peoples, "It is difficult for me to believe that the kind of change we need now can be planted within a system based on the ideology of conflict. I no longer believe law is the solution; it is the heart of the problem" (87). Canadian law (and the criminal justice system as a whole) is not based on principles of fairness and equality, despite the hubristic myths that describe it as a system whose primary mandate is to uphold justice for all. The totality of the institution, thus, must first be regarded in terms of its strategic instrumentality in the colonization of Turtle Island. Addressing this point from the perspective of an Indigenous woman growing up on the Flathead Indian Reservation, home of the Salish and Kootenai, sociologist Luana Ross (1998, 16) powerfully attests, in her book *Inventing the Savage*, "The values that ordered Native worlds were naturally in conflict with Euro-American legal codes. Many traditional tribal codes instantly became criminal when the United States imposed their law and culture on Native people. New laws were created that defined many usual, everyday behaviors of Natives as 'offenses.' The continuous clashing of worlds over the power to control Native land and resources constantly brought Native people in conflict with the legal and judicial system of the United States, which demonstrates the political intent and utility of Euro-American laws." As in the case of other patriotic myths masquerading as truth claims, particularly those of the settler colonial brand, these historical legacies are elided to "cover the tracks" of a criminal justice system that has directly functioned in the work of Indigenous dispossession and elimination.

Repositioned in this light, both the Royal Canadian Mounted Police (previously the North-West Mounted Police), as a system of regulation, patrol, and law enforcement for Indigenous peoples, and the Indian Act, as formal colonial legislation inflicted upon Indigenous communities to ensure the material theft of land, the destruction of social relationships, and the legal abolition of indigeneity through sexist blood quantum criteria (A. Simpson 2014), were constitutive entities designed to carry out genocidal extermination, suppression, and physical containment through the pass system (see also Dickason 2002). Their actions were directed by Ottawa's policy of coerced assimilation (Jacobs 2012; Balfour and Comack 2004). Mounties, as they are popularly known in Canada, were deployed on the Canadian frontier to facilitate Indigenous peoples' subjection to colonial law and to "ensure the negation of Indigenous sovereignty and to implement effective policies of containment and surveillance" (Nettelbeck and Smandych 2010, 357).[46] Mounties were well positioned for this job; Ottawa had invested in them the power to arrest, prosecute, judge, and sentence offenders (Graybill 2007), making any notion of the legal protection of Indigenous people under the British Crown a complete illusion. In 1920, when residential school became compulsory, the RCMP were the settler state's front line foot soldiers who guaranteed the attendance of Indigenous children.[47] Gendered racism and the underlying colonial ideologies of white superiority and "Indigenous savagery," as fabricated by a newly emerging Kanata to legitimate the theft of land and natural resources,[48] are therefore encoded in the operation of the Canadian criminal justice system; they are the cruel, unjust, and bloody historical roots of its inception as a social institution, and they are the roots that make possible the contemporary, ongoing reproduction of an abhorrent desecration of humanity in the lives of Indigenous youth.

In Saskatchewan, one of the most obvious examples of the unceasing fertility of these roots can be found in the story of Neil Stonechild, the seventeen-year-old Cree university student whose frozen body was discovered by two construction workers on 29 November 1990. The body was located in an industrial area in the northwest periphery of Saskatoon, marked with cuts and bruises, although the autopsy performed at St. Paul's Hospital ultimately confirmed that Stonechild had died of hypothermia (Saskatchewan, Ministry of Justice 2004). On the night of his "disappearance," the winter temperature had dropped to a frigid −28.1°C.[49]

The Saskatoon Police Service conducted an investigation into Stonechild's death and quickly ruled out the possibility of foul play. Stonechild's family challenged the expedient closure of his file. They vociferously argued that racism factored into his death, as did activists in the city who called the police force racist. Jason Roy, a peer and friend of Stonechild, who was with him on the last night he was seen alive, repeatedly reported that he saw his friend in the back of a police cruiser, bloodied and calling for help, alleging that Stonechild had been in police custody immediately preceding his disappearance (Green 2011). Despite Roy's and Stonechild's family's allegations of police misconduct, it took thirteen years before a public inquiry was established to look into the circumstances surrounding the death of Neil Stonechild.[50]

Headed by Mr. Justice David Wright, the 2004 report of the Commission of Inquiry into Matters Relating to the Death of Neil Stonechild criticized the initial police investigation into Stonechild's death, carried out by Keith Jarvis.[51] The report called the police investigation a "superficial and totally inadequate investigation of the death" (Saskatchewan, Ministry of Justice 2004, 200) that disregarded important information and obfuscated the role of Constables Hartwig and Senger in Stonechild's gruesome demise. As a result of the inquiry, Wright confirmed that Stonechild had, indeed, been in police custody the last night he was seen alive, that evidence had been tampered with, that police officers had lied and withheld information, and that the Saskatoon Police Service as a whole, implicating a number of police chiefs, was negligent in their refusal to take seriously the testimonies of racist police misconduct voiced by Stonechild's family members and friends and investigations carried out by various media outlets. Wright's chilling final remarks are a clear reflection of the heavily strained social relations between Indigenous and non-Indigenous residents in Saskatoon: "As I reviewed the evidence in this Inquiry, I was reminded, again and again, of the chasm that separates Aboriginal and non-Aboriginal people in this city and province. Our two communities do not know each other and do not seem to want to. The void is emphasized by the interaction of an essentially non-Aboriginal police force and the Aboriginal community. The justice system produces another set of difficulties" (Saskatchewan, Ministry of Justice 2004, 208). Yet, for all of the revelations offered in Wright's report, no criminal charges were ever laid against the police officers responsible for the murder of seventeen-year-old Neil Stonechild. Justice has never been granted.

## The Invention of Criminality

A more nuanced social discourse surrounding the disproportionate representation of Indigenous youth in Canadian prisons would be incomplete without an interrogation of the invention of criminality. Indeed, shedding light on how a criminal justice system that has been historically created to dismantle indigeneity also retains the power to determine the parameters of legality and illegality signals the highly subjective and political understandings inherent in the social construction of law itself. "Criminals," are, in fact, brought into existence by examining and/or classifying individual actions against legal norms that have been devised in accordance with a white settler social order (Ogden 2005). As explained by Heidi Stark (2016), "The imposition of colonial law, facilitated by casting Indigenous men and women as savage peoples in need of civilization and composing Indigenous lands as lawless spaces absent legal order, made it possible for the United States and Canada to shift and expand the boundaries of both settler law and the nation itself by judicially proclaiming their own criminal behaviors as lawful" (2). This sentiment is also underscored by Ross (1998, 5) in her mapping of neocolonial racism and the loss of Indigenous sovereignty, whereby state and federal governments were empowered to cast Indigenous peoples as "deviant" and "criminal" and restrict the power of Native nations, inventing colonial legislation that purposefully aided occupation. "Natives were regarded as 'savages,'" she writes, "legitimizing the removal of Natives from the westward path of civilization's progress. The ideology of Native inferiority was used to justify both genocide and attempts to supposedly assimilate Natives into the dominant society" (Ross 1998, 16).

The criminalization of Indigenous youth, and the invention of criminality[52] as a form of punitive social categorization tied to Indigenous dispossession, works in tandem with systems of policing to produce the extreme incarceration rates of Indigenous youth in Canada. The typical path to imprisonment for Indigenous youth involves initial charges for relatively minor offences (Czapska, Webb, and Taefi 2008) such as shoplifting, minor theft, minor school altercations, or public disturbances, and the system treats first offences by Indigenous youth more harshly than it treats similar offences for their white counterparts

(Winsa and Rankin 2013). Furthermore, many of the crimes committed can be characterized as poverty survival strategies (property offences, drug trafficking, sexual exploitation) that speak to the structural origins of behaviours branded as "criminal" and/or "deviant."[53] Through this categorization, the settler state effectively redirects responsibility for the structural conditions producing such survival strategies, which, coincidentally, fall outside the socially constructed realm of legality – back to Indigenous youth and the thorny question of "choice" (Totten 2009; Neve and Pate 2005). This criminalization also distracts attention from the retrenchment of social programming and the swathe of cuts to public funding for welfare, housing, and health services that have disproportionately impacted Indigenous communities in Canada. "Jails are our most comprehensive homeless initiative," conclude Neve and Pate (2005, 28) as they reveal a link between the rising number of women in prison and an evisceration of social programs across systems of healthcare, education, and social services.

Adding to this, Indigenous youth are also given extremely restrictive probation and bail conditions: curfews, no go zones restricting movement throughout the city, abstaining from drug use, and refusing contact with peers. The restrictions are often so stringent that youth are unable to meet them because of their lived experiences of homelessness and poverty (Dean 2005; Czapska, Webb, and Taefi 2008; NWAC 2014b). As a result, Indigenous youth are imprisoned for breaching unrealistic conditions and enter into a seemingly never-ending cycle of incarceration and "administrative" or "non-compliance" offences, such as "breach of probation" or "failure to appear in court" (Czapska, Webb, and Taefi 2008).[54] All of this happens in spite of the introduction of a new Youth Criminal Justice Act, which came into effect in 2003 and was intended to reassert the value of keeping youth in the community rather than criminalizing those who are already marginalized. Despite this allegedly "new approach" to matters of youth crime, incarceration rates of Indigenous youth have remained steady. In fact, Indigenous youth are the demographic segment that has not experienced a decrease in imprisonment (Brown 2011; Neve and Pate 2005). Pretrial custody rates have actually increased under this legislation, and initial examinations of its impact are uncovering the racialized and gendered face of the new legislation (Calverley, Cotter, and Halla 2010; Sprott and Doob 2009). This point came across painfully clearly during one of my conversations with a former Crown prosecutor. "Mondays are the busiest," she told me when I asked her to explain the ebb and flow of youth court in Saskatoon. "All of the new arrests pile up over the weekend and then it's a zoo on Monday when youth have to make their first appearance before a judge. You get to see them paraded out, one by one, behind the wall of glass." She had only four words, not numbers, to share when I asked her what percentage of youth in custody where Indigenous. "Almost all of them," she replied.

The mainstream media also work in concert with the justice system to fabricate the notion of an "Indigenous youth threat" and bolster the perception of Indigenous youth as "criminal," "lazy," "violent," and "intellectually inferior" to settler youth (Anderson and Robertson 2011). In other words, they send the message that Indigenous youth are young people to be feared, that they are the ones who will attack you, who will steal your purse when you are walking down the street. Settler colonialism and its handmaiden racism, then, are practised through an "extreme discursive warfare" (Lawrence 2004, 309) in which the mainstream media play one of the leading roles. In concrete terms, this means that the consumption of dominant media is directed towards a normative white, middle-class citizenry and is substantially imbued with racialized depictions of those who fall outside the boundaries of this normative construction (Henry and Tator 2002). Communications scholar Yasmin Jiwani (2006, 68) argues, in fact, that media become "the invisible backdrop against which stigmatized and valorized Others are profiled."

In the case of Indigenous peoples in Canada, Joyce Green (2011, 237) attests to this constant thread of colonial imagery in public discourse when she says, "For the most part, Aboriginal peoples do not exist for the media, except as practitioners of violence or political opposition, as marketing stereotypes, or as bearers of social pathology." Indigenous resistance to the forced assimilation agenda of the settler colonial state is also consistently portrayed in a negative light in dominant media outlets. Coverage of Idle No More, for example, as well as protests and blockades against the large scale environmental degradation caused by industrial development projects throughout Canada (the tar sands as a case in point), are often tactically positioned as unreasonable outbursts of anger[55] centred on the sabotaging of federal negotiations rather than as rightful opposition to endemic colonial state violence.

The past decade in Saskatchewan has also been marked by an infiltration of the issue of "Indigenous gangs" into prairie print, radio, television, and online media (Grebinski 2012).[56] Drawing on a 2005 Criminal Intelligence Service Saskatchewan (CISS) report documenting the escalation of Indigenous gang involvement, the media mounted a campaign to vilify Indigenous youth and young adults associated with gangs, without due consideration of the social, political, economic, and cultural contexts contributing to the rise of gangs in the first place as a response to social power imbalances and material deprivation (Sinclair and Grekul 2012; Totten 2009). Ignoring context, the media have, once again, furthered the perception of Indigenous youth as threatening gangsters to be feared and have fuelled colonial tropes marking Indigenous bodies as criminal (Green 2011). Such characterizations strip the humanity from young people who are already contending with conditions of privation and systemic discrimination across a network of government agencies, including child welfare agencies, to which I turn next.

*Intersections with Toxic Child Welfare*

In the case of Indigenous children and youth, child welfare apprehension acts an extractive governing technology, with direct linkages to criminalization. In Saskatchewan, while Indigenous peoples count for 15 per cent of the population, nearly 80 per cent of children and youth in out-of-home care are Indigenous (Saskatchewan Child Welfare Review Panel 2010, 29). Indigenous children and youth are thirteen times more likely to be become Saskatchewan's Crown wards than non-Indigenous youth. This trend parallels the high rate of Indigenous youth in Saskatchewan's prisons (Malone 2013) and highlights the probability that contact with the criminal justice system will more than likely mean a pre-existing connection to colonial state agencies through child welfare.

The history of child welfare apprehension for Indigenous children and youth in Canada is grave. Federal policy changes in the 1950s ushered in what is now known as the "Sixties Scoop," a settler colonial practice that resulted in approximately 20,000 Indigenous children and youth being apprehended and removed from their home families and communities and placed in either foster or adoptive care with mostly non-Aboriginal families in Canada, the United States, and Europe. Not surprisingly, this history of forced state removal of Indigenous children and youth from their communities has created a massive sense of distrust and fear of the system for Indigenous parents and extended family members. "Many Aboriginal families," contends the Saskatchewan Child Welfare Review Panel (2010), "feel the mainstream child welfare system is a real and constant threat – to take their children, to put them first in homes that have no connection to the child's community, and to move on to adoption as soon as possible, severing all ties to the family and community" (21). Given the current scale of apprehension, this fear is not only well founded but also very real.

Scholars and child youth advocates (Sinclair et al. 2004; Blackstock and Trocmé 2005; Czapska and Webb 2005; Baskin 2011), have further been calling attention to the ways that the present-day system of apprehension is an extension of residential schooling, a new form of institutionalization for Indigenous children and youth that carries out the project of forced settler colonial assimilation disguised in the deceptive language of "protection." Powell and Peristerakis (2014) argue, in this sense, that residential schools were replaced by a child welfare system engaged in the mass removal of Indigenous children from their families and communities of origin (82). The majority of state apprehensions in Saskatchewan are designated as cases of "neglect" (Saskatchewan Child Welfare Review Panel 2010), whereby Indigenous families are accused of inflicting harm on their children as a result of the conditions of poverty, lack of housing, and an inability to provide basic needs they suffer because of inadequate resources and a lack of social programming. Through this label of "neglect," Indigenous families are once again vilified for the social conditions perpetuated by the state itself. Czapska et al. (2008, 34) observe the irony of this discursive manipulation: "In child welfare law, neglect includes: the failure to supervise children, leading to physical harm; the failure to provide for the child adequately, including failing to provide adequate nutrition and clothing; and living in unhygienic or dangerous living conditions. Given these definitions, it would seem that the Canadian government should be charged with neglect of mothers and families living in poverty."

Complicating these issues further, the NWAC (2014a) reports that two thirds of Indigenous women in Canadian prisons are single mothers.[57] Once these women are imprisoned, child welfare authorities often capture their children, effectively "condemning a new generation to the child welfare and youth criminal justice systems" (NWAC 2014a, 11). The differences in family organization and parenting styles between Indigenous and non-Indigenous formulations of kinship structure are also disregarded in the dominant child welfare model that imposes white, middle-class values on Indigenous families. The white way is the right way, and the only way. Once apprehended, Indigenous children are often placed in non-Indigenous foster homes, disconnected from the appropriate transmission of traditions and cultural practices, and can be subjected to sexual and physical abuse within their care placements (Czapska and Webb 2005) – even death (Saskatchewan Child Welfare Review Panel 2010; Sinclair and Grekul 2012, qtd. in Mas 2015; Inter-American Commission on Human Rights 2014).[58]

There is also a gendered dynamic to apprehension, as illustrated in the life story of Nitânis, whose experiences of child welfare I make reference to in the introduction. When sharing her experiences in foster care, Nitânis repeatedly lamented how she was silenced by the various social workers responsible for her case file, even when she cited instances of sexual abuse. The following interview excerpt illustrates the state's denial of the abuse she was suffering:

> N: Like the social worker was always putting me in different homes. She
>    thought they could deal with me.
> JD: What were the foster homes like?
> N: Some of them were ... some were okay I guess, and some of them were
>    really bad. Like some of them would use me, like the Dads I mean. I
>    lived in a foster home in Zenith Lake and uhm ...
> JD: How far is Zenith Lake from Saskatoon?
> N: A couple of hours. And uh, that white man there was a farmer and
>    he raped me in the barn and he tried to tell me, "What are you getting
>    mad for? You'll do it for free anyway." And so he, he kept doing it and I
>    couldn't get him to stop. I tried to tell my social worker that some of the
>    homes that we were living in weren't good but she always thought I was
>    making shit up.

Indigenous young women and girls, like Nitânis, who run away from such violence because that is the only option available to them, face elevated levels of danger from being targeted by pimps, johns, drug dealers, and other violent persons looking to exploit them and who prey on their vulnerability when they are living on the street and facing homelessness (Smiley 2012). In her research on the sexual exploitation of Indigenous young women and girls, Sikka (2009, 9) found that, "Many girls' first point of entry into the criminal justice system is a charge for an offence committed within a care facility." Sikka goes on to explain that "girls may be charged with assault on a staff member or other 'violent' offences and are often remanded to detention centres, where they come into contact with sexually exploited youth and recruiters." Experiences of colonial sexual violence sanctioned within state-controlled care placements enacting their own form of structural violence, then, directly contribute to Indigenous girls' increased susceptibility to other forms of societal and interpersonal harm.

Living in non-Indigenous foster homes or over-crowded group homes,[59] as permanent or temporary wards of the state, can also produce an array of mental health problems for Indigenous youth that make themselves manifest in trust and attachment issues as well as in a lack of clarity around personal and collective identity. "Who am I?" takes on heightened meaning within this context. Adding insult to injury, Indigenous youth must also develop coping strategies to address the instability created by a child welfare system that lacks adequate resources. In a focus group discussion I conducted in 2007 with ten Indigenous youth at Helping Out – an organization providing mentoring support for youth in care in Saskatoon – one Indigenous girl told me that she had moved care placements eleven times over a one-year period. As a result, her schooling was consistently disrupted, she was not able to make any friends, and she experienced feelings of intense isolation. In her words, "I don't trust anyone and I don't get to know anyone because you probably aren't going to see them again. When I go into a home I am really quiet. I am only in foster care until my mom gets better and the other kids in the home might run away, or I might be moved and I am scared because I have lost a lot of people in my life and I am scared that if I open up to someone then I will lose them too and they will be gone."

Another Indigenous youth spoke of the distrust his family expressed towards the child welfare system as a whole and the way his mother fought his possible adoption. He shared, "My mother grew up in foster care and she grew up hating white people and she said to them [child welfare agents] that you are never going to adopt a child of mine. My mother grew up in foster care and she was abused and treated really badly and she doesn't like white people. She said no white woman is going to adopt a Native child of ours. And the Band stopped it."

In interviews conducted with Indigenous girls in state care by the advocacy organization Justice for Girls, girls reported that government care is not a real home: "State intervention in their lives has been mostly harmful to their families, and ... state care cannot replace family because 'it's government'" (Czapska et al. 2005, 36). Clearly, the intersections between child welfare apprehension and the high degree of criminalization and incarceration of Indigenous children and youth merits deeper systematic analysis to articulate more fully the way these institutions work together as contemporary instantiations of settler colonial rule. Only when we have acquired further insight into the ways state agencies continue to constrain the lives of urban Indigenous youth, often in concert with one another, will we be able to think through strategies of defence that pay heed to the multiplicity and complexity of their experience.

\* \* \*

Throughout this chapter, I have demonstrated that urban Indigenous youth embody a set of realities that are largely not of their own making. I reject the notion that these young people simply fall through the cracks of an otherwise well-functioning set of social systems.[60] On the contrary, their marginalization is made real, brought into being, in large part, by settler colonial practices and policies and the everyday state violence to which their lives are deeply connected. The intensities and frameworks of Canadian social institutions (such as education, criminal justice, and child welfare) produce intersecting avenues of colonial harm whose cumulative impact is severe deprivation. These institutions remain aligned with the political roots and cultural underpinnings of a settler colonial state whose primary objective is to maintain the sanctity of settler sovereignty – they are not impartial entities whose agendas operate in isolation from this larger objective and mandate. They are fundamental to settler colonial continuity – organizations that enact the more genteel and acceptable forms of elimination characterizing the governing technologies of contemporary settler states. Indigenous youth, thus, live the paradox of a Canada that professes to recognize self-determination and have inklings of Indigenous sovereignty while simultaneously subverting Indigenous emancipation through ongoing territorial displacement, withholding of material resources, and violent social dispossession that is evidenced in the social exclusion of urban Indigenous youth from the Canadian "good life." In short, there is a war on Indigenous youth across Turtle Island. The lives of these youth are the lives that sit at the centre of debates over social intervention through participatory politics.

# PART TWO

## The Space That Lies In Between: Ethnographic Encounters with the Land of Living Skies

*Chapter Three*

# The Seduction of Participation:
# They Say the Best Is Yet to Come

They fed me one story. Then another, spinning it until it became the unraveling ball of wool, it always was.

— Leanne Simpson, "A Love Song for Attawapiskat"

Canada has not adequately met the needs of Aboriginal youth living in urban areas.

— *Urban Aboriginal Youth – An Action Plan for Change*

Moving on from the more theoretical discussion of the changing face of settler colonialism in Canada reflected in the preceding chapters, this chapter is a material exploration of how participation functions as a technology of settler colonial governance. More specifically, I trace the conceptual underpinnings and discursive logics of the Indigenous Alliance, a collaboration between the state and an Indigenous organization, the Indigenous Peoples Collective. The collaboration coalesces around social reforms targeted at reducing the high rates of urban Indigenous student drop out and "empowering"[1] Indigenous youth to become prosperous members of the city as a whole. I explain how the Indigenous community,[2] vis-à-vis the Indigenous Peoples Collective, becomes integrated into a state-generated blueprint for rebranding Indigenous–state relations, through a form of reconciliation politics requiring, as Coulthard (2014a, 107) describes it, that "individuals and groups work to overcome the debilitating pain, anger, and resentment that frequently persist in the wake of being injured or harmed by a perceived or real injustice." The horizon for redress for Indigenous peoples and for the urban Indigenous youth I present in this book, who have been "excluded" from the attendant benefits of white settler society in Saskatoon, is framed in terms of participatory state inclusion. Justice, in other words, is only to be found through an embodied alliance that relies on wiping the slate clean, beginning again.

My goal throughout the following pages is to demonstrate why we must interrogate the legitimacy of the "legal" and administrative frameworks that are foundational to Canadian statehood and that promote an interventionist strategy for Indigenous youth that posits indigeneity within the confines of generic citizenship rights. Relinquishing such an interrogation effectively enables a depoliticizing and delimiting of the terms of struggle between Indigenous peoples and the settler colonial state. This scheme, I argue, is infused with a settler colonial logics that at its core reflects an ongoing preoccupation with colonial relations of domination and associates urban Indigenous youth with the socialities of pathological dysfunction, fragility, and deviance from settler standards of white civility – a way of being that is in need of redemptive correction. Insofar as the conceptual bedrock of "participation" is political formations of Canadian statecraft that disable discussions of indigeneity, through what Rifkin (2015, 4) identifies as "a geopolitics askew with respect to the terms of state mappings and adjudication," the formulations of "seeking positive change" in the lives of urban Indigenous youth will continue to operate as part of a continuum of state assemblages that reinscribe colonial injury.

I begin the chapter by charting the creation of the Indigenous Alliance and its relationship with a broader set of state arrangements intent on socially engineering[3] the lives of urban Indigenous youth. Next, I trace the imprints of settler colonial governing on the social and political construction of the Indigenous Alliance by drawing out the vernacular representations of participation offered by state agents, Indigenous representatives, and youth workers engaged in developing social reforms targeting urban Indigenous youth. These propositions work to highlight the ways the political and ideological roots of the Indigenous Alliance resonate with settler colonial reconciliation politics while being celebrated as a new and innovate strategy for responding to the demands of Indigenous peoples in the city around the "crisis" facing urban Indigenous youth. My concluding discussion sets the stage for the remaining chapters, which draw more direct attention to a number of critical points I raise in this chapter.

## Imaginaries of Colonial Participation: The Indigenous Alliance Awakened

On a rainy day in early summer of 2006, I set out to accompany members of the Indigenous Alliance to a reserve outside of Saskatoon. It was the scheduled quarterly meeting between the members of the working group who are responsible for implementing the plans and strategies of this initiative – officials from the school division and local Indigenous leaders from the surrounding area, who occupy a more advisory role in its official organizational structure. Dakota stopped at my parents' house to retrieve me. He was a handsome Cree man in his early thirties, with a flair for hip urban fashion and an impressive wealth of knowledge about the latest musical talents inciting excitement and passion in the city's youth, as well as an on-the-ground member of the working group responsible for mentoring Indigenous students at an inner city high school in Saskatoon's Westside. We sprinted through the summer downpour and hopped in his jeep to make the journey.

"Man, I am soaked!" I exclaimed to Dakota. "You'd think I was back in BC with this weather!" Dakota laughed at me, a broad, winning smile across his expressive face, and said, cajoling, "But isn't it a beautiful day Jas? And, shouldn't we just be thankful that we are alive?" I looked at him, dripping wet with rain but smiling nonetheless and finally agreed that yes, he was indeed correct, we should be thankful to be alive. His response was not surprising to me, as I had come to expect Dakota's clarion call for optimism and persistent reminders of our ultimate mortality and increasingly precarious condition as human beings on the planet. His smile, in many ways, belied the social, political, and economic reality of Indigenous peoples in the province – speaking to the hope of new and restorative projects destined to chart a new course, gesturing to a world otherwise than it is.

I buckled myself into my seat and glanced up to notice the sage hanging from his rear view mirror as well as a collection of stickers, signalling Dakota's interest in youth issues, pasted across the front of the dashboard. Dakota started up the jeep and turned on the stereo, his latest musical recording filling the internal space of the vehicle with the sounds of rhythmic drumming and vocals speaking vivid tales of the present and cogent tales of the afflictions of the past. He sang along with the music, his silver hoop earrings moving from side to side as he swayed his head, his fingers drumming against the steering wheel. He was always singing.

With a few swift turns, Dakota pulled out of my parents' neighbour-hood, a fairly recent and predominantly white housing development in the north end of Saskatoon, with a suburban-like persona to match its spatial separation from the city's Westside, where most of my fieldwork had taken place. With its somewhat banal architecture, eerie quietness, and hypersanitized streets, the north end exuded a palpable sensation of normalcy and sterility, a recognizable desire for order and the strict maintenance of private property and public space. We travelled along the main road that leads from the north end to the centre of town, a road with which I am so exceedingly familiar that I could anticipate each upcoming pothole and slight curve in the road. Dakota and I made idle conversation as we drove, commenting on the intensity of the rain and our approximate arrival time at the meeting. In a few minutes, I could see the traffic lights ahead of me through the rapidly moving windshield wipers, the Robin Hood Flour Mill looming over the inter-section on my right, as we crossed the railway tracks at 33rd Street and officially entered the city's downtown.

The city had been developing quickly over the past decade. New restaurants, retail stores, and service shops now lined the downtown streets to mark the city's economic progress in competition with its counterparts in the neighbouring provinces of Manitoba and Alberta. We passed by a number of low rise signature buildings, including a large blue structure, home to the Great Western Brewing Company, and turned right at the old Hudson's Bay Company (now trendy condos), slowly making our way towards the city's Westside. Picking up speed, Dakota deftly swerved between cars, and when we stopped for a red light, I could clearly see one of the city's larger youth service organi-zations, with a mangy looking group of school-aged youth huddled outside the front door, shielded from the rain by an old wooden canopy and smoking cigarettes. The building resembled a factory warehouse space; there were few visible windows, and it was painted a drab shade of deep orange, with a substantial amount of pine siding lining its outer walls. A few yards away, a young mother pushed her baby carriage towards the group, likely seeking protection from the wet weather and whatever meagre assistance the organization might be able to provide for her and her child.[4]

Leaving the city behind us, Dakota and I drove the distance to the reserve across winding roads etched between beautifully lush green fields peppered with the hues of yellow and brown crops, while watch-ing a spectacular thunderstorm roll in across the big prairie sky; a geographic backdrop that itself provided a palpable entry point into questions of social programming for urban Indigenous youth that are often tied to migration from on-reserve to off-reserve. As we drove, I focused for a few moments to take in the splendour and beauty around me – reminding myself of my own connection to this land and its complicated history – absorbing the peace and serenity of the vast and expansive space that one can only encounter on the open prairie terrain.

I had come to know Dakota quite well at this stage in my research. I often sat with him during lunch and accompanied him to the many meetings he attended to do with the development of a pilot mentoring program for Indigenous youth. As we drove, we talked informally about his work with the Indigenous Alliance and how he understood what was important in the lives of Indigenous youth in Saskatoon. He made a point of explaining that, while he believed it was of value for them to learn the skills and knowledge that were required to be part of "city life," it was also deeply important that they remember their place on the land and "be proud of where they come from." This idea of collective remembrance of struggle as a moral responsibility for Indigenous youth had come up repeatedly in my conversations with him, as well as the role of youth programming in promoting an understanding of the relationship between past, present, and future for Indigenous peoples in Canada. It seemed that professing pride in one's historical struggle largely defined the discourses through which he articulated his work in the Indigenous Alliance – a testament, arguably, to the difficulty Indigenous youth often confront when navigating the social, economic, and political spaces of urban life. This is especially pronounced in prairies cities such as Saskatoon, where neighbourhoods have been clearly racialized and gendered violence abounds.

The drive to the reserve took about two hours, a fair distance from the hustle of Saskatoon's core neighbourhood. Dakota and I turned off the main road onto a smaller dirt thoroughfare at the edge of the reserve and began weaving through a very narrow, muddy, and snaking path enveloped by trees, en route to the lakeside lodge where the meeting was being held. The rain was coming down with noticeable force by this time, and there were a couple of moments when Dakota's jeep almost became stuck. Knowing that others would be facing similar difficulty, Dakota and I chuckled about how everyone from the city would be complaining about having to trek out to the reserve to attend the meeting when there were plenty of places where this meeting could have taken place within the city limits. The availability of space in the city, however, was not the point.[5] Holding the meeting on the reserve was understood as an attempt by the Indigenous Alliance to "equalize" relations between Indigenous peoples and the state – while the majority of the work associated with the Indigenous Alliance took place within the official boundaries of Saskatoon, there were also supposed to be interruptions in this traditional practice, where meetings occasionally moved to Indigenous spaces on reserve.[6]

We parked near the top of a hill where it would be easy to turn Dakota's jeep around. From my vantage point, I could see a large wooden patio where the Director of Education for the school division, a high school principal, youth workers, local Indigenous leaders, and members of the Indigenous Alliance working group had started mingling and getting reacquainted. As we made our way down towards the lodge, umbrellas in hand, I mentioned to Dakota how stunning the surroundings were, what a refreshing change it was from the sterile boardrooms where I commonly attended meetings. Dakota smiled in agreement and replied that he too was relieved to be on the reserve and that it was important for the people from the cities who were in charge of "all of this stuff" to remember where Indigenous youth were coming from. "I don't do this work because I want to help them," Dakota explained. "I don't even think of myself as working for the Indigenous Alliance; I work for my people. We need our kids to remember who we are, our place on this land, to learn the drumming and dancing. You know, this is about us." When I asked him who or what it was that he meant by "them," he responded by telling me "you know, all those bureaucrats in the city, I feel like all they do is go to one meeting after another. I don't mean any disrespect, but they get so caught up in their own things that they forget about the real issues. Sometimes, I feel like the work is just going nowhere."

This particular exchange I had with Dakota caught my attention for several reasons and typifies a number of core tensions that form the basis of the Indigenous Alliance – tensions that find their social and political ancestry in a trail of state-manufactured initiatives to "right the wrongs" of Canada's historic treatment of Indigenous peoples. What were the "real issues" that Dakota was speaking of? How did this state–Indigenous "joint effort" take up the social issues facing urban Indigenous youth? Where did the power lie to make decisions about what direction the Indigenous Alliance would take? Who did the Indigenous Alliance, in fact, represent? What were its ultimate goals?

I was accustomed to hearing similar remarks about the importance of reviving Indigenous culture (as indicated by Dakota's gesturing towards drumming and dancing) and drawing attention to the history of colonization in Canada by various community advocates in non-profit organizations, Indigenous and non-Indigenous alike. Yet, I was surprised to hear Dakota articulate his position so clearly. After all, the Indigenous Alliance he worked for was a government-sponsored initiative and the official mission and vision of the union clearly celebrated the blending of Indigenous and government entities to resolve the social issues facing urban Indigenous youth. Given my experience as an advocate, I had to wonder whether these issues were solely about cultural retention. Was the reason that so many Indigenous youth were struggling in Saskatoon the incommensurability of Indigenous culture with mainstream state institutions?

Dakota's assertion that bureaucrats in the city were not connected to the "real" issues suggested that some form of Indigenous representation in the Indigenous Alliance was required to achieve a degree of authenticity in the quest for social reform but that this representation was not necessarily reflective of all Indigenous polities. His references, then, spoke to a bounded understanding of the state and the urban Indigenous community and to the complicated questions of place, belonging, and Indigenous sociopolitical identity that exist within the settler city of Saskatoon, that was consistently positioned as non-Indigenous space. Coupled with these points, Dakota's comments also signalled that he distinguished himself and his work from the state, although potentially viewing the Indigenous Alliance as a medium through which he could reach out to urban Indigenous youth. His remarks made me consider the possibility that he was, in fact, harnessing some of the power of the state to advance his own agenda and to work with Indigenous youth in a manner he deemed appropriate. The location of the meeting on reserve land, held in an unfinished lakeside lodge with no electricity and no running water (we used a portable toilet outside), was the least the state should be doing, in his mind, in order to symbolically move towards supporting social programs for Indigenous children and youth on different terms then they had in the past. Consequently, I began to wonder about how this ostensibly hybrid institutional form managed to reconcile potentially competing ideas about how best to support urban Indigenous youth, particularly within the context of destabilized power relations that required individuals, families, and communities to take back powers and responsibilities that, since the nineteenth century, had been acquired by states, politicians, and legislators. And finally, Dakota's remarks illustrated the thorny history of Indigenous–state relations in which this collaboration was deeply embedded and the complexity involved in thinking through how the creation of participatory strategies was implicated in larger questions of Indigenous political entitlements.[7]

## Coming into Being

The Indigenous Alliance is homed in the Indigenous Peoples Collective, a large Indigenous organization serving seven member nations located within a 200 km radius of Saskatoon. The Indigenous Peoples Collective provides support for Indigenous nations across the areas of children, family, and community programs; education and health and wellness services; environmental and engineering services; affordable housing; labour force development; and technical and business advisory services. It is an organization known for becoming a "valuable participant" in the Saskatoon community via contributions made in these areas, and this includes a substantial focus on youth programming offered through the organization's department dedicated to supporting a rapidly growing Indigenous urban populace. In order to fulfil its mandate of "gathering together, honouring the past, and building the future," in step with its member nations, the Indigenous Peoples Collective is an avid proponent of joining forces with the state. The road to greater quality of life, the organization believes, is through strengthening such allegiances.

The Indigenous Peoples Collective, however, is only one of many Indigenous organizations throughout Canada that has become actively involved in crafting social programming for urban Indigenous youth under an explicit agreement with the federal and provincial governments. Recall from the introduction, that the Urban Aboriginal Youth Strategy (UAYS), in particular, has fostered the creation of numerous collaborative efforts between the state and Indigenous organizations, with the goal of addressing "the needs" of urban Indigenous youth by recognizing the importance of having Indigenous participation to ensure change. As stated within the eighty-seven page report *Urban Aboriginal Youth – An Action Plan for Change*:

> Governments need to acknowledge that *urban Aboriginal people know what their problems are*, that they are in a much better position to identify

appropriate solutions, and know that they need adequate resources applied in accordance with their own priorities to implement locally developed initiatives. That said, governments should not hold to a purely passive funding role. Urban Aboriginal communities should not be expected to find all the solutions to their problems which exist in the broader context of Canadian society. Therefore we strongly urge governments to acknowledge that community designed initiatives are often more effective than programs developed in centralized government ministries. Accordingly, in structural terms, government departments need to delegate to Aboriginal service providers the authority to customize services and react flexibly to local circumstances. (Canada, 2003, 33; emphasis added)

Reading between the lines of these amnesic[8] statements, however, is a concrete sense that the state is interested in reinforcing the notion that there is no colonial present responsible for producing "the suffering we currently see reverberating at pandemic levels within and across Indigenous communities today" (Coulthard 2014a, 121). Instead of addressing the structural conditions that will continue to produce harm in the lives of Indigenous youth, the state issues an appeal to Indigenous peoples to "identify their own problems and their own solutions." Indeed, apart from a few cursory remarks at the beginning of the report, there is no mention of colonialism throughout the document at all. It is also important to note that the label of "risk" is what demarcates the parameters of settler state intervention in the lives of urban Indigenous youth through this federal strategy, even with the active participation of Indigenous representatives sitting at the table. According to UAYS, the federal government "develops and funds specific initiatives for young Aboriginal people on the basis that they are one of the most 'at-risk' groups" (Canada, 2003, 10). This notion of "risk," then, is a significant part of what drives the agenda to intervene in the lives of Indigenous youth, and it is central part of the rationale for "rescuing" them.

The Indigenous Peoples Collective has been the recipient of funding from the UAYS, as well as of monies from a program of INAC dedicated to creating educational partnerships (the Educational Partnerships Program) between Indigenous nations and provincial school divisions. On the educational front, the tying together of the state and Indigenous community organizations has been lauded, in relation to Indigenous youth, as a mechanism to enhance Indigenous student retention, family and community support, and involvement in educational and social programming; and in relation to employees working within areas that intersect with the lives of Indigenous youth, as a mechanism for curriculum and professional development. The Indigenous Peoples Collective formulated the Indigenous Alliance under the auspices of the Educational Partnerships Program that was generated through INAC and in partnership with Sask Learning.[9] However, it is important to note for analytical reasons that much of the Indigenous Alliance's work with youth traverses into related youth programs of the Indigenous Peoples Collective, operating through funding from the UAYS and other provincial agencies (such as the Ministry of Corrections and Public Safety) caught up in the work of participation and inclusion. This includes programs that fall under the rubric of "urban justice," since so many Indigenous youth are caught in the criminal justice system and serve time in secure or open custody facilities (as I explained in chapter 2). As a result, youth fluidly move in and out of these programs, often accessing multiple programs at the same time. For example, an Indigenous youth may be engaged in an initiative based in the Indigenous Alliance that focuses specifically on education, but since she may have also recently been released from prison, she may also be connected to a youth justice program that is focused on her "reintegration" back into the settler city. From the perspective of fieldwork, this meant that, even though I spent the majority of my time with the Indigenous Alliance, I also found myself in other youth programs of the Indigenous Peoples Collective that were equally ensconced in the participatory politics of the state – and, as I reveal later in the book, sometimes members of the Indigenous Alliance were called upon to provide guidance and direction to the Indigenous Peoples Collective on matters pertaining to urban Indigenous youth, even though those matters could be considered to fall outside the formal purview of education. This also meant that members of the Indigenous Alliance often intersected with youth workers assigned to other youth programs of the Indigenous Peoples Collective.

The Indigenous Alliance officially came into being in 2003. An official memorandum of understanding (MOU) was signed between the state and the Indigenous Peoples Collective, acting as a representative body for the urban Indigenous community in the city. The MOU outlined a series of principles upon which the state and the urban Indigenous community were to come together in this new participatory alliance. These included recognizing and supporting treaty knowledge within the educational system to support healthy relations among students, creating an equitable governance council to ensure that decision making was a shared process representative of all stakeholders, and recognizing and celebrating common interests and uniqueness. The MOU also contained directives regarding the design of an array of educational supports and programs for Aboriginal education and directives to honour Indigenous knowledge and revitalize Indigenous culture and language within these programs with honest and respectful participation.

The formal organizational structure of the Indigenous Alliance was comprised of two layers. A working group was responsible for undertaking the on-the-ground work of conceptualizing and implementing initiatives. And an education council served an advisory role, providing mission direction and formal approval of strategies and initiatives. The working group was comprised of representatives from the Saskatoon School Division, from the Indigenous Peoples Collective, and from the urban Indigenous community of the city, as well as youth workers attached to the various initiatives (usually about six or seven were present at the meetings). Two co-chairs – one from the state (in this case a member of the Saskatoon School Division) and one from the Indigenous Peoples Collective – were in charge of organizing and facilitating working group meetings and were responsible for approving all of the programs, events, and initiatives for the Indigenous Alliance. On paper, the education council consisted of all members of the working group and included also provincial state agents, urban Indigenous representatives, and individuals from the Métis community – its elders, parents, and students. The education council was supposed to meet quarterly, but during the years I was conducting my fieldwork, they met noticeably infrequently, usually because the availability of members to meet was limited (and the meetings were poorly attended when they did occur). This resulted in a substantial amount of power being concentrated in the hands of the working group in terms of the day-to-day operations of this inclusionary effort. The working group formally met on a monthly basis, although there were sporadic, informal meetings between different members of the working group carrying out specific projects as well.

The specific types of strategies and initiatives undertaken by the Indigenous Alliance conjoined around four main goals:

1. Developing and implementing sustainable Indigenous curricula to ensure the inclusion of Indigenous perspectives throughout the public school curriculum and to encourage youth organizations to adopt Indigenous cultural practices such as smudging – an attempt to indigenize the spaces where Indigenous youth found themselves in Saskatoon

2. Supporting anti-racism education and awareness of contemporary Indigenous issues in Canada through professional development workshops and the establishment of policies and procedures for dealing with "racial incidents" and offering workshops around "stereotyping" for all staff, students, and parents
3. Improving the learning outcomes of urban Indigenous youth through a variety of support mechanisms, including the development of mentoring programs
4. Implementing Indigenous workforce development dedicated to increasing the hiring of Indigenous teachers in public schools and improving Indigenous teacher retention

Yet, while all four were goals of the Indigenous Alliance, not all of them came to fruition to the same extent. Working group members were actively engaged in selecting certain areas to which their time and resources were directed (as I explain in more detail in chapters 4 and 5), while others took a backseat. Moreover, the ways that members of the Indigenous Alliance articulated their conceptions of the purpose of this participatory coalition between the state and the urban Indigenous community lend considerable insight into the political rationale under-girding these efforts.

Before delving into a series of ethnographic episodes that reveal the political rationale of the participatory coalition, I would like to move to a brief discussion of how the Indigenous Alliance was constructed in alignment with broader state mandates to alter relations between the governing and the governed, and how these mandates rely on the normative story of linear progress to mobilize state agents and community representatives towards colonial goals. Peering closely at enunciations in official state documents unveils Canada's intensely statist settler colony mission in crafting these alliances. It is a mission that reeks of modern governing sentiments about future social mobility, about selective inclusion that assumes that freedom from suffering for Indigenous youth can occur within state institutions, and about a desire to recreate urban Indigenous youth subjectivity in alignment with the preservation, most importantly, of a white settler state.

## Saskatchewan's Claim to Trying Something New: The Discursive Landscape of Participation

In 2003, the province of Saskatchewan embarked on a journey to develop educational alliances between Indigenous communities and local school divisions. The alliances were supposed to elicit Indigenous participation as a way to address the "low educational attainment levels"[10] of Indigenous youth drop outs, to promote the "success" of Indigenous youth in Saskatchewan's public schools, and to advance social programming that enabled Indigenous youth to become vital and contributing members of the province. Under the direction of Judy Junor, Minister of Learning in the provincial cabinet, Saskatchewan released its policy framework to inform systematic and "authentic" collaboration between Indigenous communities and public school divisions across the province. The policy framework was entitled *Building Partnerships: First Nations and Métis Peoples and the Provincial Education System – A Policy Framework for Saskatchewan's Prekindergarten to Grade 12 Education System*[11] and called for the province to enlist cooperation, equity, and community as vital guides in the advancement of new and strengthened ways of working with First Nations people (Sask Learning 2003, 1–2). This policy document is a state archetype that outlines Saskatchewan's "commitment to promoting collaborative working relationships among the provincial education system and First Nations and Métis authorities and communities. It puts forward the vision, goals, and principles for school divisions as they transform their working relationships and the governance of the existing system through partnerships."

*Building Partnerships* cites three "compelling reasons" to promote the participation of Indigenous communities around social and educational reform:

1. "To improve the learning outcomes for First Nations and Métis students" by fostering "mutual understanding and respect between and among Aboriginal and non-Aboriginal children, youth, and adults" and create "mechanisms to facilitate the full participation of First Nations and Métis people in education planning and decision making"
2. "To strengthen the integrity of the provincial educational system" to address the "unparalleled growth in the number of First Nations and Métis people and the decline in the number of non-Aboriginal people." The province also recognizes that this "shift is occurring at a time when First Nations and Métis people are expressing a desire for increased control over the education of their children" in urban centres[12]
3. "To build a shared and prosperous future for Saskatchewan," recognizing that education is "the social institution with the

mandate and capacity to foster mutual understanding, respect, and community among diverse peoples. In preparing young First Nations and Métis people to become caring and contributing citizens, education has a critical role to play in creating a society that is inclusive, equitable, and prosperous."

At first glance, Saskatchewan's slick policy call for the annexation of Indigenous communities to the state, with its origins in INAC, appears to be a benign instrument for promoting the overall social utility of education and related social programming and for responding to Indigenous nations' requests for greater control over programs impacting their children and youth. Yet, upon closer scrutiny, the decontextualized fostering of state–Indigenous collaborations takes what is rightly a political problem and repositions it in the neutralized space of "blended interests," where colonial goals are masked under the cloak of neutrality – a key feature of modern power (Shore and Wright 1997, 8). In this way, this document takes on an authoritative, futuristic power through its discursive presentation of "coming togetherness," and is armed with a benevolent posture of caring. The inevitable questions arise, then, around the political terms of this caring and the gains by the state – what are these terms? and what does the state gain by granting Indigenous communities the opportunity to participate?

First, for the state, the creation of alliances with Indigenous peoples is a way to channel more decision-making power to the urban Indigenous community itself, especially in the wake of the well-cited "educational disengagement" of urban Indigenous youth and growing demands for Indigenous autonomy. That is, the alliance becomes conceived as an avenue through which the government can appear to abdicate some degree of power over Indigenous youth by eliciting assistance from Indigenous community members. From this vantage point, Indigenous communities are presented with an opportunity to partake in programs for their youth, even if those are tied to improving state-sanctioned standards of success. However, Nikolas Rose (1999, 174) reminds us that, in new governing regimes, "the state is no longer required to answer all society's needs for order, security, health and productivity. Individuals, firms, organizations, localities, schools, parents, hospitals, housing estates must take on themselves – as "partners" – a portion of the responsibility for resolving these issues, whether this be permanent retraining for the worker, or neighbourhood watch for the community.

This involves a double movement of autonomization and responsibilization." In the case of programs for urban Indigenous youth, the Canadian state envisions the urban Indigenous community as an active partner in creating efforts at reforms that target Indigenous students but do not draw attention to the ways government language and practices may construct the terms under which participation can happen. In other words, participation does not readily imply "general" or "neutral" opportunities that are devoid of nationalist social and political agendas – as evidenced in the official document, the state is preoccupied with finding a way to address the "Indigenous youth problem" in education as both a matter of necessity and, from the settler state's perspective, national stability.

Second, the language behind "learning outcomes" in and of itself recalls quantitative measurement tools through which standards of success are tied to fixed indicators, such as graduation rates and transition to post-secondary institutions, honing in on a continued focus on the economic utility of education for Indigenous children and youth. In his work on the links between economics and self-determination, Michael Marker (2000, 30) draws attention to the way "economic issues frame the context for imagining cultural outcomes from the education process." Thus, when examining the parameters through which partnerships will be conceived, the idea of "improving learning outcomes" is something that merits careful analysis.[13]

Third, these passages from the policy document contain a direct recognition of the state's interest in linking education and Indigenous youth social programming with the formation of citizenship, although new configurations of citizenship that will address the protracted social and political conflicts between Indigenous peoples and "the rest of Canadian society." It follows, then, that these alliances will promote some version of the "good life" through which all citizens in Saskatchewan will prosper and that this end is a moral obligation to which we all should aspire. However, whose version of the "good life" is never brought into question. Instead, it is assumed that we are all uncritically marching towards the same glorious future, Canadian flags in hand. A quick Google search with the terms "Indigenous," "Canada," and "Future" will immediately cast doubt on this colonial illusion.

Created through the directives provided in Saskatchewan's provincial policy framework, a parallel emphasis on western colonial narratives of transformational change can be found in the conceptual construction of the Indigenous Alliance. The following passage, taken directly from the MOU (2003; emphasis added),[14] highlights the consistency of these notions:

> The most important opportunity and challenge we face in Saskatoon and in this province is the creation of a shared harmonious and prosperous future for all. This future must be one in which everyone experiences prosperity and personal well-being. Education is recognized universally as the key to helping create a society that is dynamic and productive, one that offers opportunity and fairness to all. The Saskatoon Public School Division is committed to inspiring and sustaining learning, and to being accountable to all children and youth so they may discover, develop, and act upon their lives potential, thereby enriching their lives and our community. We have clearly rededicated ourselves to being a school division that is inclusive, responsive, accountable, and effective. We can only achieve these goals by working together in partnerships to foster insight, understanding, and respect for the strengths and contributions of all those who attend our schools. To be effective we must provide numerous opportunities for shared leadership and management. We must strengthen our relationships, to ensure an equitable voice in planning and decision-making. We must rethink and transform our existing systems, procedures, decision-making, leadership, and management structures. All that we say is merely words that will be lost in the wind if we do not make a positive difference for the youth of our First Nations. Our past is not one to be proud of; our future hangs in the balance.

The remainder of this chapter focuses directly on how these sentiments of settler colonial transformational change are evidenced in the narratives of participatory collaboration articulated and enacted by members of the Indigenous Alliance.

### Empty History and Blended Futures: Breaking Away from "Us" and "Them"

It was springtime in Saskatchewan. People breathe a sigh of relief at this time of the year, just starting to recover from the isolation of the long cold winter that is so characteristic of the prairies. One cannot escape the persistent talk about weather in Saskatchewan; it is one of the constant reminders that you are in a place where daily life is dependent on climactic conditions – whether your car will start, if you are going to need a shovel to get your car moving on the road, if the highways are safe from black ice.

This was how I began my conversation with Sam when he offered to meet with me to share his perspective on the creation of coalitions between Indigenous peoples and provincial and federal governments in Canada. As part of an executive team for the Ministry of Education that deals directly with Indigenous education, Sam was a high level bureaucrat involved with conceiving the overarching policy directions for social and educational programs pertaining to Indigenous youth in the province. Of equal significance was that his department was one of the official government bodies through which the rationale and ideas for participation came into being. Given the shifting population demographics of cities like Regina and Saskatoon, his work was increasingly moving in the direction of addressing social issues facing urban Indigenous youth.

Sam's office was in Regina, the provincial capital of Saskatchewan. On a sunny day in April, I made the two-and-a-half-hour drive on Highway 11 leading south out of Saskatoon to the "beautiful oasis on the prairies," the city where Saskatchewan's colonial legislative edifices stand and government officials broker deals impacting the fate of Indigenous peoples in the province. I pulled up at Sask Learning's building, a rather plain looking structure near Regina's city centre, and parked my car. Making my way to Sam's office through the beige and gray hallways, I couldn't help but notice the sterility and formality of this space. With the exception of Ministry logos and a few posters with the faces of smiling children sporadically decorating the interior, the walls offered nothing to the imagination. It didn't take long to locate Sam's office. I entered to find a short, middle-aged, and quite rotund man, with a full beard and a hearty laugh to match his size. A sea of books and papers surrounded him, quite literally, as he worked feverishly at his desk. I introduced myself and thanked him for meeting with me. One of the co-chairs of the working group of the Indigenous Alliance had put me in touch with Sam, who, on occasion, made his way to Saskatoon to attend Education Council meetings. I wanted to meet him to learn more about how he understood the notion of participation within the context of Indigenous—state relations.

Over the course of thirty minutes or so, the time he was able to spare in his hectic schedule as a government agent, Sam laid out for me the rationale behind the push to foster the active participation of Indigenous communities in programming for Indigenous youth (in education and elsewhere). From Sam's perspective, the primary impetus behind the participation strategy was to be able to get the state to "engage"

First Nations youth in more meaningful ways, and the initial dollars for these initiatives were to be spent as a catalyst for beginning a process whereby the government and Indigenous communities could "learn more about each other," a step towards figuring out how to build more effective collaborations. I was puzzled by this comment about catalyst dollars being used to "learn about each other," so I asked Sam to clarify what he meant by this. He went on to explain that the initial funding was to be used to foster the creation of a more significant relationship between a local government agency and an Indigenous community, one that went deeper than a surface awareness of each other's issues. And with respect to the specific context of education, he attested, it was also vital for the Indigenous community in a city like Saskatoon to understand why it was so important that they work with the local state agencies (such as the school division) to ensure that Indigenous youth succeeded in school in the same ways that other youth did. He believed such an understanding could be reached through a process of direct consultation. I later discovered that, in the creation of the Indigenous Alliance, these initial stages were used to cultivate a set of reference points against which the lives of urban Indigenous youth could be measured, and I take these stages up in greater detail in the next chapter.

Perhaps the most striking aspect of our entire conversation, however, was a series of comments Sam made about his belief in participation as a way of blending the interests of the state with those of the urban Indigenous community – a fusion, he argued, that could be accomplished in a seamless way, his argument foregrounding the assumption that there was one set of unified interests upon which everyone could agree. "This is part of getting to that shared and harmonious future people are always talking about," he said when I asked him to articulate his stance more fully. "We are now finally getting to that place where you can't tell who is working for the First Nations and who is working for the government," added Sam. "It's not an 'us' and 'them' perspective anymore, we are now really listening to our First Nations communities, we are learning what they think and incorporating their perspectives into the ways that we do things."

Sam's remarks about the creation of participatory alliances between Canada and Indigenous communities opens an unmistakable window onto state attempts to quell Indigenous political difference – even if this may be an unintentional aim – and exhibits how such attempts operate from the social and political belief in the power of the settler colonial state to reach a coveted completion of the process. What happened in the past, then, was simply a reflection of "bad listening skills," a flawed strategy, on the part of the state, to actively engage Indigenous peoples in questions of their own future – a form of exclusion of Indigenous perspectives that made it impossible for the settler colonial state and Indigenous nations to reach consensus on any number of social issues. According to Sam, these new alliances hold the potential to rectify past colonial blunders with the aid of a revised policy framework designed to bring Indigenous polities into the protective arms of the state, and to reframe this as an opportunity to move forward together towards a fresh tomorrow.

What this requires, however, is emptying history.[15] It requires an optics of erasure that wilfully disregards the "imperial debris" upon which Canada rests (see Ann Stoler 2008). And from the perspective of a fieldworker, it requires being attentive to what is *not* being said, to recognize the way colonial silence feeds into Indigenous deletion. Throughout the entire discussion with Sam, I was alarmed by the absence of any direct reference to the history of residential schooling or the many other abhorrent settler colonial tactics that were (and are) being used by Canada to effectively extinguish Indigenous existence. Despite an interest in advancing the ability of urban Indigenous youth to achieve higher rates of graduation and thus be armed with the skills and knowledge required to engage more productively[16] with white settler society within the parameters of an urban context, no emphasis or importance was placed on the collective remembrance of a deeply troubling history or on a present-day social reality still reflecting settler colonial atrocities. Gillian Cowlishaw (2003, 107) captures how current incarnations of state governing of Indigenous peoples carry ghosts of the past. She remarks, "Gestures such as the Reconciliation Council, Aboriginal units in many professional organizations, and thousands of individuals, expert or not, whose jobs involve liaising between Aboriginal communities and state institutions, are the expression of the nation's goodwill toward Indigenous people, but these have not erased older responses of fear, hostility, and mistrust of an irremediable otherness lurking at the margins." With the exception of Dakota's emphasis on the vital responsibility of resurrecting social histories and placing them front and centre in the space of social programming for urban Indigenous youth, the majority of those associated with the creation of the Indigenous Alliance were largely preoccupied with an approach to social reform fixated on the future, without a significant retelling of the past.[17] Indeed, by focusing on the "future" and using descriptors such as "harmony" and "shared," Sam conjures up a sense that the state is "moving in the right direction" and that we can look forward to a brighter tomorrow, regardless of what has occurred in the past.[18] Put another way, his prognostications dovetail with consistent state attempts to locate colonial oppression in the recesses of a buried past, to manipulate a critical consciousness of the present by hijacking claims to the future.

In his critical research on participation as a social reform enterprise, Thomas Popkewitz (2004) speaks to the paradoxical nature of state–community alliances that attempt to bring marginalized communities into the decision-making apparatus of social institutions through the devolution and decentralization of state authority. He argues that the invocation of participation suggests that there is a consensus between collaborative partners (in this case, between Indigenous organizations and the state) around the roots and construction of the social problem that is the focus of cooperative efforts, thereby facilitating an agreement about the types of solutions, programs, or policies that are generated to rectify these social conditions. This promotion of "participation" as politically impartial space where people unify to work towards common goals, then, is particularly significant within the context of social reforms targeted at urban Indigenous youth, as it veils the historical and contemporary relations of power and regulation within the context of settler colonial nation states and disregards the important questions of how competing constructions of Indigenous voice and authority are taken up within a participatory vision. Canada only exists through an ongoing dispossession of Indigenous territory and ways of being. A new strategy for blending political interests that are inherently at odds with one another, thus, can only be implemented by eliminating points of dissension and by fostering alliance building that works to keep the colonial dimensions of power intact.

## Participation as Giving Voice? As Political Power?

The idea of "giving voice" to Indigenous peoples involved in participatory social reform via the Indigenous Alliance surfaced repeatedly in my interviews and field observations. In fact, in many of my conversations with working group members it seemed that there was a firm belief that participation in the Indigenous Alliance was going to lead to positive changes in the lives of Indigenous youth and, in turn, for the Indigenous community in the city as a whole.[19] Both members of the Indigenous community organization and the government officials working for local state agencies construed participating in the Indigenous Alliance as a deliberate choice. They often spoke unequivocally of the Indigenous Alliance as a good thing, something that was moving urban Indigenous youth development forward in a way that could create meaningful changes in young lives – once again reiterating an assumption of progress.

Based on the testimonies provided by members of the Indigenous Alliance working group, the rise of this collaborative entity corresponded directly with concerns voiced by representatives from the Indigenous community about the alienation Indigenous youth were facing in the city's public schools and other youth organizations they frequented. During one of our many discussions, Dave, a Métis man and one of the co-chairs representing the state through his position in the school division, explained the impetus for the creation of the Indigenous Alliance as follows:

JD: Do you remember what the impetus was for undertaking the
   Indigenous Alliance?
DAVE: There were various studies that were going on in the province and
   one of the recommendations that came from them was about meeting
   the needs of Aboriginal students and what a disgrace it was and I think
   our board was really sensitive … and one of the recommendations was
   that there be more community consultations and this was part of the
   board's doing that and then responding to what the community said at
   that meeting. And so, probably the strongest message that came from
   that community consultation was the lack of voice. That we get studied
   to death but who listens and what do you do with it? What do you do
   with the information that we give you? And, and … the accountability
   piece, who are you answering to? You know, they went away and that's
   when we realized that a partnership could provide that voice and if we
   [meaning the school division] were working with them [Indigenous
   peoples] in partnership, then there would be an authentic voice and an
   accountability piece because the school division was not going to blow
   off or dismiss the words of a partnership so readily and that made sense.

Dave's account of the evolution of the Indigenous Alliance is important, not only because it points out that, from his perspective, the Indigenous Alliance grants access to a form of power for Indigenous peoples and increases accountability for the state in matters concerning

Indigenous youth, but also because his comments raise the question of how the Indigenous Alliance has become the authoritative voice for representing a diverse Indigenous community in Saskatoon. In this instance, then, Dave discursively lays the groundwork for an investigation into questions of representational authority through the privileging of certain conceptions of the urban Indigenous community (a topic that forms the basis of the chapter 4).

This positioning of Indigenous participation in state entities as a form of political power was also reiterated in an interview I conducted with another member of the Indigenous Alliance, Sally, a superintendent for the school division, where she revealed her perceptions about the reasoning behind the creation of the Indigenous Alliance:

> Well and I think the reason that we moved away from our old model is because if we kept doing what we were doing we would have kept getting what we were getting and when you have community engagement forums and First Nations peoples are sharing concerns that there are issues of racism and their students walk into schools and they don't feel welcomed and they don't feel that their stories are being told and they are being honoured or even acknowledged ... so when you hear that, uhm, you have to look at a different model and I think there were things that we were doing well but I think, uhm, the decision to move to participation was quite a deliberate one because we felt, uhm, we needed to do things differently and we thought ... well the province has a commitment to partnership – they put out protocol and policy and encouragement on working in partnership and of course, working in partnership means not only that you are working with the Saskatchewan government but you are engaging the federal government and so it's very complex but I think over the years, uhm, the concerns that people have said in those meetings is just the reality today.

Expressed in these statements is the idea that, from the state's viewpoint, it was time to try something different; that the state was unsuccessful in getting the results they wanted through the methods they were currently employing, and so it was time that a new strategy be adopted. "Policies not only impose conditions, as if from outside or above," contend Shore and Wright (1997, 6), "but influence people's Indigenous norms of conduct so that they themselves contribute, not necessarily consciously, to a government's model of social order." The comments of Sally also exemplify how the initiation of this alliance was primarily state directed and the alliance itself was crafted with particular goals that were not misaligned with the interests of the settler state but rather very much in keeping with the sometimes contradictory governing policies of neoliberalism.[20] For example, recalling the documentary evidence provided earlier in this chapter, one can argue that the impetus for these inclusionary tactics was directly tied to the labour force utility of Indigenous children and youth and a recognition that the increasing number of Indigenous students in the education system was something that the state had no choice but to contend with as a matter of economic and political stability for the province. The Indigenous Alliance, then, has become an administrative technology that can be used by the Ministry of Education to regulate and direct the lives of urban Indigenous students.[21]

This notion of participation as a form of inclusionary power also poignantly surfaced when I was invited to attend a community gathering on social issues facing urban Indigenous youth. The event was hosted by another Indigenous community–based organization in Saskatoon and was co-sponsored by the Indigenous Alliance as part of their community outreach initiative. I entered the gymnasium, where the forum was being held, with Dave and a couple of other working group members. We took a seat near the front of the gym where I could more easily scan the room and determine who was present from the broader Indigenous community in the city. Since the Indigenous Alliance had partly funded the gathering, Dave was invited to say a few words at the start of the event.

Addressing a crowd of people whose day-to-day lives were largely concerned with designing and implementing social programs for urban Indigenous youth, Dave began to speak earnestly and enthusiastically about the power of participation and the ability to work together with the state in the face of great adversity. He explained:

> We need to find a way to come together in dealing with our [First Nations] kids and the high drop out and all of the other issues they have. These are our kids and there is so much that we need to do to make sure that they have the chances that other kids have. There needs to be First Nations and Métis content and perspectives in all of our classrooms and we are making that happen through the work of the Indigenous Alliance and through all of the work that the leaders and youth workers present here today are doing. We can pull from the resources that the province has to reach our students and help them learn the skills that they need to rebuild our communities.

Participants at the forum listened intently while he spoke, some jotting down notes and others looking somewhat confused about his comments. However, it became clear that the Indigenous Alliance was being represented by Dave as a new way of interacting with the state, one that had the potential to result in different outcomes for Indigenous youth than previous state attempts at reform.

Dave's articulation of the power of participation also intimated that working in concert with the state was as a form of distributive justice whereby more government resources could be channelled to urban Indigenous youth. For Fraser (2004), this channelling conjures up material recognition and redistribution of support for urban Indigenous youth that would improve their likelihood of graduating from high school and move them away from lives of destitution. On our drive back from the gathering to the offices of the local school division where Dave was stationed, I asked him how he thought Indigenous collaboration with government entities might be perceived by those members of the Indigenous community who called for a distinct separation from the state. He lamented that First Nations peoples needed to do this work from "all sides" and insisted that the government had the resources to make a change in the lives of kids and that was what mattered most to him. Dakota's comments about participating in the Indigenous Alliance also resounds with this belief; the engagement with the state heralded certain benefits for urban Indigenous youth that would otherwise be out of reach. Voicing a word of caution in this regard, however, Popkewitz (2004, 28) reminds us that "there is no state without a civil society; and there is no self-governing without the conditions of the state that produce the calculus of governing action and participation." Accordingly, what we must be careful to question is what participation means in terms of shifts in the social reality of Indigenous students and the broader political goals of Indigenous peoples in Canada more generally.

Further, the shift in relations between the governing and the governed can be construed as a way to construct a form of citizenship for the Indigenous peoples that would compete with political conceptions that emphasize a gulf between the state and Indigenous political entitlements and interests. Hence, the inclusionary strategy is offered up as a vehicle for the realization of self-governance with strings, where Indigenous peoples can envision their interactions with the state in ways that appear independent and non-partisan, while at the same time being held accountable to a particular vision of urban Indigenous youth reform. Rose (1999, 174) associates the problematics inherent in this move by saying, "Organization and other actors that were once enmeshed in the complex bureaucratic lines of force of the social state are to be set free to find their own destiny. Yet, at the same time, they are to be made responsible for that destiny, and for the destiny of society as a whole, in new ways. Politics is to be returned to society itself, but no longer in a social form: in the form of individual morality, organizational responsibility and ethical community." Adopting Rose's frame, Indigenous peoples are placed in two mutually exclusive positions: the objects of settler state worry and the consultants for their own problems. And all of this takes place, of course, by stepping into the state and speaking within a hegemonic discourse through which the terms of indigeneity are being constructed under conditions of massive political contestation.

What, then, does "giving voice" really mean within the context of settler colonial power relations? I am reminded, here, of Glen Coulthard's (2014a) recent critique of *This Is Not a Peace Pipe* by Dale Turner, a book in which Turner argues that critically undermining colonialism requires Indigenous peoples to find more effective ways of engaging the political and legal discourses of Canada – to strengthen an ethics of participation to ensure that Indigenous peoples can "shape the legal and political relationship so that it respects Indigenous worldviews" (Turner 2006, 111). This, Turner attests, evolves out of a dialogue between Indigenous peoples and the Canadian settler state. He makes his case, confident of the unavoidable fact that the rights of Indigenous peoples will, for the foreseeable future, be caught up in state mechanisms of adjudication. Given this awareness, he claims that paving a path for a decolonial future relies on Indigenous peoples' ability to engage the political and legal discourses of the state through more effective participation, aided, in part, by the development of an intellectual community of Indigenous "word warriors." The primary function of these word warriors, he explains, is "to make greater inroads into mainstream Canadian legal and political practices while generating a more vigorous intellectual community" (Turner 2006, 72).

In *Red Skin, White Masks*, Glen Coulthard (2014a) argues against this inclusionary stance, showing how Turner's emphasis on interjecting the unique perspective of Indigenous peoples and their ways of knowing into state mechanisms always carries a great risk of assimilation and dilution. In particular, he takes issue with Turner's "quasi-Foucauldian" theoretical assumption that Indigenous discourses employed by these word warriors might "pack the power" necessary to transform the legal and political discourses of the state into something more amenable to Indigenous languages of political thought" (Coulthard 2014a, 46). In the face of the legal and political power of the settler colonial state, with its longstanding and well-honed practices of facile accommodation, it stands to reason, Coulthard asserts, that Indigenous knowledges and critiques could (and will) become absorbed into mainstream, dominant renditions of societal change and progress – a process of assimilation, he asserts, that receives little attention in Turner's book.

Consequently, even though there may be Indigenous participation in the development of social programs for urban Indigenous youth that is coming from a place of indicting the state, there is a very good chance that fundamental challenges to state structures will be manipulated away.[22] Furthermore, Coulthard rightly points out how Turner's analysis elides the place of non-discursive configurations in reproducing colonial relations. On this aspect, he writes, "my concern here is that the problem with the legal and political discourses of the state is not only that they enjoy hegemonic status vis-à-vis Indigenous discourses, but that they are also backed by and hopelessly entwined with the economic, political, and military might of the state itself" (Coulthard 2014a, 47). Harkening back to the material power of the state to continue to enact forms of structural, colonial violence as evidenced in the previous chapter, Coulthard's words are a vital cautionary call to examine more deeply how local Indigenous knowledge about urban Indigenous youth's social realities are usurped by powerful state agendas and their concomitant claims to participatory empowerment, not to mention the importance of thinking through a diversity of forms of decolonial practice that exist outside of state institutions. It also calls attention to the ways Indigenous youth sociality may be misrecognized and misrepresented.

## Redemptive Talk: Casting Personhood and Saving Urban Indigenous Youth from Decay

It was dark and immensely frigid outside. I quickened my pace to get out of the cold and inside the basement space where Dakota and I were gathering with others to discuss the creation of a pilot youth-mentoring program initiated by the Indigenous Alliance. The idea had emerged after a day-long workshop in the Spring of 2005, where the working group had met with members from the Saskatoon School Division and Indigenous community members to contemplate educational support for urban Indigenous youth. Dakota and I were meeting on this cold evening with representatives from youth service agencies in Saskatoon, since he was pulling a makeshift advisory group together to help guide the direction of the program. This came about as a direct result of a goal held by the Indigenous Alliance to network with community groups across the city and ensure that issues pertaining to educational success did not fall off the radar of policy and program development geared towards Indigenous youth in the core neighbourhood.

When I was about a block away from the old church on 20th Street, which also served as a community meeting space, I saw a figure standing on the corner of the street. The young woman was huddled into herself, arms wrapped tightly around her body and a bright-coloured purple toque pulled down over her forehead. "Hey there, are you alright?" I asked. She glanced at me, nervously looking from side to side, avoiding eye contact. She was dressed inadequately for the extreme weather: jeans that barely reached her ankles, sneakers and a thin jacket that fit close to her body. "Why don't you come inside for a bit?" I asked her, "There will be food and something warm to drink." She shook her head and told me that she needed to stay outside. I reminded her of some of the youth service organizations in the city where she might be able to get some assistance and told her that if she changed her mind and would like to come in, she would be more than welcome.

When I entered the meeting space, Dakota was setting up drinks in the back of the large cavernous room, and after I set down my things, I began an informal conversation with a couple of youth service workers who had already arrived. Eager to learn about how these (white) youth workers were thinking about offering assistance to urban Indigenous youth, I asked them what they thought were the most important things for the Indigenous Alliance to consider as the collective went about its preparation for this pilot mentoring program. The following dialogue ensued:

YOUTH WORKER 1: There are so many supports services for students in the city already but we need something that will help them [Indigenous youth] see the value of going to school and staying there. Schools dis-invite students too … I am not saying that that's not the way it is … but life out there [gesturing outside] is rough and if you don't go to school it's going to stay that way.

JD: What do you mean it is rough?

YOUTH WORKER 1: Well, I mean there are gangs, drugs, there is pregnancy … you know all that stuff … and it's worse for First Nations kids.

JD: Why is it worse for them?

YOUTH WORKER 1: Because they are all in the core and it's in their families too. It's a difficult run for them.

YOUTH WORKER 2: Yeah, there are tons of risks out there and they [Indigenous youth] need to learn how to deal with those. There are different choices they can make but without school there is not much out there.

YOUTH WORKER 1: And a lot of these First Nations kids are really messed up. They are always in trouble with the cops, stealing, doing things they shouldn't be doing. Even when you give them chance after chance, they don't follow through.

YOUTH WORKER 2: I know. These kids have so many problems. It's hard to know where to start. I feel sorry for them [shaking his head].

When I was later reflecting on this exchange, it seemed ironic that, as I was about to enter into a debate about a pilot program whose primary objective it was to find ways of supporting urban Indigenous students to become "more successful," I was confronted with the stark reality of impoverishment and overdetermined choice that, more often than not, came along with being an Indigenous youth in the social spaces of urban life – images of the young woman I had just encountered on the street flickered through my mind. These comments also suggested that "survival skills" for urban Indigenous youth could be taught within the parameters of formal state education or youth programming, as if they could be packaged up and handed over through the right kind of social experiences and that the colonial stronghold mediating their lives would somehow melt away if we could only design the right program. Recollect from chapter 2 that the rhetorical device of "choice" works to obscure the structural, colonial constraints in which urban Indigenous youth live and consistently renders them individually responsible for their life trajectories.

In fact, witnessing the casting of Indigenous youth personhood through the labels of "broken," "lost," "dysfunctional," and "troubled" was a recurrent experience in my dealings with the Indigenous Alliance. This trope crystalized when I first met Dakota on the day he was being interviewed as a potential candidate for the design and implementation of the pilot mentoring program. I was seated with Donna and Dave, the two co-chairs of the working group of the Indigenous Alliance, in a small boardroom at the main offices for the Saskatoon School Division. Dakota entered the room on crutches, since he was just recovering from a knee injury. His face was gentle, his dark eyes smiling. He sat down and held out his hand to me as way of introduction. I liked him right away.

The interview began with a series of questions about Dakota's education and employment record. He adeptly answered them all, explaining that he had an undergraduate degree from the University of Saskatchewan and had been doing recreational activities, such as volleyball and a cardio regiment, with Indigenous youth at one of the local youth organizations in Saskatoon. Dakota was also a registered member of an Indigenous band in close proximity to Saskatoon and spent a considerable amount of time moving back and forth between the reserve and the city.

About half way through the interview, Donna, a Cree woman in her mid-fifties who had spent the majority of her life working for the provincial education system, started speaking about how important it was for Dakota to find a way to help Indigenous youth. "Our youth are in trouble," she lamented. "They have lost their way. They don't know how to cope with life in the city, they don't have any of the skills they need. All of the studies keep telling us this. They are making bad choices, in trouble with the law, eh. Education has to be key to everything we do. We need services that will prevent them from ending up on the street." Dave was nodding his head in agreement and contributed, "We want them to celebrate their culture but they also have to take responsibility for their lives. Many of them aren't even taking advantage of the opportunities that are being offered. We're not blaming them, but dysfunctional behaviour isn't helping any of us." When Dave started explaining that one of the key features of the mentoring program would be developing strong relationships with Indigenous youth, Donna added, "And we can't help all of them. Some of them are just too far gone, so you have to figure out who you are going to focus on developing relationships with."

Dakota seemed nervous during this aspect of the interview, slightly shifting in his chair and periodically glancing over in my direction as if looking for a lifeline. "They aren't bad kids," he simply said. "They just need some direction." The interview carried on for another thirty minutes or so, and during this time, Donna and Dave continued to reinforce the notion that Indigenous youth had the ability to carve out a better life for themselves, to live in a "good way," if they could only break away from being poor decision makers and engaging in deviant behaviour that was getting them nowhere.

After the interview ended, Dakota and I lingered behind and chatted for a while longer. He told me that he didn't think either Dave or Donna knew what "these kids" [Indigenous youth] were really up against. When I asked him to say more about this, he remarked, "They are stuck in so many of these systems – there are police everywhere, they usually aren't living with their families. There is almost no way out. And this city, it's so racist. Can't you feel it? Even I used to drink all the time to get away from it. But then I stopped because that shit is poison."

In a sense, Dakota's rejection of Dave and Donna's comment can be understood as an interruption of the story they were trying to tell about Indigenous youth in Saskatoon, a story that has multifaceted and intimate connections with broader settler colonial narratives indexing the depravity of Indigenous lives in Canada. Dave and Donna's representations of urban Indigenous youth sociality in Saskatoon also reflect the paucity of critical analysis in white settler society about Indigenous youth in general and augment a settler colonial chronicling of their lives that functions to characterize the personhood of these young people as inherently broken, in need of fixing and rehabilitation. As evidenced in their interviewing of Dakota, they viewed the work of the Indigenous Alliance, and their participation in it, as an avenue to cultivate social interventions that held the potential to eradicate these pathologies – strategies rooted in a rescuing rationality set on expunging a kind of "troubledness" that had (magically) found a home in Indigenous youth bodies. Only a "curing" of this social dysfunction, they believed, could lead to the rightful bestowal of settler citizenship.

This depiction of Indigenous youth, however, also accomplishes something else: it legitimizes the need for the state to step in and save the day. In other words, the consistent reinforcement of Indigenous youth as pathologically lost and unable to cope with the "legacy" of their colonial heritage only serves to legitimate the redemptive rationales of the state. The answer to the urban Indigenous youth crisis, then, is found in more state intervention, although this kind of intervention comes with a participatory stamp that signals Indigenous community agreement with state measures of social control. In these portrayals of urban Indigenous youth experience, it is not the state that comes under scrutiny or indictment, but the social behaviours and actions of the Indigenous young person whose body bears the physical and psychological inscription of settler rule. Intrusive colonial state intervention becomes justifiable, even morally defensible, when Indigenous youth are consistently portrayed as deviant, criminal, suffering from FASD (fetal alcohol spectrum disorder), neglected, and weak.

Critical scholars of education (Lipman 2003; Delpit 2006; Ladson-Billings 2007) have also outlined how these notions of intrinsic pathology translate directly into educational experience – an argument worth noting, given Donna's emphasis on education as the answer to avoiding life on the street. Surfacing in the 1950s and 1960s, cultural deficit theories in education suggested that children and youth of colour, or racialized youth, were "victims of pathological lifestyles that hindered their ability to benefit from schooling" (Ladson-Billings 2007, 4). These theories reinforced the idea that the "failure" of youth of colour was rightfully attributed to the families and communities of which they were a part, bolstering the belief that parents just didn't care, that these children and youth had limited life experiences or exposure to learning opportunities, and that children and youth of colour and their families simply didn't value education. Writing in opposition to these theories of paradigms of failure, however, Ladson-Billings (2007, 7) reminds us that the problem of "educational failure" associated with low-income children and children of colour, including Indigenous children and youth, is the result of centuries of neglect and structural violence, coupled with a systematic denial of educational opportunities that are positively grounded in and directed by communities themselves. Following in step, Pauline Lipman (2003), in her research on the Chicago school district, redirects the critique of the educational failure of students of colour towards an analysis of how accountability intersects with questions of race, class, and power. More specifically, she examines how school policies steeped in the ideology of deficit theories parallel the containment and policing of youth of colour in their neighbourhoods and produce "failure" through the militarization of educative spaces and discriminatory disciplinary policies (Lipman 2003, 94).

At this point it is useful to turn the work of Tania Li and her investigation of "improvement schemes" within the larger milieu of international development. The analytic insights yielded by her detailed inquisition into the diagnostic components of state programming have significant purchase within the context of state social interventions for Indigenous urban youth. In particular, in *The Will to Improve*, Li maps how the process of social programming involves the focused and deliberate work of two elements. The first is problematizing, a social practice that involves identifying deficiencies that need to be rectified (Li 2007, 7). In the case of the Indigenous Alliance, working group members relied on a vast array of social science (primarily psychology) and governmental "research" that downplayed the role of state institutions and the broader context of colonialism in creating marginality in the lives of urban Indigenous youth. Of significance here is that the calculation of state intervention is not the product of a singular intention or will. Rather, Donna and Dave's modes of perception about urban Indigenous youth were situated within an administrative apparatus and field of documentation that works to congeal urban Indigenous youth into problems that need to be solved. This intervention creates a bureaucratic intelligentsia through government commissions, reports, academic research, and vocabularies of risk and deficit that foreshadow new state interventions to ostensibly improve their lives. It is based on a broad circulation of discourses generated by state agents, researchers, the media, and Indigenous peoples themselves that work to socially construct "the problem" as one within the bodies, minds, and spirits of Indigenous youth themselves. Even the UAYS finds its justification in the notion that urban Indigenous youth "needs" (educational, recreational, etc.) are precisely what the state has failed to properly identify and address with programs, a foundational premise that belies the social and political histories of this generation.

Once the process of problematizing is complete, social programming can proceed to the next step, which Li (2007, 8) identifies as rendering technical – a process that actively produces an intelligible arena for intervention and anticipates the form of intervention that will take place. The process assumes that the social problem identified through problematization can be solved through calculated means (such as a mentoring program) and the scope of intervention becomes directly aligned with the parameters of the problem. Part of what the rendering of these stories of dysfunction and failure about urban Indigenous youth does, then, is to translate the ongoing messiness and injury caused by settler colonialism into linear narratives of problem solving and solution building – and when the colonial state is in charge of setting the terms of these narratives, the outcomes are self-evident. What we learn from all of this is that claims to sympathy and understanding of "the needs" of urban Indigenous youth can entail gross misrecognition and also offer deeply problematic solutions that reinforce a form of domestic humanitarianism that elevates the goodwill of the settler state while downplaying colonial relations of domination.

When I consider some of Donna and Dave's comments, with reference to the interview with Dakota, I also recall Li's (2007, 5) remark that "when power operates at a distance, people are not necessarily aware of how their conduct is being conduced or why." Neither Donna nor Dave were ill willed in their desire to "help" urban Indigenous youth, however misguided their efforts may seem. Their desire to improve the lives of urban Indigenous youth through what may be perceived as "the white man's way" is situated within the field of power that Michel Foucault called "government" and an attempt by the government to shape human conduct by calculated and measured means. Donna, for example, had a sensibility about the world that was cultivated through her life growing up on a reserve. Members of her family were survivors of residential schools, and she herself had come face to face with racist provocation in Saskatoon numerous times. Her desires for Indigenous youth to become fully functioning members of the settler state were not born out of malice against them. Rather, they were born out of a genuine belief that this was the only way to survive. Indigenous peoples working in collaboration with state agencies, or within them, are also framed and produced through the power and the multiple discursive fields of settler colonialism, and their subjectivities are reflective, at least partly, of the internalization of settler state ideals and notions of social change.

As individuals who work closely or within state structures, both Dave and Donna have effectively adopted the hegemonic frames of analysis and modes of operation that are characteristic of colonial state institutions. Neither of them ever described their work with the Indigenous Alliance as an avenue to advance a political resistance campaign.[23] The promises they were offering to urban Indigenous youth, in fact, do not even hint at the larger political reality in which these young people live – a social existence mediated by the material reality of vigilant settler colonial policing, state apprehension through child welfare systems, a colonial education system, and a palpable and racist hostility towards them on the city streets. For them, the issues facing urban Indigenous youth were primarily ones of material disadvantage that could be rectified if Indigenous youth simply had access to the right programs and tried harder. But as I have demonstrated throughout this book thus far, the question of material disadvantage only scrapes the surface of what's at play: the existence of these youth is a reminder to the settler state of Canada of an ongoing need to disavow Indigenous alterity, to actively curtail the potential for political resistance that in the very near term will largely rest in the hands of Indigenous youth. How, then, can Indigenous youth be what they want to be when that very being is structured by dispossession? It seems to me that this goal recalls Laura Berlant's (2011) "cruel optimism," a dream that has very little chance of finding solid ground when the terms of the game continue to be set by the colonial state itself.

* * *

I have argued, in this chapter, that inclusionary formulations such as the Indigenous Alliance can be read as attempts by the settler state to recast colonial goals through the discourse and practice of participation. The Canadian settler state is able to fashion itself as a "transformed" and more responsive governing entity by advocating collaboration with Indigenous communities, precisely when its ability to assert sovereign control over Indigenous affairs and to deliver on the promise of social change and equality is compromised. By taking on the "unstately" task of working in partnership and purposefully seeking the inclusion of an Indigenous voice, the state conceals its colonial aspirations and is able to send the message that this is not governing as usual. Instead of being tied to its historical precedent of top-down social program development, the state's commitment to urban Indigenous youth is expressed through the ability of marginalized Indigenous subjects to take back responsibility for themselves and their communities. Thus, participation becomes a vehicle for "self-governance" through which urban Indigenous peoples can envision their participation in ways that appear independent and non-partisan, while at the same time embodying accountability to particular visions of colonial statecraft. The shift to discourses of collaboration, then, paves the way for settler colonialism to be instantiated as a more responsive form of governance, as a superior kind of governing actor that learns and bends with Indigenous input.

The question remains, however, how does the Indigenous Alliance come to represent the broader urban Indigenous community? What sorts of challenges, contradictions, and tensions are raised? What types of programs are undertaken in the name of shared responsibility between the state and Indigenous peoples with respect to urban Indigenous youth? What types of experiences recede and what comes into view?

## Chapter Four

# Policing the Boundaries and Debates over What's "Real"

Another friend tells you you have to learn not to absorb the world. She says sometimes she can hear her own voice saying silently to whomever – you are saying this thing and I am not going to accept it. Your friend refuses to carry what doesn't belong to her.

– Claudia Rankine, *Citizen: An American Lyric*

As a society, Canadians and their governments continue to fail these vulnerable children. Despite spending millions of dollars each year, we see marginal, if any, impact on outcomes.

– Canadian Council of Provincial Child and Youth Advocates, *Aboriginal Children and Youth in Canada: Canada Must Do Better*

Nitânis and I were having lunch at a small diner in the Westside, having just finished a meeting about sexual exploitation in Saskatoon.[1] We had been doing advocacy around the importance of developing a non-profit organization that would be directly informed by the experiences of urban Indigenous girls, a focus that was noticeably lacking in all of the youth organizations in the city. Nitânis had committed herself to being part of this initiative, since she herself had had numerous encounters with sexual violence. She wanted to lend her experiential insight into social programs that were designed to "help" urban Indigenous youth, and she was principally attentive to the ways that youth organizations had muted the stories of Indigenous girls. As we sat back against the slippery vinyl cushions of our booth, coffees sitting on the formica table in front of us, she recounted her own past and moaned about how she felt as though there was nothing available for her in terms of advocacy or support. Thinking about her comments several years later, I found resonance with Claudia Rankine's (2014, 63) piercing words, "The world is wrong. You can't put the past behind you. It's buried in you; it's turned your flesh into its own cupboard. Not everything remembered is useful but it all comes from the world to be stored in you."

Nitânis went on to explain, "There was no programming for us, nothing at all. There weren't fifty people sitting at a round table, whatever those do, trying to figure out how to help me or help my friends. We were just out there on our own. There was nothing at all until that talking group for girls who had been sexually exploited started. That was the first thing in the city that was for girls and it wasn't in an Aboriginal organization either." When I asked Nitânis if she or any other Indigenous youth she knew had ever been asked to take part in the initiatives of the Indigenous Peoples Collective, including the Indigenous Alliance, she shook her head and answered back with, "I don't even understand what they do. I mean, who are they supporting? It's not girls like me."

Nitânis's questioning of the substantive mission of the Indigenous Peoples Collective in terms of addressing a diverse and heterogeneous range of urban Indigenous youth experience aligned with my own observations within the first few months of conducting fieldwork on the Indigenous Alliance. Early on, two things repeatedly struck me. First, I was surprised that there was no obvious representation from the Indigenous feminists in the city (activists and/or scholars), since they were the ones who were, primarily, taking up the issues of poverty, violence, homelessness, and criminalization facing Indigenous women and children. Second, there seemed to be no direct questioning of who or what comprised the urban Indigenous community in the city – the composition appeared a taken-for-granted assumption, determined a priori. Indeed, this registered as especially problematic, given the persistent claim that the Indigenous Alliance was centred on promoting a more inclusive and open form of settler governance that would "empower" Indigenous peoples and draw on their local knowledge. Yet, the more time I spent understanding its social and political work, the more it surfaced that the construction and deployment of "the urban Indigenous community" was, in fact, central to the mandate and implementation of the Indigenous Alliance.[2] Consequently, my interest in the field, for some time, became one of extending my investigation of the relationship between the colonial settler state and Indigenous peoples to an analytical inspection of the "urban Indigenous community" that was vital to this new technology of governing. Without an urban Indigenous community with which the state could align itself, a politics of recognition activated through participation would simply not fly.

In *Powers of Freedom: Reframing Political Thought*, Nikolas Rose (1999, 168) undertakes a deconstruction of "community" as a third space[3] of governing, which appears as a natural, extra-political zone of human relations and, simultaneously, as an object and target for the exercise of political power, a counterweight to it. He writes, "Whilst the term community has long been salient in political thought, it becomes governmental when it is made technical" (Rose 1999, 175). Departing from the dominant interpretations found in the embrace of a social politics where "community" is considered in opposition to state bureaucracy, Rose argues that the state and civil society are, in fact, sometimes collapsed through the institution of community and that community must be considered an entity saturated with effective power. Positioning it as an invented third space whose vectors and forces can be mobilized, enrolled, and deployed in novel programs and governing techniques, Rose (1999, 176) terms it "government through community."

Borrowing from Rose's analytic framework, I assert that fostering the creation of participatory alliances between the settler colonial state and Indigenous peoples as a way to recognize Indigenous demands for greater control over the social programs that impact urban Indigenous youth raises the question of whether the "urban Indigenous community" itself may become constituted as a trajectory of state authority, through the policing of the terms of these collaborative ventures and concealed control over the knowledge that informs them. The participatory alliances, then, could also be read as a way for the state to reinvent itself through the auspices of Indigenous community organizing. With respect to analysing the inner workings of community, Rose (1999, 189) offers, "Boundaries and distinctions have to be emplaced; these spaces have to be visualized, mapped, surveyed, and mobilized." Rose's critical appraisal also pushes us to think critically about how a socially constructed consensus on matters pertaining to urban Indigenous youth is necessarily achieved through the fracturing of Indigenous political subjectivity in Saskatoon – some perspectives on Indigenous–state relations gain critical currency while others are strategically screened out.[4] To maintain its sanctity as a settler state while being actively challenged about the legal terrain of its sovereignty, Canada must disguise its colonial goals through subversive means. Following Rose (1999, 177), "community," thus, postures social relations that appear non-artificial and direct, in matrices of affinity that appear more natural.

The first goal of this chapter is a descriptive one: to submit a portrait of how the creation of the Indigenous Alliance works to construct the parameters of an urban Indigenous community that is both able and willing to participate with the state in urban Indigenous youth social reform. The drawing of this portrait includes an exploration of how this seemingly bounded entity is developed through a precise process of working group member selection, the fostering of social cohesion through relationship building, and the facilitation of community meetings to invent consensus, and a discussion of the way the Indigenous Alliance activates itself as an authoritative voice in the city on social issues pertaining to urban Indigenous youth. The second purpose of this chapter is to reveal how political resistance to the structure and programmatic content of the Indigenous Alliance – a refusal to accept the singularity of urban Indigenous youth experience and its depoliticization of Indigenous–state relations – becomes tactically contained by members of the working group. Simultaneously, I foreground how the Indigenous Alliance excludes narratives of colonial gender violence that explicitly challenge the projection of a benevolent settler state.

## Manufacturing an Urban Indigenous Community through Participation

The evolution of the Indigenous Alliance can be traced back to prior to the official signing of the MOU.[5] However, gathering historical evidence about its precursors was difficult, since many of the key players associated with its creation no longer lived in Saskatoon and were impossible to track down. Yet, based on the accounts I was able to collect through a few brief descriptive documents and my interviews with members from the working group, I learned that the initial seeds were planted after a series of community consultations. A local state agency, the Saskatoon Public School Division, conducted the consultation in order to determine "what was happening" with Indigenous youth in the city, in terms of social issues and barriers to completing high school. Dave explained to me that the biggest issue raised in the community consultations was the lack of a voice for Indigenous peoples in terms of the planning and development of social initiatives for urban Indigenous children and youth. As a result, members from the local school division who were designated as part of the agency's departmental unit addressing matters pertaining to Indigenous youth were asked to assemble a group of experienced and interested representatives from the city. This initial group would then become part of a collective tasked with crafting an alliance between the local school division and what came to be understood as the "urban Indigenous community" that could speak on behalf of the wider urban Indigenous populace.

An important point to clarify in relation to the construction of the Indigenous Alliance, however, is that, while the formal agreement was between the Saskatoon School Division and the Indigenous Peoples Collective, the Indigenous Peoples Collective was not the sole source of representational authority. Representation occurred through a more collective process, which involved a series of community meetings in the Westside of the city, where a compilation of "key issues" that urban Indigenous youth face were debated by a broader cross section of Indigenous people and I speak to these meetings in the sections that follow. The Indigenous Peoples Collective became a place for this alliance to be housed organizationally, since some type of entity needed to be involved in the signing of the memorandum of understanding between the state and the "community." The Indigenous Peoples Collective was chosen because it represents a selection of member First Nations in the area and consequently was said to have a broad and deep understanding of the issues facing Indigenous children and youth, both on reserve and in the city. What I am interested in exploring in the next section is how the composition of the working group itself, along with the process of establishing a sense of cohesion among members, coupled with the garnering of a consensus around issues pertaining to urban Indigenous youth social reform, become part and parcel of Rose's government through community.

## Working Group Fabrication

The working group for the Indigenous Alliance was, in essence, the lifeblood of this participatory initiative. The individuals who comprised the working group were on-the-ground foot soldiers and represented the working "face'" of the Indigenous Alliance to the city as a whole. While each of the individuals participating in the working group possessed her or his own unique role, my purpose here is to chart generalized characteristics that all participants embodied to some degree or another and the way these characteristic enlisted certain types of behaviours or ways of interacting with the idea of altering the social reality of urban Indigenous youth. I also want to be clear that the status of the working group members as non-Indigenous or Indigenous is not the primary factor through which I came to understand their relationship with the Indigenous Alliance. Instead, it was their commitment to the notion that it was possible to make changes in the lives of urban Indigenous youth through models of social and educational reform centred on a distinct union between Indigenous peoples and the state that I was interested in understanding.

As a case in point, all working group members demonstrated a belief in the transformational power of joining forces with the state in order to alter the contours of educational and social programs for Indigenous children and youth in Saskatoon. As I outlined in the previous chapter, where I mapped the vernacular representation of participation as an avenue for accessing political power, working group members believed that the Indigenous Alliance would ultimately work towards creating more just and equitable conditions in all educational institutions, with the likelihood of spin-off in other social institutions as well. In other words, there was agreement that coalitions between the urban Indigenous community and the state were a way to actualize a politics of recognition that made good on state promises. Working group participant Dave clearly stated this belief when he said:

I think they [the school division] recognized that we needed to go in a new direction and they recognized the reality for First Nations, Inuit, and Métis youth in our school division and it wasn't pretty. They recognized that this was sort of public knowledge and what they were doing wasn't working, we are going to fix you and this is what we are going to do. And so one of the administrators, in what I think was my first meeting with him, he used the word "abysmal." How we have treated Aboriginal youth in our school division is abysmal and that has got to stop. It has got to change. And that was my mandate, whatever it takes to bring about a change, that is what we are going to do. And he [referring to a superior in the provincial education system] told me straight out, in our meeting, I want to know if somebody gets in your way and if somebody is throwing up barriers; I want to know it because it is just not going to happen anymore, we've got to stop that mentality. And so he was adamant. I walked out of that meeting empowered. Up until that point, I knew what I wanted and I knew what the literature was saying, but I didn't know what the Saskatoon School Division was saying about just how far I could go. And after that meeting I knew, there was some freedom. I wasn't shackled.

What this signalled, in effect, was that working group members' theories of social change resided within the protective arms of the state itself and were augmented by a belief that the state was ultimately working in the best interests of Indigenous youth. Such a stance, I would argue, is easily accepted when the social problem is located within the bodies of Indigenous youth.

Next, the working group members, with the exception of two, had been deeply involved with the provincial public education system in Saskatoon for some time and were consequently older in age and occupied a particular generational status. Through their social positionality as older members of the community, they were also considered, to some extent, leaders. Even though many of the working group members were critical of the lack of "cultural responsiveness" in the Saskatoon public schools and youth organizations that were serving Indigenous youth, they nonetheless were tied to the idea that the social realities of urban Indigenous youth could be improved, a view that reflected their professional commitment to an overarching belief that state institutions could be fundamentally transformed. An extremely active member of the partnership, Sally, who was also a superintendent, explained her history with public education:

> I am completing my 27th year. I have a BA, BEd, MEd, and my career path was that of elementary teacher, and then I got into school-based leadership as vice-principal and then a principal and I have been in this position for over three years. The opportunity to work in the First Nations, Métis, and Inuit areas is quite new to me although I have always been a supporter of championing for diversity; I feel very strongly about that, and over the years personally I have learned some more about that and I just believe it is part of our goal – to make sure all of our students experience a well-rounded education and that includes understanding treaties and understanding from where they come in Saskatchewan.

Another member, Donna, commented:

> And so I have seen a real development happening through the years and I have always been involved in some aspect of education for the last thirty-two years. I have been a teacher educator, I have been a high school teacher, I have been a principal, a vice-principal, superintendent, and now a director. I had the opportunity to work for my own reserve for fifteen years and I also had an opportunity to work in the Saskatoon Public Schools back in the eighties.

The above declarations suggest that working group member's "inside" knowledge of how state systems work might benefit them in developing a critical understanding, to some degree, but it also means that they are drawing on the lexical tools and hegemonic discourses of the settler state, which are central to social institutions like the education and criminal justice systems. Participatory entities like the Indigenous Alliance, then, are predicated on the assumption that the integration of "local Indigenous knowledge" will significantly alter the social polices of state institutions that are fundamental to the ongoing dispossession of Indigenous peoples from their territories.[6] Furthermore, the notion of "integrating" Indigenous knowledge does not challenge how those who are in a position to craft the parameters of what counts as valid knowledge or construct the presentation of local knowledge may mediate the representation of urban Indigenous experience and inadvertently modify larger political goals. In other words, because these alliances came into being under the framework of recognition politics, their priorities were undoubtedly influenced by the wider institutional mandates and protocols of settler social institutions that are actively engaged in curtailing Indigenous resistance. Was it any wonder that the working group, the very entity that was carrying out the activities of this state–Indigenous coalition, was composed of people who believed in the power of the colonial state to shift the social realities of Indigenous youth from within?

Speaking at length with Dave over the course of almost two years, I also learned how the professional status of "teacher" had the potential to trump his positioning as a self-identified Indigenous person. Dave describes his identity as a teacher for colonial state institutions first and foremost, in the following 2006 interview excerpt, where he explains to me how he came to view his role as an educator in Saskatoon, after being away from the country for a number of years:

So I have moved around the city and one of things that I wanted when I came back from England ... England for me was an epiphany because of how I saw myself when I went to England. I saw myself as an Aboriginal teacher. When I got there, nobody cared that I was Aboriginal; it meant nothing to them and so it was like those stereotypes and everything just dropped off me, and I realized I was a teacher who happened to be Aboriginal and in this context it didn't make a difference – all that they cared about was that I was professional, that I cared about what I was doing, and that I did it well. That is all that mattered, and that I did it well didn't just impress them, it impressed me – that I rose to the challenge and presented myself in a very professional manner where they bought into that, and I thought why do I think that I can only teach in the inner city? Why do I see myself that way? I have to see myself as a professional who is Aboriginal and so, when I came back they placed me at Fairhaven, which is a perimeter school and I thought that is fine, and I told my Superintendent that when I am done here, I want to go to the Eastside – my biggest fear, I wanted to now deal with that. I wanted to get over there and I wanted them to see that I was a teacher first and the perk was that I was Aboriginal and that I was going to bring a different perspective. But I wanted them to see that I was a teacher first and that everything I did was professional and appropriate and it was for them, it was for everybody.

This juxtaposition of a "professional status" with the idea of an "authentic Indigenous community organizer" also became apparent to me when I had a meeting with an Indigenous scholar, Tammy, working at the University of Saskatchewan. I had encountered Tammy at several local events in Saskatoon where local activists were raising awareness about murdered and missing Indigenous women and girls and calling attention to critiques of colonial child welfare practices. I had lunch with her one day to talk about her involvement with the Indigenous Alliance. She explained her rationale for not being more active with their work by saying, "They are not very critical over there. I don't think they are operating with a critical perspective and that bothers me, so I don't really get involved in it."

A Cree youth worker, Chuck, had voiced a similar concern to me about how some local Indigenous leaders that were active in the Indigenous Alliance were from an older generation and had "bought into the state system." "They are scared." he said. "All they want to do is to find a way to work in the system so they can have job security. They are not going to go against it. We need the younger generation to take over. They are the ones with all of the new ideas." Both Tammy's and Chuck's comments, then, intimate a perception of the Indigenous Alliance as espousing a more conciliatory approach towards Indigenous–state relations and downplaying the persistent facets of settler colonialism that are ever present in everyday life for the majority of the urban Indigenous youth they were purportedly supporting.

Representational authority in the working group was also enhanced through an emphasis on relationship building and on establishing personal connections between people who were "working together." This relational character was repeatedly reiterated by working group members, who argued that one of the reasons that this alliance was able to bridge the historical divide between non-Indigenous and Indigenous peoples in Saskatoon around urban Indigenous youth social reform was because they had cultivated trusting and lasting associations with one another through a range of experiences. In her account of the historical development of the Indigenous Alliance, one of the working group members, Karen, talked at length about personal investment and the affective dimensions of participation:

> There was a lot of investment and I really give credit to the people that came before. And you know, when you talk about the work that was done by people over the years, I mean awhile back, you know how people have all worked towards this day and had courageous conversations – people often working in isolation just to bring this willingness to look at what we were doing well, but also to look at what we needed to do better. So I would really like to give credit to the people that did all that foundational work and did it in such a respectful way that when the needs from this group came forward we were able to say that we can't do this alone, we can't do this well – how could we better meet the needs of Aboriginal youth? Well, our belief was that we could do it through partnership and it made sense to come together in relationship for a common purpose and that was what happened.

Josh, a high school principal also on the working group, commented:

> And if it wasn't there, this alliance, there would still be good things happening but they would be happening a lot slower and you wouldn't see the same kinds of resources and the trust factor in terms of the relationship. Even though it is a little uneven right now in terms of the power, I would like to believe from listening and watching that there is a trust because there are personal relationships.

Those carrying out the day-to-day work of the Indigenous Alliance, then, were not simply aligned with it through facile participation; they developed a more intimate connection to advancing its agenda because they had personally bought into the agenda. This was achieved through relational tactics such as beginning every meeting or event of the Indigenous Alliance with food and informal talk (we usually devoted about thirty minutes at the start of every meeting), organizing group dinners at working group members' homes, and creating space for working group members to collectively take part in Indigenous ceremonies and cultural practices, such as sweats, feasts and giveaways, and round dances. These social engagements were often led by members of the Indigenous Peoples Collective, offered up as a mechanism to promote the "cultural understanding" of non-Indigenous state agents who were active members in this alliance.

While one might argue that this connection is desirable for carrying out the programmatic work of the Indigenous Alliance, I would contend that it creates a link between the state and the members of the urban Indigenous community in a way that moves beyond professional association and into the realm of affective relations. There, it opens the doorway to the possibility of further appropriation – an appropriation set against traumatic histories of genocide and colonization in which settlers have sought to seize control of every aspect of Indigenous life and absolve themselves of their own complicity in the continued dispossession of both Indigenous territory and existence (Barker et al. 2015). The building of a cohesive and blended state–Indigenous unit designed to shape the future of urban Indigenous youth, then, seems unquestionably dangerous when we recall this history. As Rose (1999) reminds us, the community of the third space is not primarily a geographic space, a social space, a sociological space, or a space of services, although it may attach itself to any or all such spatializations. It is a "moral field binding persons into durable relations. It is a space of *emotional relationships* through which *individual identities* are constructed through their bonds to *micro-cultures* of values and meanings ... And it is through the political objectification and instrumentalization of *this* community and its 'culture' that government is to be re-invented" (Rose 1999, 172–73; emphasis in the original).

## Community Meetings and the Politics of Who Speaks

The Saskatoon School Division took the lead on organizing the series of community meetings that were conducted to determine the most crucial issues facing urban Indigenous youth. To organize the meetings, it relied on support from a few, selected Indigenous representatives living in the city, including Dave, who was working for the public school division at the time. These representatives were asked to facilitate three meetings to generate a sense of what the focus and direction of the Indigenous Alliance would entail. The present-day strategic areas of intervention outlined by the Indigenous Alliance were said to be reflective of the issues raised at these meetings, and the foci emerged around the following areas: curriculum development, anti-racism education, workforce recruitment and professional development, and improving learning outcomes for students broadly speaking (including a pilot mentoring program). In essence, gathering information about key issues through a series of meetings made the urban Indigenous community in the city real for the purposes of constructing the Indigenous Alliance. "Over the second half of the twentieth century," Rose (1999, 189) reveals, "a whole array of little devices and technologies have been invented to make communities real. Surveys of attitudes and values, market research, opinion polls, focus groups, citizens' juries and much more have mapped out these new spaces of culture, brought these values and virtues into visibility and injected them into deliberations and authorities." The province vis-à-vis the school division was now able to have a concrete referent with which claims about values and virtues in education and social programming for the "urban Indigenous community" in the city could be made. "For to govern communities, it seems one must first link oneself up with those who have, or claim, moral authority ... in the 'local community'" (Rose 1999, 189).

Curiously, when I asked several members of the Indigenous Alliance if there was any official record of these events, which happened a number of years prior to the beginning of my fieldwork, no one was able to produce a written record, apart from a brief planning template and a succinct bullet point summary of the responses that were gathered. According to the brief planning template that I was given, Indigenous representatives were asked a series of questions regarding "gaps in services" – identifying community and government agencies who would be in a "good position" to take the lead on key initiatives and determining the resources that would be required to "fill these gaps." Obviously, the framing of the questions in these terms leads the conversation down a particular path – the discussion did not begin with a critical investigation of Canada's treatment of Indigenous people but reinstated the "problem" of urban Indigenous youth as one of failed service delivery.

When I inquired about who was present at these meetings, I was told that the turnout at the meetings had been low, although a substantial effort had been made to find ways to get people to come out and talk about the challenges facing urban Indigenous children and youth in terms of educational and social experience. One afternoon, I had returned to the school division office after attending a city-wide meeting about the initiatives of Saskatoon's Urban Aboriginal Strategy. I ran into Sally shortly after my arrival back and relayed to her a brief synopsis of the meeting, which included a description of some dissent among those in attendance about how not all community organizations in the city had an equal say in designing Indigenous youth programming. Seizing the opportunity to discuss this aspect of my fieldwork, I pushed Sally to explain how the "Indigenous community" in Saskatoon had been represented in the early days of developing the Indigenous Alliance. Sally reported, "There were a couple of teachers, some parents, but mostly just a few of us who were interested in finding ways to support Aboriginal students in local schools. The community piece is definitely something I think we need to work on." Another partnership member, Todd, explained that it was his personal experience and knowledge that identified him as valuable resource for the alliance. He told me, "I was somebody who was, I think, in some ways was identified by the central office people as someone who had a knowledge base in history and someone who has taught native studies and history and therefore had a historical context to work from and has also done some reading and research around cross cultural education." Dave mentioned to me as well that, while they did not have as great of a turnout at the meetings as they would have liked, they did use the information that was gathered respectfully to create the basis for the program development and initiatives, which I could now witness, within the purview of the Indigenous Alliance's mandate. Situated as an expert entity, the Indigenous Alliance was now in a position to advise the public school system and Indigenous peoples in Saskatoon about matters pertaining to the educational and social realities of urban Indigenous youth.

Hence, I would argue that the initial "community consultations" enabled the Indigenous Alliance to claim authority in speaking on behalf of urban Indigenous peoples in Saskatoon. While some of the members who sat on the working group self-identified as Indigenous, it was not their authority alone that became the basis for program development. Rather, it was the series of community meetings where the "authentic" Indigenous voice conveying local knowledge was able to provide the experiential directive. The point here is not whether these foci were good or bad choices, but rather that they have come to signify the material presence of urban Indigenous experience in education and other social institutions, and consequently, license the local leadership on social reform. "These experts are now on hand to advise on how communities and citizens might be governed in terms of their values, and how their values shape the ways they govern themselves," asserts Nikolas Rose, "as community becomes a valorized political zone, a new political status has been given to the 'Indigenous' authorities of community" (Rose 1999, 189). Given the composition of the working group, which includes only a few select members from "the community" (meaning Indigenous peoples living in the Westside who self-identify as Indigenous), I had to wonder about how the social interventions set forth by the Indigenous Alliance would shift the social and political realities for urban Indigenous youth. Members of the alliance, then, also became subjects of the state, as the ideas that were raised in the series of community meetings took on increased purpose and authority and grew into the authoritative knowledge base from which decisions about program development were made. "The disciplinary forms of [the] power of the state, then, are constantly engaged in a perpetuated reproduction of the state, its institutions, its hierarchies, its own languages and forms of identities produced and sanctioned by its procedures" (Hansen and Stepputat 2001, 6). The specific task of government through community becomes particularly clear in the following section, where one is readily able to witness how the Indigenous Alliance becomes an apparatus by which state authority can be vetted through multiple channels of Indigenous youth development that actively exclude stories concerning colonial gender violence.

### Policing the Boundaries and Refusals to Toe the Line

The remainder of this chapter is dedicated to the increasingly precarious nature of Indigenous social inclusion apparent in the discourses and practices of participation. I rely on ethnographic vignettes from my fieldwork to demonstrate how the urban Indigenous community in Saskatoon was not, in fact, a unified and bounded entity with which the state could uniformly "partner" to design social interventions for Indigenous youth.

### *Invoking Indigenous Authority and Quelling Dissent*

Just as important as the way a series of three community meetings, held during the early stages of the development of the Indigenous Alliance, became the social and historical knowledge base upon which this inclusionary entity drew to make decisions about its work, these meetings were also instrumental in garnering a commanding status for the alliance in the field of Indigenous youth development in Saskatoon more broadly. The Indigenous Alliance become a way for the state to infiltrate other aspects of Indigenous youth social policy and program development, as a result of its ability to enter these city-wide spaces as a reliable "Indigenous voice."

During my fieldwork, I was asked by the Indigenous Alliance to co-facilitate a strategic planning meeting for the development of programs for the urban Indigenous youth who frequented CHARM, a non-profit offering life skills development and trades opportunities to street youth. I was to facilitate the meeting with the assistance of a young Cree woman, who moved across a number of youth service organizations in the city to represent the experiences of Indigenous youth. The programs at CHARM were not direct initiatives of the Indigenous Alliance, but the alliance had become involved in the work of this organization as a result of its recognized authority in the city on issues pertaining to Indigenous youth education and social programming. Thus, representatives from the Indigenous Alliance attended this type of planning meeting in order to maintain the importance of education within the broader scope of youth programming and to ensure that the urban Indigenous community would be represented adequately. The planning meetings also provided a larger context for understanding how youth service organizations were constructing the needs and experiences of Indigenous youth in Saskatoon, and how this fit with the "needs" and "service" emphasis that was central to many aspects of the Indigenous Peoples Collective, of which the Indigenous Alliance was a part. This larger milieu, then, forms part of the backdrop against which the Indigenous Alliance grows and executes its plans and strategies and attempts to suture together broader purposes and goals among youth initiatives in the city. Many of the youth who will participate in programs of the Indigenous Alliance are the same youth who will be entering CHARM to access the services they have as well.

CHARM, itself, stood at the corner of a lettered avenue and 20th Street, a central location in the Westside. I walked into the building and was greeted by the sounds of youth in the back wood shop. They were creating furniture for sale as part of a program providing trade skills for marginalized young people and a space to foster "self-awareness and political actualization."[7] CHARM was going through a renewal process, with a recently appointed director and some turnover in staff, and part of what I had been asked to do was chair the meeting and take notes about the new directions the organization might take.

Moments after I arrived, a young woman walked towards me – tall, dark flowing hair, and dressed in a printed long skirt and blue t-shirt. She introduced herself to me as Cedar and spoke for a few moments about the reserve where she came from, about an hour southwest of Saskatoon. She looked me over carefully as we spoke and I, correspondingly, took in her slow evaluation of my presence. Sensing her unease and uncertainty, I introduced myself to her and explained why I was there, offering that I was happy to help out with whatever she needed me to do. I also mentioned that I had been working with Dakota, since I knew he was in and out of many of the youth service organizations and that this association might help explain my presence. Smiling back after I offered this short overview, she began speaking proudly to me about her role as a community worker in the Westside of the city, and she quickly took me by the hand to one of the offices in the back of the building.

We entered a room painted bright yellow and adorned with various cultural symbols of her identity as a Cree woman and artefacts of her political advocacy. I set my bags on the ground and looked around to discover a photograph of her on her desk with an older gentleman. I asked her about the picture, and she told me about her grandfather, a very famous First Nations actor and Indigenous advocate in Canada. I immediately became curious about how she became involved with CHARM and how she viewed her role in relation to Indigenous youth more specifically. We began an informal conversation about her work and she began her jeremiad:

> I am so tired of being the only First Nations person at so many of these meetings. What do they think? That I represent all First Nations people? I know what the government is doing and I am not for the government. I am here to help my people and to get people to think about what is happening, how we lost our land, what belongs to us. I was at this city council meeting and this councilwoman asked me to tell her what I think First Nations people need. It's always about our needs. I am so tired of this.

Unlike members of the Indigenous Alliance, Cedar was voicing a political critique of the state that was not common in forums about urban Indigenous youth. Even more so, she was fully aware of the token nature of her participation at many of these meetings and the lack of support she felt, in doing this work, from the organizations that often invited her to come to the table to represent the interests of Indigenous youth in the city.

I glanced at my watch and told her that we had better make our way to the meeting. We would be late if we didn't hurry. "Wait, before we go into this meeting we have to smudge," she told to me. I stood there waiting for her to light the sweet grass and spread the sweet smelling smoke over her. I took my turn as well, having learned the protocol associated with this ceremonial, cultural practice. "I am so glad I brought this today," she then told me. "My mom gave this to me this morning, and it is going to help us during the meeting to open everyone's minds to what we have to say and to dispel any bad feelings that people might be having about why we are here." I gratefully accepted the little piece of white tissue she handed me and opened it to find a tiny piece of liquorice root. "Eat it right before you go in and don't tell anyone about it. It's just between us." I smiled in agreement and obliged, thankful to have her gift in my pocket.

Cedar and I proceeded to the meeting in the boardroom of CHARM. There were several staff members present as well as representatives from various community organizations, including a representative from the Indigenous Alliance, who were involved in reconfiguring the mission and purpose of CHARM. Cedar and I had conferred and decided that she should take the lead in facilitating this meeting, since she was there as an Indigenous young woman representing Indigenous youth in Saskatoon. Consequently, I took a backseat at the start.

The meeting began with a prayer spoken by Cedar and everyone was supposed to spend the following few minutes gathering their thoughts about what they were hoping to accomplish. However, before she moved ahead with the agenda for the day, Cedar decided to spend a few minutes voicing her concerns about how she thought programs for Indigenous youth were often being constructed. With a slightly elevated voice she remarked, "I think we need to stop for a minute. Where are the Aboriginal youth at this table? This is another meeting where we are talking about our kids but none of them are here to speak their experience. I know you people here are trying to fix things but there are a lot of problems with the way things are happening."

Caught off guard, most people in the room starting shifting in their chairs, twirling their pens. One of the staff members from CHARM, Deborah, interrupted her. "We are trying to work on things here at CHARM Cedar, and we need to start from a positive place. I don't think it is going to be helpful to be negative and just talk about all of the things that are going wrong. We need to think about ways to move forward and not all of the things that have gone wrong in the past." I was becoming increasingly uncomfortable, at this point, because this staff person was obviously trying to silence Cedar and did not want to open the floor to debating her concerns. It was also notable that, throughout this meeting, where there was no other representation from the Indigenous community, Cedar became both the essential Indigenous voice and also the contained Indigenous voice. The terms of debate, it seemed, were not open for discussion, and while she had been asked to co-facilitate this meeting, the power to determine the agenda rested elsewhere.

I attempted to interject, arguing that we needed to pay attention to Cedar's concerns and work through what she had to say before moving on. It was at this moment that the representative from the Indigenous Alliance, Sara, jumped in and began invoking the authority of the urban Indigenous community through the collaborative vessel. "We have heard from the community forums we conducted with the Aboriginal people in the city about what the issues are and we need to be respectful of that too Cedar. We really need to honour that or elsewhere is our accountability to those people who came to those meetings?" Sara was also giving a naturalness to the idea of urban Indigenous community derived through the community meetings, its legitimacy axiomatic. "In this apparently natural space," Rose (1999, 189) writes, that "the authority of community authorities, precisely because it is governed by no explicit codes and rules of conduct, is often even more difficult to contest than that of experts or professionals."

There was loaded silence in the room for a few moments, and then Cedar backed off and stepped away from the front of the table where we were both standing. Another participant at the meeting then suggested we move on in the agenda for the sake of time, since everyone was busy and there were certain items that needed to be discussed – Cedar's remarks not being one of them. The meeting proceeded with an overview of the broader mission of CHARM and the types and range of programs and services it should provide for inner city youth, who in Saskatoon were primarily Indigenous. There was consensus around these programs (mentoring, life skills, trades development) being a source of "empowerment" for Indigenous youth. A staff at CHARM concurred, "Youth need to be empowered and realize what their potential is. I think these programs need to give them the tools to move beyond where they are and to realize what their life purpose is." I looked anxiously over at Cedar who, by this stage in the meeting, refused to look up from the ground. The underlying assumption behind the consensus was that young peoples' partaking in these pro-grams was going to empower them to identify their roles in a white settler society and also to have a better sense of themselves. The com-position of the staff at CHARM was all white, except for a young Indig-enous woman who sat at the front desk, greeting people upon entry to the space. There was also a cursory debate about how to include more "First-Nations people and culture" in the organization, through the use of elders and increased parental involvement in some of the programs, but this was the extent to which this topic was discussed. Cedar remained silent during this conversation as well, avoiding the role of facilitator, and I was left to direct the conversation.

About halfway through the meeting Cedar's daughter ran into the room and sat on her lap (one of her family members had dropped her off). She reached for some food across the table and was visibly happy to see her mom. Some of the participants in the meeting looked puzzled about the presence of Cedar's daughter in the room, although they did not say anything directly to Cedar. Cedar stayed for a few more min-utes and then whispered to me that she needed to leave to get her little girl ready for a Pow Wow she was going to later that day. I hugged her, thanked her for her time, and told her I would look for her at the Pow Wow. Apparently, the liquorice root had not worked as well as she had hoped.

In the meeting's final phase, we moved into a more focused discus-sion of the board's role and staff training, and at the end of this discus-sion, I thanked the group for inviting me to their space and quietly made my exit, bewildered and admittedly angered by the whole expe-rience. Later on that day, at the school division office, I approached Sara and asked her what she thought about the gathering at CHARM. "Everyone has their own thing," was her reaction; and she continued, "We can't possible take on all of the issues out there. We need to focus on the things that will help these kids stay in school, get good jobs, be stable."

Visible to me as I reflected on this experience, was that the Indig-enous Alliance had a very fixed and deliberate direction it wanted to move in with respect to conceptualizing the purpose of educational and social interventions in the lives of Indigenous children and youth. Discourses of empowerment, risk, and success were all laden with par-ticular values about how these youth could become better citizens and members of the settler city. Also, the power of the representative from the Indigenous Alliance to block Cedar's overt contestation of the lack of Indigenous youth at the table, as well as Cedar's direct questioning of the "empowerment programs," by invoking an alternative form of Indigenous authority drawn from the community meetings was exceptionally disconcerting. I was perplexed by how this representation of the "urban Indigenous community" through the auspices of the Indigenous Alliance became a vehicle through which state interests could be deployed at any time to manage dissent or critique, since the alliance seemed to possess legitimacy and own the moral high ground when it came to identifying the "key issues" facing urban Indigenous children and youth – plainly a technique of settler colonial governance. Even though the conversations were loaded with assumptions about who these Indigenous youth were, in terms of their social and political histories and life circumstances and what they needed in order to alter their life trajectories, the assumptions were not something open for discussion.

The quelling of dissent also surfaced in a similar vein at a working group meeting a few months after the incident at CHARM. I walked into the boardroom at the Saskatoon School Division, relieved to see only three or four people in the room, since I was arriving late. Todd, the coordinator of events for the Indigenous Alliance, and Dave greeted me. "Have some soup and bannock Jas," Dave suggested, reminding me of the social practice of eating and chatting before the meeting began. I thanked him for the offer and made my way to get some food.

After a short time, several other working group members arrived, and we welcomed one another in the usual fashion – hugging or placing a hand on a shoulder, another instantiation of the relational practices that were central to the working group. Donna began the meeting by reciting a prayer, and just as she was finishing, the door to the boardroom opened. A petite woman entered, carrying a coffee cup in one hand and a leather bag overflowing with papers in the other. "Welcome Tina," Dave said. "We were just getting started." Dave introduced Tina to the group as a representative from the Aboriginal community. She worked part time in one of the elementary schools in the Westside and as a volunteer in one of the local friendship centres. I motioned to Tina to take a seat in the empty chair next to me.

Dave proceeded with the meeting agenda and the group began to engage in a discussion about the upcoming round dance that was going to be held to promote the work of the Indigenous Alliance across Saskatoon. "Communication is a key strategy to making this partnership work, so we need to get the word out there," declared Denise, a working group member. The topic then shifted to a dialogue about work for the upcoming months. Dave announced, for example, that he had been in conversation with Sask Learning, and the government was suggesting the Indigenous Alliance should be documented through a community research project.

At this point in the meeting, Tina raised her hand and asked if she could interject and pose a question. At Dave's approval, who was also chairing the meeting, she expressed doubt over the substantive focus of the Alliance's work:

> I know I am new here and I don't want to be too critical or nothing like that, but how are we coming to these decisions? We need to really ask ourselves what our values are and what we are going to be responsible for. Is what we are doing here at these meetings, through this initiative, helping our First Nations peoples? The kids I work with have bigger problems then what you're talking about here. We have a broader perspective here, but we need to have a community perspective. Let's ask parents what they think. I have to be an advocate for our kids at this table and I represent them. Our kids are becoming addicts at 11 and 12. They're being jailed. And that's just the start. We are skirting around the issues.

There was silence in the room for a few moments; an obvious tension had slowed the flow of the discussion. Dave looked around while the rest of us remained silent. After a few moments, he spoke, echoing a stance similar to the one I had heard voiced at CHARM. "Tina, we had a series of community meetings when the Indigenous Alliance was developed and the work we are doing here is what the community told us they wanted. If we don't listen to that we lose the whole mission for this." With a fairly dismissive riposte, Tina added, "Well maybe we should redo those community meetings and see what new stuff comes up." Dave nodded and told her we would have to take that up at a later date.

The meeting resumed with business as usual, and at a break, I asked Tina if I could come by and visit her school where she helped out. I told her I thought she had raised an important point in the meeting. She said, "I can feel that things have become too formal here, everyone is too concerned about the big political organizations and their own personal agendas. This isn't helping us." I only saw Tina at a couple more working group meetings before she stopped coming altogether, speculating that her confrontation with Dave had curtailed her attendance.

I include this encounter to once again demonstrate how the Indigenous Alliance is able to exercise its authority despite the concerns, in
this iteration, raised by participating individuals who explicitly challenged its ostensibly apolitical mission and positioning of the "problems" facing urban Indigenous youth within the purview of technical
state intervention. The Indigenous Alliance can be read, then, as a third
space of negotiation between the state and Indigenous peoples, almost
acting like a filter for the issues in the city and a medium through which
the state can determine the terms of engagement. The acute difference
between this state technology and the more overly assimilative ones
espoused by the settler state is that the decisions appear to be made
by Indigenous peoples themselves, albeit in direct conversation with
the state. We already witnessed how disciplinary forms that stabilize
the discourses of inclusion and participation undermine demands for
access to decision-making power. In this way, state practices of collaboration provide the allusion of inclusion but in practice allow for social
fabrications in which traditional meanings of "local control" and "by
the people" do not mean equality of representation, lived experience,
and/or political voice. These are technologies aimed at welcoming into
state structures capable Indigenous bodies that govern themselves in
liberal ways and perform consent to settler sovereignty.

## Colonial Scripting and the Exclusion of Colonial Gender Violence

In the writing of this book, I have been careful to walk the line of
revealing enough while being attentive to the voyeuristic dangers of
ethnographic research. I have made an effort to reduce the number
of individual stories recounted by various people over the course of
my research, stories rife with suffering, abuse, and pain, in attempt to
limit the sensationalizing and unnecessary exposure of such experiences. It was never my intention to produce "damage narratives" (Tuck
2009, 409) through my explication of the Indigenous Alliance. On the
contrary, I was moved by a desire to think critically about what I was
doing in my own work as a youth advocate and to look at the state
mechanisms through which purported changes were being brought
into the lives of urban Indigenous youth, set against, of course, a shifting backdrop of settler colonialism. In revealing the following event
and in the subsequent discussion, then, I wish only to demonstrate the
degree of ongoing colonial state violence with which we must contend
if we choose to engage in social reforms impacting Indigenous children

and youth. The exclusion of colonial gender violence from the scope of work advanced by hybrid governing entities such as the Indigenous Alliance can only be deliberate. In *Seeing Like a State*, James Scott (1998) exposes how states can administer effectively only by simplifying and homogenizing the local context so as to make it legible to the state. With respect to the everyday realities of Indigenous women and girls, a narrowing of the alliance's focus also serves, I would argue, to reinscribe the Canadian settler state's long history of violence enacted against Indigenous women and girls. Omission is complicity. Pushing against this complicity, I turn now to another encounter during my fieldwork.

As a result of my longstanding work in the area of youth advocacy in Saskatoon, much of which directly involves advocacy alongside Indigenous young women, I became well acquainted with the small number of activists in Saskatoon who were undertaking public awareness and program development around issues of violence facing Indigenous women and girls. In fact, while I was conducting research on the Indigenous Alliance, I was simultaneously working on developing a youth organization that would be directly informed by the experiences of Indigenous girls. Consequently, it wasn't unusual for me to be working alongside these activists, and it was from them that I learned of a biweekly meeting being held by small group of Indigenous women in the city's Westside. Locating the funding and political energy needed to tackle the gravity and breadth of colonial gender violence was not an easy task, by any stretch, so I was compelled to learn more about this group, and I inquired about whether or not it would possible for me to attend one of their meetings. An acquaintance made a couple of calls on my behalf, and a few days later, called to inform me where and when the gathering was going to be held.

The following week, I was behind the wheel, driving one evening to nearly the end of the Westside on 22nd Street, where the highway meets the city perimeter. I followed the directions for the meeting location and pulled into a residential neighbourhood. I approached the building with a little unease, unclear about what the group had been told about my attendance. I walked around the structure looking for a side entrance, since I had been told that the meeting would be held in the basement. I found the door unlocked and entered. Old, cracked linoleum led the way to a short staircase, and I descended to find an open space where five women were sitting around a small round table. "Are you Jas?" one of them asked me. I introduced myself and shook hands with each of them, thanking them profusely for allowing me to step into their gathering and learn about some of the initiatives they were undertaking. The physical space itself was intimate, and after my short introduction, I made a decision to ask them a couple of questions about how they perceived social programming in the areas of education and justice intersecting with the work they envisioned. I also made the decision to exit quickly and respectfully, so they could carry on with their business without feeling the presence of someone they did not know very well intruding on their time together.

I briefly clarified that I was doing research on the Indigenous Alliance and asked them if they had heard of this collective and some of their initiatives for urban Indigenous youth in Saskatoon. One of the women, an older lady, with dark, graying hair and glasses, looked at me and said, dismissively, that she didn't understand where the programs were coming from. Citing the stories of Indigenous girls who had repeatedly experienced sexual abuse and were being harassed on the street on their way to school, her face communicated dismay at the mentioning of yet another government initiative; her awareness and insight prompted me to wonder how uncritical mentoring programs and a series of anti-racism workshops alone were going to support Indigenous youth living in poverty, dealing with addiction, and facing sexual violence every day on the street – the materiality of colonial violence that I knew so well. According to her, the attention needed to be refocused to directly involve critical challenges to the state, by allowing Indigenous women to be the ones that offered support and guidance to Indigenous girls.

Another among the women began talking about the issue of the sexual exploitation and criminalization of young women and girls, highlighting the ways Aboriginal girls had become dehumanized through this exploitation, enduring levels of violence that were so severe that the programs of the Indigenous Alliance were not going to address the powerlessness, hopelessness, and struggles they faced. "We live here, in this community every day, and this is what we are dealing with. I don't think the people working over there [motioning towards the centre of the city] really know what's going on. They have no clue." One of the women who had been quiet until this point chimed in, "They are going with what the government has always done. What does it matter, are they going to listen to what we have to say?"

The perspectives and knowledge of the Indigenous women I met that night poignantly punctured the claimed singularity of the urban Indigenous community in Saskatoon – and the lived experiences that comprise it. How is it that the insights of these Indigenous women have been excluded from dialogues and debates about social reforms targeted at urban Indigenous youth? What harm is the Indigenous Alliance enacting by erasing these experiences from the purview of a participatory mandate centred on exploring "the needs" of Indigenous children and youth? Through their challenges, then, these Indigenous women were urgently questioning the ability of the Indigenous Alliance to adjudicate or authorize claims made on behalf of the urban Indigenous community, despite the Alliance's professing to speak in an "authentic Indigenous voice." More explicitly, they questioned the lack of a gendered analysis in the mandate of the Indigenous Alliance by calling to account programs that paid little heed to the rampant violence against Indigenous women and girls across Turtle Island. And they are far from alone in their critique. In *Mohawk Interruptus* (2014), Audra Simpson explains how the bodies of Indigenous girls have historically been rendered less valuable because of what they are taken to represent: land, reproduction, kinship, and governance, and an alternative to heteronormative and Victorian rules of descent. "Their bodies carry a symbolic load," she argues, "because they have been conflated with the land and are thus contaminating to a white, settler social order" (A. Simpson 2014, 156). State failures to respond to instances of abuse and the implementation of social policies that eclipse the layered realities of Indigenous women and girls, is an indicator, then, of how the state itself is a driving force behind violence enacted upon Indigenous peoples historically, and in the present, is the primary perpetrator in fact (A. Simpson 2016; Smith 2005).

Sadly, there is no shortage of evidence documenting the ongoing colonial gender violence experienced by Indigenous women and girls in Canada (Dhillon and Allooloo, 2015; Amnesty International 2004). Tina Fontaine. Loretta Saunders. Cindy Gladue. Pamela George. Bella Laboucan-McLean. These names are halting signposts of colonial gender violence in Canada. They are part of a growing, state-generated epidemic of murdered and missing Indigenous women and girls across Turtle Island – an unmistakable rendering of settler state power juxtaposed with its claims of munificence and postcolonial calm.[8]

In January 2015, the Inter-American Commission on Human Rights (IACHR) released a 127-page document outlining the egregious levels of violence experienced by Indigenous women and girls in Canada. According to the report, the number of murdered and missing Indigenous women and girls is overwhelming in its scope, tallied at approximately 1,200 cases. Indigenous women and girls are eight times more likely to die of homicide than non-Indigenous women (Inter-American Commission on Human Rights 2014, 49). Given that Indigenous women and girls comprise only 4.3 per cent of the overall Canadian population, this revelation is particularly alarming.

I would caution, however, against getting caught up in the numbers game: the constant focus on numbers does a particular kind of work in delimiting the focus of the problem. It remains vital to remember that these numbers are not just abstract figures or horrific, sensationalized stories that appear in newspapers or across TV screens in the form of nightly news. Every single one of those "numbers" corresponds to a life. These statistics are Indigenous girls and women who were integral parts of their communities, human beings who withstood brutal assaults on their bodies and spirits, and daughters, mothers, sisters, students, cousins, aunties, friends, and partners, whose lives were extinguished in unconscionable ways. This vicious story of elimination, then, casts light on the devastation and collective wreckage endured by so many Indigenous families and communities across Turtle Island who are suffering immense loss and righteously demanding justice for their loved ones and for Indigenous peoples more broadly. It also renders a clear, ominous picture of where Indigenous women and girls stand in the eyes of the settler colonial state of Canada.

It is my contention that Indigenous girls and women continue to "disappear" and be murdered in Canada because the state is actively engaged in ensuring that this continues to happen. Violence against Indigenous women and girls is not an inexplicable phenomenon but the modus operandi of the Canadian criminal justice system. Reworking it into a "crime problem" disguises the fact that colonial gender violence has been targeting Indigenous girls and women since the point of first contact, since before Canada became Canada. It is the effect of a criminal justice system that was instrumental in the historical disempowerment of Indigenous women and girls and that is relentless in its pursuit of colonial gender violence as a central feature of settler sovereignty. "Gender violence and murdered and missing Indigenous women are a symptom of settler colonialism, white supremacy and genocide," attests Leanne Simpson (2014a), "symptoms of the dispossession of Indigenous peoples from our territories." The settler state of Canada has something very material to gain – the continued seizure of territory, coupled with a dismantling of Indigenous political efforts centred on decolonial mobilization – with a continuation of colonial gender violence. And it is made real through a number of cunning technologies of governance.

For example, state omissions lead to killings and disappearance without consequences – the complete and utter failure of the police, specifically, to respond to violence against Indigenous girls and women has created a culture of impunity for men to rape and murder at will. State actions (including violence) work in concert with targeted acts of male violence that are effectively born of state neglect and complicity. Both the provincial police and the RCMP have failed to adequately prevent this and protect Indigenous women and girls from a continuum of violence (the extinguishing of life itself being the concrete endpoint) and have abdicated responsibility for thoroughly investigating acts of violence when they are committed.[9] "Family members of murdered and missing women have described dismissive attitudes from police officers working on their cases, a lack of adequate resources allocated to those cases, and lengthy failure to investigate and recognize a pattern of violence" (Inter-American Commission on Human Rights 2014, 12). Confirming allegations of Indigenous women and girls' exclusion from state protection, the *Report of the Aboriginal Justice Inquiry of Manitoba* has also reiterated the ways that police have come to view Indigenous peoples, not as a community deserving protection, but as a community from which white society must be protected. This has led to a situation often described as one of Indigenous communities' being "over-policed" but "under-protected" – positioning Canadian white society as in need of protection from Indigenous nations (Aboriginal Justice Implementation Commission 1991).

The projection of criminality onto Indigenous women and girls also further fuels state failure to protect them and solidifies the elision of their lived experience. During a conversation I had about policing in the lives of Indigenous girls, Annabel Webb explained how the positioning of Indigenous girls as "criminals" makes them more prone to becoming targets of male violence.

The criminalization of Aboriginal girls is defined by a pervasive assumption of delinquency, one that ensures that girls will come into frequent contact with police and are more likely to be questioned, searched, arrested, detained, and subjected to the brutality of criminal justice procedures such as strip searches, imprisonment, and solitary confinement. Perpetrators, whether they happen to be police officers or other men in the community, act with impunity because the positioning of Indigenous girls as "criminal" means that the first impulse of criminal justice response to her victimization will be to question the child's credibility.

Thus, a breakdown in police protection and investigation, coupled with the projection of criminality onto Indigenous girls, works to sustain violence against Indigenous women and girls because male perpetrators believe they will be exempt from the legal ramifications of their actions (and they often are).

The failure of the Canadian public to stand up and demand answers in relation to violence against Indigenous women and girls is an indication of the value Canadian society places on their lives.[10] In many ways, they serve as the "unmournable bodies" (Cole 2015),[11] bearing the lethal consequences of Canada's quest to maintain the territorial power and broad-reaching control required to keep Canada a sovereign, industrial, and capitalist nation.[12] On the disposability of life in the context of relations of domination, Judith Butler (2015, para. 2) attests, "What we see is that some lives matter more than others, that some lives matter so much that they need to be protected at all costs, and that other lives matter less, or not at all. And when that becomes the situation, then the lives that do not matter so much, or do not matter at all, can be killed or lost, can be exposed to conditions of destitution, and there is no concern, or even worse, that is regarded as the way it is supposed to be."

It follows, then, that murder and other forms of colonial gender violence are the state's most concrete triumphs over Indigenous resurgence in the greater geopolitics of settler colonialism (Balfour 2014). The homogenizing of urban Indigenous youth experience by the Indigenous Alliance through this lack of critical analysis further obfuscates state violence and reinforces the fracturing of an Indigenous political subjectivity searching for freedom.

* * *

I have argued throughout this chapter that the Indigenous Alliance depends on the cultivation of a cohesive representation of the urban Indigenous community through which it is able to advance forms of programming for urban Indigenous youth in Saskatoon. Gupta (2001, 74) gives insight into the utilization of "community" by new technologies of governance when she says, "Community participation [was] essential if government was not to be seen as something external and imposed but as an intrinsic mode of discipline that led to regular and predictable patterns of conduct that grew out of, and came 'naturally' to communities and selves." However, as my discussion reveals, systems of participatory inclusion, in addition to systems for disciplining, also entail concomitant methods of exclusion that function to constrain the social means through which questions of social intervention for urban Indigenous youth can be addressed. Dhaliwal (1994, 43) draws our attention to this concern by saying,

> The privileging of inclusion politics does not account for the ways inclusion can still oppress or fail to alter structures of domination. The inability of radical democratic inclusion politics to deal with inclusion retaining peripheralization is a key limitation, especially given that, in many liberal democratic societies, many democratic groups have been "included" by being accorded certain formal rights like the right to vote. If inclusionary attempts reaffirm a hegemonic "core" to which the margins are added without any significant destablization of that core or continue to valorize the very centre that is problematic to begin with, then it is clear that the motivation to include needs questions.

The remaining two chapters shift the focus from understanding the political relationship between the Canadian state and Indigenous peoples to more pragmatic questions of social and educational programming for Indigenous youth, where the implications of a manufactured and tightly bound "urban Indigenous community" come to light.

# PART THREE

## Pushback on the Plains:
## Tensions and Trials of Participation

## Chapter Five

# Justice in a Binder: Cultural Currency and Urban Indigenous Youth

The idea that Indian culture is "lost" and that Indians have lost their culture is a deceptively benign but very common way to refer to the effects of colonial and racial oppression on Aboriginal people.

> – Verna St. Denis, "Rethinking Culture Theory in Aboriginal Education"

Many Aboriginal peoples have lost and/or been denied the use of their cultural heritage, traditions, customs, beliefs, values, and languages since the Indian Act was passed by the Canadian government in 1876.

> – The Indigenous Alliance, Planning Document

At 5:30 p.m. on a windy Friday in March 2007, my sister and I stepped gingerly across a snow-dampened field on the grounds of what was then the First Nations University of Canada to attend a round dance. Precariously balancing our numerous gifts and kitchen supplies, long skirts dangling in the mud, we cautiously made our way to the sidewalk and through one of the side doors of the old stone building, laughing and almost colliding with a Métis woman named Karen, a member of the working group I had come to know through my research. Karen was similarly weighed down with supplies and trying to wade through the characteristically wet Saskatchewan spring weather. "Don't you girls look nice! It will be a miracle if we make it in there without dropping all of this, but I am so glad I brought the extra containers because you can never eat all the food they give you. And, you can't throw it out, so you have to take it home with you," she remarked, with the packages unstable in her arms. I had already been briefed about the protocol associated with a round dance, feast, and giveaway at a meeting with members of the Indigenous Alliance working group earlier in the day, so I was aware of the rule about leaving with uneaten food in hand. Reflecting the solemnity of this practice, I had been told that, when we were sitting down and eating at the round dance, we would be eating for all of the people who came before us – many of whom had died of starvation.

We followed Karen down a long hallway, the walls bedecked with community notices about local Indigenous events, information about school enrolment, and phone numbers advertising local organizations that provide services to Indigenous peoples in the city. The smell of sweet grass became palpable as soon as we entered the building, and small children were running up and down the hall, joyful at the prospect of receiving candies and gifts, a custom at round dances. As we excitedly watched, some of the children halted momentarily, only to begin dancing to the sound of the drumming coming from the end of the hall. In a few moments, we had reached a small group of people gathered around the entrance to the gymnasium where the round dance was being held. Dakota, who told me that he would be singing in a couple of hours, stepped over and warmly greeted me when he saw that I had arrived. Dakota always went out of his way to make me feel welcome and to ensure that I was informed about the various events hosted by the Indigenous Alliance. He extended a form of generosity that reflected the mutual consideration and respect between the two of us that had been built over time and through many conversations about the social realities facing Indigenous youth in Saskatoon. I was grateful for it. "You better be ready to dance because I am going to be sure to bring you in," he told me, looking at me directly in the eye, his hand on my arm and a smile on his face. I laughed and told him that I was ready and that, if he pulled me in, he'd better pull my sister in as well.

After leaving Dakota to prepare for his singing, my sister and I continued to make our way through the bodies at the entrance and finally entered the large space. There were about seventy people seated around the perimeter of the gym, circling a group of men sitting in the centre of the room, where sweet grass was being burned through a pipe and drums were vibrating at a variety of sonic frequencies. The men, Karen told us, were praying to the ancestors and summoning good spirits to come and watch over the dance. We followed Karen across the room and spread our blanket out on the floor to sit down next to her. I turned around to find a group of elderly women elevated on chairs behind us, and we smiled at one another. "I am so happy you were able to come to this," Karen said to me, enthusiasm in her voice. "It gives us a chance to share with everyone all of the hard work that is being done to help people in our community. We are finally starting to make things happen for ourselves." I smiled at her and told her that it was a privilege to be able to attend and that I wouldn't have missed it.

Shortly thereafter, another member from the working group, also one of the superintendents for the local Saskatoon school division, approached us with a cordial welcome. She asked me to come and sit with her and some of the others, motioning to another area in the gym, but I explained that we had already made a place for ourselves next to Karen and I would catch up with her in a little while. I glanced and saw the staff from the school division, as well as other representatives from youth organizations, seated to the left of us on the floor, distinguishable by their button-up shirts, suits and ties, and predominantly white faces. I remembered that I had brought some supplies for the giveaway, mostly candy and small toys for the children, and my sister and I quickly found out who we were supposed to hand them off to and then made our way back to our spot on the floor.

We sat down, and a few moments later, a man introduced to us as a Cree elder stood up on the stage at the front of the gymnasium, microphone in hand. The room quieted as he began talking. In fact, this older, graying man, wearing a brimmed leather hat, commanded the attention of nearly everyone in the room with surprising ease. I was anxiously waiting to hear what he had to say and curious about how he would frame the work of the Indigenous Alliance and this event in particular. He began speaking softly through the microphone, a couple of small children who had run onto the stage clinging to his side.

> I want to thank you all for coming today to help us celebrate. This is a very special day for us, for our children, for our communities. Many of you have come from afar … from Regina, Prince Albert, North Battleford, and Mistawasis, and other places to help us celebrate this coming together of the schools and our people to try and make things better. This is the first time something of this kind has happened here. We are grateful for all of you coming. We need education to rebuild our communities and for our children to learn the skills that are needed to live here in the city and on our reserves. Please enjoy everything that happens here tonight and thank you again.

I glanced around me to look at the faces of the people listening trying to determine a collective reaction. I saw teachers and youth workers whom I had met on my research excursions, state officials from the school division, five or six female Indigenous elders who were seated directly behind me, parents, children, and members of the broader community – most people were listening intently, nodding in agreement.

The elder finished speaking, and my sister and I repositioned ourselves on our floor mat, trying to squeeze ourselves into the tiny space we were occupying on the floor. A few minutes later, the superintendent came over, once again, to check in and see how we are making out. I told her that we were fine and that it was helpful for me to listen to the elder speaking about the work of the Indigenous Alliance. She spoke for a few moments, saying how delighted she was at how well she thought the event was going and how important she believed it was that they had undertaken this round dance effort. She went on to explain that these were "our kids" hanging out on street corners and getting involved with gang activity and that it was up to everyone to make sure that schools and youth organizations were being culturally responsive and meeting the needs of all of the students.

The beginning of the round dance that I describe was only one among a number of cultural events the Indigenous Alliance hosted as a way to publicly mark its existence in Saskatoon and to demonstrate a commitment, on behalf of the settler state, to a renewed approach towards addressing the social realities of Indigenous youth in the city. The event was widely advertised in schools, non-profit organizations, and through various social and media networks. It was touted as symbolic representation of the settler state's attempt to culturally realign itself with the urban Indigenous population through the creation of state initiatives ensconced in the language of celebrating difference, of shared responsibility for integrating Indigenous cultural practices into schools and other state agencies and promoting the common good.

In weighing in on the emphasis on "culture" as a central feature of the Indigenous Alliance, let me first spend a moment speaking more generally about this concept. Endless volumes have been written about the slippery facets of "culture" from within the disciplinary field of anthropology and beyond.[1] "Culture" is one of those concepts that prompts epistemological jitters within the ranks of social science research. It is rigorously criticized as unbounded, contested, and connected to relations of power; as the product of historical influences rather than evolutionary change but also as something that gains traction in individuals' self-making and remaking. In *Human Rights and Gender Violence: Translating International Law into Local Justice*, Sally Merry (2006) offers a succinct overview of "culture" as a discursive construct that can be moulded and shaped, pushed and pulled, to serve a range of social and political ends. She charts, for example, its association with antiquated, static notions of tradition that play into the modernity game; its equation with national essence, drawing a distinction between the external trappings of a civilization and the inward, spiritual reality of a certain societal grouping; and its simultaneous deployment as fluid and shifting, embodying a changing set of values and practices that alters across social and political contexts and jumps through spaces in time. "Cultures consists not only of beliefs and values," Merry (2006, 15) explains, "but also practices, habits, and commonsensical ways of doing things. They include institutional arrangements, political structures, and legal regulations. As institutions such as laws and policing change so do beliefs, values, and practices." Culture, as rendered by Merry, then, is not homogenous and "pure," but produced in historical, political, and relational social contexts.

In the field of critical Indigenous studies, important and scathing critiques of anthropology's tainted hand in (re)producing accounts of the essential and objectified "Indigenous tribal culture" have cast light on how academic depictions of Indigenous civilizations feed into settler colonialism – the story of the primitive, the savage, the backward – and more specifically, how these accounts have been used by the settler state to legitimize conquest and dispossession en route to elimination (L. Simpson 2014a; St. Denis 2011). Anthropologists in search of "Indian culture" (St. Denis 2011, 180) produced and circulated a plethora of colonial narratives of indigeneity that made legible to the colonial state how Indigenous peoples could be made to disappear, their land stolen, and their children reconstituted as subjects of the settler state through deplorable colonial schemes such as residential schooling. Colonial narratives by anthropologists were (and some still are) perpetrators of a kind of erudite, studied violence that made use of the power–knowledge nexus (Foucault 1982) to foster statist, colonial modes of perception about who and what Indigenous peoples represent in the contested political space of settler sovereignty. As a case in point, Audra Simpson discusses the historical and anthropological literature promoting an authenticating discourse on the Iroquois as a cultural group. She attests that "the literature on the Iroquois is a realization of early anthropological desire – a desire for order, for purity, for fixity, and for cultural perfection that at once imagined an imminent disappearance immediately after or just within actual land dispossession" (A. Simpson 2014, 70).

Yet, there is a curious historical moment unfolding in settler states like Canada. We are now in an era where Canada, under the political framework of liberalism and the auspices of participatory entities such as the Indigenous Alliance, does not profess an overt interest in eradicating something the colonial state recognizes as Indigenous culture but rather seeks to tactically draw upon it and employ it as a motif of justice. Of equal importance, then, is the way the round dance event creates an experiential sense of the celebratory and progressive zeal of the Indigenous Alliance's public representation of itself to the settler city of Saskatoon. It lays bare how the Indigenous Alliance endorses particular conceptions of indigeneity that operate in concert with long-standing governmental and scholarly traditions of redirecting Indigenous political struggles with the colonial state through the terrain of Indigenous cultural incommensurability with white settler society, a reframing of history as a politics of difference. In her book *Red Pedagogy*, Sandy Grande (2004, 1) terms this reframing "culturalization" and asks the important question of how this preoccupation obscures the social, political, and economic reality facing Indigenous peoples and substitutes a politics of representation for one of radical social transformation. Audra Simpson (2014, 97) also signals the problematics of culture decisively, when she says, "Culture described the difference that was found in these places and marked the ontological endgame of each exchange; a difference that had been contained into neat, ethnically defined territorial spaces that now needed to be made sense of, ordered, ranked, governing, and possessed." According to current liberal tropes of tolerance, Indigenous "culture" must be accommodated and hailed within the social institutions of the settler state as a symbolic and material signpost of progress on the thorny path towards reconciliation.

The balance of this chapter takes up the bristly question of "culture" within the purview of social interventions for urban Indigenous youth launched by the Indigenous Alliance. My intent here is to demonstrate how a critical examination of culture yields important insights into how the work of the Indigenous Alliance functions to depoliticize and constrain the field of action (Foucault 1982) around Indigenous politics in Canada and, in doing so, reifies timeless, static, and narrow portraits of indigeneity.

### Culture, Power, and the Indigenous Alliance

Step into any one of the many youth organizations in Saskatoon's core neighbourhood or in the city's downtown, most of which are not explicitly positioned as Indigenous organizations, and you will be met with an assortment of "Indigenous culture" programs in which Indigenous youth can partake. These take a spectrum of forms, including drumming sessions, talking circles, beading workshops, cultivating skills for setting up a teepee, field trips to the Wanuskwein Heritage Park, attending a Pow Wow, or learning how to sing ceremonial songs. Some of these are facilitated by individuals who self-identify as Indigenous, and some are carried out by white settlers, a fact that has raised an eyebrow or two. Most of the programs run intermittently, depending on youth interest and the availability of instructors.

In sync with youth organizations across the city, the Indigenous Alliance has correspondingly designed and implemented a number of projects operating from the same basic premise: integrating more "Indigenous culture" (as if this were easily recognizable and/or quantifiable) into the institutional spaces where urban Indigenous youth find themselves will mitigate a host of challenges – intense poverty, imprisonment, dropping out of high school, sexual violence – that currently govern their lives. As I detailed in the overview of the Indigenous Alliance's programmatic areas in chapter 3, the mandate of the Indigenous Alliance concentrates on the adoption of "cultural practices" that reflect the "backgrounds and histories" of urban Indigenous youth,[2] bolstering the belief that the social problems of urban Indigenous youth are tied, in part, to a lack of cultural responsiveness that has triggered cultural identity loss. As a result, the Indigenous Alliance crafted social interventions aiming to rectify this omission. Although the Indigenous Alliance made cursory reference to the need for anti-racism workshops, the projects that primarily emerged from this participatory effort coalesced around the promotion of cross-cultural understanding as a way to ensure that white society was more understanding of Indigenous peoples and sensitive to peoples' particular ways of being.

Materially, these social interventions took place in two ways. First, reforms were introduced to a curriculum about Indigenous peoples that was to be used in both schools and youth organization. Then, opportunities were opened up for public schools and youth organizations to invite the Indigenous Alliance's cultural resource coordinator to offer lessons about the cultural practices of Indigenous peoples and "to promote cross-cultural awareness and understanding of First Nations, and Métis history, languages, culture, tradition, and protocol, and information on contemporary First Nations and Métis issues."[3] In fact, developing cultural programming for the state was one of the primary goals the Indigenous Alliance had sketched in their strategic work plan, a plan peppered with the notion of valuing diversity. The emphasis on promoting cross-cultural awareness was also evident in many of the informal practices of the Indigenous Alliance, including the sponsoring of the round dance as a way to improve Indigenous–white relations in Saskatoon. Other practices with a similar objective included holding meetings on reserves, opening working group meetings with a prayer led by an Indigenous member, and holding sweats and cultural retreats for members of the working group and broader staff from both the Ministry of Education and Corrections and Public Safety.

In the arena of curricular shifts, the Indigenous Alliance initiated a lengthy curriculum development project that was informed by a broad guideline. The following passage is worth quoting at length, since it exemplifies the central assumptions about culture that are foundational to the mission of the Indigenous Alliance:

> Many Aboriginal peoples have lost and/or been denied the use of their cultural heritage, traditions, customs, beliefs, values, and languages since the "Indian Act" was passed by the Canadian Government in 1876. Aboriginal cultures were portrayed as being insignificant and unimportant. The "idea" was to "civilize and Christianize" which would lead to the assimilation of Aboriginal peoples into the European society. The need to assimilate the Aboriginal peoples led to the discontinuance of Aboriginal languages, customs, traditions, beliefs, and values. Many Aboriginal peoples refused to discontinue their languages and cultures and continued to speak their languages and practice their cultural ways in secret. Over one hundred years have gone by for these peoples. Despite the extreme methods used by the Government of Canada to assimilate the Aboriginal peoples, most of the languages, customs, traditions, beliefs, and values have survived. Aboriginal peoples are now reclaiming their cultures as an integral part of their lives. Aboriginal Elders and leaders have worked diligently and at great personal costs to get the Canadian government to recognize their cultures. Since the early 1970s, the federal government recognized the importance of Aboriginal peoples to have their own education systems that promoted their cultural worldviews. This revitalization and renewal of Aboriginal cultures is considered one of the factors that promote increased high school graduation rates, decreased absenteeism and more post-secondary graduates among Aboriginal peoples. Aboriginal children need to identify themselves as Aboriginal in order to develop a positive self-esteem and confidence. To do this, they require curriculum that recognizes and validates their cultures. They also require teachers that actively acknowledge Aboriginal cultures in a positive way as part of their teaching repertoire. Aboriginal students need to be given

the same opportunity as other students to have their cultural heritages recognized and validated as an integral part of their learning. This can be accomplished through the inclusion of Aboriginal content and perspectives in the Saskatchewan Learning curricula ... to do this, we need to recognize and validate these cultures, in particular, the Aboriginal cultures, by teaching Aboriginal content and perspectives in conjunction with the dominant Euro-Canadian culture. We need to ensure that our children and grandchildren live in peace and harmony as envisioned by our ancestors (Aboriginal and European) at the signing of the Saskatchewan Treaties. (Indigenous Alliance, unpublished)

The practical culmination of this focus on curriculum modification was the creation of distinct units of study, or what the Indigenous Alliance called "justice binders," for teachers and youth workers to use in the public schools and throughout youth organizations in Saskatoon. Each justice binder contained an assortment of lesson plans about traditional modes of social organization and Indigenous governance, albeit with abbreviated lessons on history and colonization, that individuals working with Indigenous youth could draw upon as a "cultural resource." The justice binders were created in concert with a number of "cultural immersion" programs to enable youth, teachers, and youth workers to acquire an "authentic understanding" of how Indigenous knowledge related to particular subject areas as well as to learn about specific ceremonial practices. The idea here was additive at its core – the Indigenous Alliance was not bent on supplanting the colonial social institution but on fostering a space within it where a form of indigeneity could be performed and expressed.

One of the most poignant representations of this attempt at the cultivation of cultural awareness was an experience I had participating in the Indigenous Alliance's annual Traditional Knowledge Keepers Camp, held in the summer of 2007, where youth (white and Indigenous) from Saskatoon were bussed to a nearby reserve for a day-long event. The overall purpose of this camp was to offer an experiential medium through which youth could come to appreciate and value an Indigenous perspective on many of the topics they were learning in school and to promote a sense of shared understanding through the bridging of Indigenous and western worldviews. In preparation for the day, one of the working group members described the camp to me as "an excellent way for all the students in Saskatoon's publics schools to celebrate what the Aboriginal culture has to offer."

The reserve was located about a twenty-minute drive outside of the official city limits. The grounds contained a number of smaller buildings, as well as substantial outdoor space, where students were able to gather in seminar-style spaces to receive what was positioned as Indigenous perspectives on various topics they were learning about in their city class-rooms. Students were also given the opportunity to listen to Cree sing-ing and to participate in talking circles where they could ask questions. Tipis had been erected in one of neighbouring fields next to the reserve, and I attended a session in one of these, where an Indigenous Elder was explaining to a group of youth the way science was approached from an Indigenous perspective, alerting students to the holistic way Indigenous peoples understand their place in the universe and their relationship to the land. The Elder was careful to point out that different practices were relevant across the range of First Nations peoples but said that, on the whole, their perspective was distinct from that of a western worldview.

I must clarify at this juncture. My argument throughout this chapter does not mean to suggest that Indigenous ways of knowing, contested as they may be within a heterogeneous indigeneity across Turtle Island, are not worthwhile or necessary for Indigenous peoples in places like Saskatoon or elsewhere. In fact, numerous Indigenous scholars, includ-ing Leanne Simpson (2014a), Alfred (2009), and Coulthard (2014b) have argued for a resurgence of Indigenous knowledge that is rooted in land-based cultural practices fostered by re-establishing First Nations connec-tions to their homelands. Others have also pointed out how attempts at the eradication of tribal knowledge suffered through centuries of coloni-zation has created enormous pressures for Indigenous scholars and tribal leaders to focus on restorative projects that affirm and sustain the value of Indigenous knowledge and language (Grande 2004, 2). Politically trou-bling, however, is how the *sole* (and in many instances a watered down and essentialized version) focus on "culture" by the Indigenous Alliance encouraged a trivializing of the ongoing impact of settler colonialism by attributing a large part of the problem facing urban Indigenous youth to their lack of a positive cultural identity. Even though we may under-stand this preoccupation with "culture" as a type of liberal decolonizing project, we need to pay careful attention to the possibility that it redirects our attention away from the foundational elements of colonial violence that sustain Canada's dominance over Indigenous peoples, impels us to look away from the history that reverberates through power and knowl-edge. In "Rethinking Culture Theory in Aboriginal Education," Verna St. Denis offers a stark exploration of how an analysis situated in cultural responsiveness, as opposed to a critical race or anti-colonial analysis, recasts political contestations over land, power, and colonial violence as mere differences in cultural values. She argues that this not only constrains our ability to see and think critically about Indigenous–state relations in our current historical moment, but also fuels the old story of cultural discontinuity, playing into the idea that Indigenous peoples are on the brink of vanishing, dying out (St. Denis 2011, 184).

A focus on "culture," then, actively works to depoliticize the terms of struggle between Indigenous people and the settler state of Canada when things couldn't be more political. It renders Indigenous–state relations as in need of technical intervention, not fundamental political realignment. Let us not forget that Indigenous peoples stand in the way of settler colonialism, contesting settler entitlement to the land and throwing into question settler legitimacy (Razack 2015, 7). Positing dispossession, the theft of land, and the rampant assault on Indigenous women and girls (to name only a few examples of ongoing colonial injury) as simple reflections of a white settler society that just needs more cultural awareness in order for the past to be rectified is politically reckless when we consider the stakes. "Culture," as a static and fixed object, is something that can be easily adopted, co-opted, and manipulated by the settler state to provide the allusion that things are changing, without the material transference of power (and as I mentioned previously, it was used as an instrument of conquest). In fact, separating Indigenous culture from Indigenous political existence and supporting the former while erasing the latter seems exceedingly convenient, set against the backdrop of Canada's quest for settler colonial completion. Taiaiake Alfred (2009, 50) offers the following counsel: "Whatever the particular situation, Indigenous peoples' basic relationship to the state is as members of nations in a colonial relationship with a dominating external power." The bureaucratized state, functioning through participatory entities such as the Indigenous Alliance, remains a powerful force through which "difference becomes apparent; political aspirations are articulated; and culture, authenticity, and tradition become politically expedient resources" (A. Simpson 2014, 18).

## Salvation from Cultural Deterioration and the Problematics of Authenticity

The emphasis on "Indigenous culture" by the Indigenous Alliance was also informed by the rhetoric of cultural decline and deterioration – the notion that there must be a concerted effort to "save" Indigenous ways of knowing and being in the world. In their description of the work of the Indigenous Alliance, working group members lauded the seemingly progressive approach to Indigenous youth social reform advanced through cultural responsiveness.[4] Underlying this idea, however, was a belief that, without this deliberate attention to "culture," Indigenous knowledge and social practices were at risk of being lost.

During an interview I conducted in 2007 with Sally, we discussed her perception of the success of the Indigenous Alliance with respect to a focus on culture:

JD: You spend a good deal of energy focusing on what you call First Nations culture in your work. How do you understand this as part of the Indigenous Alliance's success?

S: When you ask for successes I mean I think of the Cree language and culture program, I mean that is a success – which is huge. And it validates the reclaiming of language and when you reclaim language it signifies that you are preventing the loss of culture – because language and culture go together. So when we do that in our community and our parents see that, that we value that in the partnership, then that is a good example of where it is connecting directly with those families and those students. But, more importantly, I think that program has impacted on that entire school. So, you have "O Canada" sung in Cree and kids are learning songs in Cree and staff are taking conversational Cree you know it bubbles out.

Another member pointed out how she thought the ability to provide culturally relevant experiences for Indigenous students was central to their ability to rise above difficult life circumstances and that it was this potential loss of cultural connection that was responsible, in part, for the inability of urban Indigenous youth to "make the right choices." In reiterating this point, Donna clarified that for Indigenous kids without family, or if they had parents who were "sick," being able to participate in cultural programs would be beneficial. "There is so much poverty and neglect and all kinds of social issues," Donna said in softly spoken words,

And like we can't save the world but we can do our part and I really do have a soft spot in my heart. You know many times when I drive down 20th Street and I see the people that the elders call "the lost" and these are you know the homeless people and the girls that are out on the street and people who are consumed by alcohol. They call them the "lost ones" because they have had so many traumas in their lives that they are no longer able to hope. They have no more hope. I mean it used to really bother me when I lived in Prince Albert because the same thing used to happen on Central Ave. And you know sometimes I drive by and see a man walking on the road or on the sidewalk and he would be drunk in the middle of the day and you know I would cry for that person because in my heart it pains me to see that because they have lost hope and because I see people being so rude and ignorant and that hurts me too. You know because we all come to places where we make choices in life and some people don't have the roots or family support and many of them suffer and I always get so angry at people when they treat them bad and yeah, even in my own family I have cousins who live like that and even though, you know, we have tried to help them and they didn't want it and it is their choice to live that way but it still hurts me to see that.

What happens when the colonial state becomes an active agent in the preservation of "Indigenous culture," when it becomes responsible for preventing urban Indigenous youth from becoming "lost?" How does this, once again, signal a dependency of Indigenous peoples on the colonial state, particularly if the state is positioned as a mechanism to rescue Indigenous knowledge, language, and history? In this configuration, not only is the role of the settler state in perpetrating ongoing colonial violence disregarded, but also it becomes positioned as a hero in the story of saving a version of Indigenous culture from potential demise. In this old colonial tale, both the settler and the settler state are hailed as vindicators in their efforts to assist Indigenous peoples' entry into modernity while preserving a palpable and depoliticized version of indigeneity. How, then, might this also be considered a colonial assault on meaningful Indigenous existence?

The preservation of "culture" also opens the doorway to a litany of questions about authenticity with respect to the Indigenous Alliance's representations and deployments of Indigenous culture as tactical attempts at resolving the crisis facing urban Indigenous youth. What counts as Indigenous cultural practices or ways of knowing? How have these practices and knowledge forms changed and shifted across time and through colonial experiences, in both past and present? What I am getting at here is that "saving" or "reviving" Indigenous culture reinforces static notions of culture that are not reflective of the fluid dynamics of social life, particularly when we consider the context of ongoing dispossession. St. Denis (2011, 181) brings this point home when she states,

> The idea of culture as an entity outside of people provides a foundation for the belief in the potential of "cultural revitalization" and the very idea that culture can be retrieved. While the idea that culture resides deep inside one's "core" may be reassuring the in the early stages of an engagement with cultural revitalization, when the "traditional" culture fails to appear to reveal itself, it can be very troubling. This failure of culture to appear becomes a very different kind of problem. It is a problem long familiar to those anthropologists who have been keenly interested in "authentic" and "real Indians" or the "primitive," and for whom evidence of cultural change would suggest otherwise, namely that culture is mutable.

People create culture, make it real, breathe life into it. It is not something that operates outside of people or their social, political, and historical experiences. It is not an object that can be separated out from the relational context in which it originates. The problem here, as articulated by Coulthard (2014a, 147), is that the cultural practices that the colonized (or the colonized and the state, in this instance) may cling to as a source of pride and empowerment can easily become a cluster of antiquated attachments that divert attention away from the present and future needs of Indigenous peoples. We must ask questions, then, about how the culturally based interventions of the Indigenous Alliance navigate the avenues of government-mandated rules, regulations, procedures, and governance structures and if this actually moves Indigenous peoples towards emancipation and cultural reclamation. Is there an "authentic" Indigenous culture to be returned to that has not been transformed through colonial encounters? These reform efforts also downplay the possibility of the blending of the state and Indigenous communities in the self-construction of "Indigenous culture," and the impact of this unification in terms of broader claims to Indigenous political sovereignty and freedom from colonial rule. Moreover, at no point do working group members question the likelihood of "Indigenous culture" being dislodged from the discursive and material practices of white settler institutions that actively produce and circulate notions of what it means to be "Indigenous." Laclau (1995, 103) reiterates the importance of thinking this through more deeply when saying, "If a racial or cultural minority, for instance, has to assert its identity in new social surroundings, it will have to take into account new situations which will inevitably transform that identity. The main consequence that follows is that, if the politics of difference means continuity of difference by always being the other, the rejection of the other cannot be radical elimination either, but constant renegotiation of the forms of his presence."

The focus on authentic "cultural programming" was also challenged from within the Indigenous Peoples Collective, taken to task by some of its own members. Chuck, for example, was often asked to facilitate "cultural" events for Indigenous youth circling through his own program (revolving around criminal justice issues)[5]and those of the Indigenous Alliance. Chuck had a reputation for being a "cultural guy," in Saskatoon, that was the way Dakota first described him to me. He was an accomplished Cree singer and drummer, had spent numerous years on the Pow Wow trail, and had learned his cultural and ceremonial protocols from his father and grandfather while growing up on a reserve about a two-hour drive from Saskatoon. He was also responsible for initiating a Cree language program that ran at various locations in the city.

I accompanied Chuck one afternoon to a Pow Wow on one of the local reserves. He had been asked by his supervisor to take a group of youth from the Indigenous Peoples Collective on a cultural experience and asked if I would help to supervise the excursion. Sitting on metal benches, eating "Indian tacos," and watching a string of colourful fancy dancers roll in and out of the spotlight, Chuck expressed dismay at the lack of integrity he felt characterized so much of the cultural programming offered by the Indigenous Peoples Collective. "They don't even know what they are doing, none of them have been taught the right way. They want to do it because that's what they think they should be doing. But hardly anyone that works there knows anything about Aboriginal culture. It's tokenistic, it's not real eh?"

Now, Chuck may himself endorse a stable and fixed understanding of Cree culture, a set of beliefs, practices, and knowledges that was passed down intergenerationally through his own family. His testimony, however, points to the way that this thing that has come to be understood as "culture" within the Indigenous Alliance can quite easily disaggregate into a variety of narratives, rather than one comprehensive official story, about who Indigenous peoples are, depending on who you are talking to (see A. Simpson 2014, 97). In terms of the Indigenous Alliance, it forces us to think harder about the kinds of stereotypes and colonial representations of Indigenous peoples that might (un)wittingly be reproduced through their programs and the larger political work that the colonial state may be doing in rendering the "problem" of Indigenous peoples in Canada through a cultural lens.

## Resolving Conflict with White Settlers

Linked to the notion of using culturally relevant programming as a way to save Indigenous culture from further deterioration was the Indigenous Alliance's advancement of the idea that promoting cultural understanding and awareness in and of itself was a desirable goal because of its appeal to liberal notions of justice and equity. In other words, attempts at cultural inclusion served the purpose of making individuals feel as though they were doing the right thing, that social conditions were changing for the better, and that conflicts between settlers and Indigenous peoples could be solved by settlers understanding "the Indian way."[6] Liberalism, in part, relies on our ability to be respectful of others. When speaking to this point, Cathryn McConaghy writes (2000, 193), "Rather than cultural difference as perceived in terms of deficits, cultural relativism purports to perceive cultural difference in more positive terms." A liberal notion of pluralism requires us to profess tolerance and blindly provide the appearance of equality of perspective without thinking twice about the capacious network of colonial power that still exists.

This sentiment was captured succinctly by Sara, an Indigenous woman in her thirties, whose primarily responsibility in the Indigenous Alliance was the development of a cultural curriculum. Sara made clear that she believed one of the chief problems in Saskatoon was that white people just did not value the perspective of First Nations people. She equated the intense and widespread experiences with racism that was often cited by urban Indigenous youth as a result of a lack of information about Indigenous peoples and believed that if white teachers and youth workers were taught about Indigenous peoples through a series of workshops, that these "misunderstandings" could be resolved. "When you only think of one cultural way of knowing and one cultural group," Sara declared, "it automatically, through omission, denigrates the other ways of knowing and we have just had enough of that, that has just got to stop." She went on to explain, "I say quite explicitly in my workshops with teachers, that if they only teach from one perspective then we give the impression to our young people that that cultural group, their ways of knowing, what they do, how they do it is so much more important and that fuels that whole question of privilege and entitlement and that everybody's else's ways are not as valuable and I think there is a lot we can learn from each other. Actually, I think we need to learn from our Indigenous community."

Dave adopted a similar stance in his discussion of "authentic cultural experiences," such as sweats, for white settlers, as a vehicle for personal growth:

> Dave: Yeah it is awesome. And it is another way of building relationships and providing professional development they would never (emphasis) get anywhere else and it is also about personal growth and personal understandings and knocking down barriers that people have. I have had people who came into the sweat who said "I have never been to a sweat before, I don't know what to expect." It is that personal growth and you get through that first round and all your fear just drops away and you see the look on their faces of accomplishment and it is like they have overcome a barrier. And suddenly they are open to other opportunities. You know and there are teachings that are happening in there and they are asking questions, you know, why do you do this, why do you do that? Things that they never would have got to ask before. So, there isn't a single time that I don't come away just awestruck and amazed. And I watch these teachers and youth workers who are changed. They walk away changed.
>
> JD: So that is what you have found to happen? That they have changed?
>
> Dave: Yes. I have to tell you that it might have been three sweats ago. I had this teacher who informally told me that she hoped she was never placed in a community school because she could not even empathize with Aboriginal kids, so she would have no idea how to support them, she would not understand their culture and there was nothing she could do to help them and so if she was ever placed in a school she might have to resign or go on sick leave or something, she didn't know how she would cope.
>
> JD: She said that?
>
> Dave: I was aghast. I was just like how can you say that? You can't even empathize? I just thought where are you coming from and what is your level of ignorance that you already decided that you can't work with Aboriginal kids. I just couldn't believe it. Anyway, three sweats ago, there she was and she had come to this sweat and she is talking on and on and on. She has no idea what to expect and she is sitting beside me and she is scared.
>
> JD: What did you say to her?
>
> Dave: I said to her, "I am sitting right beside you and I am here and I am going to give you some sage to hold on to and you can hold on to the sage

and it will be fine and if you have any questions or anything I will help you through this." And when the first door opens and it happens and she is sitting there and it is almost like she is floating on air. She had this emotional experience and by the time the sweat was over, I don't know how many times she thanked me, again, and again, and again and that suddenly she understood that there was so much she needed to learn but she just needed to be open to it and she just needed to take a step out of her comfort zone and she had done that and for her that was powerful and she was just looking forward to further opportunities and I thought thank you god ... thank you god that you sent her here to allow her this opportunity because she might have gone the rest of her career thinking there was nothing she could do for Aboriginal kids or our people.

It is helpful at this juncture to turn to the writing of Fazal Rizvi (1993) and his explication of how particular constructions of race and racism, particularly racism as individual pathology, have a utility in the managing of social difference. Rizvi points out that individualist approaches focus on the negative, prejudiced attitudes of the individual and the existence of racism. Connected most often with the project of multiculturalism, this approach locates race and racism within the ignorance, irrationality, and pathology of a singular subjectivity and downplays the ways that subjects are produced within and through social and political histories (Rizvi, 1993). This theory of racism, then, is predicated on a set of normative assumptions about what constitutes the nature of the rational, socially accepted, and unprejudiced individual. Aligned with this view are social interventions, such as those of the Indigenous Alliance I sketch here, aimed at achieving more sensitive understandings of "cultural difference" and endorsing the demand for cultural competence in educators and youth service providers. In terms of the scope of programming for urban Indigenous youth, this conception has gained considerable traction and resulted in numerous attempts at curriculum review and the creation of professional development workshops that emphasize "diversity awareness" and fostering a change in the belief systems of individuals so they can become more aware of their own biases and prejudices and consequently become active agents in the (re) adjustment of larger processes of social change. This theory of racism as a matter of individual pathology, however, has been rightly criticized for its failure to problematize the structural nature of the systemic disadvantage of particular social groups (Dei 1996). How, then, does an argument about cultural misunderstanding or deficit in the Indigenous knowledge held by white settlers address the relations of domination framing Indigenous–state relations in settler states like Canada or the material power exercised by the state over urban Indigenous youth in institutions of education or criminal justice? Where is the material and political privilege and the attendant benefits of Indigenous dispossession for white settlers deliberated? How is the complicity of white settlers taken up within a tolerance framework? The answer to all of these is that it doesn't and isn't.

It is also worth noting that the testimonies of both Dave and Sara ran contrary to the words of a long-time activist in Saskatoon, Jane, who had worked for the Indigenous Peoples Collective, as well as a number of social service organizations in Saskatoon. As a white woman in her fifties, Jane had extensive experience navigating Indigenous–white relations in this prairie city. She often found herself in the middle of territorial arguments about funding and service delivery (some people in Saskatoon believed that only Aboriginal organizations should be "serving" Aboriginal youth),[7] and in the precarious space of having to navigate through what she called "a divided city," divided along racial and colonial lines. Nitânis and I were both working alongside Jane as she advocated for an organization in Saskatoon that would be informed by the lived realities of Indigenous young women and girls. I had come to know her quite well over the years.

On an afternoon in 2006, Jane and I drove out to Wanuskewin Heritage Park, a protected valley cut into the flat lands of Saskatchewan, with 6,000 years of Indigenous history,[8] to conduct a meeting about the possibility of creating this organization with representatives from a cross-section of youth organizations in Saskatoon. At the meeting there were representatives from the Indigenous Peoples Collective (Jane was associated with this organization at the time) as well as from several other Indigenous community organizations that offered programs to urban Indigenous youth and from youth organizations that did not explicitly frame their programming for Indigenous youth but ended up "serving" them, nonetheless, because the majority of youth accessing youth agencies in the core neighbourhood and downtown were Indigenous. There were approximately ten attendees in total.

The point of the gathering was to elicit feedback about guiding principles that could be used in the development of this new organization for Indigenous girls. What ensued over the next hour was what someone from the outside might describe as a yelling match. I would assert, however, that it was a contestation symbolizing the deeply political and historical relations that frame Indigenous–white relations in a settler city like Saskatoon. It is memory, resistance, and refusal rising to the surface.

During the course of the meeting, one Indigenous woman who worked at the local friendship centre exclaimed there was no way she was going to be involved in creating an organization for Indigenous girls if "colonizers were running it." A white service provider retorted back that white people wouldn't have to be involved with this effort if the Aboriginal community just paid attention to their own kids. And another Indigenous woman directed an accusation saying, "You have destroyed our communities and now you want to be part of the 'helping'?"

As we pulled out of the park grounds, on our drive back to the city, Jane referred to the eruptions at the meeting as par for the course in doing advocacy for urban Indigenous youth in Saskatoon. "White people and Aboriginal people just don't get along. We [white people] haven't taken the time to come to grips with the history, with everything we have done and are still doing. It's hard work, it's depressing work. Some days, I feel like the only thing that unites the white people of Saskatoon and Aboriginal people is Wanuskewin." Jane's assertions clearly indicate that a focus on the promotion of "Indigenous culture" is grossly insufficient in advancing a revolutionary struggle that seeks to end the socio-economic exploitation and political domination of Indigenous peoples by the Canadian settler state. It elides history. It masks ongoing colonial harm. And it projects the dangerous illusion that colonial relations of domination have significantly shifted.

\* \* \*

This chapter has demonstrated how a focus on "culturalization" (Grande 2004, 1) has resulted in the (re)inscription of liberal forms of tolerance and pluralism that firmly posit Indigenous–state relations as a matter of cultural misrecognition that needs to be rectified through state accommodation. Such an approach implies that there is some way to step outside the lens of historically sanctioned power relations to view the social issues facing urban Indigenous youth with a degree of impartiality. McConaghy (2000, 196) raises the inherent contradiction embedded within this liberal aim when examining the primacy of cultural relativism in Indigenous politics in Australia:

We don't live in a "horizontally" integrated community. Rather, we live in communities that are characterized by social hierarchies and numerous forces for dis-integration. As a central contradiction, the legitimation structures upon which cultural relativism draws its claims to epistemic authority, colonialism and bourgeois liberalism, have created a hierarchy of values. Cultural relativism's authority is only possible within this very hierarchy which it claims to be undoing. Further, those who use cultural relativism to develop projects for social justice and tolerance often do so from a position of considerable elevation within the colonial hierarchy.

Perhaps, it would behove us to consider the potential limitations of this approach to altering the social realities of urban Indigenous youth in settler states like Canada as well.

# The Dislocation of Self

I feel most coloured when I am thrown against a sharp white background.
  – Zora Neale Hurston, *How It Feels to Be Coloured Me*

Cover your tracks.
Whatever you say, don't say it twice.
If you find your ideas in anyone else, disown them.
The man who hasn't signed anything, who has left no picture
Who was not there, who said nothing:
How can they catch him?
Cover your tracks.
  – Bertolt Brecht, "Ten Poems from a Reader for Those Who Live in Cities"

On 20 April 2013, the headlines of the *Star Phoenix*, Saskatoon's premier newspaper, read, "Teen Receiving 16 Year Term in 'Appalling Case.'" The story was about the death of Mervin Clarence McAdam, a twenty-two-year-old First Nations young man, who had been murdered and then thrown into a dumpster, his body subsequently lit on fire. McAdam was completing 12th grade at the time he died as a result of strangulation and severe head trauma, after an altercation had broken out at a house where he was "partying" in Saskatoon. He was from the Ahtahkakoop First Nation, the youngest of four siblings, and had a toddler-aged son.

Bobby Dean Hannah, the First Nations young man who received the sixteen-year carceral term for McAdam's murder, was arrested and sentenced after pleading guilty to manslaughter and offering an indignity to human remains. According to media reports, Hannah had become involved with a gang[1] in Saskatoon at a young age, the

Indian Posse, as a way to obtain "a sense of family and belonging" (see "Teen Receiving" 2013). The comment thread following the article in the *Star Phoenix* contained a litany of references to Hannah's character, ranging from "unproductive" and "threatening" to "uncivilized" and "savage." Notably, there was a statement declaring that Hannah was an "uncivilized Indian savage," as well as one remark asserting that settlers shouldn't be blamed for defending themselves against people like him. Hannah was a youth at the time the crimes against McAdam were committed, although he was sentenced as an adult when the case came to trial and had been in and out of the justice system many times prior, for a host of offences, including what the state terms "aggravated assault." His weeping mother and younger siblings were present in the courtroom at the time of sentencing.

The stories of these two young Indigenous men, whose life trajectories are heartbreaking and immensely troubling, each in its own right, are clear examples of the high stakes facing participatory youth programs operating through organizations like the Indigenous Peoples Collective. Indigenous youth absorb the shock of conquest, both past and present. They carry the painful load of living in a settler colonial reality that, as I have written elsewhere, is intent on mutilating Indigenous bodies, dislocating them, holding them in captivity, and ultimately, making them disappear (Dhillon 2015). "The body has memory," writes Claudia Rankine (2014, 28). "The physical carriage hauls more than its weight. The body is the threshold across which each objectionable call passes into consciousness – all the unintimidated, unblinking, and unflappable resilience does not erase the moments lived through." Building a deeper, anti-colonial critique of what happens in the lives of young Indigenous men like Mervin McAdam and Bobby Hannah requires being vigilant about the way we unravel the normative frameworks that structure their everyday worlds. It demands that we look far, far beyond what we see in the headlines. And it compels us to look closely at the programs that are ostensibly designed to support them.[2]

In the spirit of such an inquiry, this chapter takes us to the ground of a criminal justice youth program of the Indigenous Peoples Collective, Journeying Forward, operating in conjunction with the educational mandate of the Indigenous Alliance. I am interested in providing a window into how social reform projects formulated through participatory politics are not simply suspended in the city's air but enter into the daily lives of urban Indigenous youth. "Power exists only when it is put into action," Foucault (1982, 788) observes, "even if, of course, it is integrated into a disparate field of possibilities brought to bear upon permanent structures." My purpose in this chapter is thus twofold. First, I set forth a descriptive account of Journeying Forward, revealing how this program can be read as inherently disciplinary while simultaneously positioned as functioning in "support" of urban Indigenous youth. Second, I make visible how Indigenous youth workers caught in the messy layers of program implementation find themselves in the contradictory space of having to navigate the ideologies of a colonial settler society while maintaining their own politics and beliefs about what is in the best interest of urban Indigenous youth. Struggling to make connections with these youth in a context where the threat of material deprivation haunts every corner of social interaction, I showcase how youth workers were repeatedly confronted with discourses of risk and the use of social science expert knowledge (Cruikshank 1996) when assembling an epistemological framework for assessing lived reality that could support an Indigenous youth colonial subjectivity.

The remainder of the chapter proceeds as follows. I begin by offering a descriptive account of Journeying Forward – providing program background, outlining its relationship to the Indigenous Alliance, and tracing the program's mission and goals. In the next section, I delineate Journeying Forward's preoccupation with advancing a settler colonial agenda in the lives of Indigenous youth by exploring how the notions of self-sufficiency, service delivery, and healing factor into the program's work. The rest of the chapter deals specifically with one youth worker, Chuck, and how he pushed back against the ideological framework of Journeying Forward through his support of and advocacy for an Indigenous youth, whom I call Derek. Chuck's ability to flex and twist the parameters of the program to align with his own understanding of the sociopolitical and economic context facing Indigenous youth suggests that, while these programs may be designed to serve the interests of the colonial state, some youth workers will, nonetheless, find a way to splinter them from within (although these actions are never without consequences). I equate this "pushing back" with an attempt at what Gayatri Spivak terms "affirmative sabotage."[3] In the end, I argue that the tensions emerging through my exposition of Journeying Forward signal the larger frictions experienced in the settler city of Saskatoon around the containment of Indigenous political claims, resistance to an ongoing settler colonial enterprise, and demands for social programs that meet the material needs of Indigenous youth navigating multiple settler social institutions and coping with extreme marginalization.

## Mitigating "Risk" and Scaffolding "Empowerment"

I have already mapped the ongoing criminalization and incarceration of Indigenous youth in Canada at numerous junctures throughout this book. It suffices to say that the Indigenous Peoples Collective, while spending a great deal of energy on educational interventions, was also involved in social programming for Indigenous youth coalescing around the criminal justice system – the mounting tensions between Indigenous youth and settler colonial institutions of policing a significant contributing factor. Conceived as a joint operation between the Ministry of Corrections, Public Safety, and Policing and the Indigenous Peoples Collective, Journeying Forward builds on the goals of both the UAYS and Corrections and Public Safety to "develop community capacity" by partnering with Aboriginal organizations. In addition, given the oft-quoted statistics regarding the disproportionate representation of Indigenous youth in Canadian youth prisons, the state was forced to respond, in some way, to this crisis – developing programs in direct relationship with Indigenous community organizations was part of this response.

With respect to an explicit set of objectives, Journeying Forward was posited as way to provide support services and "community connections" for a selected group of youth and young adults, aged twelve to twenty-four years, who had been categorized by Corrections and Public Safety as moderate to high risk to reoffend and had an active file with the Ministry of Justice. The "risk to reoffend" was determined by state agents employed by Corrections and Public Safety, through an examination of the youth's family history of intergenerational crime, family support, positive connections, addictions/substance abuse issues, mental health issues (usually equated with the classifications "learning disabilities," "anti-social behaviour," and "violence"), and connection (or not) to education. The story went something like this: these were Indigenous youth, many of whom were wards of the state, whose path into the criminal justice system was already well worn. This program, at least on the surface, was intended to (re)direct them from this path onto another one, where they would be able to shed their criminogenic tendencies and begin anew.

Journeying Forward also put a precise emphasis on educational programming for Indigenous youth as they transitioned out of detention centres back into the colonial social fabric of Saskatoon. Educational programming was, in fact, considered to be central in the healing of

Indigenous youth "in conflict" with the justice system, particularly the possibility for educational interventions to "restore cultural/First Nations" identity, as I mapped out in the preceding chapter. What this meant in practical terms, was that Indigenous youth were connected to multiple programs operating through the Indigenous Peoples Collective at the same time – since a significant component of the community safety plan for youth completing prison terms involved their reconnection with educational programming of some sort, the work of the Indigenous Alliance necessarily involved these youth, even though the impetus for a focus on education was being derived, in this instance, from the joint work of the Indigenous Peoples Collective and the criminal justice system. Moreover, given the Indigenous Peoples Collective's authoritative voice on matters pertaining to urban Indigenous peoples in Saskatoon, they were once again conceived as an "ideal partner" with which the state could engage through participation.

According to the coordinator of Journeying Forward, both young men and young women were permitted access to the program, although the majority of youth referred to it were young Indigenous men (approximately 75 per cent) – another indicator of the lack of gendered analysis in youth organizations across Saskatoon. The day-to-day operations of the program were headquartered at an Indigenous community organization located in the core neighbourhood so youth workers could be in close proximity to other state agencies and could be located in the area of Saskatoon where most Indigenous families resided. The program's primary target was youth who would be completing criminal justice sentences at youth detention facilities in Saskatoon (there were two main ones) in the near term or were already on probation. It was the responsibility of the state (through a state social worker or justice worker) to recommend youth to the Journeying Forward program. Once someone was referred to the program, a youth worker from Journeying Forward was asked to review his or her case file in collaboration with a state agent from Corrections and Public Safety in order to collectively determine a "community safety plan" for the Indigenous youth moving forward. The case file for the youth would be "co-managed" from that point on, and this meant regular check-in meetings between workers from Journeying Forward and Corrections and Public Safety. There were three or four youth workers employed by Journeying Forward at any given time, although employee turnover was high, and each one had a caseload of up to ten youth. All of the youth workers, as well as administrative staff overseeing the program, self-identified as Indigenous.

Jonathan, one of the higher level bureaucrats from the Indigenous Peoples Collective administering Journeying Forward, provided an analogy for the way he viewed the mandate of the program. "I liken it to the idea of crossing bridges," he told me one day while I was sitting in his office. "We offer services to the Aboriginal youth who are really struggling in their lives. We give them opportunities to be part of meaningful cultural experiences and other activities consistent with increasing our ability to control the risks in their lives. We help them figure out their strengths so that they will be the Aboriginal youth that will have the guts to cross the bridge to the Eastside." Jonathan's words were synonymous with the greater vision of the Indigenous Peoples Collective: to foster a better quality of life and culturally sensitive programs for urban Indigenous peoples in Saskatoon through programming that (attempted) to take into account their unique "needs" and, to some extent, their history. His statement also referenced the spatial, racialized poverty that separated the wealth and prosperity of the Eastside of Saskatoon from the struggle and crime associated with the Westside (as I have addressed in chapter 2). Some of the other activities that were considered consistent with reducing risk included securing housing for the youth upon release (a serious challenge in a city with a major housing shortage); connections to leisure activities; access to drug and alcohol programs, positive choice, and problem solving workshops; and facilitated connections to "healthy" family members.

In terms of the daily workings of the program, youth workers were expected to develop close relationships with their youth based on a mentorship, relational model, infused with what one worker described to me as a "non-threatening and friendly approach that gives youth hope." After establishing a community safety plan in collaboration with the state, a youth worker would arrange a series of visits to the detention facility, if the youth was still in closed custody, or set-up a series of activities during the week so that she or he could get to know the individual youth better. Through this relationship building, it was expected that the youth worker would draw on the youth's particular history and background when developing a plan for "reintegration"[4] post-incarceration. One of the most significant components of a youth worker's duties was the creation and ongoing revision of a "profile" of each of the youth whom he or she was supporting.

The creation of a "profile" involved a series of steps that began with the youth worker compiling a detailed history of the youth, including as much narrative description about his or her family as possible. Since the

program goals revolved around reduction of recidivism, youth workers were supposed to document any signs of the youth in their charge
exhibiting what the state called "pro-criminal" or "anti-social" behaviour – social actions that were defined by the state as being unlawful or
inconsistent with the dominant (white) norms of social order. The initial process included recording how a youth narrated and made sense
of his or her "negative behaviour patterns," which included things like
(according to the formal documentation guidelines) skipping school,
stealing, taking drugs, lying, hanging out with "bad kids," exhibiting
signs of anger management problems, and maintaining connections
to family members who might be involved with gang activity – basically anything that could be considered a contributing factor for future
"criminal activity." The youth worker would continue to ask questions
about the youth's life and interactions with family and friends and
record responses over a span of time. Youth workers were required to
make note of anything that signalled the likelihood that a youth would
reoffend as well as alert supervisors in both the Indigenous Peoples
Collective and Corrections and Public Safety when this happened.

The overall rationalization for the program was grounded in the
logic that, with the knowledge and skills offered through the activities
of the Journeying Forward program, coupled with the direct assistance
of youth workers, these young persons would be able to "have their
voices heard" and "see their crime patterns" over time and, in turn, be
empowered to create a series of short- and long-term goals. The goals
could then be phased in to allow for the young persons to make different, healthier life choices – choices that would apparently allow them
to lead a "positive" life in an urban centre like Saskatoon. In keeping
with the program's directive for a balanced and holistic approach to
supporting Indigenous youth entrenched in the criminal justice system,
these ambitions for individual change were outlined according to the
four quadrants of the medicine wheel that charts physical, emotional,
mental, and spiritual dimensions of life. The youth worker was supposed to direct youth in designing short- and long-terms life goals in
accordance with this framework.

Wedged in the logics of the program, then, was the idea that urban
Indigenous youth, and in this case youth who had committed crimes,
must be individually capacitated – youth needed a collection of skills,
knowledge, and rehabilitative experiences that would lead them down
the road of becoming more productive "citizens" of Canada. This perspective further assumed that these youth were acting from a position

of deficit whenever police apprehended them – that their entanglements with the criminal justice system were singularly a result of their
own wrongdoing and were not conscious acts of opposition to a neoliberal, colonial social order.[5] Jonathan made this clear to me when he
explained how youth coming into the Journeying Forward program
just needed to be put on the right path because they had grown up
without really knowing right from wrong and "their families were so
dysfunctional" with "no one to teach them these things." Viewed in this
light, the program tells of the state's commitment to saving Indigenous
youth from further social disintegration – a disintegration that was
fuelled, in part, at least according to Jonathan, by dysfunction within
Indigenous families and communities. It was about influencing the
way they came to think about themselves and their relationship to the
racialized and gendered space around them and the role they believed
they might play as individuals in creating their own destinies. What
was conveniently missing from this scenario, however, was how the
state circumscribed the choices that were made available to Indigenous
youth and the myriad ways structural forms of violence have actively
worked towards directing their conduct to align with particular ends.

On the surface, this program may seem "responsive" to urban Indigenous youth who are contending with the harsh realities of the criminal justice system and incarceration, affording them an opportunity to
"share their story by granting them voice." I would suggest, however,
that these empathizing interventions can also be critically assessed as
part of a continuum of settler colonial technologies of surveillance.
This is an especially important point, considering that the creation of
the program was premised on a direct line of communication between
the state and the youth workers employed by the Indigenous Peoples
Collective, even though the program itself is housed within an Indigenous community organization. While this is not an overtly disciplinary
tactic, to ask Indigenous youth who have been subjected to the abhorrent structural violence of ongoing settler colonialism to share their
histories, innermost thoughts, and future intentions paves the way for
their stories to become "objects of knowledge" (Foucault 1977, 24) –
knowledge that that can be drawn upon and manipulated by the state
to advance colonial goals and regulatory state functions. The compilation of detailed notes and oral stories[6] about who these youth and their
families are, then, served as part of the field of documentation used to
structure future decisions about their lives – an effective, potent means
of maintaining power as opposed to providing a conduit towards their

ostensible liberation. For example, if a youth disclosed that she or he had family members (and this could be parents, siblings, and/or cousins, associated with "gang activity"[7]), the youth was actively discouraged from contacting them, even though they might be the only source of social support. Formal disconnection from family and friends could even be integrated into a youth's probation orders.

Not surprisingly, one of the main sticking points during staff meetings of Journeying Forward was how youth workers were not doing a good enough job of "getting youth to talk." During once such staff meeting, Jonathan was complaining about how the workers were failing at having youth properly identify their "risk and protective factors"[8] and craft overall sets of goals that seemed realistic to achieve. One of the youth workers responded to this critique by saying that it was difficult to develop relationships with youth who were in prison, that it took time because they were so fearful of everything. In the youth worker's words, "They are scared of their own feelings and they don't want to tell us about their families. They don't just trust us right away." Is it any wonder that Indigenous youth who are caught in the dehumanizing captivity of prison are not willing to open up to yet another youth worker about their lives, Indigenous or not?

To argue for a critical gaze on the underlying assumption that Indigenous youth will be better supported by divulging their intimate thoughts and experiences to the youth workers of Journeying Forward does not imply encouraging the reverse: that youth should be silent about their lived experience. Rather, I am cautioning that a form of "empowerment and granting voice" that is sanctioned by the state, the very same entity actively involved in perpetuating conditions of Indigenous dispossession, may not, ultimately, be in their best interest. Moreover, the articulations of "negative behaviour" and individualized failure, which are so often associated with discourses of risk and crime prevention and often central to the project of personal change, work in tandem with upholding a normative settler colonial social order. They do not make linkages between everyday experiences, including the situations that resulted in an individual youth's incarceration, and the historical, political, and economic contexts that define Indigenous–state relations in Canada. And in no way are they reversing the gaze from "problematic Indigenous youth" to mapping the political geography and footprints of colonial policies and practices (child welfare programs, gentrification, criminalization, territorial seizure, gender violence, to name a few) that unquestionably mediate young Indigenous lives. In fact, as I explain in the next section, some of the staff of Journeying Forward actively reinforced notions of Indigenous pathology by channelling their work through the language of service delivery and by deliberately downplaying urban Indigenous youths' political critiques of the Canadian settler state.

## Service Delivery, the Trope of Individual Healing, and the Role of Expert Knowledge

I was taken aback the first time I heard one of the Indigenous youth who was part of Journeying Forward being referred to as a "client." It was during a brief exchange I had with the coordinator of the program while standing outside in the warm summer sun in a parking lot, early on in my research on the program. I had driven in at the same time as the coordinator, and we were walking into the building together. I asked her how she was doing and what she had on her agenda for the day. She mentioned to me, in passing, that one of the youth workers needed help with a "client" because there was an issue with the transition from secure to open custody, and she needed to attend to it as soon as she got to her desk. I was confused when she first said it, thinking that she meant the youth worker was having an issue with someone at another youth organization. After I asked her to clarify though, it was obvious that she was speaking about a young Indigenous man in prison, a young man that one of the youth workers from Journeying Forward had been assigned to support in his development of a community safety plan to be used upon his release.

The deployment of the term "clients" to refer to Indigenous youth is, perhaps, one of the clearest indicators of colonial state influence on the conceptual framework and subsequent operationalization of the Journeying Forward program. Advancing a program that works in the interests of the colonial state requires reframing the way the lives of Indigenous youth intersect with Indigenous politics in Canada more generally, as well as the way these young people factor into forms of resurgence demanding Indigenous sovereignty. Language factors into this reframing in important ways as power "relayed through external instruments" (Foucault 1982, 786). I am aware that this may seem an obvious point to some, but I would urge us to think more expansively about the work this reframing does in furthering the settler colonial state's desire to quell Indigenous political resistance in Canada. Having youth workers and the bureaucrats who administer the program in partnership with the state think through the lens of "clients and service delivery" positions urban Indigenous youth first and foremost as subjects of the state, in need of support. Indeed, the language of service delivery, often associated with developing programs designed in reactive response to allegations of poverty and social neglect, functions to disconnect the political and economic realities circumscribing the lives of Indigenous youth from their carceral experiences, even if these experiences are very much intertwined. What I am gesturing towards, here, is that, although this program was formulated under the direction of an Indigenous organization purportedly concerned with advancing the interests of urban Indigenous peoples, the reliance on state language of "offering services to urban Indigenous youth" and positioning them as clients is itself yet another tactic of deceptive depoliticization. Alfred (2009, 51) offers a grave warning in this regard:

> In such a colonial relationship, impositions of power and authority by the regime may be absorbed, tolerated, or accommodated by Indigenous people in various ways over time, but the conquest of the Indigenous population becomes inevitability only when settlers' imperial claims to legitimacy are accepted and normalized by Indigenous peoples. Legitimation (acceptance and support for colonial institutions) is a fundamental mandate of the colonial regime. The most important and immediate imperative once the seizure of land is accomplished is to assimilate those Indigenous peoples who have survived the initial assault on their existences. Without an autonomous and authentic Indigenous identity and cultural foundation, there is no memory store or intellectual base upon which to maintain oneself as an Indigenous person or for communities to maintain their cohesion and to challenge the colonial regimes continuing efforts to marginalize and disempower.

It follows, then, that a focus on "clients" and "service delivery" would lead to interventions in the program that privileged the individual healing of urban Indigenous youth, with a particularly heavy emphasis on their enrolment in rehabilitative educational programs that would enable them to find their lost First Nations identity and culture. A case in point is the answer offered by Shannon, one of the youth workers from Journeying Forward, when I inquired about how she approached "serving" urban Indigenous youth who were involved with the criminal justice system. Shannon explained to me that she focused as much attention as she could on their "personal healing," as opposed to "getting all political." In fact, "When they start talking about their families' experiences with residential schooling," she insisted, "I tell them to stop. All of them want to use that as an excuse for their behaviour. I tell them they're making their own choices and all they have control over is their own future. All of this bigger political stuff, I don't even know. They can't get mixed up with that. They can't even take care of themselves."

In this specific instance, Shannon was alluding to a young Indigenous man she had been working with over the course of six months. During their relationship building, this young man had expressed interest in learning about what Shannon characterized as the "political issues" facing Indigenous peoples in Canada. The young man wanted to know more about the history of residential schooling and how it had affected his family. When I asked Shannon if she thought that she might reconsider helping this young man acquire more information on this topic, she told me it wasn't part of the mandate of the program. "It's a hefty load working with these youth," she retorted. "You have to stay concrete and goal-oriented. I can't get sidetracked with every little thing they want to do. When they get out of a jail, they will need a job to support themselves. They need life skills. Otherwise, they will end up back in the same place as before."

Another youth worker shared an experience she had when one of her youth "became passionate" upon learning about Bill C-45.[9] In this case, the youth worker had been more responsive to the interests of this young man and provided additional resources for him to learn more, even while he was completing his prison sentence. This young man was so compelled by what he was learning, in fact, that he took it upon himself to write a letter to Stephen Harper expressing his views. The letter was published in the *Star Phoenix* several weeks later, with the support of the youth worker. When this youth worker mentioned to her supervisors that this had happened (which curiously, she did not record in her formal notes about the youth), they responded by telling her she needed to stay focused on the program goals and not bring her own theories into the work.

The insights of both of these youth workers signal how the Journeying Forward program functions as another site of political erasure in the lives of urban Indigenous youth, another way to uproot and distort the roots of the social problem so that their existence in a settler colonial sociopolitical reality is downplayed and their perceived deficit and dysfunction are what rises to the surface.[10] In deliberating on deracination in America, Keguro Macharia (2013) writes of it as a "persistent undoing," an elision of the intertwining stories of precariousness and social disorganization that lace the day in and day out of a life lived in colonialism's long, billowing shadow. Through programs such as Journeying Forward, urban Indigenous youth are unanchored from their historical lineage in a settler city whose very existence was born of genocidal dispossession – a circular process of elimination for which there is no state accountability. They are attempting "reintegration" into a settler colonial space that is, first and foremost, inhabited and fortified by institutional assaults on Indigenous families through racist social policies across the child welfare, health, education, and justice systems; racial epitaphs and jokes about the "drunken, lazy Indians"; grotesque colonial gender violence that carries on unabated; and a social service landscape where they are repeatedly cast as a crisis in need of state solutions. The focus is on their "rehabilitation" and "individual healing," as opposed to an acknowledgment of the political and collective healing that needs to take place between Indigenous peoples and the white settler state. "Repairing the psychologically injured or damaged status of Indigenous peoples," (Coulthard 2014a, 121) through the "discourse of healing" has been studied by Sam McKegney (2005, 85) as part of the state's agenda to position Indigenous peoples as the "primary objects of study rather than the system of acculturative violence." And in the parlance of Taiaiake Alfred (2009, 45), "Current approaches are often based on concepts of healing, reconciliation, or capacity building. Problematizing the people and not the state's behaviour, such approaches are not intended to alter the underlying, colonial, causes of unhealthy and destructive behaviours in First Nations communities." From this vantage point, Indigenous youth are the dirty wounds in need of settler colonial cleansing.

Adding to this, a host of literature written by social scientists informs the tools used by Journeying Forward in assessing the "risks of recidivism" for Indigenous youth and creating "service plans." These tools were drawn from the fields of developmental psychology and youth justice and were based on the conceptual models of social vulnerabilities associated with delinquency, with the aim of "identifying offending trajectories."[11] For example, in staff meetings, Jonathan would often refer to a list of tools outlined by Public Safety Canada that could be used to identify certain problem behaviours that were said to be precursors of reoffence. Risk factors were separated into two types: static and dynamic factors. Static factors referred to "historical characteristics" that could not be changed through intervention, such as history of violent behaviour and parental criminality. Dynamic risk factors, on the other hand, were characteristics that could change over time as a result of "treatment" and included things like school disconnection, substance abuse, and association with delinquent peers. Youth workers from Journeying Forward were supposed to be attentive to the dynamic factors, where it was possible for them to make a difference in reducing the overall criminogenic profile of a given youth.[12]

Now, while the potential usefulness of social science research in the creation of programs for urban Indigenous youth could be argued (albeit very contentiously from where I am standing), I would suggest that this research dangerously produces a singular epistemological framework for understanding their lived experiences. It also works to make claims about social interventions based solely on a framework that focuses on individual behaviours as the source of social breakage. Nowhere in these tools is there acknowledgment of or attention paid to how the Canadian criminal justice system was created by a settler colonial agenda, or to the ways that the system itself is structured through a racist legal policy and practice. For instance, I outlined in chapter 2 how Indigenous youth were being stalked, hunted, and criminalized by law enforcement agents in Saskatoon, which arguably increases their contact with the institutions of policing and justice, thereby making them "delinquents" in the eyes of the state. How is this inherent discrimination accounted for? When does the settler state itself become positioned as a "risk factor," given that its existence is predicated on the theft of land and the elimination of an entire people?

There have also been substantial critiques levied by critical scholars working in the fields of education and social work against the discourse of "at-risk," exemplifying the damage it does in terms of reifying the raced, classed, and gendered deficit perspectives of youth. Pica-Smith and Veloria (2012, 34), for example, argue that the notion floats through professional and academic contexts as a *tangible* construct instead of socially constructed one, the locus of dysfunction found in individuals of colour, single parent families (especially mothers who are not married), low income communities, and people with disabilities. Simply put, by downplaying institutionalized structures of inequality and building a systemic analysis of *what* places youth "at risk," this discourse functions to cultivate a social identity that once again pathologizes youth of colour and low-income youth (Fine 1995). Cruikshank (1996, 237) takes this one step further by outlining the utility of social science knowledge in the realm of modern governing, when she reminds us that:

> The social sciences can be seen as productive sciences; the knowledges, measurements, and data they produce are constitutive of relations of governance as well as the subjectivity of citizens. In devising the methods for measuring, evaluating, and esteeming the self, social science actually devises the self and links it up to the vision of the social good and a programmer of reform. In short, social scientists have helped to produce a set of social relationships and causal relations where there were none before.

In the case of the Journeying Forward program, then, social science research was called upon to produce a composite about who these youth were, largely because of its ability to offer directive insight into how to alter their political subjectivities and patterns of social conditioning. To put it another way, it is this knowledge base that, in part, produced the urban Indigenous youth as the "criminal" subject, as the one who lacks self-esteem, the one who needs to be "treated" through inventive social programming designed in partnership with an Indigenous organization.

## Containing Anger and Indexing Injury

The youth prison sat on quiet, inconspicuous residential avenue. Its back edge paralleled Highway 11, the road leading to the provincial capital of Regina. To reach the prison from downtown Saskatoon, I drove across one of the city's many bridges and made a few turns before parking my car in front of a rather generic looking house on a tree-lined street.

I was meeting Chuck. He had been working in Journeying Forward for about a year, and one of his "case files" represented the story of a young Indigenous man named Derek who was soon to be moved from secure to open custody for the remainder of his sentence. Chuck was assisting Derek in coming up with a plan for what would happen when he made this transition. Release from secure custody was often tied to a set of conditions with which the youth must comply. The conditions often included requirements to attend a school/education program, prohibition from no-go zones (neighbourhoods considered "off-limits" because of prior "criminal activity"), zero tolerance for the use or trafficking of drugs and alcohol, obligations to perform community service, banning of association with other "criminals" (read the youth's entire peer network and family), and observing strict curfews, often enforced by police presence.[13] If a youth failed to comply with these conditions, he or she would be "breeching" court orders and might be apprehended by city police and sent back to prison by a judge. Successive breaches could cumulatively result in a substantial extension of time served in secure custody.

Chuck was standing outside and leaning against his car when I arrived, arms crossed against his chest and looking rather relaxed on this warm and sunny summer day – tall, handsome, with jet-black short spiky hair. He was casually, but nicely, dressed in a light-coloured button-down shirt and jeans. The prospect of witnessing kids in cages didn't seem to rattle him in the slightest. He'd been to this institution a hundred times before.

"I'm sorry I'm a few minutes late," I said, quickly grabbing my things from the car and hurrying across the street. "I took a wrong turn back there and ended up having to ask someone for directions. I missed that sharp turn you have to take to get onto this avenue; it's not easy to see." Chuck smiled at me, saying nothing about my tardiness. "I didn't want to make you late for meeting Derek; I am sure the guards are particular about timing."

"Here," he said, and handed me a piece of fry bread wrapped in clear plastic. "Do you like bannock? I picked this up for you while we were at the Pow Wow. And just chill, everything will be fine."

I was smiling now too, holding the bannock in my hands. "Thank you for this."

"*Tapwe*,"[14] Chuck replied. "No problem."

The complex looked forbidding, as most prisons do. The grounds were encased in heavy-duty metal fencing, towering thirty feet at the highest points. The barricade of industrial-like buildings immediately facing the street made it difficult to see anything beyond the exterior walls; the territory inside hid and stayed hidden. A quick Google Earth search revealed the aesthetics of the prison from above: a large red roof set it apart from any other structure in the vicinity. A matching red dumpster sitting on the outer edge of the institution's perimeter was the only thing that escaped the protection of powerful steel latticework. Everything was still.

A rectangular sign staked into the ground with a large white pole triggered my curiosity as we walked up the sidewalk to the first of three security doors we needed to cross before being able to see Derek:

Admey Hall Youth Centre. Restricted Area. Trespassers Will Be Prosecuted.

The sign designated this institution as a youth "centre," distancing itself from the pejorative characterization of a prison or jail. The use of "centre" over jail or prison was a strategic discursive move, diverting attention from the hard realities of incarceration and penal discipline that were undoubtedly contained within these walls. It spun Admey Hall in a more positive light, towards the possibility of state-sponsored social regeneration that could make these youth into different people than when they arrived. It assumed they could be better citizens, rehabilitated state subjects who would more clearly align with the archetype of the ideal Canadian living in a sovereign Canada.

Chuck hit a small button on the concrete wall outside the first door. In a few moments, we heard a loud buzzing sound. He pulled it open, and we stepped through the first doorway. A heavy door slammed shut behind us, echoing through the building. The warmth and light of the day were sealed off. The outside world was gone. Another door. It, too, buzzed open for us, and we crossed the second threshold.

Inside everything was gray – walls of concrete blocks, metal doors, and cold cement flooring. We approached a window that had been cut into one of the walls, and a male guard, middle-aged, white, and slightly balding, was standing in the window behind a counter. "I have an appointment to see Derek," Chuck informed the guard. The guard looked down at a schedule on the counter and glanced at me. He was rattling his keys. "She's with me," he said. The guard nodded and told us to sign in and put all of our belongings in the cubbies immediately behind us. Cell phones, keys, wallets – everything was supposed to go into the wooden locker box. After we were finished, the guard led us down a hallway to the third and final door.

The door opened onto a small enclosure that measured about 8 × 8 ft. – more concrete walls; more cement flooring. There were benches erected along the bottom portion of the room's three sides, which served as seating for inmates and their visitors. A small Plexiglas window, defaced by frantic scratches and scribbles, was mounted in the top right corner of the wall immediately opposite us as we entered. It looked as though someone had taken a screwdriver and scraped back and forth across its entire surface, trying to break free. There was nothing else in the room except for Derek, who was waiting for us and leaning back against the wall, with one of his legs resting on the bench. His eyes were pointed towards the ground.

Derek was wearing a plain white t-shirt, gray sweatpants (issued to him by the detention facility), and relatively worn, low-cut basketball shoes. He was noticeably smaller than Chuck in height, with medium-brown wavy short hair. Glasses shielded his eyes, and he looked very youthful. Derek has been locked up for a number of years now and had to serve one more year of his multi-year sentence.[15]

As I stepped into the room, I noticed the movement of his hands right away. In a rhythmic beat, Derek was drumming his fingers against the bench and occasionally integrated his palm whenever the beat called for it. He smiled when he saw Chuck, and we sat down on one of the benches. The guard walked out of the room after telling us he would be back later.

"*Tansi*. So, how've you been *napew*?" Chuck asked. "And the *moniyâwak*? They treating you okay?"[16]

"Yeah, I'm good. Gettin' outta here soon." Derek's fingers were still drumming against the bench and occasionally he slapped his four fingers down at once. They never stopped moving.

"Oh yeah. We gotta get a plan going for that. This here is my friend Jas. She's lives back east but grew up in Saskatchewan. She's all right, though, she's okay," he said cajoling. "Done a lot of work with youth. Been hanging out with me." I assumed Chuck was teasing me as a way for us to ease into a conversation with Derek. He often used humour.

"Nice to meet you Derek," I said, offering a subtle smile. "Thanks for letting me come and visit." Derek nodded at me, somewhat uninterested, and turned his attention back to Chuck, his fingers were still drumming.

"Has anyone come to visit you here recently or what?" Chuck questioned.

"No, my Auntie came but that was like six months or so ago. She might come again."

"Do you have some clothes for when you are transferred to the new place? You know you will be able to go out during the day."

"No, not really."

"I will hook you up with some when you get out," responded Chuck. Derek nodded and then changed the subject.

"Can you get me another book to read? I finished the last one." Chuck told Derek that he would bring another book for him on his next visit. A few days prior, I learned that Derek had been asking Chuck for books about Indigenous history. The one he just finished was about the Riel Rebellion.

"That's cool you enjoy reading books Derek." I added, feeling a bit like an intruder at this point. I likely represented another adult who would come in and out of his life without anything about his reality really changing at all.

"I don't have much to do," he replied. "And we didn't learn anything like that in school."

"Like what?" I asked.

"Native studies and stuff. Like stuff about our people. I never had a class like that." He glanced towards Chuck. "And Chuck's been teaching me about that. And how to sing and drum."

"*Tapwe*. Pow-wow singing with the big drum," he was smiling broadly now. "And Dakota taught him [Derek] round dance with the hand drums. Should we sing something right now *cî*.[17] We have a guest here."

A few minutes later, after some discussion about what to sing and who should begin, Derek and Chuck broke out in a Cree courting song. Sung loudly, the following words erupted from a place the sterile and dehumanizing space of the prison had not been able to reach:

When the sun goes around to
The other side of the world,
And the moon comes out to play
With the stars at night
That is when I think of you
Think of you *neechimos*.[18]

Derek continued to drum his fingers against the bench while singing, only this time in concert with the sound of harmonizing voices that broke the stillness.

As we made our way out of the youth prison a short time later, Chuck turned to me and said, "What's sad is that jail is the safest place for Derek. He has nothing once he steps out of here, only the clothes on his back. He is like so many other Aboriginal kids I know. It's a tough go. Most of them will move from youth prison to the adult penitentiary. We are failing them over and over again. We are failing them."

The fact that Chuck conceived of prison as a "safe place" for Derek was, in itself, a staggering statement. And let me be clear that this perspective was not indicative of Chuck's lack of caring for young people like Derek. He was an extremely dedicated youth worker. Rather, he was acutely aware of what Derek was up against when he stepped outside the walls of a carceral institution and landed back on the streets of a settler city where he had little support. Derek had been a ward of the state since he was young, had no stable housing, and the majority of his family was inaccessible to him, according to the conditions of his transfer to open custody, as a result of ostensible gang involvement. Chuck's statements spoke to the grim reality that marked the world of urban Indigenous youth whose lives were caught up in the dirty work of colonial disposability. Somehow, in all of this, prison has become understood as an inevitable part of their destiny.

Over the course of a few months of getting to know Chuck and his work with Derek, I asked a great number of questions about how he navigated the Journeying Forward program. At numerous points, Chuck had expressed an overt critique of the program's mission, arguing that it was impossible for Indigenous youth to step out of the cycle they were caught in by simply filling out forms that charted long- and short-term goals. "It's a joke. This is a white system," Chuck said to me on one occasion. "It is not set up to accept these kids. Even if they did get themselves together in the ways that the organization wants, they would still lose. This is a very racist city; people aren't just going to hire Aboriginal youth in good jobs. And these kids have been caught in the criminal justice system now, which is so not good. They are going to try to survive in whatever ways they can."

Chuck was a youth worker, then, who wasn't interested in playing by the rules set out for him by Journeying Forward. Instead, he adopted an approach to relationship building that he argued was predicated on a sense of humanity and a historical awareness of the way colonial violence had impacted his people. "I treat these young people like human beings, like I would treat my own children. That's what this takes," Chuck told me one afternoon as we drove to a youth service organization in Saskatoon's downtown to meet up with another one of the youth in his caseload. "It's not a 9 to 5 job where you can just show up and ask a few questions and then leave," he continued. "These youth need us to be guides, but we have to treat them with respect first. They are not bad kids; they are kids that are caught in a system that is totally rigged. Aboriginal peoples in Canada have had a rough go of it. Colonization and residential schooling – that shit's real. It hasn't gone anywhere."

Chuck's more overtly politicized take on Indigenous–state relations translated directly into the way he approached working with Indigenous youth tangled in the criminal justice system. His advocacy for Derek, as a case in point, was not centred on identifying what risk factors would keep Derek from committing another "crime" but on helping him develop some sense of the social and political trajectory through which his life had moved, activating his political sensibility and historical memory. Chuck described to me, for example, how, when Derek was finished reading a book, the two of them would have a conversation about Indigenous politics and some of the "hot topics" gaining currency in the country. "I want to feed his mind," Chuck disclosed to me. "This kid could be anything he wants to be." Chuck also made a special effort to explain to Derek how his idea of "culture," of learning how to drum and sing, was also tied to a set of politics he had about what it meant to be an Indigenous person: that drumming and singing were not just about performance but part of ceremonial protocols tied to the land where his people were from and had been from for centuries.

Throughout the time we spent together, Chuck was also visibly frustrated with how Indigenous youth, who engaged with Journeying Forward, were frequently diagnosed by social workers as having "anger management" problems – a generic classification which could be derived from a whole range of actions, including fighting back against the local police or raising your voice too loudly to security guards, programming staff, probation officers, or other authority figures. This classification, Chuck clarified, regularly led to prescribing of drugs by local mental health practitioners. "Every last kid I have worked with has been diagnosed with something," Chuck told me his face stern. "They are sent to this white doctor and given a bunch of pills. It's really troublesome. They ingrain in the minds of these youth that they have mental problems when they are just reacting to the environment that they have to live in. Who wouldn't be angry? Instead, they keep getting told that this is wrong with you or that's wrong with you." Chuck then recounted one of the first case conferences about another Indigenous young man on his caseload:

> I walked into the room and there were ten people sitting there on one side of the table and this young man was on the other. There were social

workers, justice workers, police, a psychiatrist, a principal, and a teacher, all of them sitting there and staring at this poor kid. I sat down next to him and said, "Wow, this must be hard for you." I don't know how he survived it. And at that meeting, this doctor kept pushing for this young man to take his pills because the doctor kept saying, he [the kid] had violent tendencies, and this young man kept saying that he didn't want to. I finally convinced them to re-evaluate his diagnosis in a couple of months after I had some more time to work with him.

Chuck's critical stance on the pathologization of Indigenous youth, particularly the perceived exhibition of "anger" by Indigenous youth who are being asphyxiated by colonial state institutions, is in keeping with a growing movement to rethink how anger becomes both conceived and interpreted within the context of relations of domination. Glen Coulthard's *Red Skin, White Masks*, as a case in point, contains an entire chapter ("Seeing Red") dedicated to exploring the ways that "under certain conditions Indigenous peoples' individual and collective expressions of anger and resentment can help prompt the very forms of self-affirmative praxis that generate rehabilitated Indigenous subjectivities and decolonized ways of life in ways that the combined politics of recognition and reconciliation has so far proven itself incapable of doing" (Coulthard 2014a, 109). Leanne Simpson (2014a) espouses a similar view, writing on Indigenous and black resistance in the aftermath of the Ferguson riots,

I am repeatedly told that I cannot be angry if I want transformative change – that the expression of anger and rage as emotions are wrong, misguided, and counter-productive to the movement. The underlying message in such statements is that we, as Indigenous and Black peoples, are not allowed to express a full range of human emotions. We are encouraged to suppress responses that are not deemed palatable or respectable to settler society.

In a piece inspired by Coulthard's work, Jarrett Martineau (2014) similarly raises ideas of how righteous rage "affirms life by refusing to keep calm, to remain docile." While Chuck did not deliberately position his response to the issue of "anger management" in this way, his critique does have inklings of the need to revise and refine our understanding of what, I would assert, is an entirely appropriate manifestation of Indigenous youth resentment directed at the structural and symbolic violence enveloping their lives. Yet, the principles of Journeying Forward were doing little to challenge the way "anger" manifested in the actions of Indigenous youth was either critically understood or contextualized.[19]

## Not a Team Player

Chuck was often in trouble with his supervisors for not adhering to the guidelines for youth workers as laid out in the Journeying Forward program, for what he called "rocking the boat." I was at the office with him the day he received formal notification of his one year evaluation, which first came in the form of a letter and was followed by a meeting with his supervisors. We were supposed to be heading out to lunch when he received the notice. Chuck, shaking his head, quickly grabbed his things and asked me to meet him outside. I was curious about what had happened, since we had both been sitting quietly at his desk and catching up on a few things, the day uneventful up until that point. I left the office and waited next to the entrance to the organization as he had asked. Chuck emerged a few moments later. "It's my one-year evaluation," he said grimacing. "It's pretty rough."

Over lunch, Chuck laid bare the contents of his evaluation. "They keep telling me I am not a team player, that I am not following the rules," he said. "I don't care. I'm going to just keep doing my own thing." One of the primary points of contention for his supervisors was that Chuck refused to complete the large amount of paperwork associated with each youth on his caseload, including filling out all of the risk assessment protocol and goal sheets that were central to the operation of Journeying Forward. "I'm not doing any of that," Chuck said, standing firmly in his decision. "I am not convinced that doing all of that stuff is going to help these youth one bit, and I have no idea where that information is going either. They want me to tell them everything that my youth and me talk about? How are they going to trust me at all? These are smart kids. They know what's up. My job is to help them see there's another way, but I am not going to make shit up. We talk real."

Chuck offered a number of justifications for disregarding Journeying Forward's directives and the duties for youth workers. First, he made it clear to me that he considered Journeying Forward's emphasis on risk assessment to be void of an understanding of what Indigenous youth were facing in the back alleys and open streets of white settler society. "Who created all that risk indicator stuff anyway? It was Joe

Smith from Michigan," he said smiling slyly. "And he doesn't know shit about Aboriginal youth. There has to be another way to do this; I guess that's what I'm trying to figure out." Through his challenging of the conceptual underpinnings of Journeying Forward, it seemed as though Chuck was rejecting the portrait of individualized pathology that framed so much of the program, even though it embraced building "cultural and community connections" for Indigenous youth who had been, or were, incarcerated. He was also suspicious of what the state was going to provide, materially, for Indigenous youth at the end of the day, and he was critical of his fellow youth workers when he thought they were simply toeing the party line. As a result, among co-workers, Chuck was considered a bit of an outlier. Another youth worker for the program put it to me succinctly, saying, "He is always bringing his own political opinions into everything and when you're part of a team that doesn't really work."

Chuck also expressed how he felt a responsibility for the young people he was working with that went beyond the way the parameters of the job were laid out to him. And this sense of responsibility compelled him to push back against the idea that the structural conditions of violence organizing the lives of the Indigenous youth on his caseload were going to be easily rectified through a simple checklist of activities. This is not to say that Chuck didn't offer opportunities for the youth on his caseload to partake in some aspects of the programming offered through Journeying Forward. He did plenty of that too, but he always had an eye on the realities of what it meant to be Indigenous while growing up in a settler city. "Some of my youth have told me that when they get out of prison, they will probably go back to their gang. What am I supposed to say that? It's all they know and it's all they have. The best I can tell them is to try not to get killed and to not kill anyone else." Chuck was not naïve about how the settler state would come through and save they day for Indigenous youth, especially for youth who were already marked as "criminal" by the justice system. In the case of Derek, Chuck said, "Derek has no safety blanket. He has no fantasy life to hold on to that offers security or a clear sense that the system works. That life isn't going to be handed to him by the government."

Despite repeated confrontations with his supervisors, Chuck was able to hold on to his job, although it was obvious that he found it difficult to work under the auspices of Journeying Forward. Eventually, he ended up leaving on his own. After his departure, he explained to me that he felt as though he was unable to justify his position in the program any longer – a program that he believed was ultimately aiding the further destabilization of Indigenous youth in Saskatoon.

* * *

Throughout this chapter, I have argued that participatory programs like Journeying Forward are designed to reinforce the individual patholo- gization of urban Indigenous youth and to effectively depoliticize the social contexts that contribute to their entanglements with Canada's colonial criminal justice system. Even though Chuck attempted to shape the program in accordance with his own beliefs, the program itself was powerful in terms of its ability to keep criticism at bay and to employ youth workers who were uncritical of settler colonial social institutions as a whole. This program, then, was not simply about pro- viding services to urban Indigenous youth whose lives were caught in the barbed wire of the justice system. It was also about the telling of partial stories, discouraging critical thought about settler colonialism's persistent pressing down on Indigenous peoples, and suppressing all the ways urban Indigenous youth were made to feel inferior. This was a program contributing to the ongoing breaking of young Indigenous lives, to a kind of colonial living Macharia (2013) characterizes as "rapid erosion." Through Journeying Forward, urban Indigenous youth were being conditioned to just hang in there and keep hanging on while the world continued to fall apart all around them.

# Conclusion: Red Rising

Even in my disconnection from song, from dance,
I am not tragic
Even in seeing you as privileged,
As an occupier of my homeland in my homeless state
Even as men abduct as I hitchhike along these new highways
To disappear along this lonely colonial road
I refuse to be tragic

> – Lee Maracle, "Blind Justice"

There are other worlds. Other kinds of dreams.

> – Arundhati Roy, *The End of Imagination*

*Prairie Rising* began with an entry into the world of urban Indigenous youth and the constellation of discourses of crisis, risk, and recognition that circulate around them. These discourses, I have argued, scaffold a network of participatory social interventions ostensibly designed to alleviate their social suffering and set them on the path to an alternative destiny. By way of conquest, and more recently, a strange incarnation of necrophilic settler benevolence, Indigenous youth in Canada have become the involuntary recipients of state-sponsored "care" and redemption – young people engulfed by "solutions" to the dehistoricized "crisis" that has befallen them, "answers" powered by the state-projected irrecoverability of Indigenous life. Yet, Indigenous youth are simultaneously anti–settler state subjects who must bear the heavy weight of colonial (re)booting, bodies, spirits, and minds caught in the cyclical, spinning wheels of what Sherene Razack (2015, 28) calls

Canada's "annihilative impulse" to make Indigenous peoples disappear. They are the most discernible barriers to the long awaited endpoint of Indigenous elimination that seals the deal, so to speak, on Canadian sovereignty, the most clear and present danger to the continuation of white settler society.

In shining an anti-colonial light on the ways that Indigenous youth have been bound up in the colonial logics and institutional cages of state-run education, criminal justice, and child welfare systems, this book has tried to detail how crisis stories about Indigenous youth come into being in the first place. One of my central preoccupations in writing this, then, has involved adjusting the aperture through which we come to understand and make sense of the everyday lived realities of these young people and of the hegemonic, normative structures, buttressed by colonial violence from above, that so powerfully govern their lives. In doing so, I have tried not to lose sight of the materiality of what it means to be an Indigenous youth living in a Canadian city, not to minimize the brutality that comes with having one's body be the site of colonial imprint over and over again. I have attempted to remind us that these ongoing colonial assaults are lived, breathed, and fought against by Indigenous youth every single day. These vicious strikes are very real, and they are far from receding. Engaging in such revelatory work is a challenging task to undertake while being attentive to the incredible strength, compassion, and imagination that is ever present in so many of the Indigenous youth I have encountered. It is true that colonialism orders their lives, but in the end, it is not what defines them. I am reminded, here, of Nitânis, who, even after contending with years and years of structural violence in state institutions and on the street, shows remarkable grace, kindness, and ingenuity in her interactions with everyday people. She simply refuses to give up her humanity.

By this point, it should be clear that this book was never intended to make a series of knowledge claims about indigeneity itself. It should be read, first and foremost, as an indictment of the Canadian settler colonial state. Perhaps most obviously, then, this book has endeavoured to problematize how federal and provincial governmental strategies, generated under the liberal, pluralist politics of recognition and inclusion, have fostered a host of state–Indigenous alliances aimed at "improving" the lives of urban Indigenous youth. Enlisting the "participation" of Indigenous communities in the design and implementation of social programs for Indigenous youth in urban centres across Canada and the subsequent state–community alliances, as I have shown throughout this book, is a deeply fraught endeavour. It is part of a long line of man-agement solutions to what the colonial imaginary views as the recalci-trant "Indian problem," which has shown itself to be more resilient than expected. Consequently, these alliances, which are extolled as marks of linear social progress while their exponents vociferously seek to negate Indigenous presence from within, are a flashing, neon WARNING sign to those engaged in the hard work of decolonization. Translated into more basic terms: look in the other direction if you so choose, but do so at your own risk. This is a ship with cavern-sized leaks.

The larger structure of dominance framing Indigenous–state relations is fundamental to the inner workings of participatory governing strate-gies. Wildly unequal power relations regulate the boundaries of who partakes in these projects and the substantive parameters under which they take place – Canada's emergence as a settler state, born of blood and occupation, cannot be separated from them; nor can the countless ways that settler societies continue to benefit from the marginalization, abjection, and subjugation of Indigenous peoples be downplayed. The social construction of the "problem" of Indigenous youth, as portrayed by these alliances, warrants intellectually rigorous and unrelenting interrogation so that we don't lose sight of the present-day acts of ter-ritorial seizure and Indigenous dispossession that tell a very different story about what's really going on.

As an advocate and scholar who thinks a great deal about how to thread together critical knowledge and reflection to produce strategic political action, or what Paulo Freire (1970, 51) demarcates as "praxis," I am aware that a sustained politics of encounter with all of the above demands a sustained politics of transformation; the old refrain rever-berates – Where do we go from here? How does the critique set forth throughout this book push us to revisit the question of justice and free-dom for Indigenous youth? Where are the decolonial points of rupture in the state systems in which we find ourselves? How does decolonial praxis[1] shift when we put Indigenous youth at the centre of our politi-cal strategies for radical social transformation? How do we make space and care for the existence and persistence of decolonial potentiality within our present world? What risks are we willing to take? What and where are the lines of sacrifice?

As a non-Indigenous person growing up on Cree land in Saskatch-ewan, I am in no position to be directive towards Indigenous nations about shifting political strategies and the multivariate forms of resis-tance to colonial occupation that already exist; Indigenous nations have always resisted – without the aid of settlers, I might add. What I offer are some provisional points for consideration, harnessed from my work as both an advocate and a scholar, and these became clearer to me as I went about the business of researching and writing this book. I offer them in the spirit of allyship, in solidarity, and with acknowledgment and the utmost respect for all of the Indigenous scholars whose incredible intellectual prowess, evidenced throughout the chapters of this book, has strengthened my arguments, forced me to tussle with my own thinking, and made me realize all of the things that I still don't know and may never know. Their guidance has been crucial; their wisdom remarkable. As Jodi Byrd (2011, 229) eloquently points out, "Indigenous scholars engaged in Indigenous critical theories that draw from the intellectual traditions of their own histories and communities to contravene in, respond to, and redirect European philosophies can offer crucial new ways of conceptualizing an after to empire that does not reside within the obliteration of Indigenous lives, resources, and lands." I believe this to be true.

The considerations I offer are also based on important, vital lessons I have learned from Indigenous and non-Indigenous comrades working alongside Indigenous youth in non-governmental organizations and in the messy and politically charged spaces of state agencies and institutions of higher education – all of us are implicated in one way or another. It also merits stating that these speculations are by no means exhaustive or complete. They are a series of loose starting points for deliberative dialogue – beginnings and more beginnings – about inciting decolonial imaginaries and fuelling the anti-colonial resistance that is informed by an Indigenous relationship to land and life. The conflicts and tensions produced by settler colonialism are not easily resolved with a set of fabricated "solutions" or quick lessons learned, but that doesn't mean we aren't obligated to push ourselves into new spaces of anti-colonial disruption, to tunnel our way through to alternative possibilities of social and political existence that advance Indigenous resurgence and freedom.[2]

Finally, in outlining the propositions that form the body of this conclusion, I reflected on my own insights as a person of colour who knows she is living on stolen territory. I have learned a great deal over the years about the ways that Indigenous histories and struggles have been elided within the dominant anti-racism discourses of social change. People of colour are situated in and through incongruous terrain in Canada, as collectives marginalized by a white settler nationalist project, while at the same time being invited to take part in the pervasiveness and harmfulness of ongoing settler colonialism (Lawrence and Dua 2005). Following Razack (2015, 27), here, I contend that "rather than focus on our individual histories of dispossession and migration, and thus handily avoid the question of what it means to live in a settler colonial state, people of colour and white settlers alike must confront our collective illegitimacy and determine how to live without participating in and sustaining the disappearance of Indigenous peoples." Thus, the propositions that follow are an ethical articulation of the political responsibility I have inherited as someone who carries a Canadian passport and calls Canada home. I hope we can build from them.

## Outside In and Inside Out

It is predictable and justifiable that the first inquiry someone might make after reading this book is whether or not I am calling for a wholesale dismissal of working within, or in collaboration with, settler state agencies in advancing decolonization and Indigenous sovereignty and in shifting the brutal realities facing so many Indigenous youth. There is no uncomplicated answer to this question, and undoubtedly, this is a matter of political strategy that warrants deep and careful consideration, trepidation with no end. Still, the critique set forth in this book involves elevating the importance of a critical decolonial praxis that acts from outside the so-called justice and freedom offered through state mechanisms of recognition and redress. Glen Coulthard (2014a, 3) captures this succinctly when saying, "The politics of recognition in its contemporary liberal form promises to reproduce the very configurations of capitalist, racist, patriarchal state power that Indigenous peoples' demands for recognition have sought to transcend." While I recognize the need for ongoing advocacy to change social policies and practices from within domestic government agencies, legal systems, and institutions (and I speak to this shortly), as well as through international treaty bodies and declarations, I would argue it is short-sighted and dangerous to assume that the settler state is simply going to step in and right its own wrongs – regardless of how many more inquiries are called or reports commissioned or participatory strategies developed. If, as Andrea Smith and Taiaiake Alfred have warned, the state is the chief perpetrator of violence in Indigenous nations, its institutions, agencies, and programs cannot be the place where justice is found, nor can strategies for eradicating colonial violence and fostering decolonial futures be rooted in these power structures. "There is no freedom to be found in a settler state, either one that would seek to give it or take it away," writes Jarrett Martineau (2014, para. 19). Alternatively, there must be a turning away from state protestations of assistance and a turning towards the longstanding strength, artistic practice, intergenerational wisdom, and epistemologies that are central to Indigenous ways of life. There must be an arsenal of resistance to colonial violence (including violence that is targeting youth) that is rooted within Indigenous nations themselves – a flourishing, in the words of Leanne Simpson (2011, 17), "of the Indigenous inside." This would be a future world and a decolonial movement, in other words, operating on Indigenous frequencies.[3]

Yet, Indigenous youth continue to be caught in the strangulating webs of settler state institutions – there is no escape route that will be quick, no jetpack immediately ready to launch that will free them from the colonial state's death grip. As Coulthard (2014a, 179) rightly observes of the sociopolitical and economic realities confronting Indigenous peoples across Turtle Island, "Settler-colonialism has rendered us a radical minority on our own homelands, and this necessitates that we continue to engage with the state's legal and political system." Coulthard goes on to argue that this present condition demands that we begin to approach our engagement with the settler state apparatus with a high degree of critical self-reflection, scepticism, and caution – vital components of an Indigenous resistance movement mounted on hostile terrain. Furthermore, this means we need people working in settler state spaces and agencies that embody a politicized understanding of Indigenous–state relations and the strong hold state institutions have on the lives of Indigenous youth through micro, everyday actions. We must advocate for the creation of youth organizations that relinquish the language and practice of service delivery and instead foreground the social and political histories and present-day realities of colonialism when considering program creation and advocacy for Indigenous youth.[4]

For those of us within institutions of higher education, this also means we have an obligation to make substantive, critical changes in the areas of curriculum, hiring, and public programming.[5] The social workers, youth workers, probation officers, nurses, doctors, aid workers, criminologists, and police, along with many novice researchers, are being "trained" within our post-secondary institutions, an intellectual and learning space from which they derive a portion of their knowledge about the world. What forms of critical pedagogy are we using to challenge the dominant modes of address invoked in everyday references to Indigenous peoples across Turtle Island? How are we ensuring that the whitewashing of our fields of study and program areas is not feeding into the production of a new set of "professionals" willing to take up the goals of the settler colonial state? At stake in accomplishing these critical changes, then, is the way we conceive of our teaching itself as a political act. We need to seriously consider the discursive ammunition we are offering to our students, who are active agents in the world (see e.g. Césaire 2001). We need to add this to our matrix of strategies and tactics if we haven't already.[6]

## Decolonizing Youth Studies

Researching and writing this book, I was repeatedly confronted by the utter lack of critical thinking and writing about Indigenous youth from both within and outside the academy. While there is no shortage of governmental reports charting the challenges facing Indigenous youth within colonial state institutions, youth studies scholars and social policy makers have paid very little attention to the ways that the distinct political and material formation of settler colonialism has mediated the scope and frames through which we understand Indigenous youth experience in settler states (Lesko and Talburt 2012). Thus, one of the most prominent insights emerging from this book is that there is an urgent need to decolonize and politicize youth studies and (re)position the centrality of Indigenous youth within the purview of critical Indigenous studies and Indigenous feminism. When we position Indigenous youth at the centre of our work we see an entirely different way of engaging; we have an entirely new perspective on what it means to move forward while looking back. The political rationales that undergird these fields of study are not without consequence. They are part of the way we evolve an alternative frame for sense making in the greater landscape of decolonization.

Decolonizing and politicizing youth studies includes taking a giant step away from the grossly homogenized renditions of Indigenous youth experience in the quest for Indigenous sovereignty – a crucial corrective to the cursory lip service paid to the diverse nature of the materiality of the social (Farmer 2004). As I have made visible throughout this book, settler colonialism impacts bodies differently, depending on their social markings and the political subjectivities that have attached themselves to a colonial consciousness. Indigenous youth differentially experience injustice, lack of protection, policing, social regulation, as well as state intervention, containment, and disciplinary punishment – these things operate in different ways depending on how they are read by the state and society (take Indigenous girls, as a case in point). In a striking example of this multiplicity of experience, Billy-Ray Belcourt's (2015) talk "Queer Bodies, Failed Subjects," at the North American Indigenous Studies Association Meeting, highlighted the fundamentally affective impact of settler colonialism on queer Indigenous bodies that serves as "an affective rupturing of our attachments to life, to each other, and to ourselves." In doing so, Belcourt's incantation, which summons the figure of the queer Indigenous poltergeist, demands that we rethink the criteria for membership in a decolonial future and pay heed to the numerous ways that settler colonialism winds itself around Indigenous bodies, including through the destructive work of heteronormativity. In a similar vein, Robert Innes and Kim Anderson's (2015) edited collection, *Indigenous Men and Masculinities: Legacies, Identities, Regeneration*, crucially draws our attention to the colonial manifestations of masculinity that intersect with indigeneity in a series of profound twists and turns.

I would also argue that decolonizing youth studies will push us to make connections between Indigenous youth's lived realities in settler states and the environmental degradation (vis-à-vis extractive processes) that is occurring on their homelands at rapid fire pace. Indigenous lands are under constant threat from domestic and international fossil fuel companies and the provincial and federal governments in Canada – the tar sands are only one example of this devastation.[7] Indigenous youth who will, in the not so distant future, become the leaders of their nations are unquestionably tied to and implicated within these struggles. Keeping them locked up in state detention facilities, assaulting and murdering them on the streets, and holding them in conditions of intense deprivation and poverty only supports colonial goals of ongoing land dispossession for the purposes of capitalist accumulation.[8] How might knowledge about the linkages between Indigenous dispossession and extractive processes compel Indigenous youth to self-mobilize in different ways?[9] Without making an explicit attempt to politicize and decolonize the field of youth studies, this relationship will remain grossly under-theorized and largely unexplored.

## Indigenous Futures,[10] Imagination, and the Rise-Up Generation

Powerful words rang out on the banks of the South Saskatchewan River during a protest in Saskatoon on an exceptionally brilliant and luminous day in December of 2012.

> This is the rise of Indigenous awareness, the Indigenous presence. And the reality is that the potential of who we are as Indigenous peoples hasn't been fully realized yet. The potential for what our children are bringing, for what our young people are bringing has yet to be witnessed by Canadian citizens and yet to be witnessed by the world. And we can see that among our young people who are here today. I feel that this is a stepping-stone for our young people to witness and experience for they are the ones who are going to carry on.[11]

The activist who spoke these words was one among many who came together at Vimy Memorial that day. Despite the deep snow and sub-zero climactic freeze, parents, children and youth, community members, activists, academics, artists, and other allies joined the rally organized as part of a growing Indigenous resistance in Canada. This grassroots movement,[12] widely known as Idle No More, is a national platform to bring Canada's history as a white settler colony to the centre of the country's political stage and support the rebuilding of a nation-to-nation relationship based on Indigenous sovereignty – an entitlement that forms the basis of treaty agreements between the Crown of the Dominion of Canada and Indigenous peoples at the time of Canada's colonial founding.[13]

I arrived at the protest with a colleague and friend of mine, Jane, having just flown into the Treaty Six (Cree) territory of Saskatoon from the north-eastern United States. I was doing my best to adjust to the glacial temperature – eyes watering, breath seizing, and extremities beginning to numb after only a few minutes of exposure to the icy air. Rather quickly though, my feet fell in rhythmic step with the beat of the round dance, and I focused my attention on the variety present in my immediate surroundings – ceremonial songs, drumming, prayer, and awareness-raising speeches were at the core of this gathering, all of these peaceful activities revolving around Indigenous demands for territory, dignity, political autonomy, and a natural world where things continued to grow in abundance. People were embracing one another with enthusiastic and unfettered words of solidarity, suggesting a unified front. I listened to conversations laced with nascent hope for this northern and geographically diverse land of towering trees and canopied forests, of arctic ice bound to ancient truths – a terrain rich with aging rock fields spanning an otherwise solitary expanse of Canadian shield, where acres of pale yellow and green grasses undulate in the warm prairie winds in summertime and youthful mountain tops reaching high into night skies, speckled with billions of stars, at all times of year – a vast country, many have said, with scattered, threatened waterways that hold the makings of life itself.

As a conduit for political organizing, Idle No More is raising fundamental, urgent questions about decolonization, ecological destruction, and the tenuous and fraught relationship between the first inhabitants of this land and the sanctioned entity of the Canadian settler state. Originating in Saskatoon,[14] Idle No More initially coalesced around a nationwide interrogation of the legislative omnibus Bill C-45 but has expanded its reach to raise awareness with respect to a vast array of social issues. In doing so, it articulates a framework for political change positioned both as a counter-attack against structural violence and a visionary discourse, charting a thorny path towards "what could be." Through organized teach-ins, protests and rallies, blockades and flash mobs, and consciousness-raising arts and documentary projects, Indigenous peoples and their allies are shining a judicious spotlight on historic and contemporary social realities that deftly and deeply intertwines the politics of land rights (territory) with a politics of place and culture – a rejection of the decontextualized usage of "culture," I described in chapter 5 of this book. Bill C-45,[15] specifically, removes the environmental protections of a vast number of Canada's rivers and lakes in order to facilitate the nation's economic development (through the amendment of the Navigable Waters Protection Act), contentiously evidenced in the expansion of tar sands mining and the proposed building of pipelines to carry carbon-intensive oil from Northern Alberta to the Pacific and Gulf coasts for overseas shipment. The omnibus bill also includes provisions to bypass important consultation procedures with Indigenous peoples around resource extraction projects taking place on, or moving through, Indigenous territory, thereby potentially easing corporate access to ancestral land. A sampling of the additional material stakes (re)surfacing in the rippling tides of this movement include inadequate housing, high poverty rates, rampant violence against Indigenous women and girls, limited access to medical care in many remote communities, contaminated drinking water and environmental degradation, the underfunding of education for Indigenous children and youth, the over-representation of Indigenous peoples in the criminal justice system (both youth and adults), and alarming apprehension statistics for Indigenous children in the child welfare system.

In the midst of this passionate activity, my colleague was stopping every few feet to introduce me to someone new, laughing with them (and me) about how I was having trouble handling the weather, despite the hand and foot warmers she had placed in my boots and mittens. Personal cell phones and other handheld technological devices were memorializing the event. Media crews quickly assembled their equipment to facilitate the creation of "made-for-TV" bits and pieces that would later tell partial stories to eagerly awaiting, and perhaps sombre, members of the Canadian populace. There were legions of people who had come out to support the event in the frigid cold, and the obviously jubilant and energizing atmosphere immediately struck a chord with me. A march of winterized feet mapped critical questions through pristine blankets of snow, attempting to historicize amnesic public debate on the "Indigenous question." Somewhere in the sky above, the sound of brave birds reverberated through unforgiving air. I watched as smiling children played in the powdery whiteness, imprinting the ground with snow angels and running up and down the steps of the memorial gazebo, either side of the white circular-like structure flanked with large Idle No More banners. Many people held posters and placards stamped with phrases:

I Will Fight for My Rights
This Government Is NOT Representative of Us as First Nations
You Forgot Our Permission
Education NOT Prison for Our Youth
I AM the Embodiment of Treaty
Our Land Is Sovereign Land

A range of Indigenous flags flew high amid Canadian, American, Saskatchewan, and British flags, occupying a powerful and rightful place among these symbolic representations of colonial governance, occupation, and capitalist ownership.

There was a soft, delicate mist drifting up from the snowed in and glowing frozen river, the trees covered in thick white frost, creating a kind of metaphorical and spiritual backdrop that suggested inevitable

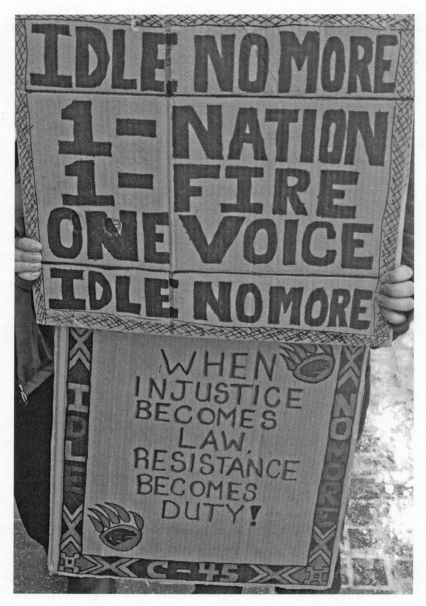

Figure 6. Signage from Idle No More Rally, 2012 (Photo credit: Jaskiran Dhillon)

change was coming, even in the presence of seemingly intractable social conditions.

Most notably, however, there was a youthful presence that could not be undermined. A presence that called attention to hard lessons learned from those whose lives are lived on serrated edges. The young people participating in this rally were fervently contesting the dissonance between the alleged privileges and benefits of growing up in Canada and the social policies and laws through which they perceived their lives to be regulated and restricted. On this day, they were not passive on-lookers in their rejection of an unjust political order, and they were certainly not silent – one couldn't reach the sky, no matter how close it seemed, with wings crafted from desperation alone.

What Idle No More has most visibly ushered in, is an awareness that Indigenous youth are already on the front line of the fight for decolonization in Canada and are rising to this challenge with passion and power. "Youth engagements in Indigenous participatory politics has been a crucial thread of the Idle No More Movement" writes Karyn Recollet (2015, 142), "where youth develop a critical consciousness through the creation of new media and the use of technology to mobilize." While movements like Idle No More are not an ideal type, in the Weberian sense, or a refined blueprint for decolonialization within settler states like Canada (for an insightful reflection on Idle No More, see Martineau [2015]), they nonetheless pave the way for new ways of being to come to light, for visionary forms of Indigenous futurism to enter into our imaginations, to be seeded, and to grow.[16] Finding ways to support Indigenous youth who are part of this front line resistance work should be foundational to the way we are thinking about decolonization and Indigenous resurgence. If we are going take seriously the leadership role that can be assumed by Indigenous youth in the fight for Indigenous freedom, then we need to identify concrete ways to bring those opportunities into being, for their leadership to flourish.

On a related point, there is a growing cadre of scholars who are opening up space to (re)imagine, (re)invent, and (re)vision how Indigenous creativity, the act of creation itself, is a necessary strategy for survivance, for new ways of imagining the world, reclaiming Indigenous presence, and transforming reality. In *Creative Combat: Indigenous Art, Resurgence, and Decolonization*, Jarrett Martineau (2015, 10) alludes to the importance of Indigenous creativity when he remarks that "we must not only locate creativity within the anti-colonial struggle, we must inhabit sites of generative indeterminacy: emergent spaces of creation from which

Figure 7. Idle No More Protest, 2014 (Photo credit: Marcel Petit)

to imagine and perform decolonial possibilities into being." Through-out the pages of *Creative Combat*, Martineau charts the way Indigenous creativity, both past and present, resists colonial ruses and snares. He pursues the vital question of how Indigenous art, broadly conceived, contributes directly to decolonial thought and political action. In sync with Martineau, Recollet's (2015, 143) *Glyphing Decolonial Love* guides us to consider how "creative solidarity challenges the influence of mul-ticulturalism's narrowly defined Indigeneity, and offers up geographies of resistance which manifest in relationship with traditional caretakers of the land within distinctive Indigenous urban spaces." To my mind, this work holds important implications for connecting and supporting Indigenous youth throughout Turtle Island. What if we harnessed our resources towards these ends, towards producing spaces of creative engagement that could become ammunition, in Martineau's and Recol-let's formulation, in the struggle to decolonize? How might this aid in the envisioning, by Indigenous youth, of a different kind of future? I am not suggesting this is a simple matter of developing a few art programs to be scattered across colonial institutions here and there (although those too serve a function), but that we think long and hard about how the arts may be the place where we can foster critical consciousness and perhaps draw upon an armoury of Indigenous inventiveness that still lies sleeping. Perhaps it's time, as Martineau (2015, 51) suggests, that we "look for new weapons" to nurture the rising red tide.

### #ItEndsHere

In February 2014, I was asked to participate in a blog series, *#ItEndsHere*, documenting the horrific reality of murdered and missing Indigenous women and girls in Canada. The frozen body of Loretta Saunders, an Indigenous young woman attending university in the Maritimes, had just been found. I was joined by a host of other writers and thinkers – Siku Allooloo, Leanne Simpson, and Tara Williamson among many others – all attempting to shine a much needed spotlight on how brutal assaults on the lives of Indigenous women and girls continue while many of us wilfully ignore what is happening, how the isolation persists, and how the exploitation and murder continues to be positioned, strategically, as a problem of their own making. In an opinion piece published in the *Northern Journal*, Allooloo (2015, para. 5) passionately writes, "As long as the status quo prevails, more of us will continue to be killed. Meanwhile, we must also endure the ongoing violence of a society and judicial system that have yet to affirm our rights as human beings. This barbarity could not continue if enough people were in touch with their own humanity."

Perhaps it goes without saying, then, that colonial gender violence in Canada is alive and well. It has not recessed into historical record or taken a back seat to other forms of violence enacted upon Indigenous nations. What much of this book tells us, rather, is that there is a war raging against Indigenous women and girls across Turtle Island. And an awareness of the material, everyday violence that is a core feature of being an Indigenous woman or girl in Canada pushes us, as Sarah Hunt (2015) urges, to rethink conceptions of what is politically significant within the context of Indigenous struggles for sovereignty and self-governance. It calls for a suturing together of the microdynamics of daily life with macropolitical struggles for land. It demands that we bring gendered violence, police brutality, the carcerality of everyday life, the death of kids in care, and a willing neglect of Indigenous communities into the realm of the political, and that our strategies of defence be always attentive to this materiality (Hunt 2015, 4). In concrete terms, this also means that we must be moved to mobilize every time an Indigenous woman or girl is subjected to state violence and to support Indigenous communities in developing alternative pathways for addressing violence in their own communities in ways that minimize state contact. "It's in all our best interests to take on gender violence as a core resurgence project, a core decolonization project, a core of any Indigenous mobilization," attests Leanne Simpson (2014c, para. 10), in her contribution to the blog series *#ItEndsHere*. I believe this call to action is unmistakably clear.

* * *

The story of one remarkable Indigenous young woman unleashed the ideas of this book into the critical chapters that form its core challenge to the settler state of Canada. The last time I saw Nitânis, in the spring of 2015, when she stopped by my family home in Saskatoon for a visit, she was contemplating what she was going to do next in her life, ever reaching for possibility, always standing her ground. In many ways, her life compels us to (re)cast Saskatoon as an *Indigenous city*; a city that bears the traces, scars, and open wounds of settler colonialism, but also a place where both the strength and fight of Indigenous youth are ever present, inseparable from Indigenous peoples' resistance and spirit to foster brave new worlds. It is from them that all of us will learn what it means to rise, and keep rising, in the wake of a colonial battle still raging.

# Notes

## Introduction

1 I use the word "disappeared" to signal a range of issues regarding Nitânis's removal from her biological parents by child welfare authorities. Adherence to principles of confidentiality and anonymity prevent my disclosing further details.

2 "Structural violence" refers to "violence that is exerted systematically – that is indirectly – by everyone who belongs to a certain social order … in short, the concept of structural violence is intended to inform the study of the social machinery of oppression" (Farmer 2004, 307).

3 See, e.g., Canada's parliamentary report on *The Sexual Exploitation of Children in Canada* (Canada, Standing Senate Committee on Human Rights 2011); MacDermott (2004). With respect to children and youth, the discourse of sexual exploitation has largely replaced that of prostitution in the social service and legal arenas in Canada. This formal distinction highlights the particular vulnerability of children to sexual procurement practices along a continuum of power and violence. "Commercial sexual exploitation" is also used to acknowledge the financial gain accrued, often by an adult, through this violence and to demonstrate that the use of children and youth for sexual acts is abuse and is inherently exploitative. Indigenous young women and girls are disproportionately represented among this population – an extension of the gendered and sexualized violence of colonialism, a point I take up later on in this chapter.

4 In the same vein, Johan Galtung (1990, 294) argues that "a violent structure leaves marks not only on the human body but also on the mind and the spirit."

5 In the poignant words of Andrea Smith (2005, 5), "Despite the more than 500 years of genocide that Native peoples have faced, they continue to survive

and organize, not only on their behalf but on behalf of all peoples." Lorenzo Veracini (2011, 4) argues that "it is resistance and survival that make certain that colonialism and settler colonialism are never ultimately triumphant." And twenty-five-year-old Lakota hip-hop artist, Frank Waln (2014) asserts, in his 27 November *Guardian* article, "America's colonial project failed. We're still here, and we're keeping our ceremonies and traditions alive."

6 I am indebted to my colleague Timothy Pachirat for kindly allowing me to borrow the structure of one of his sentences.

7 In making this point, it is not my intention to downplay the suffering Nitânis has experienced or the constellation of factors that have produced her individual experience within the legacy of colonialism in Canada. Rather, I wish to underscore that a focus on her singular experience negates the larger political issues at play and misses the whole point of including her story within this broader context. For further evidence of this collective experience of deprivation as lived by numerous Indigenous youth in Canada, see chapter 2 below.

8 Sherene Razack (1998) offers a compelling discussion of how "race" works ideologically as racism to reify culturalist explanations for alienation and marginalization that bypass the important questions of how colonial power relations have, in fact, created massive social inequalities.

9 Indigenous writer and academic Leanne Simpson (2013b), in her 22 October *Huffington Post* exposé, reports on the recent RCMP attacks on Indigenous protestors at Elsipogtog, New Brunswick. In doing so, she offers an overview of recent (as of time of writing) land contestations in Canada, and related struggles between Indigenous peoples and the Canadian state. Her trenchant words echo: "Over the past several centuries we have been violently dispossessed of most of our land to make room for settlement and resource development. The very active system of settler colonialism maintains that dispossession and erases us from the consciousness of settler Canadians except in ways that (*sic*) deemed acceptable and non-threatening to the state. We start out dissenting and registering our dissent through state-sanctioned mechanisms like environmental impact assessments. Our dissent is ignored."

10 The notion of an "authentic" Indigenous identity, as regulated by the state, has been critically explored by several scholars, including Sarah Maddison (2013), whose article "Indigenous Identity: 'Authenticity' and the Structural Violence of Settler Colonialism" offers an insightful synopsis of some key points.

11 See Statistics Canada (2002). In Western Canada, these cities are Saskatoon, Regina, Winnipeg, Calgary, and Edmonton. Statistics Canada's 2002 report,

*Youth in Canada,* indicated that the largest concentrations of Aboriginal youth are found in the western provinces: 16 per cent in Manitoba, 14 per cent in Saskatchewan, 6 per cent in Alberta, and 5 per cent in British Columbia.

12 References to the "crisis" facing Indigenous youth can be found across academic writing and within community-based and government reports centring around the social and economic realities facing Indigenous peoples in Canada. See the many sources cited here, the *Action Plan for Aboriginal Youth* (Canada, Standing Senate Committee on Aboriginal Peoples 2003), and the many publications emerging from the Native Women's Association of Canada (NWAC) and provincial ministries across Canada. I take this up in greater detail in chapter 2.

13 Yasmin Jiwani (2006, xii) succinctly defines "discursive" as "the parameters defining particular subject matter in terms of how it is thought of and talked about."

14 See Coulthard (2007), for an excellent, well-developed critical analysis of liberal settler multiculturalism within the context of Canada, and the resultant problematics and limitations.

15 See, e.g., Povinelli (1998); Cowlishaw (2003); Muehlmann (2009) on the complicated terrain of Indigenous desire.

16 Bill Cooke and Uma Kothari's (2001) edited volume provides a collection of essays that speak to the various ways the discourse and practice of participation intersects with modern approaches to global development.

17 It should be noted that my focus on explaining theoretical frames in this section is intentionally abbreviated. While it is undoubtedly important to map out the analytical terrain and repositories of scholarship upon which this book builds, my overall purpose in writing this account is to highlight, in descriptive and rich detail, the empirical realities that enable us to consider and consider again many of these concepts. The nuances and microinteractions that make up everyday life are then essential to refining and reshaping the space of the theoretical; and as Nadine Naber (2012, 14) argues, when thinking about the way scholarship can become disconnected from the public, "We have lost sight of empire's subjects."

18 I am aware that the emerging field of settler colonial studies has been regarded by some scholars as a white attempt to think through contemporary colonial relationships and hence entails several political and ethical risks. Nonetheless, in its assertion of settler nation states as particular political formations that demand specificity in our understanding of colonialism and as distinct from other colonial societies in many respects, I believe it usefully shifts the conceptual register toward

examining a type of jurisdictional power and sovereignty exercised by the state over Indigenous people within a context of ongoing governmental authority, predicated on the dispossession of land and control over people from "within" national boundaries. This does not mean, of course, that, as an analytic tool, it is not without its inherent weaknesses or that we should not critically engage in a careful and rigorous assessment of its utility within concrete Indigenous political struggles and social movements. For the purposes of this book, however, I am relying on the broader contributions this theory makes with respect to disrupting mainstream understandings of the Canadian state's historical and present-day relationship to Indigenous peoples. See Alissa Macoun and Elizabeth Strakosch (2013), for a more nuanced discussion of these points

19 In the introductory chapter to his *Settler Colonialism*, Lorenzo Veracini (2010, 1) offers an in-depth explanation of the concept of a settler colony and provokes a series of reflections when stating, "Colonizers and settler colonizers want essentially different things."

20 See, e.g., Flannigan (2000), for a dominant account of Canada's making as a nation.

21 While it can be claimed that the treaty process in Canada is an attempt to offer redress for land seizure, I would argue that a Crown-sanctioned process of granting portions of Indigenous land "back" to the original inhabitants of Canada, a process that has been mired in years of court delays, requires ongoing, critical assessment (Milloy 2008).

22 See Sarah Carter (1997) on cultural imagery.

23 Razack (2002) is especially useful in illuminating these points.

24 See "A Brief History" (2009), for a succinct summary of the marginalization of Indigenous women in Canada.

25 See, e.g., Jamieson (1978); Silman (1987); Barman (1997–98) on these issues.

26 In her review of the justice system's responses to extreme levels of violence as experienced by Indigenous girls, Kelly MacDonald (2005, 15) writes, "In our work as advocates, we have been alerted to situations where Aboriginal girls have been disbelieved, treated abusively, or criminalized by the police in response to their reports of male violence."

27 These points are underscored by my previous research highlighting the problematics associated with the homogenization of the urban youth experience in general (Dhillon 2011).

28 See, e.g., Foucault (1991; 1982) for additional clarification. A detailed elaboration of Foucault's theory of governmentality is not possible within the limited scope of this introduction.

29 Adding to this discussion, Hindess (2000, 119) says, "Government, in Foucault's view is a special case of power: it is a matter in other words

of acting on the actions of others (or even oneself). But the governmental regulation of conduct also involves a significant element of calculation and a knowledge of its intended object, neither of which is necessarily present in every exercise of power."

30  In its mapping of the implications and resulting contradictions and tensions of these inclusionary projects within a larger discussion of Indigenous political claims and lived experience, *Prairie Rising* finds linkages with scholars in anthropology and in work on Indigenous and minority rights in other contexts, especially Povinelli (2002); Garcia (2005); Postero (2006); Kowal (2008). I also contribute to a cadre of committed but sceptical scholars who are concerned with understanding how modern governing practices shape and frame the lives of marginalized peoples; see, e.g., Gupta (2001); Popkewitz (2004); Levin (2004); Sharma (2006); Fairbanks (2009); Lukose (2009); Ticktin (2011); Fassin (2012).

31  Timothy Mitchell (1991, 78) signals the way modern techniques of governing account for the prominence of the state idea without attributing to the state a "coherence, unity, and absolute autonomy" that it does not have.

32  Rose goes on to describe five fundamental effects of the new technologies of advanced liberal governments, which include making economic life more like a market, fragmenting the social into a multitude of markets, making employees into entrepreneurs, and "designing in control."

33  David Goldberg's (2009, 336) work also lends insight into the way racial meaning has animated neoliberal attacks on the welfare state and reinforced the notion that those who are deserving, those who belong in society, are racially coded as white. The remaking of the state through neoliberal tactics of privatization, coupled with the promotion of the trope of self-improvement and individual merit divorced from social and political contexts, partly comes into being, then, through *racial* neoliberalism, where race remains a key structuring technology in modern state formation.

34  Tania Li's (2007) scholarship on improvement schemes and the way colonial social practices position people as subjects with various capacities for action and critique is also instructive in provoking a set of questions about how governmental programs are devised, what various techniques they assemble, and ultimately, how they are transformed or fall apart. In *The Will to Improve*, she emphasizes the importance of making visible the way seemingly unassuming tactics of education, persuasion, motivation, and encouragement operate at a distance, yet powerfully, and rely on processes of translation to reify state authority, invoke expert knowledge, and adapt social projects in attempt to "improve the human condition," projects that in this case are specifically targeted at urban Indigenous youth.

35 The concept of "relations of ruling" was created by Dorothy Smith (1988) to argue for a feminist sociology that draws attention to the patriarchal forms of our contemporary experience alongside the dynamic advance of the distinctive forms of organizing and ruling contemporary capitalist society.

36 While the inclusion of a detailed history of the relationship between Indigenous peoples and non-Indigenous peoples in Saskatchewan is not possible within the scope of this chapter, a brief commentary on this history is worth noting; see Carr-Stewart's (2003, 223) work on the history of Indigenous peoples in Saskatchewan,

> between 1871 and 1905 the Cree, Saulteaux, Dene, Dakota, Nakota, and Lakota peoples entered into treaties with representatives of the British Crown. In exchange for imperial commitments and services, First Nations agreed to share their traditional land with the newcomers who journeyed to their vast prairie territory. Today the land known as Saskatchewan is home to a population of one million people of whom in 2001, 13.3 percent self-identified as Aboriginal. The larger non-Aboriginal portions of the population are mainly descendants of settlers who moved from eastern Canada and Europe. Despite a century of residing together within provincial boundaries, the two communities – Aboriginal and non-Aboriginal – have mostly remained apart geographically, economically, socially, and educationally: separation fostered by culture, languages, lifestyles, and rural versus urban living, and legally by reserve boundaries, the Indian Act, and the Constitutional division of powers between the federal and provincial governments.

37 See Lawrence (2002). Also, see Savage (2012), an excellent deconstruction of the settlement saga of the Western plains; and Daschuk (2013), on the spread of disease in Indigenous communities across the Western plains.

38 Including Manitoba, Saskatchewan, and Alberta, the term "prairie provinces" denotes the vast lands between Ontario in eastern Canada and the Rocky Mountains in the west. These provinces constitute the largest wheat-producing region in Canada and are a major source of petroleum, potash, and natural gas. More recently, the prairies have been associated with oil production via the tar sands; the largest extractive industrial development project in the world is housed in Fort McMurray, Alberta.

39 In 2007, the Provincial Partnership Committee on Missing Persons conducted a review of long-term missing persons' cases in Saskatchewan and found in its final report that 60 per cent of the missing women in the province were Indigenous, even though Indigenous women make up only 6 per cent of

the total population. Notably, there have also been numerous murders of Indigenous girls and women in Saskatchewan. Laura Robinson (2004) has written on the lack of diligence in solving crimes against Aboriginal women and girls in her 24 June *Globe and Mail* article, "The Women We've Failed."

40  E.g., at the end of 2010, a Canadian Broadcasting Corporation's (CBC) radio program, *The Current*, ran a three-part series about Indigenous youth in Saskatoon, highlighting the enormous shifts in demographics and related concerns over employment, incarceration, and gang activity.

41  The notion of "race-based privilege" has most recently been associated with former Saskatoon Member of Parliament Jim Pankiw, a Reform and Canadian Alliance MP who calls for equal treatment for all in Canada and speaks out against Indigenous claims to special status within the country ("Controversial" 2010).

42  Opposition to the federal compensation of now close to C$2.8 billion (and growing) to Indigenous peoples as a result of the Truth and Reconciliation Commission's (2012) inquiry into residential schooling and related claims of physical and sexual abuse, cultural disintegration, and family breakdown (to name a few) are also commonplace. See Truth and Reconciliation Commission of Canada. (2012).

43  According to the web entry "Origin of the Name 'Canada'" on Canada's government website, which gives the etymology, the name "Canada," comes from the Iroquois word "Kanata" meaning "village" or "settlement" ("Origin of the Name" 2013).

44  The relevance of including this section in the introduction, in addition to locating myself within this research, is linked to Joseph Maxwell's (1996) idea of the integration of experiential knowledge into the development of a conceptual context for a research project. In other words, tracing the history of my work in this area is part of the process through which the conceptual orientation for this project was developed. In addition, I do not wish to position myself as a dispassionate researcher merely engaged in the process of research for the sake of research. Instead, I seek to situate this project within my broader trajectory of youth advocacy across multiple locations in Canada.

45  See Walia (2013) for an excellent discussion of the immigrant rights movements in Canada in conjunction with issues of capitalism and settler colonialism.

46  As defined by the Government of Canada, a youth is identified as someone between the ages of 15 and 24. This range changes slightly depending on how it is taken up by certain government departments. Please see the United Way's *Environmental Scan* (2010) for further information.

47 I use this term in quotation marks to illustrate the lack of consensus around how best to support an Indigenous youth on the road to self-actualization. Youth service workers often have varying perspectives on how best to address marginalization across multiple fronts. For example, in my work I have often come across discussions of the merits of skills-based training as opposed to accessing formal education.

48 This is not meant to suggest an essentialized understanding of Indigenous children and youth in relation to educational experience. My work as an advocate for young women living in poverty has made me acutely aware that gender, class, and sexuality intersect with these experiences in equally important ways.

49 For a recent overview on this point, see "Negative" (2016).

50 I am grateful to my colleague and friend Miriam Ticktin for her insight in helping me think through the ethnographic methods that are central to this project and for her guidance about the crafting of this section.

51 Robert Innes's (2004) article "American Indian Studies Research Is Ethical Research" was instructive in providing guidance around the research terms of engagement.

52 This chapter is especially important for a readership outside of North America who may be unfamiliar with the specificities of this location and is also valuable in setting the stage for comparative analysis.

## Chapter One

1 Another account of the same rally estimates that over a hundred police officers were present (Klein 2014a, 299).

2 I have chosen to use the word "protectors" over "protestors" to signal, discursively, that Indigenous people engaged in political resistance against extractive projects are doing so as part of an ancestral ethic to protect and defend the land that is rooted in Indigenous epistemology. This resistance often becomes positioned by the colonial state as an act of "protest" that is violating the safety of a (white) "public and law and order" as established by the settler colony. For further information on this point, please see Heidi Stark's (2016) "Criminal Empire: The Making of the Savage in a Lawless Land" in *Theory and Event*.

3 Media representations of the protests in Elsipogtog are reflective of the stereotypical imagery associated with Indigenous peoples in Canada. As writer and academic Leanne Simpson (2013b) has importantly pointed out, in her 22 October *Huffington Post* article, these representations consistently recycle images of the angry, armed, and dangerous Indigenous protestors

who have no legal land rights, thereby reinscribing the notion that "they deserved to be beaten, arrested, criminalized, jailed, shamed and erased." See Mitch Wolfe's (2013) article from 22 October in the *Huffington Post*, for the type of media reporting to which Simpson refers.

4 Patrick Wolfe (2011, 34) argues, in fact, that assimilation itself is the most efficient settler colonial technique of elimination, for "in neutralizing a seat of consciousness, it eliminates a competing sovereignty."

5 Ironically, in the international realm Canada is also constructed as a "peacekeeping nation" that exists outside larger imperialist agendas. This national mythology masks the history of colonization and discriminatory immigration legislation in Canada and also works to create an authoritative position from which Canadian state officials can speak about worldwide atrocities without being held accountable for social conditions in Canada. *Dark Threats and White Knights* by Sherene Razack (2004) is an excellent deconstruction of Canada as a nation of "peacekeepers."

6 See the work on equality rights by Public Service Alliance of Canada (2013) as documented on their official website.

7 See news report by CBC ("Robert William Pickton" 2007), for an overview of the Pickton Trial. Information on the provincial commission on missing women can be found on the official website of the Missing Women Commission of Inquiry (2013).

8 In my overview of Indigenous–settler state relations, I use the term "the state" to refer to the formal political and bureaucratic apparatus through which "technologies of government" are enacted (Scott 1995, 192). The vast majority of literature describing the relationship of Indigenous peoples and the Canadian nation employs this more Marxist and Althusserian definition, treating "the state" as "up there," with stored powers ready for deployment and domination over citizen and non-citizen subjects (Nash 2000). Part of the theoretical work of this book is to complicate this notion by including an analysis of those schemes that work on and through the practices and desires of the target population across numerous sites, such as the Indigenous Peoples Collective, which operate outside formal state structures and political institutions (Li 2005). However, to map the historical trajectory of Indigenous–settler state relations in Canada, one has to assume some degree of spatially concentrated power of "the state," especially in the early stages of Confederation and nation building, where domination and coercion became characteristic of the types of political strategies and tactical measures used by the newly forming nation when confronting the existence of the peoples who were already living on the land. Ferguson and Gupta (2002) have written on the construction of the

state and the social and imaginative processes through which it is made effective and authoritative.

9  Some of the scholars who have written entire books on this history include Newell (1993); Pettipas (1994); Nadasdy (2003); Belich (2009); Smith (2009).

10  A compilation of essays by Lisa Ford and Tim Rowse (2013) offers a number of reflections on the co-constitutive nature of these interactions, however unequal they may be. Writing in opposition to scholars like Patrick Wolfe and many others cited throughout this book, Ford and Rowse (2013, 2) reject the positioning of settler colonialism as a "structure bent inexorably on dispossession, subordination, erasure, or extinction." However, while I see the value in critically investigating the incompleteness of settler states and the various roles played by their "Indigenous interlocutors," I would argue that the empirical evidence of the present suggests, overwhelmingly, that the structures of colonialism, as lived by the descendants of the Indigenous communities of contact, continue to govern the lives of so many and make only certain ways of life possible. This book is one of these empirical representations.

11  See Bird and Engelstad (2002), on the various interpretations of the merits of the Royal Proclamation.

12  After the American War of Independence and the War of 1812, the British settlement of the Maritimes and of Upper and Lower Canada greatly intensified (Shewell 2004, 7).

13  The three main objectives of the Indian Act, as projected by the nascent Canadian state, were considered to be (1) assimilating Indigenous peoples, (2) better managing Indigenous peoples, their lands, expenditures, and resources, and (3) defining which Indians were entitled to federal resources by developing the legal basis for claims to Indigenous identity and enfranchisement (Isaac 2000, 140).

14  The effects of the imposition of the Indian Act, as delineated by Adrian Tanner (2009), include disorientation, disempowerment, discord, and disease.

15  Shewell (2004, 17) concludes that liberalism involved more than a new economic order. Rather, it was a way of thinking and behaving rooted in new ideas about individualism, property, and the politics of free choice. It thus redefined the relationship between the individual and society, and it propelled the emergence of the modern secular state.

16  In Canada, a "reserve" is defined by section 2.1 of the *Indian Act*, RSC 1985, c I-5, as a "tract of land, the legal title to which is vested in Her Majesty, that has been set apart by Her Majesty for the use and benefit of a band." The Act also specifies that land reserved for the use and

benefit of a band, which is not vested in the Crown, is also subject to the Indian Act provisions governing reserves. A reserve is similar to a Native American reservation, although the histories of the development of reserves and reservations are markedly different. While the American term "reservation" is occasionally used, "reserve" is usually the standard term deployed in Canada (Miller 2000). In outlining some of the economic implications of reserves, Calliou and Voyageur (1996, 118) also explain that "the Canadian state, through its federal and provincial jurisdictions, has legislated access to the land and its resources for the benefit of corporate interests and to the detriment of Aboriginal peoples."

17  "Colonialism's project, in Michael Stevenson's words, 'was, and still is, to lay waste a people and destroy their culture in order to undermine the integrity of their existence and appropriate their riches.' It is pursued via 'total war' legitimized not only through racist construction but through creation of language celebrating colonial identities while constructing the colonized as the antithesis of human decency and development, thereby establishing a justification for their physical, historical, and cultural annihilation. This language 'becomes the basis for the forming of national identity and for providing the state with an organizing ideology' whose racist, imperialist concepts become institutionalized as the 'democratic nation-state' in which hatred of the Other is bureaucratized. That is, racism becomes part of the structural base of the state, permeating the cultural life of the dominant society both by its exclusive narrative of dominant experience and mythology, and by its stereotypical rendering of the 'Other' as peripheral and unidimensional" (Green 1995, 88; quoting Stevenson 1992).

18  In the literature I have reviewed on this topic, there is very little written on the range and forms of political resistance employed by Indigenous people during this specific historical period. However, it would be naïve to assume that this did not, in fact, occur. As Miller (2000, 314) points out, "In the twentieth century, Indian political movements would become better organized and more effective in bringing their grievances to the attention of both government and the Canadian public. Although the bureaucrats and politicians continued to act until the 1960s and 1970s as though Indians were childlike and incapable of influencing policy for the better, the Indians eventually forced an unresponsive Ottawa to pay them heed." Perhaps this is the legacy of a particular type of scholarly preoccupation. Audra Simpson's recent book, *Mohawk Interruptus: Political Life across the Borders of Settler States* (2014) is an excellent contribution to the contemporary instantiation of political resistance and assertion of Indigenous sovereignty.

19  It should be noted that, even though the Canadian government was outwardly moving towards a different governance style in relation to First Nations people, discriminatory practices continued. For example, non-Aboriginal soldiers returning from combat received much more support for resettlement than Aboriginal soldiers (who enlisted voluntarily in World War I). The right to vote in a federal election was not granted until 1960 (Maaka and Fleras 2005, 189).

20  See, e.g., Thornberry (1991). The principle of self-determination first surfaced in international instruments in the United Nations Charter of 1945, and in 1960, the United Nations Declaration on the Granting of Independence to Colonial Countries and Peoples made this principle a right. These were followed up by two international covenants, the International Covenant on Economic, Social, and Cultural Rights and the second International Covenant on Civil and Political Rights. Both documents begin with the following lines: "All peoples have the right of self-determination. By virtue of that right they freely determine their political status and freely pursue their economic, social and cultural development."

21  This piece of legislation may be replaced by the controversial Bill C-33, *An Act to establish a framework to enable First Nations control of elementary and secondary education and to provide for related funding and to make related amendments to the Indian Act and consequential amendments to other Acts*, 2nd Sess., 41st Parl., 2103–2014 (first reading, 10 April 10 2014), () introduced by the Harper government. Mass Indigenous resistance was organized around this bill, and on 2 May 2014, Shawn Atleo resigned as National Chief from the Assembly of First Nations on the grounds that he would no longer mediate disputes between Indigenous leaders over this bill, even though he supports it and Prime Minister Harper's efforts. In an article published by CBC, Nepinak (2014) reported that some leaders had called the proposed bill an "illusion of control," evidenced by "the fact that the minister maintains an 'Indian agent' role and can take control of a community education program based on performance outcomes that are not determined by Indigenous communities, but by standards developed within provincial education systems that we have historically had no input in developing."

22  The Sechelt Nation of British Columbia was the first to take advantage of this framework and negotiate a self-government agreement within the constitutional framework of Canada.

23  Similar apologies were also offered in Australia and the United States.

24  See Moore (2014). In early 2014, Canadian provinces were required
    to release the death records of children and youth who died during
    residential schooling. The documents have been handed over to the Truth
    and Reconciliation Commission and the numbers are much higher than
    previously thought.

25  See the concluding statement issued by United Nations Special Rapporteur
    on the Rights of Indigenous Peoples, James Anaya, after his visit to Canada
    in October of 2013. The statement contained the following observation,
    among other scathing reflections about the state of Indigenous peoples
    in Canada relative to settler society: "From all I have learned, I can only
    conclude that Canada faces a crisis when it comes to the situation of
    Indigenous peoples of the country. The well-being gap between Aboriginal
    and non-Aboriginal people in Canada has not narrowed over the last several
    years, treaty and Aboriginals' claims remain persistently unresolved, and
    overall there appear to be high levels of distrust among Aboriginal peoples
    toward government at both the federal and provincial levels" (Anaya 2013).

26  This point was recently reiterated in a conversation I had with an Idle
    No More co-founder and Indigenous leader, when she stated, "To be
    honest, I'm really worried about the Assembly of First Nations elections.
    According to AFN mandate, they speak for all of us, even if we say
    individually they don't represent us. According to this white government,
    they represent us."

27  Coulthard offers a very astute and groundbreaking analysis of the politics
    of recognition in Canada through numerous pieces of work I am not able
    to address fully within this chapter. In addition to *Red Skin, White Masks*,
    also see his 2014 co-edited book *Recognition versus Self-Determination*.

28  The research and writing of Shiri Pasternak (2013), *On Jurisdiction and
    Settler Colonialism*, has begun to touch on the possibilities of reserves
    themselves as spaces that may promote the development of a counter-
    hegemonic political sensibility. Also see Taiaiake Alfred and Lana Lowe's
    (2005) research paper, "Warrior Societies in Contemporary Indigenous
    Communities."

29  I had the opportunity to bear witness to the role of educational institutions
    in the perpetuation of the multicultural imaginary of Canada as recently as
    December of 2012. I attended my nephews' Christmas concert celebration
    at their (largely white) elementary school in a downtown section of
    Saskatoon called City Park. At one point in the evening, the children
    from the older grades marched onto the stage to tell the mosaic story of
    Canada; each child spoke about the way that his or her family fit into

the overarching rainbow of people, cultures, and histories that made up "the strength of this great country." Ironically, given that almost no Indigenous children attend this school, a function of the racialization and spatialization of poverty that marks housing patterns across the city, there was no mention of the Indigenous nations in Saskatchewan, or anywhere else in Canada for that matter, that are also an essential, some might argue the most essential, component of this nation's story.

30 See Wolfe (2011) on this point.

31 See, e.g., Povinelli (2002); Markell (2003), on the strategic containment of Indigenous political difference.

32 In making this assertion, it is not my intention to position Indigenous communities and their allies as helpless pawns before the power of the state. Clearly, those of us who engage in advocacy and social justice work are constantly thinking and rethinking about how to transcend such conditions. This is not easy work, however, and my point here is that the state periodically reinforces its domination through overt forms of violence.

33 Murdocca (2013, viii) outlines an array of reparative practices attempting to address historical forms of injustice towards Indigenous peoples, including apologies, royal commissions, public inquiries, and a truth and reconciliation commission.

34 See, e.g., Wright (1988) and Scott (1995), on the depoliticization of culture; also chapter 5 below.

35 See the reporting by David Ljunggren (2009), for media coverage of Harper's speech.

36 I am indebted to Elizabeth Strakosch and Alissa Macoun (2012) for their insightful article, "The Vanishing Endpoint of Settler Colonialism," which clearly delineates the relationship between temporality and shifts in colonial logic in Australia, which has considerable import in Canada.

37 There were four of us who made this journey: myself, a director from Justice for Girls, and two teenage girls who had written their own submissions and were conducting advocacy with our support. One of these teenage girls is a Musqueam young woman from Vancouver and the other a biracial young woman, originally from British Columbia and also my daughter.

38 See *Justice for Girls and Justice for Girls International* (2012) for the full submission to the United Nation Committee on the Rights of the Child, including the two submissions by the teenage girls.

39 See, e.g., "UN Review Finds Canada Falling Short on Child Rights" (2012), for media coverage on the UN review. The Canadian federal government was, of course, quick to respond to the allegations contained in this report, and I was interviewed by the press about these proceedings.

40  I am fully aware that international activism is fraught with its own problematics and tensions – including debates over the merits of universality, cultural relativism, and western domination – and a critical assessment of these issues is a worthy and needed endeavour. Nonetheless, my emphasis in this chapter is on connecting Canada, as a white settler nation state, to a larger sociopolitical network of international Indigenous activism and to demonstrate that this fight does not end within the formal boundaries of Canada and sometimes gains strength outside of the nation's geopolitical borders. Questions of "authenticity" in this realm and the ways in which these discourses may themselves contain forms of negotiation and ambivalence are important, of course, but are beyond the scope of what I am able to offer here in this limited exposition.

41  Within the international domain, and the UN Working Group on Indigenous Peoples in particular, "territory" refers to an all-encompassing space consisting, not only of land, but also of its resources, including water, the sea, the ice, the air, animals, and plants, and so forth.

42  The Six Nations delegation was unsuccessful in securing a hearing with the President of the Council of the League of Nations, Hjalmar Branting, but did arouse sympathy and interest from a number of countries. England was still in a position of strength at this time and succeeded in removing the grievance of the Six Nations from the official agenda. Interestingly, while the United States was not directly implicated in this controversy, it was also opposed to self-government, and since the Six Nations straddle the US–Canada border, if successful, their case would have had implications for the Iroquois on both sides of the border (Niezen 2000).

43  See, e.g., Martínez Cobo (1986); Wright (1988); Tennant (1994); Muehlebach (2001) for an historical overview of international activism by Indigenous peoples at the United Nations

44  This international movement has not escaped the invoking of anti-essentialist critiques with respect to an analysis of Indigenous cultural politics – there are always chains of claims being made and social identities concomitantly formed. However, Muehlebach (2001) maintains that a close analysis of the WGIP reveals Indigenous delegates' strategic use of cultural politics vis-à-vis "Indigenous place" as a subversion of the dominant language and framing of Indigenous peoples. See, e.g., Wright (1988); Thornberry (1991); Turner (1993); Coombe (1999); Raffles (1999), for additional debates on this point.

45  Alongside a UN focus on "place making" has been a related emphasis on the "unmaking" of place. International Indigenous organizing has also been marked, then, by a systematic unveiling of the displacement

practices, resettlement, forced relocation, and transmigration policies that have deeply impacted Indigenous communities. In Canada, Tanner (2009) has termed this the "sedentarization" of Indigenous peoples.

46 In a similar vein, Coulthard (2010) advocates a relational understanding of land: "Seen in this light, we are as much a part of the land as any other element ... [E]thically, this means that humans hold certain obligations to the land, animals, plants and lakes in much the same way that we hold obligations to other people."

47 Ronald Niezen's (2000) work on the James Bay Cree in Northern Quebec and their ability to pressure the government, within the context of Quebec desires for succession, to uphold Indigenous peoples' distinct claims to self-determination is another example of international politics influencing domestic matters.

48 For a more detailed account of the terms of the UN inquiry, see "Cedaw" (2016).

49 See article "Report Calls for National Inquiry into Missing and Murdered Aboriginal Women" (2013) for media coverage on the launch of the report also in Saskatoon and the accompanying series of community meetings and media events. After one of the community gatherings, numerous young women approached me about similar experiences in Saskatoon and throughout Saskatchewan, implicating both city police and RCMP.

50 See NWAC (2014b), documenting these instances.

**Chapter Two**

1 The Canadian Council of Provincial Child and Youth Advocates (2010, 6) has stated, in fact, that the possibilities for Indigenous children and youth in Canada to exit the cycle of poverty are very limited and the "connection between poverty and child welfare involvement is well known in the literature and experience."

2 See Jaskiran Dhillon (2014) as part of the online compilation series #ItEndsHere, created by Indigenous Nationhood Movement in response to the disappearance and murder of Loretta Saunders in New Brunswick, Canada.

3 For a meditation on the question of denial, see Jiwani (2006), whose book offers a crucial account of the politics of denial and erasure regarding systemic and interpersonal violence as experienced by women and girls of colour in Canada.

4 While Vancouver is the site of my encounter with this young woman, and I am including it here because I am marking the start of my research and

advocacy in the area of youth development, I have engaged in similar
work in Saskatoon, where issues of sexual exploitation for Indigenous
young women and girls are equally prevalent. I also wish to underscore
that the conditions I draw attention to in Vancouver and Saskatoon are
found in numerous cities throughout Canada. For further information on
sexual exploitation as it relates to the lives of urban Indigenous youth,
some of which I address later on in this chapter, see, e.g., Schissel and
Fedec (1999); Kingsley and Mark (2001); Czapska, Webb, and Taefi (2008).
Also, see Hunt (2010), for an analysis of the deep roots of sexualized
colonial violence in Canada.

5 "Youth safe houses" refers to temporary transitional housing (state
funded) for young people living in poverty and experiencing
homelessness.

6 It should be noted that the Internet has changed the face of commercial
sexual exploitation. See Perrin (2010), for further information on this point.

7 It is important to make the distinction here between "survival" and
"survivance." Against the backdrop of ongoing settler colonial social
realities, survivance is more than simply surviving. According to Vizenor
(1994, 53), survivance involves "moving beyond our basic survival in the
face of overwhelming cultural genocide to create spaces of synthesis and
renewal."

8 See also Bourgois (1996, 250), "Youthful street culture may offer an
alternative space for resisting exploitation and subverting the ideological
insults and hierarchies of mainstream society, but it is also the site where
drugs are purveyed, boys kill one another, infants are battered, and young
women are gang-raped."

9 Also see the Cherry Smiley's podcast in *Feminist Current* (Smiley 2016),
for a discussion in 2014 of a campaign for solidarity between the Feminist
Alliance for International Action (FAFIA) and Indigenous women and girls
regarding missing and murdered women.

10 I realize this may be an obvious point to some. However, I am consistently
disturbed by the general lack of empathy and compassion I witness in the
corridors of the academy, where scholars theorize about poverty and "life
on the street" from a detached, and rather righteous, position, without
giving due attention to the immense hardship that such a life entails.
Bourgois (2001, 11906) speaks starkly to this disconnect when he says,
"At the turn of the millennium, much of the world's population survives
precariously in shanty towns, housing projects, tenements, and homeless
encampments where mind-numbing, bone-crushing experiences of
poverty engulf the socially vulnerable. Meanwhile, concerned academics

continue to fiddle in their ivory towers, arguing over how to talk correctly about the structural violence of poverty." My ongoing engagement with young people through direct advocacy serves as an essential reminder of what is at stake.

11 Numerous activists and scholars have extensively theorized violence across social movements and fields of study. For an excellent discussion on the social and cultural dimensions of violence and its continuum, please see Scheper-Hughes and Bourgois' (2004) edited volume *Violence in War and Peace*, Hannah Arendt's (1969) classic reflections in *On Violence*, and Lawrence and Karim's reader *On Violence* (2007).

12 According to sociologist Anthony Giddens, structure refers to "rules and resources, recursively implicated in the reproduction of social systems. Structures exist only as memory traces, the organic basis of human knowledgeability, and as instantiated in action" (Giddens 1984, 377). Social historian William Sewell has repositioned Giddens's theory of structuration to reflect structure as a profoundly cultural phenomenon, and it is within that framing that my arguments here are also positioned. According to Sewell (1992, 27), then, "Structures are constituted by mutually sustaining cultural schemas and sets of resources that empower and constrain action and tend to be reproduced by that action. Agents are empowered by structures, both by knowledge of cultural schemas that enables them to mobilize resources and by the access to resources that enables them to enact schemas." The literature on this concept is vast and includes large bodies of work, in both sociology and anthropology, where contrasting uses of the term are considered against competing notions of "culture" and "power." A detailed discussion of this debate is beyond the scope of this chapter. See, e.g., Bourdieu (1977); Giddens (1984); Sewell (1992); Ortner (1984), for some excellent discussion of these points.

13 Spivak alluded to the importance of approaching the question of agency with due caution in a recent interview, where she remarked,

> I don't think there is any such thing as a free agent. The idea of freedom of agency itself is existentially impoverished. We must use that idea when we are casting our votes because the vote is an arithmetical reduction of the notion and everybody has one vote. Therefore, except for voting, we must exceedingly carefully consider this impoverished notion of freedom of choice and freedom of agency. To say you can join any institution and that way you are an agent, I think it's a very knavish or foolish thing to say. Agency is institutionally validated action and, therefore, it is necessary to

develop the criticism of institutions that offer validation, and this is
the role of the intellectual. (Spivak 2014, 4)

14 See Gazzola (2012) for an overview of the project in an article published in
the Saskatoon based magazine, *Planet S*.

15 See Cyndy Baskin (2011), for a discussion of the complicated terrain of
service provision to Indigenous youth.

16 See Amnesty International (2009), for further information on this point,
as well as UN Rapporteur James Anaya (2013), for his statement upon
concluding his visit in Canada.

17 In her work on the systemic violence of social policy as it relates to
children and youth, scholar and advocate Valerie Polakow (2000, 2)
writes, "Public policies make and unmake young lives." The increasing
racialization and criminalization of poverty has led to an onslaught of
arrest and confinement for marginalized youth, as well as an explosion of
public discourse casting racialized children and youth who fall outside the
"mythical norm" as pathological, deviant, and human beings to be feared;
see, e.g., Dohrn (2000) and Giroux (2006).

18 The "culture of poverty" theory (Lewis 1967) has buttressed "blaming
the victim" narratives. For example, Bourgois writes (2001, 11906), "From
a theoretical perspective, the legacy of the culture of poverty debate has
impoverished research in the social sciences on the phenomena of social
suffering, everyday violence, and the intimate experience of structural
oppression in industrialized nations." In the United States, Pauline
Lipman's work (2009) has demonstrated how "culture of poverty" theories
continue to pathologize black urban space. As recently as December 2014, a
Winnipeg schoolteacher, Brad Badiuk, was challenged for his reinscription
of Indigenous deficiency, exactly proving the point I am trying to make
here. See CBC's news report published 11 December ("Brad Badiuk" 2014).

19 On this point, the late Mohawk legal scholar Patricia Monture-Angus
(1995, 80) says, "My concerns about law are similar to my concerns about
education. Both the systems of law and education that we now live
[under] have been forced on us. Law and education are two of the central
institutions or processes through which First Nations have been colonized
and oppressed."

20 The literature drawing linkages between education, society, and culture,
dating back to enlightenment thinkers John Locke (1964), Jean Jacques
Rousseau (quoted in Boyd 1963), and philosopher John Dewey (1916),
among others, is vast and can't be addressed fully within the purview
of this chapter. For the purposes of this ethnographic account, however,

it should be noted that I am following in the tradition of scholars and practitioners who view education, broadly conceived to include not only schooling but also educative spaces outside of formal institutions of learning, as a deeply social and political enterprise. Among the examples of this scholarship are the work of Freire (1970); Bourdieu and Passeron (1977); Willis (1977); Dei (1995); Levinson, Foley, and Holland (1996); Roman and Eyre (1997); Apple (2000); Hall (2002); Chomsky (2003). In line with this thinking, I have stated, of the relationship among social exclusion, poverty, and education highlighting, that "education and educational processes do not exist in a vacuum; embedded within a larger societal structure marked by the unequal distribution of power and resources, educational institutions are intimately connected with the (re) production of the dominant culture through the management, validation, and dissemination and construction of knowledge" (Dhillon 2011, 113).

21 The language of "promising practices" is commonly used in circles of government officials and social service providers who are attempting to find the "best solutions" or strategies for any given social problem. Specific models that have "worked" to address any given social problem are positioned as "promising practices" and often described in detail in a compendium that other jurisdictions can use as a blueprint to address similar issues in their respective localities.

22 The literature charting the relationship between education and nation building is extensive. With specific reference to the Canadian context, see, e.g., Backhouse (1999); James S. Woodsworth's "The Orientals," "The Negro and the Indian," and "Assimilation," in Woodsworth (2010 [1909]); Axelrod (1997); Osborne (1996); Francis (1997); Barman (2003); King (2003).

23 When the residential schools began to be phased out in the 1950s as a result of the concerted efforts of Aboriginal peoples, Aboriginal students began to be integrated into the schools within the provincial systems. Under the guise equal access and fairness in treatment, the Canadian government stated that Aboriginal students should be provided with the same kinds of services that other Canadians were offered. This move towards integration became reified in the 1969 White Paper, and it was this policy statement that prompted the National Indian Brotherhood to write a response that served as the catalyst for Indian Control over Indian Education (Hare and Barman 2000, 346).

24 The desire of Indigenous peoples for greater educational control is, as I argue throughout this book, a product of colonial histories of cultural and linguistic proscription, particularly within education, that must be regarded as being at the most extreme end of such practices.

25  Discussions of the "educational crisis" facing Indigenous communities can be found across academic disciplines and within community-based and government reports cohering around the social and economic realities facing Indigenous peoples in Canada. See e.g., Canada, Standing Senate Committee on Aboriginal Peoples (2003), and the work by NWAC.

26  This description of Indigenous education precontact with European colonizers should not be viewed as an exhaustive examination of Indigenous peoples' educational philosophies and approaches. I simply wanted to debunk the notion that "education" was a contribution or gift extended by the colonizers and further convey that Indigenous peoples themselves hold particular conceptions of what education has been and should be in the future. To develop this section, I have drawn on some of the leading scholars providing historical accounts of Indigenous education in North America.

27  For a more detailed discussion on the notion of the "other" within postcolonial literature, see, e.g., Said (1978); Bhabha (1994); Young (1995).

28  The history of the social and political process that accompanied the strategic assimilation and reconstruction of Aboriginal identity within Canada is long and complex. Among the literature detailing the history of assimilation and identity reconstruction in Canada, see Milloy (1999); and on the policy debates regarding industrial schools, day schools, and residential schooling, Enns (2009).

29  It is estimated that about 125,000 children passed through eighty residential schools (Thornton 2001,14).

30  As (Hare and Barman 2000, 333) point out, in 1994, "the Assembly of First Nations divided Aboriginal children's experience at residential schools into the emotional, mental, physical, and spiritual realms and demonstrated, through individual recollection, how students were wounded by having their feelings ridiculed, their creativity and independent thinking stifled, their bodily needs ignored or violated, and their ways of life denied."

31  Cheryle Partridge (2010) offers a compelling and personal portrait of this impact.

32  Recent documents released to the Truth and Reconciliation Commission indicate that this number may be higher. See reporting on residential school deaths by Connie Walker (2014) for CBC on 7 January.

33  The last residential school in Canada closed in 1996 as a result of the concerted efforts and lobbying of First Nations communities (British Columbia Human Rights Commission 2001, 14).

34  The establishment of a Truth and Reconciliation Commission to address the atrocities of residential schooling is indicative of the enormity of

its impact (both past and present). See the Commission's website, http://www.trc.ca/websites/trcinstitution/index.php?p=3, for further information.

35  This alienation takes many shapes, as Hampton (1995, 38) shows: "The structure of North American schools is hostile to Native cultures in ways that seem unavoidable to white educators. Age-segregated classrooms; natives as janitors and teacher aides; role authority rather than kin and personal authority; learning by telling and questioning instead of observation and example; clock time instead of personal, social, and natural time; rules exalted above people and feelings; monolingual teachers; alien standards, educated ignorance of cultural meanings and non-verbal messages; individual more than group tasks; convergent thinking; all these and more are structural features that undermine the Native child's culture." Also see Doug Foley (1996).

36  William Pinar's (1993) work on understanding curriculum as a racial text, has demonstrated how curricular programming is a highly significant form of representation of self and society that communicates implicit and explicit messages about racial identity.

37  Indigenous scholar Michael Marker (2006) addresses this chasm in an article examining the racist backlash against the Makah tribe for their treaty-protected right to hunt whales. The pre-eminence of "place" in Indigenous epistemology and the emphasis on the sustainability of living in a place defined as a homeland is also taken up in contrast to the kind of knowledge systems circulating in dominant institutions of education.

38  In terms of future employment and income brackets, in relation to educational attainment, for Indigenous peoples, the British Columbia Human Rights Commission (2001, 14) states, "The lasting impact of residential schools and their assimilation policies can be seen in the barriers to equality and full participation in Canadian society faced by Aboriginal people. Of all groups, Aboriginal peoples are the most disadvantaged in education, employment, and income ... Even when Aboriginal peoples and foreign-born minorities have a university education, they are still less likely than non-racialized groups to have incomes in the top 20 per cent of the income scale."

39  See Sasha Polakow-Suransky (2000), regarding the ascendance of zero-tolerance policies in schools.

40  In their analysis of white, female preservice teachers, Finney and Orr (1995) succinctly unmasked this saviour mentality when all of their participants from a cross-cultural understanding course shared the following story: "Although I have a better understanding of some of the Aboriginal philosophies, I would still like to help some of the [Aboriginals] create better hygiene practices for their children ... I felt very sad and disgusted

when I was shopping the other day and I saw a little native girl running around the store wearing no shoes or warm clothes … My heart wanted to help that little girl by taking her away from that situation and caring for her myself. My initial thought was, why don't these people look after their children?" (quoted in Gebhard 2012, 6). Here, Gebhard highlights how the teacher blames the parents and imagines saving the child from her parents and culture as opposed to critically thinking about why this child has no shoes. A provocative reflection on how white teachers construct race can be found in the writing of Christine Sleeter (2004).

41 As Albert Memmi (1965, xii) asserts, "Privilege is at the heart of the colonial relationship."

42 Sioux scholar Nick Estes (2016) offers an essential critique of cities as white settler space.

43 For a brief glimpse into gentrification on the Westside of Saskatoon, see Casey (2014).

44 The practice of state power in rationalizing imprisonment as a way of life has been described by legal scholars and criminologists as the "prison industrial complex," and refers to a political symbiosis among police, judges, lawyers, elected officials, community groups, and the prison apparatus itself. The nexus of these multiple relations enables a complex articulation between structures, people, and places and produces a state power that exercises domination over (and ownership of) human bodies as a measure of ensuring peace, security, and social order (Rodríguez 2003, 183–84).

45 This statistic was quoted in a 2011 presentation prepared by Indian and Northern Affairs Canada, drawing on a 2004 report prepared by the Department of Justice Canada, http://www.justice.gc.ca/eng/rp-pr/cj-jp/yj-jj/yj2-jj2/yj2.pdf, that maps the demographics of Indigenous youth in prison by province and territory.

46 In their study of the North-West Mounted Police, Lorne Brown and Caroline Brown (1973, 10) state the following:

> Most people assume that the NWMP were founded in response to the Cypress Hills Massacre, when American Whiskey traders murdered several Assiniboine Indians in May 1873. This is only true in the sense that the massacre hastened the organization of the Force. The establishment of the Force had been planned and officially authorized prior to this, and the primary reason for establishing it was to control the Indian and Métis population of the Northwest. What the government feared most was an Indian war over the intrusion of whites from outside the area. Such a war would have been extremely costly to the authorities and could have delayed settlement, railway construction and economic development for many years.

47 See, e.g., Marcel-Eugene LeBeuf (2011) on behalf of the Royal Canadian Mounted Police.
48 The Report of the Aboriginal Justice Inquiry of Manitoba (1991, 593) speaks to the long history of punitive measures carried out by police and state agents against Indigenous populations in Manitoba and Saskatchewan, including capturing and executing "rebels" associated with the North West Rebellion of 1885.
49 For further information on this case, please see Tasha Hubbard's powerful National Film Board of Canada documentary *Two Worlds Colliding* (2004).
50 The inquiry was precipitated, in part, because the Saskatoon City Police's practice of taking Indigenous peoples out of town and leaving them to die could no longer be denied and was so well known throughout the city that it had acquired its own name, "The Starlight Tours." In 2000, Daryl Night was dropped outside of the city. Night fared somewhat better than Stonechild and survived and subsequently filed a complaint. Two officers were eventually charged and convicted of unlawful confinement. Again in 2000, the icy bodies of Lloyd Dustyhorn, Lawrence Wegner, and Darcy Dean Ironchild (separate discoveries) were found in the same area. The RCMP was called to investigate in 2001 (Green 2011, 234).
51 According to Saskatchewan Ministry of Justice, Wright Commission (2004),

> Jarvis made no record of the contact he maintains he had with Cst. Hartwig and Cst. Senger. There is no record as to what, if any, information he received from them. He made no record of receiving information from Jason Roy, as I have concluded he did, that Stonechild was in police custody on the evening of November 24, 1990. As I have already observed, the deficiencies in the investigation go beyond incompetence or neglect. They were inexcusable. Jarvis was clearly not interested in pursuing the investigation. On November 30, 1990, he indicates there is a possibility of foul play and recommends the investigation be transferred to Major Crimes. When the file is not transferred, he summarily concludes the file on December 5, 1990. The only new information he received on that day was a verbal report from Dr. Adolph on the results of the autopsy. In any event, it simply does not make sense that any suspicions of foul play or necessity for further investigation by Major Crimes, are dispelled by the verbal report of Dr. Adolph. What is the point of recommending the file be transferred to Major Crimes if all that he was waiting for was the result of the autopsy report? If he was expecting the body to yield the answers as to how Neil Stonechild

came to die, why would he not have inspected the body or even looked at the photographs? The only reasonable inference that can be drawn is that Jarvis was not prepared to pursue the investigation because he was either aware of police involvement or suspected police involvement. (Saskatchewan, Ministry of Justice, Wright Commission 2004, 199–200)

52 The Report of the Aboriginal Justice Inquiry of Manitoba (1991), while written decades ago, is still very relevant in light of the over-representation of Indigenous youth in Canadian prisons. On the notion of criminality, the report states that

difference in crime statistics between Aboriginal and non-Aboriginal people result, at least in part, from the manner in which the behaviour of Aboriginal people becomes categorized and stigmatized. This may happen because, to a certain extent, police tend to view the world in terms of "respectable" people and "criminal" types. Criminal types are thought to exhibit certain characteristics, which provide cues to the officer to initiate action. Thus, the police may tend to stop a higher proportion of people who are visibly different from dominant society, including Aboriginal people, for minor offences simply because they believe such people may tend to commit more serious crimes. (Aboriginal Justice Implementation Commission 1991, 107).

53 Julia Sudbury's (2005) edited volume *Global Lockdown* offers a series of compelling essays on this point in the first section, titled "Criminalizing Survival."

54 Annabel Webb and Asia Czapska are researchers and advocates with Justice for Girls, an NGO working with young women and girls living in poverty. Both Webb and Czapska have pointed out the ways that "prisons are often used as a 'protective measure,' an avenue to respond to young women's lack of safety in the absence of adequate housing, protective policing or prosecution of male violence, and/or social service intervention" (Czapska, Webb, and Taefi 2008, 30).

55 For an excellent counter-framing, see "Seeing Red: Reconciliation and Resentment" in Coulthard (2014a).

56 See, e.g., Ryan Ellis, "Gang Problem May Grow," *Leader Post*, 17 March 2005; Janet French, "Gang Members Lose Heritage," *Leader Post*, 31 May 2007; Tim Switzer, "Police Fear More Gang Violence," *Leader Post*, 15 December 2004; James Wood, "Staffers Say Gangs at War Inside," *Leader Post*, 30 August 2005; Tamara Cherry, "FSIN Says It Tried to Warn Police

about Gang Activity," *Leader Post*, 16 March 2005; Neil Scott, "Gangs
Growing: Police," *Leader Post*, 15 March 2005; and "Gangs Must Be
Quelled," Editorial, *Leader Post*, 16 March 2005.

57 "The story of how so many Aboriginal women came to be locked up
within federal penitentiaries is a story filled with a long history of
dislocation and isolation, racism, brutal violence as well as enduring a
constant state of poverty beyond poor" (Wesley Group 2012, 1).

58 See "Sask Foster Care" (2010), documenting the death of a twenty-two-
month-old First Nations toddler.

59 For additional information on this point, see the website for the
Saskatchewan Advocate, www.saskadvocate.ca.

60 "By 'social systems,' Giddens means the empirically observable,
intertwining, and relatively bounded social practices that link persons
across time and space" (Sewell 1992, 4–5).

## Chapter Three

1 The field of youth development is replete with under-theorized references
to transitioning "at-risk" to an imagined state of empowerment.

2 I am fully aware that the term "community" can be critically unpacked
with respect to the homogenization of lived experience, a critique I take
up in earnest in chapter 4 below. I am using this term here, primarily
to denote how the state is attempting to capture indigeneity through
participation.

3 See Patzer (2014), for linkages between modernity's intent to rationally
design societies and the elimination of Indigenous political difference.

4 This youth organization has recently been moved to another location in
Saskatoon's downtown.

5 Ironically, after about half an hour, the meeting was cancelled, since the
rain was so persistent and members of the Indigenous Alliance became
concerned about being stranded as a result of the muckiness of the dirt
roads leading out of the reserve.

6 This spatial distinction also reinforces the idea that cities are White settler
space, not Indigenous territory.

7 Iris Marion Young (2000) charts states' moves to increase the social and
democratic participation of marginalized communities. Her analysis,
however, pays limited attention to the specific political context of
Indigenous peoples in settler states such as Canada and the United States.

8 For more on "willful amnesia," see Robert Epp (2008, 126).

9 The Ministry of Education (also known as Sask Learning) is
Saskatchewan's provincial state agency dealing directly with education.

10 These "low levels of educational attainment" can also be read as a refusal to take part in educational institutions bent on inflicting harm on Indigenous students, as I outline in chapter 2 above.

11 The document came out of a province-wide initiative in 2001 to develop a framework for cooperation across government ministries and a strategy related to First Nations peoples living off-reserve.

12 By 2016, it is projected that close to 50 per cent of children entering kindergarten in Saskatchewan will be Indigenous (Sask Learning 2003, 2).

13 For a detailed conversation linking capitalist expansion to the dispossession of Indigenous land and the exploitation of labour, see Pflug-Back's (2015) review of *Red Skin, White Masks* by Glen Sean Coulthard in *Briarpatch Magazine*.

14 Untitled internal document on file with the author.

15 Chomsky (2009, 16) got it right when he said the following about historical amnesia: "Historical amnesia is a dangerous phenomenon, not only because it undermines moral and intellectual integrity, but also because it lays the groundwork for the crimes that lie ahead."

16 The notion of "productivity" was largely relegated to being able to participate in a settler economy – reminiscent of the vast array of state-generated "employment programs" for Indigenous peoples across Canada.

17 The markedly different stance taken up by Dakota is revisited in chapter 6 below, when I explore some of the challenges and tensions he faced in attempting to implement a pilot mentoring program.

18 On the modern temporal imaginary, Bruno Latour (1991, 76) writes, "We have never moved either forward or backward. We have always actively sorted out elements belonging to different times. We can still sort. It is the sorting that makes the times, not the times that make the sorting."

19 My ability to keep an open mind and to always be conscious of my own biases about and interpretations of a state–Indigenous partnership was a consistent struggle throughout this research. The idea that participation could be viewed as a form of accessing power seriously caught me off guard, as I was accustomed to hearing community advocates speak out against the state on so many issues affecting Indigenous communities in Canada.

20 Ahiwa Ong (2006, 3) captures the multiple dimensions of neoliberalism well when she says, "neoliberalism is often discussed as an economic doctrine with a negative relation to state power, a market ideology that seeks to limit the scope and activity of governing. But neoliberalism can also be conceptualized as a new relationship between government and knowledge through which governing activities are recast as non-political and non-ideological problems that need technical solutions." Morrow and

Torres (1999) also point out the contradictory elements of neoliberalism that call for individual autonomy on the one hand and the public responsibilities of citizens on the other.

21 See Alvin Finkel (2006) for an excellent exposé on the impact of neoliberal approaches to governance in Canada.

22 In step with Coulthard's critique, Alfred calls our attention to how the majority of the political and social institutions, such as band councils and government funded service agencies, that govern and influence the lives of First Nations today, have primarily been shaped to serve the interests of the Canadian state. He writes, "Their structures, responsibilities, and authorities conform to the interests of Canadian governments, just as their sources of legitimacy are found in Canadian laws, not in First Nations interests or laws" (Alfred 2009, 44).

23 Alfred alludes to the political consequences of this seemingly "apolitical" stance, when he observes, "But the acceptance of being such an 'Aboriginal' within the larger social cultural mainstream of Canada is as powerful an assault on meaningful Indigenous existences as any force of arms every brought upon First Nations by the colonial regime" (Alfred 2009, 44).

## Chapter Four

1 The sexual exploitation of Indigenous children and youth in Saskatoon is well documented by non-governmental youth organizations, media outlets, as well as numerous state agencies.

2 See Uma Kothari (2001) for excellent insight into the problematics of participation.

3 On third space, see Burchell, Gordon, and Miller 1991, 141.

4 Complementing the need for critical scrutiny of "community," ethnographers have also charted and debated the ways that authority is claimed and legitimated under the auspices of community representation. Anthropological studies, then, have begun to theorize how the concept of community becomes taken up within state-centered formulations that relate certain identities to spaces, time sequences, cultural practices, and particular locales (Alonso 1994; Urban and Scherzer 1991; Chatterjee 1993).

5 See chapter 3 above, subsection "Saskatchewan's Claim to Trying Something New."

6 See chapter 2 above for a discussion on how social policies of state institutions perpetuate the dispossession of Indigenous people in Canada.

7 This information is taken from one of CHARM's pamphlets outlining its program areas.

8 For a detailed overview of missing and murdered Indigenous Women and Girls in Saskatchewan, see the NWAC's summary available at "MMIWG" (2016).

9 The story of Bella Laboucan-McLean is particularly revealing in this regard. See Klein (2014b) for the details of Bella's case.

10 See Angus (2013), for a glimpse into white Canada's perception of Indigenous peoples' struggle for self-determination.

11 In this article, Teju Cole charts how state sanctioned violence in multiple places throughout the world positions some human life as more valuable, more mournable, than others.

12 Echoing this sentiment, Naomi Klein spoke the following words at a speech on murdered and missing Indigenous women and girls she delivered in Toronto, Ontario on 18 December 2014: "Here is one link to consider: the greatest barrier to our government's single-minded obsession with drilling, mining and fracking the hell out of this country is the fact that Indigenous communities from coast to coast are exercising their inherent and constitutional rights to say no. Indigenous strength and power is a tremendous threat to that insatiable vision. And Indigenous women really are "the heart and soul" of their communities. The trauma of sexual violence saps the strength of communities with terrifying efficiency. So let us not be naïve. The Canadian government has no incentive to heal and strengthen the very people that it sees as its greatest obstacle." See Klein (2014b), for a version of this speech.

**Chapter Five**

1 See, for example, the oft-quoted *The Interpretation of Cultures* by Clifford Geertz (1973) as well as James Clifford's (1988), *The Predicament of Culture*. On ethnographies that take up the intersection between Indigenous politics and culture, see Maria Garcia's (2005) *Making Indigenous Citizens* and Nancy Postero's (2007) *Now We Are Citizens*.

2 See the overview of the Indigenous Alliance's programmatic areas that I detail in chapter 3 above.

3 I derive this commentary from a collection of official partnership documents as well as my fieldwork over the course of numerous months, where I observed deliberations about the types of reform efforts that the Indigenous Alliance deemed would be most "effective" at shifting the social reality (high school drop outs, etc.) of urban Indigenous youth.

4 Cathyrn McConaghy has written extensively about cultural relativism within the context of Australia. Her book *Rethinking Indigenous Education:*

*Culturalism, Colonialism and the Politics of Knowing* (McConaghy 2000) was especially instructive for my thinking.

5 I explore this program in chapter 6 below.

6 This notion of the "Indian way" was used numerous times by Indigenous youth workers when they explained the importance of white settlers' acquiring knowledge about Indigenous communities.

7 An article, "Survey Reveals Comfort Levels of urban Aboriginal People" (2014), published 15 November in *Eaglefeather News*, illustrates this sentiment well.

8 In Cree, "*wanuskewin*" means living in harmony. See Tammemagi (2014) for more on Wanuskewin and how it stands as a Canadian national historic site.

## Chapter Six

1 For critical take on Indigenous youth involvement with gangs, see Chris Anderson (2007).

2 According to youth workers from Journeying Forward, Bobby Dean Hannah had, at one point, been receiving "services" from a criminal justice youth program operating through the Indigenous Peoples Collective.

3 For a detailed explanation of affirmative sabotage, see Spivak (2012).

4 By "reintegration," I mean the program's emphasis on a seemingly restorative approach to transitioning the youth from detention facilities back into a society shaped and organized by Canadian law, not by First Nations interests or law.

5 Gillian Cowlishaw (2003) offers an important counterpoint to portrayals of Indigenous "deviance" in Australia.

6 Youth workers from Journeying Forward would often speak about their youth in the main office where all of their work cubicles were located.

7 I use this term in quotations to mark how loosely "gang activity" was conceived in the operation of this program. It seemed there was no consistent understanding, at least among youth workers, about what this activity looked like, what degree of involvement meant a youth could no longer contact her family member, or what range of social actions could be classified as "gang activity."

8 Protective factors are those elements which will influence youth to maximize their "capacity," such as developing a lasting relationship with an adult, a healthy peer relationship, etc. (van der Woerd and Cox 2003, 65).

9 *A second Act to implement certain provisions of the budget tabled in Parliament on March 29, 2012 and other measures*, 1st Sess., 41st Parl., 2011–12 (assented to 14 December 2012), http://parl.gc.ca/HousePublications/Publication. aspx?DocId=5765988. I explain Bill C-45 in the concluding chapter.

10 This sentiment is well articulated in the following statement from the *Urban Aboriginal Youth – An Action Plan for Change*: "For many young Aboriginal people, cities have been their only home. Some are second and third generation urban dwellers. Despite systemic barriers and personal challenges which they may face, many manage urban life successfully. For other Aboriginal youth, city life can be an overwhelming experience. Their foothold is uncertain; their future uncertain. While cities may seem to offer great promise, countless arrive ill-prepared to take advantage of these opportunities, and promise eventually falls to despair" (Canada, Standing Senate Committee on Aboriginal Peoples 2003).

11 See Public Safety Canada (2010) for the compendium of tools used for assessment of recidivism.

12 Many of these tools originate in the United States where the juvenile justice system has been using them since the early 1990s. For more information, see US Department of Justice (2013).

13 This movement has intensified with police programs like such as the Serious Habitual Offender Comprehensive Action Plan (SHOCAP) (read targeted enforcement): the Saskatoon Police Service SHOCAP Unit, in partnership with agencies serving youth throughout the city, "*tracks the activity* of a select group of young persons" (Saskatoon Police Service 2016; emphasis added).

14 *Tapwe* means "yes" in Cree.

15 In order to maintain confidentiality and anonymity, I am unable to disclose the reason for Derek's incarceration or the circumstances immediately surrounding his arrest.

16 *Tansi* means "hello" in Cree, *napew* stands for "man," and *moniyâwak* for "white people."

17 In Cree, *cî* is used as a question marker.

18 In Cree, *neechimos* is used to refer to a sweetheart or lover.

19 Claudia Rankine (2014, 24) offers an alternative perception of "anger," when she says, "You begin to think, maybe erroneously, that this other kind of anger is really a type of knowledge: the type that both clarifies and disappoints. It responds to insult and attempted erasure simply by asserting presence, and the energy required to present, to react, to assert is accompanied by visceral disappointment: a disappointment in the sense that no amount of visibility will alter the ways in which one is perceived."

## Conclusion

1 On "decolonizing praxis," Jeff Corntassel (2012, 89) argues that "decolonizing praxis come from moving beyond political awareness and/or symbolic gestures to everyday practices of resurgence."

2 I am using "resurgence" here in accordance with the invocation offered by Coulthard (2014a, 24), which positions it as a politics "premised on self-actualization, direct action, and resurgence of cultural practices that are attentive to the subjective and structural composition of settler colonial power."

3 In the conclusion to *Red Skin, White Masks*, Glen Coulthard (2014a, 165–79) offers five theses on Indigenous resurgence and decolonization that embrace this "turning away" from the state and channeling collective labour towards the revitalization of Indigenous political values and practices. These include focusing our understanding on the necessity of direct action, supporting the development of Indigenous political-economic alternatives to capitalism, addressing systems of dispossession that shape Indigenous peoples' experiences in both urban- and land-based settings, stopping violence against Indigenous women and girls, and thinking beyond the nation state.

4 Both the Native Youth Sexual Health Network and Justice for Girls are excellent examples of this kind of organization that engages in political advocacy at both the personal and systemic level, and both include a central focus on Indigenous politics. Detailed information on the work they do is available on their official websites: http://www.nativeyouthsexualhealth.com; http://www.justiceforgirls.org.

5 The work of Sara Ahmed comes to mind when deliberating over the power operating within institutions of higher education; see Ahmed (2012).

6 For an example of critical curriculum, please the #StandingRockSyllabus created by the New York Stands with Standing Rock Collective http://www.publicseminar.org/2016/10/nodapl-syllabus-project/#.WBiWkFISD8E.

7 See Black et al. (2014) for further information on the tar sands.

8 During a lecture at the University of Victoria, Leanne Simpson (2013a) evocatively pointed out,

> Canada has a vested interest in disconnecting Indigenous youth from their lands, culture, elders, and political traditions – when you are disconnected from the lands, it is easier to exploit them, when Indigenous people do not know their history and political tradition, it is easier for the government to sell the idea that their idea is the only possible way out of the myriad of social problems they caused in the first place. When Indigenous people do not know their languages and traditions of leadership, it is much easier to control leaders by exerting pressure and political agendas on band councils, regional

and national Aboriginal organizations. When Indigenous people do not know that we are strong, it is easier to continue to position us as weak. Colonialism is always deliberate and so resurgence must be deliberate as well.

9 The power of Indigenous youth organizing around colonialism and climate is not to be underestimated. See Dhillon (2016) for further discussion.

10 See Lindsay Catherine Corum (2015) for an excellent overview on Indigenous futurism.

11 Quoted from the author's field notes.

12 See the official website of Idle No More for more information on the history and substantive focus of this movement: http://www.idlenomore.ca.

13 Wab Kinew (2014, 96) characterizes Idle No More as a movement that "now encompasses a broad range of conversations calling for recognition of treaty rights, revitalization of Indigenous culture and an end to legislation imposed without meaningful consultation."

14 The formal founding of Idle No More is associated with Jessica Gordon, Sylvia McAdam, Sheelah McLean, and Nina Wilson, four women from Saskatoon who spearheaded the advocacy against Bill C-45.

15 See Bill C-45 news database (2014) for an excellent overview and Pedwell (2012).

16 See Elaine Coburn's (2015) edited volume *More Will Sing Their Way to Freedom* for essays on the challenges and possibilities of Idle No More.

# References

Aboriginal Affairs and Northern Development Canada. 2008. *Statement of Apology to Former Students of Indian Residential Schools*, 11 June. https://www.aadnc-aandc.gc.ca/eng/1100100015644/1100100015649.

———. 2010. *Response of the Government of Canada to the Sixth Report of the Standing Senate Committee on Aboriginal Peoples*, 15 September. http://www.aadnc-aandc.gc.ca/eng/1100100014383/1100100014384.

Aboriginal Justice Implementation Commission. 1991. *Report of the Aboriginal Justice Inquiry of Manitoba*. Winnipeg, MB: Queen's Printer.

Adam, Betty Ann. 2013. "Teen Receiving 16 Year Term in 'Appalling Case.'" *Star Phoenix*, 20 April. www.pressreader.com/canada/the-starphoenix/20130420/281505043705469/TextView.

Ahmed, Sara. 2012. *On Being Included: Racism and Diversity in Institutional Life*. Durham, NC: Duke University Press.

Alfred, Taiaiake. 2009. "Colonialism and State Dependency." *Journal of Aboriginal Health* 5 (2): 42–60.

Alfred, Taiaiake, and Lana Lowe. 2005. *Warrior Societies in Contemporary Indigenous Communities*. Research report for the Ipperwash Inquiry. https://www.attorneygeneral.jus.gov.on.ca/inquiries/ipperwash/policy_part/research/pdf/Alfred_and_Lowe.pdf.

Allooloo, Siku. 2015. "Reclaim Justice, End the Violence." *Northern Journal*, 20 April. http://norj.ca/2015/04/reclaim-justice-end-the-violence/.

Alonso, Ana Maria. 1994. "The Politics of Space, Time and Substance: State Formation, Nationalism, and Ethnicity." *Annual Review of Anthropology* 23 (1): 379–405. http://dx.doi.org/10.1146/annurev.an.23.100194.002115.

Amnesty International. 2004. *Stolen Sisters: A Human Rights Response to Discrimination and Violence against Indigenous Women in Canada*. http://www.amnesty.org/en/library/info/AMR20/003/2004.

———. 2009. *Canada: Follow Up to the Concluding Observations of the United Nations Committee on the Elimination of Discrimination against Women.* London: Amnesty International.

Anaya, James. 2013. *Statement upon Conclusion of the Visit to Canada*, 15 October. Report of the United Nations Special Rapporteur on the Rights of Indigenous Peoples. http://unsr.jamesanaya.org/statements/statement-upon-conclusion-of-the-visit-to-canada.

Anderson, Benedict. 1991. *Imagined Communities.* London: Verso.

Anderson, Chris. 2007. "Aboriginal Gangs as a Distinctive Form of Urban Indigeneity." Paper presented at the Annual Meeting of the Association of Canadian Geographers, 76th Congress of the Humanities and Social Sciences, Saskatoon, SK.

Anderson, Mark, and Carmen Robertson. 2011. *Seeing Red: A History of Natives in Canadian Newspapers.* Winnipeg, MB: University of Manitoba Press.

Angus, Charlie. 2013. "Stand Up to Online Bullying and Racism against Aboriginal Peoples." *Rabble* (blog), 17 July. http://rabble.ca/blogs/bloggers/charlie-angus/2013/07/stand-to-online-bullying-and-racism-against-Aboriginal-peoples.

Ahearn, Laura M. 2011. *Living Language: An Introduction to Linguistic Anthropology.* Oxford: Wiley-Blackwell.

Apple, Michael W. 2000. *Official Knowledge: Democratic Education in a Conservative Age.* New York: Routledge.

Arendt, Hannah. 1969. *On Violence.* New York: Harvest.

Asch, Michael. 2014. *On Being Here to Stay: Treaties and Aboriginal Rights in Canada.* Toronto: University of Toronto Press.

Assembly of First Nations. 2005. *Our Nations, Our Government: Choosing Our Own Paths.* Ottawa: Assembly of First Nations.

Axel, Brian. 2002. *From the Margins: Historical Anthropology and Its Futures.* Durham, NC: Duke University Press. http://dx.doi.org/10.1215/9780822383345.

Axelrod, Paul. 1997. *The Promise of Schooling: Education in Canada, 1800–1914.* Toronto: University of Toronto Press.

Backhouse, Constance. 1999. *Colour-Coded: A Legal History of Racism in Canada 1900–1950.* Toronto: University of Toronto Press.

Balfour, Gillian. 2014. "Canada's Aboriginal Women Are Being Murdered While Officials Look the Other Way." *Conversation*, 6 November. http://theconversation.com/canadas-Aboriginal-women-are-being-murdered-while-officials-look-the-other-way-33523.

Balfour, Gillian, and Elizabeth Comack. 2004. *The Power to Criminalize: Violence, Inequality, and the Law.* Blackpoint, NS: Fernwood.

Barker, Joanne, Jodi A. Byrd, Jill Doerfler, Lisa Kahaleole Hall, LeAnne Howe, J. Kēhaulani Kauanui, Jean O'Brien, Kathryn W. Shanley, Noenoe K. Silva, Shannon Speed, Kim TallBear, and Jacki Thompson Rand. 2015. "Open Letter from Indigenous Women Scholars Regarding Discussions of Andrea Smith." *Indian Country*, 7 July. http://indiancountrytodaymedianetwork. com/2015/07/07/open-letter-indigenous-women-scholars-regarding-discussions-andrea-smith.

Barman, Jean. 1997–98. "Taming Aboriginal Sexuality: Gender, Power, and Race in British Columbia." In "Native Peoples and Colonialism." Special issue, *BC Studies* nos. 115/16:237–66.

———. 2003. "Separate and Unequal: Indian and White Girls at All Hallows School, 1884–1920." In *Children, Teachers and Schools in the History of British Columbia*, edited by J. Barman and M. Gleason, 283–302. Calgary, AB: Detselig.

Baskin, Cyndy. 2011. "Aboriginal Youth Talk about Structural Determinants as the Cause of Homelessness." In *Racism, Colonialism and Indigeneity in Canada*, edited by M. Cannon and L. Sunseri, 192–202. Toronto: Oxford University Press.

Battiste, Marie. 1995. Introduction to *First Nations Education in Canada: The Circle Unfolds*, edited by M. Battiste and J. Barman. Vancouver: University of British Columbia Press.

———. 2000. "Maintaining Aboriginal Identity, Language, and Culture in Modern Society." In *Reclaiming Indigenous Voice and Vision*, ed. Marie Battiste, 192–208. Vancouver: University of British Columbia Press.

Belcourt, Billy-Ray. 2015. "Queer Bodies, Failed Subjects: Thinking through (and within) the Decolonial Infrastructures of Queerness." Paper presented at the Annual Meeting of the North American Indigenous Studies Association, Washington DC.

Belich, James. 2009. *Replenishing the Earth: The Settler Revolution and the Rise of the Anglo-World, 1783–1939*. New York: Oxford University Press. http://dx.doi.org/10.1093/acprof:oso/9780199297276.001.0001.

Benton, Ted, and Ian Craib. 2001. *Philosophy of Social Science: The Philosophical Foundations of Social Thought*. New York: Palgrave.

Berlant, Lauren. 1997. *The Queen of America Goes to Washington DC*. Durham, NC: Duke University Press.

———. 2011. *Cruel Optimism*. Durham: Duke University Press.

Bhabha, Homi. 1994. *The Location of Culture*. London: Routledge.

Biehl, João. 2005. *Vita: Life in a Zone of Social Abandonment*. Los Angeles: University of California Press.

Bill C-45 news database. 2014. *Huffington Post*, 18 October. http://www.huffingtonpost.ca/news/bill-c-45/.

Bird, John, and Diane Engelstad. 2002. *Nation to Nation: Aboriginal Sovereignty and the Future of Canada*. Concord: Anansi.

Black, Toban, Stephen D'Arcy, Tony Weis, and Joshua Russell. 2014. *A Line in the Tar Sands: Struggles for Environmental Justice*. Oakland: PM Press.

Blackstock, Cindy, and Nico Trocmé. 2005. "Community-Based Child Welfare for Aboriginal Children: Supporting Resilience through Structural Change." *Social Policy Journal of New Zealand* 24:12–33.

Bourdieu, Pierre. 1977. *Outline of a Theory of Practice*. Cambridge, UK: Cambridge University Press. http://dx.doi.org/10.1017/CBO9780511812507.

Bourdieu, Pierre, and Jean-Claude Passeron. 1977. *Reproduction in Education, Society, and Culture*. London: Sage.

Bourgois, Philippe. 1996. "Confronting Anthropology, Education and Inner-City Apartheid." *American Anthropologist* 98 (2): 249–58. http://dx.doi.org/10.1525/aa.1996.98.2.02a00020.

———. 2001. "Culture of Poverty." In *International Encyclopedia of the Social and Behavioural Sciences*, edited by N.J. Smelser and P.B. Baltes, 11904–7. Oxford: Pergammon.

Boyd, William. 1963. *Educational Theory of Rousseau*. New York: Russell and Russell.

"Brad Badiuk, Winnipeg Teacher, on Leave after Controversial Facebook Posts on Aboriginals." 2014. *CBCNews*, 11 December. http://www.cbc.ca/news/canada/manitoba/winnipeg-teacher-sparks-controversy-with-facebook-postings-about-Aboriginal-people-1.2869065?cmp=abfb.

Brecht, Bertolt. 1987. "Ten Poems from a Reader for Those Who Live in Cities." In *Poems, 1913–1956*, edited by Ralph Manheim, 131–40. New York: Routledge.

"A Brief History of the Marginalization of Aboriginal Women in Canada." 2009. *Indigenous Foundations*. http://Indigenousfoundations.arts.ubc.ca/home/community-politics/marginalization-of-Aboriginal-women.html.

British Columbia Human Rights Commission. 2001. *Removal of Aboriginal Children from Their Families by the Ministry of Children and Families*. Vancouver: British Columbia Human Rights Commission.

Brown, Lorne, and Caroline Brown. 1973. *An Unauthorized History of the RCMP*. Detroit, MI: James, Lewis and Samuel.

Brown, Sue. 2011. "Canadian Girls in Custody." Master's thesis, Simon Fraser University.

Bruyneel, Kevin. 2007. *The Third Space of Sovereignty: The Postcolonial Politics of US–Indigenous Relations*. Minneapolis: University of Minnesota Press.

Burchell, Graham. 1996. "Liberal Government: Old and New." In *Foucault and Political Reason: Liberalism, Neo-Liberalism, and Rationalities of Government*, edited by A. Barry, T. Osbourne, and N. Rose, 19–36. Chicago: University of Chicago Press.

Burchell, Graham, Colin Gordon, and Peter Miller, eds. 1991. *The Foucault Effect: Studies in Governmentality*. Chicago: University of Chicago Press.

Butler, Judith. 2015. "What's Wrong with All Lives Matter?" Interview by George Yancy. *New York Times*, 12 January. http://opinionator.blogs. nytimes.com/2015/01/12/whats-wrong-with-all-lives-matter/?_r=0.

Byrd, Jodi. 2011. *The Transit of Empire: Indigenous Critiques of Colonialism*. Minneapolis: University of Minnesota Press. http://dx.doi.org/10.5749/minnesota/9780816676408.001.0001.

Cairns, Alan. 2000. *Citizens Plus: Aboriginal Peoples and the Canadian State*. Vancouver: University of British Columbia Press.

———. 2005. *First Nations and the Canadian State: In Search of Coexistence*. Kingston, ON: Institute of Intergovernmental Relations.

Calliou, Brian, and Cora Voyageur. 1996. "Aboriginal Economic Development and the Struggle for Self-Government." In *Social Control in Canada: Issues in the Social Construction of Deviance*, edited by B. Schissel and L. Mahood, 86–103. Toronto: Oxford University Press.

Calverley, Donna, Adam Cotter, and Ed Halla, eds. 2010. *Youth Custody and Community Services in Canada*. http://www.statcan.gc.ca/pub/85-002-x/2010001/article/11147-eng.htm.

"Canada Endorses the UN Declaration on the Rights of Indigenous Peoples." 2016. *Cultural Survival*. http://www.culturalsurvival.org/news/canada-endorses-un-declaration-rights-Indigenous-peoples.

Canada, Standing Senate Committee on Aboriginal Peoples. 2003. *Urban Aboriginal Youth – An Action Plan for Change: Final Report*, October. http://www.parl.gc.ca/Content/SEN/Committee/372/abor/rep/repfinoct03-e.pdf.

Canada, Standing Senate Committee on Human Rights. 2011. *The Sexual Exploitation of Children in Canada: The Need for National Action*, November. http://www.parl.gc.ca/Content/SEN/Committee/411/ridr/rep/rep03nov11-e.pdf.

Canadian Council of Provincial Child and Youth Advocates. 2010. *Aboriginal Children and Youth in Canada: Canada Must Do Better*. Position paper. http://www.cdpdj.qc.ca/Documents/CCCYA_UN_Report-final.pdf.

"The Canadian Population in 2011: Population Counts and Growth on the Website for Statistics Canada." 2012. *CBCNews*, 21 June. http://www.cbc.ca/news/canada/saskatchewan/story/2012/06/21/sk-immigrans-population-2012.html.

Cannon, Martin. 2011. "Revisiting Histories of Legal Assimilation, Racialized Injustice, and the Future of Indian Status in Canada." In *Racism, Colonialism, and Indigeneity in Canada*, edited by M. Cannon and Lina Sunseri, 89–97. New York: Oxford University Press.

Caplan, Pat. 1993. "Learning from Gender: Fieldwork in a Tanzanian Coastal Village, 1965–1985." In *Gendered Fields: Women, Men and Ethnography*, edited by D. Bell, P. Caplan and W. J. Karim, 168–81. London: Routledge.

Cardinal, Phyllis. 1999. *Aboriginal Perspectives on Education: A Vision of Cultural Context with the Framework of Social Studies*. Edmonton, AB: Alberta Learning.

Carr-Stewart, Shelia. 2003. "School Plus and Changing Demographics in Saskatchewan: Toward Diversity and Educational Communities." *Canadian Journal of Native Education* 27 (2): 223–34.

Carter, Sarah. 1997. *Capturing Women: The Manipulation of Cultural Imagery in Canada's Prairie West*. Montreal: McGill-Queen's University Press.

Casey, Allan. 2014. "Reviving Riversdale." *Walrus*, October. http://thewalrus. ca/reviving-riversdale/.

Cattelino, Jessica. 2008. *High Stakes: Florida Seminole Gaming and Sovereignty*. Durham, NC: Duke University Press. http://dx.doi. org/10.1215/9780822391302.

———. 2010. "The Double Bind of American Indian Need-Based Sovereignty." *Cultural Anthropology* 25 (2): 235–62. http://dx.doi. org/10.1111/j.1548-1360.2010.01058.x.

"The Cedaw Inquiry." 2016. *FAFIA–AFAI*. http://fafia-afai.org/en/ solidarity-campaign/the-cedaw-inquiry/.

Césaire, Aimé. 2001. *Discourse on Colonialism*. New York: Monthly Review Press.

Chatterjee, Partha. 1993. *The Nation and Its Fragments: Colonial and Postcolonial Histories*. Princeton, NJ: Princeton University Press.

Chomsky. Noam. 2003. "The Function of Schools." In Saltman and Gabbad 2003, 25–35.

———. 2009. "The Torture Memos." *Chomsky Info*, 24 May. http://www. chomsky.info/articles/20090524.htm.

Clifford, James. 1988. *The Predicament of Culture: Twentieth-Century Ethnography, Literature and Art*. Cambridge, MA: Harvard University Press.

Coburn, Elaine. 2015. *More Will Sing Their Way to Freedom: Indigenous Resistance and Resurgence*. Halifax, NS: Fernwood.

Cole, Teju. 2015. "Unmournable Bodies." *New Yorker*, January, 9.

Collins, Patricia Hill. 1990. *Black Feminist Thought: Knowledge, Consciousness, and the Politics of Empowerment*. Boston, MA: Unwin Hyman.

Comaroff, John, and Jean Comaroff. 1992. *Ethnography and the Historical Imagination*. Boulder, CO: Westview.

"Controversial Sask. Politician Pankiw Announces Comeback Bid." 2010. *CBCNews*, 4 February. http://www.cbc.ca/news/canada/saskatchewan/controversial-sask-politician-pankiw-announces-comeback-bid-1.968774.

Cooke, Bill, and Uma Kothari, eds. 2001. *Participation the New Tyranny?* London: Zed.

Coombe, Rosemary. 1999. "Culture: Anthropology's Old Voice or International Law's New Virtue." *Proceedings of the American Society for International Law*, 261–70. Washington, DC: American Society for International Law.

Corntassel, Jeff. 2012. "Re-envisioning Resurgence: Indigenous Pathways to Decolonization and Sustainable Self-Determination." *Decolonization* 1 (1): 86–101.

Corrado, Ray, Lauren F. Freedman, and Catherine Blatier. 2011. "The Over-representation of Children in Care in the Youth Criminal Justice System in British Columbia: Theory and Policy Issues." *International Journal of Child, Youth, and Family Studies* 2 (1/2): 99–118. http://dx.doi.org/10.18357/ijcyfs21/220115429.

Corum, Lindsay Catherine. 2015. "The Space NDN's Star Map." *New Inquiry*, 26 January. http://thenewinquiry.com/essays/the-space-ndns-star-map/.

Coulthard, Glen. 2007. "Subjects of Empire: Indigenous Peoples and the 'Politics of Recognition' in Canada." *Contemporary Political Theory* 6 (4): 437–60. http://dx.doi.org/10.1057/palgrave.cpt.9300307.

———. 2010. "Place against Empire: Understanding Indigenous Anti-Colonialism." *Affinities* 4 (2): 79–83. http://ojs.library.queensu.ca/index.php/affinities/article/view/6141/5820.

———. 2014a. *Red Skin, White Masks: Rejecting the Colonial Politics of Recognition*. Minneapolis: University of Minnesota Press.

———, ed. 2014b. *Recognition and Self Determination*. Vancouver: University of British Columbia Press.

Cowlishaw, Gillian. 2003. "Disappointing Indigenous People: Violence and the Refusal of Help." *Public Culture* 15 (1): 103–25. http://dx.doi.org/10.1215/08992363-15-1-103.

Crenshaw, Kimberle. 1991. "Mapping the Margins: Intersectionality, Identity Politics, and Violence against Women of Color." *Stanford Law Review* 43 (6): 1241–99. http://dx.doi.org/10.2307/1229039.

Crosby, Andrew, and Jeffrey Monaghan. 2012. "Settler Governmentality in Canada and the Algonquins of Barriere Lake." *Security Dialogue*, 3 October, 421–38. http://dx.doi.org/10.1177/0967010612457972.

Cruikshank, Barbara. 1996. "Revolutions Within: Self-Government and Self-Esteem." In *Foucault and Political Reason: Liberalism, Neo-Liberalism, and*

*Rationalities of Government*, edited by A. Barry, T. Osbourne, and N. Rose, 231–52. Chicago: University of Chicago Press.

Chrisler, Matt, Jaskiran Dhillon, and Audra Simpson. 2016. "The Standing Rock Syllabus Project." *PS*, 21 October. http://www.publicseminar.org/2016/10/nodapl-syllabus-project/#.WBy6Gcljak1.

Czapska, Asia, and Annabel Webb. 2005. *Memorandum of Justice for Girls Regarding the Right of Teenage Girls to Adequate Housing in Canada*, 15–17 October. Submitted to the United Nations Special Rapporteur on Adequate Housing. http://www.justiceforgirls.org/uploads/2/4/5/0/24509463/memorandum_-_right_of_teenage_girls_to_adequate_housing.pdf.

Czapska, Asia, Annabel Webb, and Bura Taefi. 2008. *More than Bricks and Mortar: A Rights-Based Strategy to Prevent Girls Homelessness in Canada*. Vancouver : Justice for Girls.

Daschuk, James. 2013. *Clearing the Plains: Disease, Starvation, and the Loss of Aboriginal Life*. Regina, SK: University of Regina Press.

Day, Richard. 2000. *Multiculturalism and the History of Canadian Diversity*. Toronto: University of Toronto Press.

Dean, Amber. 2005. Locking Them Up to Keep Them "Safe": Criminalized Girls in British Columbia. Report. Vancouver: Justice for Girls.

Dei, George. 1995. "Examining the Case for African-Centred Schools in Ontario." *McGill Journal of Education / Revue des sciences de l'éducation de McGill* 30 (2): 179–98. *http://mje.mcgill.ca/article/view/8239/6167*.

———. 1996. *Anti-Racism Education: Theory and Practice*. Halifax, NS: Fernwood.

———, ed. 2011. *Indigenous Philosophies and Critical Education*. New York: Peter Lang.

Deloria, Vine, and Daniel Wildcat. 2001. *Power and Place: Indian Education in America*. Golden: Fulcrum.

Delpit, Lisa. 2006. *Other People's Children: Cultural Conflict in the Classroom*. New York: New Press.

Dewey, John. 1916. *Democracy and Education*. New York: Free Press.

Dhaliwal, Anand. 1994. "Reading Diaspora." *Socialist Review* 4 (24): 13–43.

Dhillon, Jaskiran. 2011. "Social Exclusion, Gender and Access to Education in Canada: Narrative Accounts from Girls on the Street." *Feminist Formations* 23 (3): 110–34. http://dx.doi.org/10.1353/ff.2011.0041.

———. 2014. "Eyes Wide Open." *#ItEndsHere* (blog), 10 March. http://nationsrising.org/eyes-wide-open/.

———. 2015. "Indigenous Girls and the Violence of Settler Colonial Policing." *Decolonization* 4 (2): 1–31.

———. 2016. "Indigenous Youth Are Building a Climate Justice Movement by Targeting Colonialism." *Truthout*, 20 June. http://www.truth-out.org/

news/item/36482-indigenous-youth-are-building-a-climate-justice-movement-by-targeting-colonialism.

Dhillon, Jaskiran, and Siku Allooloo. 2015. "Violence against Indigenous Women Is Woven into Canada's History." *Guardian*, 14 December. https://www.theguardian.com/commentisfree/2015/dec/14/violence-indigenous-woman-canada-history-inquiry-racism.

———. 2016. "Dismantling Columbus and the Power of the Present." *Truthout*, 10 October. http://www.truth-out.org/opinion/item/37924-dismantling-columbus-and-the-power-of-the-present.

Dickason, Olive Patricia. 2002. *Canada's First Nations: A History of Founding Peoples from Earliest Times*. 3rd ed. Don Mills, ON: Oxford University Press.

Dohrn, Bernadine. 2000. "Look Out Kid It's Something You Did: The Criminalization of Children." In Polakow, 157–87.

Driskill, Qwo-Li. 2010. "Doubleweaving Two-Spirit Critiques: Building Alliances between Native and Queer Studies." In "Sexuality, Nationality, Indigeneity," edited by D. H. Justice, M Rifkin, and B. Schneider. Special issue, *GLQ* 16 (1/2): 69–92.

Dua, Enakshi, Narda Razack, and Jody Warner, eds. 2005. "Race, Racism, and Empire. Reflections on Canada." Special issue, *Social Justice* 32 (4).

"Edmonton Mayor Encourages Citizens to Learn about Aboriginal People." 2014. *APTN National News*, 10 April. http://aptn.ca/news/2014/04/10/edmonton-mayor-encourages-citizens-learn-Aboriginal-people/.

Elkins, Caroline, and Susan Pedersen. 2005. *Settler Colonialism in the Twentieth Century: Projects, Practices, and Legacies*. New York: Routledge.

Enns, Richard. 2009. "'But What Is the Object of Educating These Children, if It Costs Their Lives to Educate Them?' Federal Indian Education Policy in Western Canada in the Late 1800s." *Journal of Canadian Studies / Revue d'Etudes Canadiennes* 43 (3): 101–23.

Environics Institute. 2011. *Urban Aboriginal Peoples Study*. http://www.uaps.ca/

Epp, Robert. 2008. *We Are All Treaty People: Prairie Essays*. Edmonton, AB: University of Alberta Press.

Escobar, Arturo. 1992. "Imagining a Post-Development Era? Critical Thought, Development and Social Movements." *Social Text* 31 (31/32): 20–56. http://dx.doi.org/10.2307/466217.

———. 1998. "Whose Knowledge, Whose Nature? Biodiversity, Conservation and Social Movements' Political Ecology." *Journal of Political Ecology* 5 (1): 53–82.

Estes, Nick. 2016. "Off the Reservation: Lakota Life and Death in Rapid City, South Dakota." *Funambulist*, May–June. http://thefunambulist.net/2016/07/09/off-the-reservation-lakota-life-and-death-in-rapid-city-south-dakota-by-nick-estes/.

Fairbanks, Robert. 2009. *How It Works: Recovering Citizens in Post-Welfare Philadelphia*. Chicago: University of Chicago Press. http://dx.doi. org/10.7208/chicago/9780226234113.001.0001.

Fanon, Franz. 1963. *The Wretched of the Earth*. New York: Grove.

Farmer, Paul. 2004. "An Anthropology of Structural Violence." *Current Anthropology* 45 (3): 305–25. http://dx.doi.org/10.1086/382250.

Fassin, Didier. 2012. *Humanitarian Reason: A Moral History of the Present*. Berkeley: University of California Press.

Feldman, Alice. 2001. "Transforming Peoples and Subverting States: Developing a Pedagogical Approach to the Study of Indigenous Peoples and Ethnocultural Movements." *Ethnicities* 1 (2): 147–78. http://dx.doi. org/10.1177/146879680100100201.

Ferguson, James. 1994. *The Anti-Politics Machine*. Minneapolis: University of Minnesota Press.

Ferguson, James, and Akhil Gupta. 2002. "Spatializing States: Toward an Ethnography of Neo-Liberal Governmentality." *American Ethnologist* 29 (4): 981–1002. http://dx.doi.org/10.1525/ae.2002.29.4.981.

Findlay, Isobel, and Warren Weir. 2004. *Legacy of Hope: An Agenda for Change*. Regina, SK: Commission on First Nations and Métis Peoples Justice Reform.

Fine, Michelle. 1995. "The Politics of Who's 'At-Risk.'" In *Children and Families "At Promise": Constructing the Discourse of Risk,* edited by B. Swadener and S. Lubeck, 76–94. Albany, NY: SUNY Press.

Finkel, Alvin. 2006. *Social Policy and Practice in Canada: A History*. Waterloo, ON: Wilfrid Laurier University Press.

Finney, Sandra, and Jeff Orr. 1995. "'I've really learned a lot, but …': Cross-Cultural Understanding and Teacher Education in a Racist Society." *Journal of Teacher Education*, 46(5): 327–33.

Flannigan, Tom. 2000. *First Nations, Second Thoughts*. Montreal: McGill-Queens University Press.

Foley, Douglas E. 1996. "The Silent Indian as Cultural Production." In *The Cultural Production of the Educated Person: Critical Ethnographies of Schooling and Local Practice*, edited by Bradley A. Levinson, Douglas E. Foley, and Dorothy Holland, 79–92. New York: State University of New York Press.

Ford, Lisa, and Tim Rowse. 2013. *Between Indigenous and Settler Governance*. New York: Routledge.

Foucault, Michel. 1977. *Discipline and Punish: The Birth of the Prison*. New York: Vintage.

———. 1982. "The Subject and Power." In *Michel Foucault: Beyond Structuralism and Hermeneutics*, edited by H.L. Dreyfus and P. Rabinow, 208–26. Chicago: University of Chicago Press.

————. 1991. "Governmentality." In *The Foucault Effect: Studies in Governmentality*, edited by G. Burchell, C. Cardon, and P. Miller, 87–105. Chicago: Chicago University Press.

Francis, Daniel. 1997. "Your Majesty's Realm: The Myth of the Master Race." In *National Dreams: Myth, Memory, and Canadian History*, 52–87. Vancouver: Arsenal Pulp.

Fraser, Nancy. 2004. *Redistribution or Recognition? A Political-Philosophical Exchange*. New York: Verso.

Freire, Paulo. 1970. *Pedagogy of the Oppressed*. New York: Continuum International.

Frideres, James. 1998. "Indigenous Peoples of Canada and the United States of America: Entering the 21st Century." In *Images of Canadianness*, edited by Louis Balthazar and Leen Haenens, 167–96. Ottawa: University of Ottawa Press.

Frideres, James, and Rene Gadacz. 2001. *Aboriginal Peoples in Canada*. New Jersey: Prentice Hall.

Galtung, Johan. 1990. "Cultural Violence." *Journal of Peace Research* 27 (3): 291–305. http://dx.doi.org/10.1177/0022343390027003005.

Garcia, Maria. 2005. *Making Indigenous Citizens: Identity, Development, and Multicultural Activism in Peru*. San Francisco: Stanford University Press.

Gazzola, Bart. 2012. "The Real World: StreetGraphix Offers an Unvarnished Look at Youth at Risk." *Planet S*, 29 November.

Gebhard, Amanda. 2012. "Schools, Prison, and Aboriginal Youth: Making Connections." *Journal of Educational Controversy* 7 (1). http://cedar.wwu.edu/jec/vol7/iss1/.

Geertz, Clifford. 1973. *The Interpretation of Cultures*. New York: Basic.

Giddens, Anthony. 1984. *The Constitution of Society: Outline of the Theory of Structuration*. Los Angeles: University of California Press.

Giroux, Henry A. 2006. "Disposable Youth, Racism, and the Politics of Zero Tolerance." In *America on the Edge: Henry Giroux on Politics, Culture, and Education*, 175–88. New York: Palgrave Macmillan. http://dx.doi.org/10.1057/9781403984364_11.

Goldberg, David. 2009. *The Threat of Race*. Oxford: Blackwell.

Gone, Joseph. 2014. "Colonial Genocide and Historical Trauma in Native North America." In *Colonial Genocide in Indigenous North America*, edited by A. Woolford, J. Benvenuto, and A. Hinton, 273–91. Durham, NC: Duke University Press.

Grande, Sandy. 2004. *Red Pedagogy: Native American Social and Political Thought*. New York: Rowman and Littlefield.

Graybill, Andrew R. 2007. *Policing the Great Plains: Rangers, Mounties, and the North American Frontier*. Lincoln: University of Nebraska Press.

Grebinski, Leisha. 2012. "That's the Life of a Gangster: Analyzing the Media Representations of Daniel Wolfe." Master's thesis, University of Regina.

Green, Joyce. 1995. "Towards a Détente with History: Confronting Canada's Colonial Legacy." *International Journal of Canadian Studies* 12 (Fall): 85–105.

———. 2011. "From Stonechild to Social Cohesion." In *Racism, Colonialism, and Indigeneity in Canada*, edited by M. Cannon and L. Sunseri, 234–41. Ontario: Oxford University Press.

Gregory, Derek. 2004. *The Colonial Present: Afghanistan, Palestine, Iraq*. Oxford: Blackwell.

Gupta, Akhil. 2001. "Governing Population: The Integrated Child Development Services Program in India." In *States of Imagination: Ethnographic Explorations of the Postcolonial State*, edited by T. Hansen and F. Stepputat, 65–96. Durham, NC: Duke University Press. http://dx.doi.org/10.1215/9780822381273-003.

———. 2006. "Blurred Boundaries: The Discourse of Corruption, the Culture of Politics and the Imagined State." In *The Anthropology of the State: A Reader*, edited by A. Gupta and A. Sharma, 211–42. Oxford: Blackwell.

Haig-Brown, Celia. 1993. *Resistance and Renewal: Surviving the Indian Residential School*. 6th ed. Vancouver: Tillacum Library / Arsenal Pulp.

Hall, Kathleen. 2002. *Lives in Translations: Sikh Youth as British Citizens*. Philadelphia: University of Pennsylvania. http://dx.doi.org/10.9783/9780812200676.

Hampton, Eber. 1995. "Towards a Definition of Indian Education." In *First Nations Education in Canada: The Circle Unfolds*, edited by M. Battiste and J. Barman, 5–46. Vancouver: University of British Columbia Press.

Hansen, Thomas, and Finn Stepputat, eds. 2001. *States of Imagination: Ethnographic Explorations of the Postcolonial State*. Durham, NC: Duke University Press. http://dx.doi.org/10.1215/9780822381273.

Henry, Francis, and Carol Tator. 2002. *Discourses of Domination*. Toronto: University of Toronto Press.

Hesch, Rick. 2010. "Richards Rhymes with Reaction and Racism: An Analysis of Popular Policy Proposals for Aboriginal Education Reform." In "Anti-Racism Education: Missing in Action," edited by C. Smith. Special Issue, *Our Schools / Our Selves* 19 (3): 255–73.

Hindess, Barry. 2000. "Citizenship in the International Management of Populations." *American Behavioral Scientist* 43 (9): 1486–97. http://dx.doi.org/10.1177/00027640021956008.

———. 2005. "Sovereignty." In *New Keywords: A Revised Vocabulary of Culture and Society*, edited by Tony Bennet, Lawrence Grossberg, and Meaghan Morris, 329–30. London: Wiley Blackwell.

Hare, Jan, and Jane Barman. 2000. "Aboriginal Education: Is There a Way Ahead?" In *Visions of the Heart: Canadian Aboriginal Issues*. 2nd ed. Edited by David Long and Olive P. Dickason, 331–59. Toronto: Harcourt Canada.

Hastrup, Kristen, and Karen Olwig. 1997. *Sitting Culture: The Shifting Anthropological Object*. London: Routledge.

Human Rights Watch. 2013. *Those Who Take Us Away: Abusive Policing and Failures in Protection of Indigenous Women and Girls in Northern British Columbia, Canada*, 13 February. https://www.hrw.org/report/2013/02/13/those-who-take-us-away/abusive-policing-and-failures-protection-indigenous-women.

Hunt, Sarah. 2010. "Colonial Roots, Contemporary Risk Factors: A Cautionary Exploration of the Domestic Trafficking of Aboriginal Girls and Women in British Columbia, Canada." *Alliance News* 33:27–23.

———. 2015. "Violence, Law, and the Everyday Politics of Recognition." Paper presented at the Annual Meeting of the North American Indigenous Studies Association, Washington D.C.

Hurston, Zora Neale. (1928) 1989. "How it Feels to be Colored Me." In *Norton Anthology of American Literature*, edited by N. Baym et al., 535–41. New York: Norton.

INAC (Indian and Northern Affairs Canada). 2005. *Education Action Plan*. http://www.turtleisland.org/education/inac05.pdf.

Innes, Robert. 2004. "American Indian Studies Research Is Ethical Research: A Discussion of Linda Smith and James Waldram's Approach to Aboriginal Research." *Native Studies Review* 15 (2): 131–38.

Innes, Robert, and Kim Anderson. 2015. *Indigenous Men and Masculinities: Legacies, Identities, Regeneration*. Winnipeg: University of Manitoba Press.

Inter-American Commission on Human Rights. 2014. *Missing and Murdered Indigenous Women in British Columbia, Canada*. http://www.oas.org/en/iachr/reports/pdfs/Indigenous-women-bc-canada-en.pdf.

Isaac, Thomas. 2000. "No End in Sight." *Globe and Mail*, 19 September.

Jacobs, Madeline. 2012. "Assimilation through Incarceration: The Geographic Imposition of Canadian Law over Indigenous Peoples." PhD diss., Queens University.

Jamieson, Kathleen. 1978. *Indian Woman and the Law in Canada: Citizens Minus*. Ottawa: Ministry of Supply and Services.

Jhappan, C. Radha. 1990. "Indian Symbolic Politics: The Double Edge Sword of Publicity." *Canadian Ethnic Studies* 22 (3): 19–39.

Jiwani, Yasmin. 2006. *Discourses of Denial: Mediations of Race, Gender, and Violence*. Vancouver: University of British Columbia Press.

Jordon, David F. 1988. "Rights and Claims of Indigenous Peoples: Education and the Reclaiming of Identity – The Case of the Canadian Natives, the Sami and Australian Aborigines." In *Minority Education: From Shame to Struggle*, edited by T. Skutnabb-Kangas and J. Cummins, 189–222. Clevedon, UK: Multilingual Matters.

Justice for Girls. 2015. *Court Case Summaries R. v. David William Ramsay*. Accessed 15 January. http://www.justiceforgirls.org/justicesystemmonitoring/cc_Ramsay%20Updated.html.

Justice for Girls, and Justice for Girls International. 2012. *Submission to: UN Committee on the Rights of the Child at Its Sixty-First Session and Periodic Review of Canada, 17 September–5 October*. http://www2.ohchr.org/english/bodies/crc/docs/ngos/JusticeForGirls_Canada61.pdf

Kallen, Evelyn. 2003. *Ethnicity and Human Rights in Canada: A Human Rights Perspective on Ethnicity, Race, and Systemic Inequality*. Don Mills, ON: Oxford University Press.

Kauanui, Kēhaulani J., and Patrick Wolfe. 2012. "Settler Colonialism Then and Now. A Conversation." *Politica and Società* 2:235–58.

Kawagley, Oscar, and Ray Barnhardt. 1999. "Education Indigenous to Place: Western Science Meets Native Reality." In *Ecological Education in Action: On Weaving Education, Culture, and the Environment*, edited by G. Smith and D.R. Williams, 117–42. New York: SUNY Press.

Kinew, Wab. 2014. "Idle No More: It's Not Just an Indian Thing." In *The Winter We Danced*, edited by Kino-nda-niimi Collective, 95–97. Toronto: Arbeiter Ring.

King, Thomas. 2003. *The Truth about Stories: A Native Narrative*. Toronto: Anansi.

Kingsley, Cherry, and Melanie Mark. 2001. *Sacred Lives: Canadian Aboriginal Children and Youth Speak Out about Sexual Exploitation*. Vancouver, BC: Save the Children Canada.

Kirkness, Verna. 1999. "Aboriginal Education in Canada: A Retrospective and a Prospective." *Journal of American Indian Education* 39 (1): 14–30.

Klein, Naomi. 2014a. *This Changes Everything*. Toronto: Knopf.

———. 2014b. "How a Cree Woman Fell to Death, and No One Saw Anything." *Globe and Mail*, 18 December. http://www.theglobeandmail.com/news/national/how-a-cree-woman-fell-to-death-and-no-one-saw-anything/article22167039/

Kothari, Uma. 2001. "Power, Knowledge, and Social Control in Participatory Development." In *Participation: The New Tyranny*, edited by B. Cooke and U. Kothari, 139–52. London: Zed.

Kowal, Emma. 2008. "The Politics of the Gap: Indigenous Australians, Liberal Multiculturalism, and the End of the Self-Determination Era." *American Anthropologist* 110 (3): 338–48. http://dx.doi.org/10.1111/j.1548-1433.2008.00043.x.

Laclau, Ernest. 1995. "Universalism, Particularism, and the Question of Identity." In *The Identity in Question*, edited by John Rajchman, 83–90. London: Routledge.

Ladson-Billings, Gloria. 2007. "Pushing Past the Achievement Gap: An Essay on the Language of Deficit." *Journal of Negro Education* 18 (3): 316–23.

Lather, Patty. 1993. "Research as Praxis." In *Qualitative Research in Higher Education: Experiencing Alternative Perspectives and Approaches*, edited by A. Haworth and P. Scott, 131–39. Needham Heights, MA: Ginn.

Latour, Bruno. 1991. *We Have Never Been Modern*. Cambridge, MA: Harvard University Press.

Lawrence, Bonita. 2002. "Rewriting Histories of the Land: Colonization and Indigenous Resistance in Eastern Canada." In *Race, Space, and the Law: Unmapping a White Settler Society*, edited by Sherene Razack, 21–46. Toronto: Between the Lines.

———. 2003. "Gender, Race, and the Regulation of Native Identity in Canada and the United States: An Overview." *Hypatia* 18 (2): 3–31. http://dx.doi.org/10.1111/j.1527-2001.2003.tb00799.x.

———. 2004. *"Real Indians and Others: Mixed-Blood Urban Native Peoples and Indigenous Nationhood*. Vancouver: University of British Columbia Press.

Lawrence, Bonita, and Enakshi Dua. 2005. "Decolonizing Antiracism." *Social Justice* 32 (4): 120–43.

Lawrence, Bruce, and Aisha Karim, eds. 2007. *On Violence*. Durham, NC: Duke University Press. http://dx.doi.org/10.1215/9780822390169.

Laymon, Kiese. 2015. "Black Churches Taught Us to Forgive White People: We Learned to Shame Ourselves." *Guardian*, 23 June. http://www.theguardian.com/commentisfree/2015/jun/23/black-churchesforgive-white-people-shame?CMP=share_btn_fb.

LeBeuf, Marcel-Eugene. 2011. *The Role of the Royal Canadian Mounted Police during the Indian Residential School System*. http://publications.gc.ca/site/archivee-archived.html?url=http://publications.gc.ca/collections/collection_2011/grc-rcmp/PS64-71-2009-eng.pdf.

Le Guin, Ursula. 2004. *The Wave in the Mind: Talks and Essays on the Writer, the Reader and the Imagination*. Boston, MA: Shambhala.

Lesko, Nancy, and Susan Talburt, eds. 2012. *Keywords in Youth Studies: Tracing Affects, Movements, Knowledges*. New York: Routledge.

Levin, Henry. 2004. "The Public-Private Nexus in Education." In *Educational Partnerships and the State: The Paradoxes of Governing Schools, Children and*

*Families*, edited by B. Franklin, M, Bloch, and T. Popkewitz, 171–86. New York: Palgrave MacMillan.

Levinson, Brian, Doug Foley, and Dorothy Holland, eds. 1996. *The Cultural Production of the Educated Person: Critical Ethnographies of Schooling and Local Practice*. Albany: State University of New York Press.

Lévi-Strauss, Claude. 1963. *Structural Anthropology*, translated by Claire Jacobson and Brooke Grundfest Schoepf. New York: Basic.

Lewis, Oscar. 1967. "The Children of Sanchez: Autobiography of a Mexican Family." *Current Anthropology* 8:480–500.

Li, Tania Murray. 2005. "Beyond the State and Failed Schemes." *American Anthropologist* 107 (3): 383–94. http://dx.doi.org/10.1525/aa.2005.107.3.383.

———. 2007. *The Will to Improve: Governmentality, Development, and the Practice of Politics*. Durham, NC: Duke University Press.

Lipman, Pauline. 2003. "Cracking Down: Chicago School Policy and the Regulation of Black and Latino Youth." In Saltman and Gabbard 2003, 81–102.

———. 2009. "The Cultural Politics of Mixed Income Schools and Housing: A Racialized Discourse of Displacement, Exclusion and Control." *Anthropology and Education Quarterly* 40 (3): 215–36. http://dx.doi.org/10.1111/j.1548-1492.2009.01042.x.

Ljunggren, David. 2009. "Every G20 Nation Wants to Be Canada, Insists PM." *Reuters*, 22 September. http://www.reuters.com/article/2009/09/26/columns-us-g20-canada-advantages-idUSTRE58P05Z20090926.

Locke, John. 1964. *Some Thoughts Concerning Education*. New York: Columbia University Press.

Lugones, María. 2007. "Heterosexualism and the Colonial/Modern Gender System." *Hypatia* 22 (1): 186–209.

Lukose, Ritty. 2009. *Liberalization's Children: Gender, Youth, and Consumer Citizenship in India*. Durham, NC: Duke University Press. http://dx.doi.org/10.1215/9780822391241.

Maaka, Roger, and Augie Fleras. 2005. *The Politics of Indigeneity: Challenging the State in Canada and Aotearoa New Zealand*. Dunedin, New Zealand: Otago.

MacDermott, Wendy. 2004. *Evaluation of the Activities of the Working Group to Stop the Sexual Exploitation of Children*. Saskatoon: University of Saskatchewan.

MacDonald, Kelly A. 2005. *Justice System's Response: Violence against Aboriginal Girls*. Vancouver: Justice for Girls.

Macharia, Keguro. 2013. "On Quitting." *New Inquiry*, 3 May. http://thenewinquiry.com/essays/on-quitting/.

Macoun, Alissa, and Elizabeth Strakosch. 2013. "The Ethical Demands of Settler Colonial Theory." *Settler Colonial Studies* 3 (3/4): 426–43.

Maddison, Sarah. 2013. "Indigenous Identity: 'Authenticity' and the Structural
  Violence of Settler Colonialism." *Identities* 20 (3): 288–303. http://dx.doi.org/
  10.1080/1070289X.2013.806267.
Maira, Sunaina. 2009. *Missing: Youth Citizenship and Empire after 9/11*. Durham,
  NC: Duke University Press. http://dx.doi.org/10.1215/9780822392385.
Malone, Kelly. 2013. "More Aboriginal Children in Foster Care in Sask than
  National Average." *Saskatchewan News*, 9 May. http://www.ckom.com/
  story/more-Aboriginal-children-foster-care-sask-national-average/109272.
Mamdani, Mahmood. 1998. "When Does a Settler Become a Native? Reflections
  of the Colonial Roots of Citizenship in Equatorial and South Africa."
  Inaugural Lecture, A.C. Jordan Professor of African Studies, University
  of Cape Town, Cape Town, 13 May. http://citizenshiprightsafrica.org/
  when-does-a-settler-become-a-native-reflections-of-the-colonial-roots-of-
  citizenship-in-equatorial-and-south-africa/.
Maracle, Lee. 2013. "Blind Justice." *Decolonization* 2 (1): 134–36.
Markell, Patchen. 2003. *Bound by Recognition*. Princeton, NJ: Princeton
  University Press.
Marker, Michael. 2000. "Economics and Local Self-Determination: Describing
  the Clash Zone in First Nations Education." *Canadian Journal of Native
  Education* 24 (1): 30–44.
———. 2003. "Indigenous Voice, Community and Epistemic Violence:
  The Ethnographer's 'Interests' and What 'Interests' the Ethnographer."
  *International Journal of Qualitative Studies in Education* 16 (3): 361–75. http://
  dx.doi.org/10.1080/0951839032000086736.
———. 2006. "After the Makah Whale Hunt: Indigenous Knowledge and
  Limits to Multicultural Discourse." *Urban Education* 41 (5): 482–505. http://
  dx.doi.org/10.1177/0042085906291923.
Martineau, Jarrett. 2014. "Fires of Resistance." *New Inquiry*, 12 December.
  http://thenewinquiry.com/essays/fires-of-resistance/.
———. 2015. "Creative Combat: Indigenous Art, Resurgence, and
  Decolonization" PhD diss., University of Victoria.
Martínez Cobo, José R. 1981. *Study of the Problem of Discrimination against
  Indigenous Populations*. New York: United Nations.
———. 1986. *The Study of the Problem of Discrimination against Indigenous
  Populations*. United Nations, Dag Hammarskjöld Library, Dag Repository.
  http://repository.un.org/handle/11176/354767.
Mas, Susana. 2015. "Truth and Reconciliation Commission Final Report Points
  to 'Growing Crisis' for Indigenous Youth." *CBC News*, 14 December. http://
  www.cbc.ca/news/politics/truth-and-reconciliation-final-report-1.3361148.
Maxwell, Joseph. 1996. *Qualitative Research Design: An Interactive Approach*.
  London: Sage.

McCarthy, Cameron, and Warren Crichlow 1993. *Race, Identity, and Representation in Education*. New York: Routledge.

McConaghy, Cathryn. 2000. *Rethinking Indigenous Education: Culturalism, Colonialism, and the Politics of Knowing*. Flaxton, QLD: Post Pressed.

McGee, Patrick. 1993. "Decolonization and the Curriculum of English." In McCarthy and Crichlow, 280–88.

McKegney, Sam. 2005. "From Trickster Poetics to Transgressive Politics: Substantiating Survivance in Tomson Highway's Kiss of the Fur Queen." *Studies in American Indian Literatures* 17 (4): 79–113. http://dx.doi.org/10.1353/ail.2006.0006.

McLean, Sheelah. 2014. "Idle No More: Re-Storying Canada." In *The Winter We Danced*, edited by Kino-nda-niimi Collective, 92–94. Toronto: Arbeiter Ring.

Memmi, Albert. 1965. *The Colonizer and the Colonized*. Boston, MA: Beacon.

Merry, Sally. 2006. *Human Rights and Gender Violence: Translating International Law into Local Human Rights*. Chicago: University of Chicago Press.

Miller, James R. (1989) 2000. *Skyscrapers Hide the Heavens: A History of Indian–White Relations in Canada*. 3rd ed. Toronto: University of Toronto Press.

Milloy, John. 1999. *A National Crime: The Canadian Government and the Residential School System,1879–1986*. Winnipeg: University of Manitoba Press.

———. 2008. *Indian Act Colonialism: A Century of Dishonour, 1869–1969*. Research paper, National Centre for First Nations Governance. http://fngovernance.org/ncfng_research/milloy.pdf.

Minister of Indian Affairs and Northern Development. 1997. *Gathering Strength: Canada's Aboriginal Action Plan*. (Catalogue No. R32-189-1997E ISBN 0-662-26427-4). http://www.ahf.ca/downloads/gathering-strength.pdf.

Missing Women Commission of Inquiry. 2013. Archived website. http://www.missingwomeninquiry.ca/.

Mitchell, Timothy. 1991. "The Limits of the State: Beyond Statist Approaches and Their Critics." *American Political Science Review* 85 (1): 77–96.

Mohanty, Chandra. 2003. *Feminism without Borders: Decolonizing Theory, Practicing Solidarity*. Durham, NC: Duke University Press. http://dx.doi.org/10.1215/9780822384649.

Monture-Angus, Patricia. 1995. *Thunder in My Soul: A Mohawk Woman Speaks*. Halifax, NS: Fernwood.

Moore, Dene. 2014. "Tens of Thousands of First Nation Children Died in Residential Schools." *Canadian Press*, 13 March. http://westcoastnativenews.com/tens-of-thousands-first-nation-children-died-in-residential-schools/.

Morrow, Raymond, and Carlos A. Torres. 1999. "The State, Social Movements, and Educational Reform." In *Comparative Education: The Dialectic of the*

*Global and the Local*, edited by R. Arnove and C.A. Torres, 73–84. New York: Rowman and Littlefield.

Mosby, Ian. 2013. "Administering Colonial Science: Nutrition Research and Human Biomedical Experimentation in Aboriginal Communities and Residential Schools, 1942–1952." *Histoire Sociale / Social History* 46 (9): 145–72.

Muehlebach, Andrea. 2001. "'Making Place' at the United Nations: Indigenous Cultural Politics at the UN Working Group on Indigenous Populations." *Cultural Anthropology* 16 (3): 415–48. http://dx.doi.org/10.1525/can.2001.16.3.415.

Muehlmann, Shaylih. 2009. "How Do Real Indians Fish? Neoliberal Multiculturalism and Contested Indigeneities in the Colorado Delta." *American Anthropologist* 111 (4): 468–79. http://dx.doi.org/10.1111/j.1548-1433.2009.01156.x.

Murdocca, Carmela. 2013. *To Right Historical Wrongs: Race, Gender, and Sentencing in Canada*. Vancouver: University Of British Columbia Press.

Naber, Nadine. 2012. *Arab America: Gender, Cultural Politics, and Activism*. New York: New York University Press.

Nadasdy, Paul. 2003. *Hunters and Bureaucrats: Power, Knowledge, and Aboriginal–State Relations in Southwest Yukon*. Seattle: University of Washington Press.

Nader, Laura. 1972. "Up the Anthropologist: Perspectives Gained from Studying Up." In *Reinventing Anthropology*, edited by David Hymes, 284–311. New York: Pantheon.

Nash, Kate. 2000. *Contemporary Political Sociology: Globalization, Politics, and Power*. Malden, MA: Malden–Blackwell .

Nepinak, Derek. 2014. "New First Nations Education Act an 'Illusion of Control.'" *CBCNews*, April 11. http://www.cbc.ca/news/Aboriginal/new-first-nations-education-act-an-illusion-of-control-1.2607178.

Nettelbeck, Amanda, and Russell Smandych. 2010. "Policing Indigenous Peoples on Two Colonial Frontiers: Australia's Mounted Police and Canada's North-West Mounted Police." *Australian and New Zealand Journal of Criminology* 43 (2): 356–75. http://dx.doi.org/10.1375/acri.43.2.356.

Neve, Lisa, and Kim Pate. 2005. "Challenging the Criminalization of Women Who Resist." In Sudbury 2005, 19–34. New York: Routledge.

Newell, Diane. 1993. *Tangled Webs of History: Indians and the Law in Canada's Pacific Coast Fisheries*. Toronto: University of Toronto Press.

Nichols, Robert. 2014. "The Colonialism of Incarceration." *Radical Philosophy Review* 17 (2): 435–55. http://dx.doi.org/10.5840/radphilrev201491622.

Niezen, Ronald. 2000. "Recognizing Indigenism: Canadian Unity and the International Movement of Indigenous Peoples." *Comparative Studies in Society and History* 42 (1): 119–48. http://dx.doi.org/10.1017/S0010417500002620.

Noguera, Pedro A. 2003. "Schools, Prisons, and Social Implications of Punishment: Rethinking Disciplinary Practices." *Theory into Practice* 42 (4): 341–50. http://dx.doi.org/10.1207/s15430421tip4204_12.

NWAC (Native Women's Association of Canada). 2014a. NWAC Disappointed Once Again. News release, 7 March. https://www.nwac.ca/wp-content/uploads/2015/05/14.03.07-NWAC-Disappointed-Once-again-VAIW.pdf.

———. 2014b. *Special Submission to the Expert Mechanism on the Rights of Indigenous Peoples (EMRIP) on Access to Justice for Aboriginal Women in Canada*, 10 March. http://www.ohchr.org/Documents/Issues/IPeoples/EMRIP/FollowupStudyAccessToJustice/NativeWomensAssociationof Canada.pdf.

———. 2016. "MMIWG." *NWAC*. Accessed 29 September. *https://nwac.ca/mmiwg/*.

Ogden, Stormy. 2005. "The Prison Industrial Complex in Indigenous California." In Sudbury 2005, 57–66. New York: Routledge.

Ong, Ahiwa. 2006. *Neoliberalism as Exception: Mutations in Citizenship and Sovereignty*. Durham, NC: Duke University Press. http://dx.doi.org/10.1215/9780822387879.

. "Origin of the Name 'Canada.'" 2013. *Government of Canada*, 18 June. http://canada.pch.gc.ca/eng/1443789176782.

Ortner, Sherry. 1984. "Theory in Anthropology since the Sixties." *Comparative Studies in Society and History* 26 (1): 126–66. http://dx.doi.org/10.1017/S0010417500010811.

———. 2001. "Specifying Agency: The Comaroffs and Their Critics in Interventions." *International Journal of Postcolonial Studies* 3 (1): 76–84. http://dx.doi.org/10.1080/13698010020027038.

Osborne, Ken. 1996. "Education Is the Best National Insurance: Citizenship Education in Canadian Schools Past and Present." *Canadian and International Education / Education Canadienne et Internationale* 25 (2): 31–58.

"Negative Attitudes toward Indigenous Peoples Highest in Prairie Provinces: National Poll." 2016. *APTN National News*, 8 June. http://aptn.ca/news/2016/06/08/negative-attitudes-toward-indigenous-peoples-highest-in-prairie-provinces-national-poll-2/.

Palmater, Pamela. 2011. "Stretched beyond Human Limits: Death by Poverty in First Nations." *Canadian Review of Social Policy / Revue canadienne de politique sociale* 65/66:112–27.

Parkouda, Michelle. 2013. "The Aboriginal Opportunity: Optimizing First Nations and Métis Contributions to Economic Growth and Social Well-Being." *Saskatchewan Business Magazine*, March 22–23. http://www.conferenceboard.ca/Libraries/PUBLIC_PDFS/ski_sb_mar2013.sflb.

Partridge, Cheryle. 2010. "Residential Schools: The Intergenerational Impacts on Aboriginal Peoples." *Native Social Work Journal* 7:33–62.

Pasternak, Shiri. 2013. "On Jurisdiction and Settler Colonialism: The Algonquins of Barriere Lake against the Federal Land Claims Policy." PhD diss., University of Toronto.

Patzer, Jeremy. 2014. "Residential School Harm and Colonial Dispossession: What's the Connection?" In *Colonial Genocide in Indigenous North America*, edited by A. Wolford, J. Benvenuto, and A. Hinton, 166–85. Durham, NC: Duke University Press. http://dx.doi.org/10.1215/9780822376149-008.

Pedwell, Terry. 2012. "Idle No More vs. Bill C-45: First Nations Leaders Launch National Protest in Ottawa as Movement Grows." *Canadian Press*, 21 December. http://www.huffingtonpost.ca/2012/12/21/idle-no-more-bill-c-45-ottawa_n_2343396.html.

Perrin, Benjamin. 2010. "Prosecute the 'Wal-Mart of Child Sex Trafficking' – Craigslist." *Canada Free Press / Troy Media*, 23 October. http://www.canadafreepress.com/index.php/article/29106

Pettipas, Katherine. 1994. *Severing the Ties That Bind: Government Repression of Indigenous Religion Ceremonies on the Prairies*. Winnipeg: University of Manitoba Press.

Pflug-Back, Kelly Rose. 2015. "Capitalism Must Die in Order for Indigenous Nations to Live." Review of *Red Skin, White Masks: Rejecting the Colonial Politics of Recognition*, by Glen Sean Coulthard. *Briarpatch Magazine*, January/February. http://briarpatchmagazine.com/articles/view/unmasking-the-canadian-settler-state.

Pica-Smith, Cinzia, and Carmen Veloria. 2012. "At-Risk Means a Minority Kid: Deconstructing Deficit Discourses in the Study of Risk in Education and Human Services." *Pedagogy and the Human Sciences* 1 (2): 33–48.

Pinar, William. 1993. "Notes on Understanding Curriculum as Racial Text." In *Race, Identity, and Representation in Education*, edited by Cameron McCarthy and Warren Crichlow, 60–70. New York: Routledge, 1993.

Polakow, Valerie. 2000. *Public Assault on America's Children: Poverty, Violence, and Juvenile Injustice*. New York: Teachers College Press.

Polakow-Suransky, Sasha. 2000. "America's Least Wanted: Zero Tolerance Policies and the Fate of Expelled Students." In Polakow, 101–39.

Ponting, Rick. 1997. *First Nations in Canada: Perspectives on Opportunity, Empowerment, and Self-Determination*. Toronto: McGraw Hill.

Ponting, Rick, and Roger Gibbins. 1980. *Out of Irrelevance: A Socio-Political Introduction to Indian Affairs in Canada*. Toronto: Butterworths.

Popkewitz, Thomas. 1991. *A Political Sociology of Educational Reform: Power/Knowledge in Teaching, Teacher Education and Research*. New York: Teachers College Press.

———. 2004. "Partnerships, the Social Pact and Changing Systems of Reason in a Comparative Perspective." In *Educational Partnerships and the State: The Paradoxes of Governing Schools, Children and Families*, edited by B. Franklin, M. Bloch, and T. Popkewitz, 27–54. New York: Palgrave MacMillan.

Postero, Nancy. 2006. *Now We Are Citizens: Indigenous Politics in Postmulticultural Bolivia*. Palo Alto, CA: Stanford University Press.

Povinelli, Elizabeth. 1998. "The State of Shame: Australian Multiculturalism and the Crisis of Indigenous Citizenship." *Critical Inquiry* 24 (2): 575–610. http://dx.doi.org/10.1086/448886.

———. 2002. *The Cunning of Recognition: Indigenous Alterities and the Making of Australian Multiculturalism*. Durham, NC: Duke University Press.

———. 2011. *Economies of Abandonment: Social Belonging and Endurance in Late Liberalism*. Durham, NC: Duke University Press.

Powell, Christopher, and Julia Peristerakis. 2014. "Genocide in Canada: A Relational View." In *Colonial Genocide in Indigenous North American*, edited by Andrew Woolford, Jeff Benvenuto, and Alex Hinton, 70–94. Durham, NC: Duke University Press.

Public Safety Canada. 2010. *Tools to Identify and Assess the Risk of Offending among Youth*. Ottawa, CA: National Crime Prevention Centre. http://www.publicsafety.gc.ca/cnt/rsrcs/pblctns/tls-dntf-rsk-rprt/index-eng.aspx.

Public Service Alliance of Canada. 2013. "Equality Rights." *PSAC*. http://psacunion.ca/topics/equality-rights.

Raffles, Hugh. 1999. "Local Theory: Nature and the Making of an Amazonian Place." *Cultural Anthropology* 14 (3): 323–60. http://dx.doi.org/10.1525/can.1999.14.3.323.

Rankine, Claudia. 2014. *Citizen: An American Lyric*. Minneapolis, MN: Graywolf.

Razack, Sherene. 1998. *Looking White People in the Eye: Gender, Race, and Culture in Courtrooms and Classrooms*. Toronto: University of Toronto Press.

———. 2002. "Gendered Racial Violence and Spatialized Justice: The Murder of Pamela George." In *Race, Space and the Law: Unmapping a White Settler Society*, edited by Sherene Razack, 121–56. Toronto: Between the Lines.

———. 2004. *Dark Threats and White Knights: The Somalia Affair, Peacekeeping, and the New Imperialism*. Toronto: University of Toronto Press.

———. 2015. *Dying from Improvement: Inquest and Inquiries into Indigenous Deaths in Custody*. Toronto: University of Toronto Press.

"RCMP, Protesters Withdraw after Shale Gas Clash in Rexton." 2013. *CBCNews*, 17 October. http://www.cbc.ca/news/canada/new-brunswick/rcmp-protesters-withdraw-after-shale-gas-clash-in-rexton-1.2100703.

Recollet, Karyn. 2015. "Glyphing Decolonial Love through Urban Flash Mobbing and Walking with Our Sisters." *Curriculum Inquiry* 45 (1): 129–45. http://dx.doi.org/10.1080/03626784.2014.995060.

"Red Skin." 2013. "ILF2013 Mixtape." *2Hours* (online mixtape). https://sites.google.com/site/Indigenousleadershipforum/ilf2013-mixtape.

Regan, Paulette. 2011. *Unsettling the Settler Within: Indian Residential Schools, Truth Telling, and Reconciliation in Canada.* Vancouver: University of British Columbia Press.

"Report Calls for National Inquiry into Missing and Murdered Aboriginal Women." 2013. *MBC News*, 22 February. http://mbcradio.com/index.php/mbc-news/12110-report-calls-for-national-inquiry-into-missing-and-murdered-Aboriginal-women.

Rifkin, Mark. 2009. *Manifesting America: The Imperial Construction of US National Space.* Oxford: Oxford University Press. http://dx.doi.org/10.1093/acprof:oso/9780195387179.001.0001.

———. 2015. "Indigeneity, Apartheid, and Palestine: On the Transit of Political Metaphors." Paper presented at Comparative Settler Colonialism Workshop, Columbia University, New York, April.

Rizvi, Fazal. 1993. "Children and the Grammar of Popular Racism." In McCarthy and Crichlow, 126–39.

"Robert William Pickton: The Missing Women of Canada." 2007. *CBCNews*, 19 January.

Robinson, Laura. 2004. "The Women We've Failed." *Globe and Mail*, 24 June. http://www.theglobeandmail.com/globe-debate/the-women-weve-failed/article744478/.

Rodríguez, Dylan. 2003. "State Terror and the Reproduction of Imprisoned Dissent." *Social Identities* 9 (2): 183–203. http://dx.doi.org/10.1080/1350463032000101551.

Roman, Leslie. 1993. "White Is a Colour! White Defensiveness, Postmodernism, and Anti-Racist Pedagogy." In McCarthy and Crichlow, 71–88. New York: Routledge.

Roman, Leslie, and Linda Eyre. 1997. *Dangerous Territories: Struggles for Difference and Equality in Education.* New York: Routledge.

Rose, Nikolas. 1996. "Governing 'Advanced' Liberal Democracies." In *Foucault and Political Reason: Liberalism, Neo-Liberalism, and Rationalities of Government*, edited by A. Barry, T. Osbourne, and N. Rose, 37–64. Chicago: University of Chicago Press.

———. 1999. *Powers of Freedom: Reframing Political Thought.* Cambridge, UK: Cambridge University Press.

———. 2000. "Governing Liberty." In *Governing Modern Societies*, edited by R.V. Ericson and N. Stehr, 141–76. Toronto: University of Toronto Press.

Ross, Luana. 1998. *Inventing the Savage: The Social Construction of Native American Criminality.* Austin: University of Texas Press.

Roy, Arundhati. 1998. *The End of Imagination.* Kerela, India: DC Books.

Said, Edward. 1978. *Orientalism.* London: Vintage.

———. 1993. "The Politics of Knowledge." In McCarthy and Crichlow, 306–14. New York: Routledge.

Salem-Wiseman, Lisa. 1996. "'Verily, the White Man's Ways Were the Best': Duncan Campbell Scott, Native Culture, and Assimilation." *Studies in Canadian Literature / Études en littérature canadienne* 21 (2): 120–42.

Saltman, Kenneth, and David Gabbard, eds. 2003. *Education as Enforcement: The Militarization and Corporatization of Schools.* New York: Routledge.

Sandler, Janay B. 2010. "School Psychology, Juvenile Justice, and the School to Prison Pipeline." *Communique* 39 (4): 4–6.

Sangster, Joan. 2002. "She Is Hostile to Our Ways: First Nations Girls Sentenced to the Ontario Training School for Girls, 1933–1960." *Law and History Review* 20 (1): 59–96. http://dx.doi.org/10.2307/744155.

"Sask Foster Care Blasted after Child's Death." 2010. *CBCNews,* 12 June http://www.cbc.ca/news/canada/saskatchewan/sask-foster-care-blasted-after-child-s-death-1.871076.

Sask Learning. 2003. *Building Partnerships: First Nations and Métis Peoples and the Provincial Education System: A Policy Framework for Saskatchewan's Prekindergarten to Grade 12 Education System.* http://www.publications.gov.sk.ca/details.cfm?p=74081.

Saskatchewan. 1960. *Joint Committee of the Senate and the House of Commons on Indian Affairs: A Submission by the* Government of Saskatchewan. Ottawa.

———. 2004. *Report of the Commission of Inquiry.* http://www.qp.gov.sk.ca/Publications_Centre/Justice/Stonechild/Stonechild-FinalReport.pdf. Accessed 7 February 2017.

Saskatchewan Child Welfare Review Panel. 2010. *For the Good of Our Children and Youth: A New Vision, A New Direction.* Report. http://cwrp.ca/sites/default/files/publications/en/SK_ChildWelfareReview_panelreport.pdf.

Saskatchewan, Ministry of Justice, Wright Commission. 2004. *Report of the Commission of Inquiry into Matters Relating to the Death of Neil Stonechild,* October. http://www.justice.gov.sk.ca/stonechild/.

Saskatoon Police Service. 2016. *SHOCAP Serious Habitual Offender Comprehensive Plan.* Accessed 16 September. http://saskatoonpolice.ca/pdf/brochures/SHOCAP.pdf.

Savage, Candace. 2012. *A Geography of Blood: Unearthing Memory from a Prairie Landscape.* Vancouver, BC: Greystone.

Scheper-Hughes, Nancy. 1992. *Death without Weeping: The Violence of Everyday Life in Brazil.* Los Angeles: University of California Press.

Scheper-Hughes, Nancy, and Phillipe Bourgois, eds. 2004. *Violence in War and Peace.* Malton, MA: Blackwell.

Schick, Carol. 2002. "Keeping the Ivory Tower White: Discourses of Racial Domination." In *Race, Space and the Law: Unmapping a White Settler Society,* edited by Sherene Razack, 99–120. Toronto: Between the Lines.

Schick, Carol, and Verna St. Denis. 2005. "Troubling National Discourses in Anti-Racist Curricular Planning." *Canadian Journal of Education* 28 (3): 295–317. http://dx.doi.org/10.2307/4126472.

Schissel, Bernard, and Kari Fedec. 1999. "The Selling of Innocence: The Gestalt of Danger in the Lives of Youth Prostitutes." *Canadian Journal of Criminology* 41:33–56.

Schissel, Bernard, and Terry Wotherspoon. 1998. *Marginalization, Decolonization and Voice: Prospects for Aboriginal Education*. Discussion paper. http://files.eric.ed.gov/fulltext/ED467991.pdf.

Schouls, Tim. 2003. *Shifting Boundaries: Aboriginal Identity, Pluralist Theory, and the Politics of Self-Government*. Vancouver: University of British Columbia Press.

Scott, David. 1995. "Colonial Governmentality." *Social Text* 43 (43): 191–220. http://dx.doi.org/10.2307/466631.

Scott, James. 1998. *Seeing like a State: How Certain Schemes to Improve the Human Condition Have Failed*. New Haven, CT: Yale University Press.

Sewell, William, Jr. 1992. "A Theory of Structure: Duality, Agency, and Transformation." *American Journal of Sociology* 98 (1): 1–29. http://dx.doi.org/10.1086/229967.

Sharma, Aradhana. 2006. "Crossbreeding Institutions, Breeding Struggle: Women's Empowerment, Neoliberal Governmentality, and State (Re) Formation in India." *Cultural Anthropology* 21 (1): 60–95. http://dx.doi.org/10.1525/can.2006.21.1.60.

Shewell, Hugh. 2004. *Enough to Keep Them Alive: Indian Welfare in Canada, 1873–1965*. Toronto: University of Toronto Press.

Shore, Cris, and Susan Wright. 1997. *Anthropology of Policy: Critical Perspectives on Governance and Power*. New York: Routledge.

Sikka, Anette. 2009. *Trafficking of Indigenous Women and Girls in Canada*. Ottawa, ON: Institute On Governance / Office of the Federal Interlocutor for Métis and Non-Status Indians.

Silman, Janet. 1987. *Enough Is Enough: Aboriginal Women Speak Out*. Toronto: Women's Press.

Simmons, Lizbet. 2005. "Prison Schools: Disciplinary Culture, Race and Urban Education." PhD diss., University of California-Berkeley. ProQuest Dissertations and Theses. http://search.proquest.com/docview/305030433?accountid=14771

Simpson, Audra. 2007. "Ethnographic Refusal." *Junctures* 9:67–80.

———. 2014. *Mohawk Interruptus: Political Life across the Border of Settler States*. Durham, NC: Duke University Press.

———. 2016. "The State Is a Man: Theresa Spence, Loretta Saunders and the Gender of Settler Sovereignty." *Theory and Event* 19 (4).https://muse.jhu.edu/.

Simpson, Leanne. 2011. *Dancing on Our Turtles Back: Stories of Nishnaabeg Re-Creation, Resurgence, and a New Emergence*. Toronto: Arbeiter Ring.

——. 2013a. "Dancing on Our Turtle's Back: Building Resurgence from Within." Lecture, IGOV Indigenous Speaker Series at University of Victoria, BC, 13 February. https://www.youtube.com/watch?v=28u7 BOx0_9k.

——. 2013b. "Elsipogtog Protest: We're Only Seeing Half the Story." *Huffington Post*, 22 October. http://www.huffingtonpost.ca/leanne-simpson/elsipogtog-racism_b_4139367.html.

——. 2014a. "Indict the System: Indigenous and Black Resistance." *Briarpatch Magazine*, 29 November. http://briarpatchmagazine.com/blog/view/indict-the-system.

——. 2014b. "Land as Pedagogy: Nishnaabeg Intelligence and Rebellious Transformation." *Decolonization: Indigeneity, Education, and Society* 3 (3): 1–25. http://decolonization.org/index.php/des/article/view/22170.

——. 2014c. "Not Murdered and Not Missing." *#ItEndsHere* (blog), 5 March. http://nationsrising.org/not-murdered-and-not-missing/.

Sinclair, M., N. Bala, H. Lilles, and C. Blackstock. 2004. "Aboriginal Child Welfare." In *Canadian Child Welfare Law: Children, Families and the State*. 2nd ed. Edited by Nicholas Bala, Michael Kim Zapf, R. James Williams, Robin Vogl and Joseph P. Hornick 199–244. Toronto: Thompson Educational.

Sinclair, Raven, and Jana Grekul. 2012. "Aboriginal Youth Gangs in Canada: (De) Constructing an Epidemic." *First Peoples Child and Family Review* 7 (1): 8–28.

Slattery, Brian. 1997. "Recollection of Historical Practice." In *Justice for Natives: Search for Common Ground*, edited by A.P. Morrison, 76–82. Montreal: McGill-Queen's University Press.

Sleeter, Christine E. 2004. "Standardizing Imperialism." *Rethinking Schools* 19 (1): 26–9.

Smiley, Cherry. 2012. "Indigenous Girls and the Canadian State." *Justice for Girls*. http://www.justiceforgirls.org/uploads/2/4/5/0/24509463/indigenous_girls_and_the_canadian_state.pdf.

——. 2014. "FAFIA Launches Campaign of Solidarity with Aboriginal Women and Girls." *Feminist Current* (podcast), 30 November. http://www.feministcurrent.com/2014/11/30/podcast-fafia-launches-campaign-of-solidarity-with-aboriginal-women-and-girls/.

——. 2016. *Indigenous Girls and the Canadian State*. Accessed 16 September. http://www.justiceforgirls.org/uploads/2/4/5/0/24509463/indigenous_girls_and_the_canadian_state.pdf.

Smith, Andrea. 2005. *Conquest: Sexual Violence and the American Indian Genocide*. Durham, NC: Duke University Press.

Smith, Dorothy. 1988. *The Everyday World as Problematic*. Milton Keynes, CA: Open University Press.

Smith, Keith. 2009. *Liberalism, Surveillance, and Resistance: Indigenous Communities in Western Canada 1877–1927*. Edmonton, AB: Athabasca University Press.

Spivak, Gayatri. 1990. *The Post-Colonial Critic: Interviews, Strategies, Dialogues*. New York: Routledge.

———. 2012. "Aesthetic Education in the Age of Globalization." Lecture, Talinn University, Talinn, Estonia. https://vimeo.com/34600153.

———. 2014. *"Herald* Exclusive: In Conversation with Gayatri Spivak." By Nazish Brohi. *Dawn*, 23 December. http://www.dawn.com/news/1152482.

Sprott, Jane, and Anthony Doob. 2009. *Justice for Girls? Stability and Change in the Youth Justice Systems of the United States and Canada*. Chicago: University of Chicago Press.

Stark, Heidi Kiiwetinepinesiik. 2016. "Criminal Empire: The Making of the Savage in a Lawless Land." *Theory and Event* 19 (4). https://muse.jhu.edu/.

Stasiulis, Daiva, and Nira Yuval-Davis. 1995. "Introduction – Beyond Dichotomies: Gender, Race, Ethnicity and Class in Settler Societies." In *Unsettling Settler Societies: Articulations of Gender, Race, Ethnicity and Class*, edited by Daiva Stasiulis and Nira Yuval-Davis, 1–39. London: Sage.

Statistics Canada. 2002. *Youth in Canada*, 30 October. http://www.parl.gc.ca/Content/SEN/Committee/372/abor/rep/repfinoct03part2-e.htm

———. 2011. *Migration: International 2010 and 2011*. http://www.statcan.gc.ca/pub/91-209-x/2013001/article/11787-eng.htm. Accessed 7 February 2017.

St. Denis, Verna. 2011. "Rethinking Culture Theory in Aboriginal Education." In *Racism, Colonialism, and Indigeneity in Canada*, edited by M Cannon and L Sunseri, 177–88. Don Mills, ON: Oxford University Press.

Sterritt, Angela. 2007. *Racialization of Poverty – Indigenous Women, the Indian Act and Systemic Oppression: Reasons for Resistance*. Vancouver, BC: Vancouver Status of Women.

Stevenson, Michael. 1992. "Columbus and the War on Indigenous People." *Race and Class* 33 (3): 27–45. http://dx.doi.org/10.1177/030639689203300304.

Stoler, Ann. 1997. *Race and the Education of Desire*. Chapel Hill, NC: Duke University Press.

———. 2008. "Imperial Debris: Reflections on Ruins and Ruination." *Cultural Anthropology* 23 (2): 191–219. http://dx.doi.org/10.1111/j.1548-1360.2008.00007.x.

Strakosch, Elizabeth, and Alissa Macoun. 2012. "The Vanishing Endpoint of Settler Colonialism." *Arena Journal* 35 (3): 40–62.

Sudbury, Julia, ed. 2005. *Global Lockdown: Race, Gender and the Prison-Industrial Complex*. New York: Routledge.

"Survey Reveals Comfort Levels of Urban Aboriginal people." 2014. *Eagle Feather News*, 15 November. http://www.eaglefeathernews.com/news/index.php?detail=886.

Suzack, Cheryl, et al. 2010. *Indigenous Women and Feminism*. Vancouver: University of British Columbia Press.

"Tala's Story." 2016. *StreetGraphix*. Accessed 16 September. http://streetgraphix.ca/comics/tala/.

Taylor, Charles. 1994. "The Politics of Recognition." In *Reexamining the Politics of Recognition*, edited by A. Gutman, 27–73. Princeton, NJ: Princeton University Press.

Tammemagi, Hans. 2014. "Wanuskewin Heritage Park: 6,000 Years of Northern Plains History." *Indian Country*, 19 January. http://indiancountrytodaymedianetwork.com/2014/01/19/wanuskewin-heritage-park-6000-years-northern-plains-history-153171.

Tanner, Adrian. 2009. "The Origins of Northern Aboriginal Social Pathologies and the Quebec Cree Healing Movement." In *Healing Traditions: The Mental Health of Aboriginal Peoples in Canada*, edited by L.J. Kirmayer and G.G. Valaskakis, 249–72. Vancouver: University of British Columbia Press.

Tennant, Chris. 1994. "Indigenous Peoples, International Institutions, and the International Legal Literature from 1945–1993." *Human Rights Quarterly* 16 (1): 1–57. http://dx.doi.org/10.2307/762410.

Therein, Emile. 2011. "The National Shame of Aboriginal Incarceration." *Globe and Mail*, 20 July. http://www.theglobeandmail.com.

Thobani, Sunera. 2007. *Exalted Subjects: Studies in the Making of Race and Nation in Canada*. Toronto: University of Toronto Press.

Thornberry, Patrick. 1991. *Indigenous Peoples and Human Rights*. London: Juris.

Thornton, Martin. 2001. *Aboriginal People and Other Canadians: Shaping New Relationships*. Ottawa: University of Ottawa Press.

Ticktin, Miriam. 2011. *Causalities of Care: Immigration and the Politics of Humanitarianism in France*. Berkeley: University of California Press. http://dx.doi.org/10.1525/california/9780520269040.001.0001.

Tobias, John. 1976. "Protection, Civilization, Assimilation: An Outline History of Canada's Indian Policy." *Western Canadian Journal of Anthropology* 6 (2): 39–55.

Totten, Mark. 2009. "Aboriginal Youth and Violent Gang Involvement in Canada: Quality Prevention Strategies." *IPC Review* 3:135–56.

Truth and Reconciliation Commission of Canada. 2012. *TRC Final Report*. http://www.trc.ca/websites/trcinstitution/index.php?p=3.

Tuck, Eve. 2009. "Suspending Damage: A Letter to Communities." *Harvard Educational Review* 79 (3): 409–27.

Tuhiwai Smith, Linda. 1999. *Decolonizing Methodologies: Research and Indigenous Peoples*. New York: Zed.

Turner, Dale. 2006. *This Is Not a Peace Pipe: Towards a Critical Indigenous Philosophy*. Toronto: University of Toronto Press.

Turner, Terence. 1993. "Anthropology and Multiculturalism: What Is Anthropology That Multiculturalists Should Be Mindful of It?" *Cultural Anthropology* 8 (4): 411–29. http://dx.doi.org/10.1525/can.1993.8.4. 02a00010.

*Two Worlds Colliding*. 2004. Written and directed by Tasha Hubbard, National Film Board of Canada. https://www.nfb.ca/film/two_worlds_colliding

United Nations. 1948. Convention on the Prevention and Punishment of the Crime of Genocide. Paris, December 9. http://legal.un.org/avl/ha/cppcg/cppcg.html.

United Nations, Committee on the Rights of the Child. 2012. *Concluding Observations: Canada*. http://www2.ohchr.org/english/bodies/crc/docs/co/CRC-C-CAN-CO-3-4_en.pdf.

United Nations Development Program. 2014. *Sustaining Human Progress: Reducing Vulnerabilities and Building Resistance*. Human Development Report 2014. http://hdr.undp.org/sites/default/files/hdr14-report-en-1.pdf.

United Way. 2010. *Environmental Scan*. http://www.calgaryunitedway.org/images/uwca/our-work/kids/public-policy-research/environmental_scan_extended_age_definition.pdf. Accessed 7 February 2017.

"UN Review Finds Canada Falling Short on Child Rights." 2012. *Canadian Press*, 10 October. http://www.cbc.ca/news/politics/un-review-finds-canada-falling-short-on-child-rights-1.1178065.

Urban, Greg, and Joel Scherzer. 1991. *Nation-States and Indians in Latin America*. Austin: University of Texas Press.

US Department of Justice, Office of Juvenile Justice and Delinquency Prevention. 2013. *Risk/Needs Assessment for Youths*. Literature review. http://www.ojjdp.gov/mpg/litreviews/RiskandNeeds.pdf.

Van der Woerd, Kimberly, and David Cox. 2003. "Educational Status and Its Association with Risk and Protective Factors for First Nations Youth." *Canadian Journal of Native Education* 27 (2): 208–22.

Veracini, Lorenzo. 2010. *Settler Colonialism*. New York: Palgrave Macmillan. http://dx.doi.org/10.1057/9780230299191.

———. 2011. "Introducing *Settler Colonial Studies*." *Settler Colonial Studies* 1 (1): 1–12. http://dx.doi.org/10.1080/2201473X.2011.10648799.

Vizenor, Gerald. 1994. *Manifest Manners: Post-Indian Warriors of Survivance*. Middleton, CT: Wesleyan University Press.

Walia, Harsha. 2013. *Undoing Border Imperialism*. Oakland, CA: AK Press.

Walker, Connie. "New Documents May Shed Light on Residential School Deaths." 2014. *CBCNews*, 7 January. http://www.cbc.ca/news/Aboriginal/new-documents-may-shed-light-on-residential-school-deaths-1.2487015.

Waln, Frank. 2014. "My Family's Thanksgiving on the Reservation Is a Rebuke to America's Colonialism." *Guardian*, 27 November. http://www.theguardian.com/commentisfree/2014/nov/27/thanksgiving-on-the-reservation-is-a-celebration-of-our-way-of-live-and-a-middle-finger-to-americas-failed-colonialism.

Wacquant, Loic. 1989. "Towards a Reflexive Sociology: A Workshop with Pierre Bourdieu." *Sociological Theory* 7 (1): 26–63. http://dx.doi.org/10.2307/202061.

Weaver, Sally. 1981. *Making Canadian Indian Policy: The Hidden Agenda, 1968–1970*. Toronto: University of Toronto Press.

Wesley Group. 2012. *Marginalized: The Aboriginal Women's Experience in Federal Corrections*. Report for Aboriginal Corrections Policy Unit. http://www.publicsafety.gc.ca/cnt/rsrcs/pblctns/mrgnlzd/mrgnlzd-eng.pdf.

Willis, Paul. 1977. *Learning to Labour: How Working Class Kids Get Working Class Jobs*. New York: Columbia University Press.

Wilmer, Franke. 1993. *The Indigenous Voice in World Politics*. Newbury Park, CA: Sage. http://dx.doi.org/10.4135/9781483326610.

Winsa, Patty, and Jim Rankin. 2013. "Unequal Justice: Aboriginals Caught in the Justice System Trap." *Star*, 3 March. https://www.thestar.com/news/insight/2013/03/03/unequal_justice_aboriginals_caught_in_the_justice_system_trap.html.

Wolf, Diane. 1996. "Situating Feminist Dilemmas in Fieldwork." In *Feminist Dilemmas in Fieldwork*, 1–55. Boulder, CO: Westview.

Wolfe, Mitch. 2013. "New Brunswick Protestors Are More like Terrorists." *Huffington Post*, 21 October. http://www.huffingtonpost.ca/mitch-wolfe/new-brunswick-protests-terrorism_b_4137128.html.

Wolfe, Patrick. 1999. *Settler Colonialism and the Transformation of Anthropology*. London: Cassell.

———. 2006. "Settler Colonialism and the Elimination of the Native." *Journal of Genocide Research* 8 (4): 387–409. http://dx.doi.org/10.1080/14623520601056240.

———. 2011. "After the Frontier: Separation and Absorption in U.S. Indian Policy." *Settler Colonial Studies* 1 (1): 13–51. http://dx.doi.org/10.1080/2201473X.2011.10648800.

Woodsworth, James S. 2010. *Strangers within Our Gates, or Coming Canadians*. Charleston, SC: Nabu Press. First published 1909 by the Missionary Society of the Methodist Church, Canada.

Woolford, Andrew, Jeff Benvenuto, and Alexander Hinton, eds. 2014. *Colonial Genocide in Indigenous North America*. Durham, NC: Duke University Press. http://dx.doi.org/10.1215/9780822376149.

Wright, Robin. 1988. "Anthropological Presuppositions of Indigenous Advocacy." *Annual Review of Anthropology* 17 (1): 365–90. http://dx.doi.org/10.1146/annurev.an.17.100188.002053.

Young, Iris Marion. 1990. *Justice and the Politics of Difference*. Princeton, NJ: Princeton University Press.

———. 2000. *Inclusion and Democracy*. New York: Oxford University Press.

Young, Robert. 1995. *Colonial Desire*. London: Routledge.

# Index